Teach Yourself

teach yourself
WordPerfect 6

Tea
You

Teach Yourself WordPerfect 6

Mary Campbell

Osborne **McGraw-Hill**
Berkeley New York St. Louis San Francisco Auckland Bogotá Hamburg London Madrid Mexico City
Milan Montreal New Delhi Panama City Paris São Paulo Singapore Sydney Tokyo Toronto

ACQUISITIONS EDITOR
Scott Rogers

ASSOCIATE EDITOR
Kristin D. Beeman

TECHNICAL EDITOR
Marie Adams

PROJECT EDITOR
Claire Splan

COPY EDITORS
Laura Sackerman
Judith Brown

PROOFREADER
K.D. Sullivan

ILLUSTRATOR
Marla Shelasky

COMPUTER DESIGNER
Fred Lass

SERIES DESIGN
Seventeenth Street Studios

COVER DESIGN
Mason Fong

Osborne **McGraw-Hill**
2600 Tenth Street
Berkeley, California 94710
U.S.A.

For information on software, translations, or book distributors outside of the U.S.A., please write to Osborne **McGraw-Hill** at the above address.

Teach Yourself WordPerfect 6

1234567890 DOC 99876543

ISBN 0-07-881894-X

Contents at a Glance

I Essential WordPerfect Features

1 *WordPerfect's Basic Components* 3
2 *Creating WordPerfect Documents* 27
3 *Printing a Document* 55
4 *Using Features to Alter the Appearance of Text* 73
5 *Changing the Appearance of Lines and Paragraphs in a Document* 95
6 *Changing the Format of a Page* 117
7 *Search and Replace Options* 133
8 *Restructuring Your Document* 151

II Building on the Basics

9 *Using WordPerfect's Writing Tools* 167
10 *Page Breaks, Paragraph Breaks, and Other Options* 197
11 *Managing Files* 213
12 *Changing Print Options* 239
13 *Working with Multiple Documents* 259

III Special Features

14 *Merging Variable Information into a Standard Letter* 275
15 *Adding a Column of Numbers* 295
16 *Drawing Lines and Boxes* 311
17 *WordPerfect's Graphics Features* 333
18 *Creating an Outline* 365

19 *Changing Setup Parameters* 387
20 *Using Styles* 401
21 *Working with Text Columns* 433
22 *Using Tables in a Document* 457

IV Appendixes

A *Installing WordPerfect and Selecting a Printer* 497
B *WordPerfect Screen Elements* 507

Contents

Acknowledgments xiii
Introduction, xv

ESSENTIAL WORDPERFECT FEATURES

1 WordPerfect's Basic Components . . . 3

1.1 Start And End A Wordperfect Session, 4
1.2 Clear The Screen, 8
1.3 Locate And Use Special Keyboard Keys, 10
1.4 Use The Help And Cancel Keys, 16
1.5 Control The Entry Of Uppercase And Lowercase Letters, 19
1.6 Alter The Appearance Of Your Screen, 22

2 Creating WordPerfect Documents . . . 27

2.1 Use Wordperfect's Default Settings To Enter Text, 29
2.2 Replace Or Insert Characters, 34
2.3 Delete Characters, Words, And Lines, 37
2.4 Save A Document, 40
2.5 Retrieve A Document, 44
2.6 Open Multiple Documents, 46
2.7 Use Many Documents At Once, 48

3 Printing a Document . . . 55

3.1 Print The Current Document, 57
3.2 Print A Selected Page From The Current Document, 60
3.3 Preview Before Printing, 63
3.4 Print From A File, 67

4 Using Features to Alter the Appearance of Text . . . 73

4.1 Underline Text As You Type, 74
4.2 Boldface Text As You Type, 77
4.3 Center Text As You Type, 80

4.4 Reveal The Hidden Codes For Special Features, 82
4.5 Delete Hidden Codes, 85
4.6 Mark And Delete Blocks Of Text, 87
4.7 Apply Special Features To Blocks Of Text, 89

5 Changing the Appearance of Lines and Paragraphs in a Document . . . 95

5.1 Use Indentation, 97
5.2 Use The Back Tab Feature, 100
5.3 Set Tabs, 102
5.4 Use The Flush Right Feature, 106
5.5 Change Line Spacing, 108
5.6 Alter Justification, 110

6 Changing the Format of a Page . . . 117

6.1 Center Text On A Page, 119
6.2 Change The Margins, 123
6.3 Add Page Numbers, 126
6.4 Change The Paper Size And Type, 128

7 Search and Replace Options . . . 133

7.1 Search For A Word Or Phrase From The Beginning Of A Document, 135
7.2 Use Special Search Options, 139
7.3 Use The Replace Feature, 142

8 Restructuring Your Document . . . 151

8.1 Move Or Copy A Sentence, A Paragraph, Or A Page, 153
8.2 Move Or Copy A Block Of Text, 157
8.3 Move Or Copy Text To Many Locations, 161

II *BUILDING ON THE BASICS*

9 Using WordPerfect's Writing Tools . . . 167

9.1 Check The Spelling Of A Word, 169
9.2 Check The Spelling Of An Entire Document, 173
9.3 Find Double Words, 176
9.4 Add A Word To The Supplemental Dictionary, 179

9.5 Replace Correctly Spelled Words That Are Misused, 181
9.6 Look Up A Word In The Thesaurus, 183
9.7 Replace A Word With A Word From The Thesaurus, 188
9.8 Use The Grammar Checker For An Overview Of Your Document, 190

10 Page Breaks, Paragraph Breaks, and Other Options . . . 197

10.1 Control Widow And Orphan Lines, 199
10.2 Use Headers And Footers On Pages, 202
10.3 Add Footnotes, 206

11 Managing Files . . . 213

11.1 Create Backup Copies, 215
11.2 Create Directories, 218
11.3 Change Directories, 221
11.4 Delete Files And Directories, 223
11.5 Rename Files, 225
11.6 Create Document Summaries, 227
11.7 Search For A Word Within A Document On Disk, 231
11.8 Look At Files On Disk, 234

12 Changing Print Options . . . 239

12.1 Print Multiple Copies, 241
12.2 Display The Print Queue, 243
12.3 Cancel A Print Request, 246
12.4 Rush A Print Request, 248
12.5 Affect The Print Quality, 250
12.6 Change Fonts, 251

13 Working with Multiple Documents . . . 259

13.1 Change The Size Of A Document Window, 261
13.2 Move Document Windows, 263
13.3 Copy And Move Text Between Documents, 267

III Special Features

14 Merging Variable Information into a Standard Letter . . . 275

14.1 Create A Data File, 278
14.2 Create A Form File, 282
14.3 Produce The Merge Document, 287
14.4 Print The Merge Document, 290

15 Adding a Column of Numbers . . . 295

15.1 Obtain A Total For A Column Of Numbers, 297
15.2 Use Multilevel Totals, 301

16 Drawing Lines and Boxes . . . 311

16.1 Draw A Line, 313
16.2 Create A Box With Lines, 316
16.3 Erase A Line, 319
16.4 Move The Cursor Without Drawing, 321
16.5 Use A Special Character For The line, 324
16.6 Add Text To A Box, 326

17 WordPerfect's Graphics Features . . . 333

17.1 Add Graphics To A Document, 335
17.2 Place Text In A Graphics Box, 341
17.3 Edit And Delete Graphics Boxes, 345
17.4 Add A Caption, 350
17.5 Position And Size A Graphics Box, 353
17.6 Print Documents That Contain Graphics, 358

18 Creating an Outline . . . 365

18.1 Create An Outline, 367
18.2 Change An Outline, 373
18.3 Change The Outline Numbering Style, 377
18.4 Collapse And Expand An Outline, 380

19 Changing Setup Parameters . . . 387
19.1 Change Backup Options, 389
19.2 Change Display Options, 391
19.3 Change Other Options, 394

20 Using Styles . . . 401
20.1 Create A Character Or Paragraph Style, 403
20.2 Use Character And Paragraph Styles, 410
20.3 Create An Open Style, 415
20.4 Use An Open Style, 418
20.5 Modify A Style, 421
20.6 Create A Style Library, 426
20.7 Use Styles From A Style Library, 427

21 Working with Text Columns . . . 433
21.1 Create Newspaper Columns, 435
21.2 Create Parallel Columns, 444
21.3 Modify Column Entries, 451

22 Using Tables in a Document . . . 457
22.1 Create A Table, 460
22.2 Enter Text Into A Table, 465
22.3 Change The Width Of A Column, 471
22.4 Add Or Delete A Row Or Column, 475
22.5 Join Cells, 481
22.6 Change Cell Attributes, 483
22.7 Incorporate Simple Math Features Into A Table, 487

IV APPENDIXES

A Installing WordPerfect and Selecting a Printer . . . 497
A.1 Installing WordPerfect On Your System, 498
A.2 Installing Runtime, 501
A.3 Adding Printer Files, 501
A.4 Updating WordPerfect's System Files, 503
A.5 Installing WordPerfect In Windows, 504
A.6 Setting Up A Directory For Your WordPerfect Documents, 505

B WordPerfect Screen Elements . . . 507

B.1 Pull-Down Menus, 508

B.2 Dialog Boxes, 509

B.3 Button Bar And Ribbon, 511

Acknowledgments

Special thanks to Gabrielle Lawrence and Elizabeth Reinhardt for all of their help with the project, and to Marie Adams for checking our work to make sure there were no mistakes in the final manuscript. Marie was a tremendous asset as she carefully checked each chapter to insure that nothing was missed as we hurried to meet production deadlines. Their knowledge of WordPerfect's many features and their attention to detail ensured a smooth and timely manuscript delivery.

Thanks also to Scott Rogers, Kristin Beeman, and Sherith Pankratz for all of their help with the 6.0 upgrade; to Claire Splan for coordinating editorial phases; and to all the great staff at Osborne who worked on this book.

Introduction

If you have ever tried to learn a new software program on your own, chances are you were left somewhat frustrated by the experience. Even if you learned to use the program, you probably wondered if you were doing things correctly. Without an expert tutor in the office or the time and money to attend a seminar, you may have felt as if there were no solution. *Teach Yourself WordPerfect* 6 is designed to provide that solution. Instructions are clearly given for which pull-down menus to use, whether you are using a mouse or the keyboard. Function key and short-cut key approaches to completing tasks are provided when appropriate.

The short, easy-to-follow lessons in *Teach Yourself WordPerfect* 6 present a step-by-step guide to basic WordPerfect skills. Each new skill builds on the skills learned previously. Before long, you will be able to create all types of documents.

The book uses a learning-by-example approach and avoids lengthy discussions of features. The chapters are organized by lessons, each focusing on a learning objective and taking about 15 minutes to complete. As you master a learning objective, you will acquire a new WordPerfect skill.

Every chapter (except the first) begins with a Review Skills Check. The Review Skills Check exercises test your readiness to begin the chapter. The chapter and objective where you learned the needed skills are shown with each exercise. If you experience difficulty with an exercise, you can go back to the referenced section and work through the examples to improve your skill level before proceeding with the new material.

Once you have mastered the Review Skills Check, you are ready to tackle the first learning objective. A brief description of the skill is followed by the steps it involves and one or more practical applications. By following these steps you will be able to perform the applications. You will want to enter the examples at your keyboard if at all possible, since reading about the feature does not offer the same reinforcement as trying it out on the computer. The examples are followed by a set of exercises that test your ability to use the feature covered in the learning objective. Use this to assure yourself that you know how to use this new skill when individual steps are not provided.

Each chapter concludes with two additional sets of exercises: the Mastery Skills Check and the Cumulative Skills Check. Unlike the section exercises, which focus on one learning objective, the Mastery Skills Check tests your skill with all the chapter's objectives. The Cumulative Skills Check brings together your new skills and skills mastered in earlier chapters. Again, chapter and objective references where these skills were introduced are provided for easy review.

As you complete a chapter, you will find that you can use the skills immediately to create a wide variety of documents. After completing the last chapter, you will have acquired both beginning- and intermediate-level skills with WordPerfect. You will have gained these skills through hard work and repetition but without the frustration so often associated with learning a new software package.

HOW THIS BOOK IS ORGANIZED

Teach Yourself WordPerfect 6 is divided into 4 parts containing 22 chapters. Parts I and II are designed to be worked through in sequential order. Part I covers the basic skills needed to create WordPerfect documents. Part II covers intermediate-level features that enhance the appearance of your documents and add flexibility to your basic skills. Part III focuses on special topics. You may be interested in all of these topics or just a few. The chapters in Part III can be read in any sequence you choose, since each topic is not dependent on other special topics.

In Part IV, Appendix A covers installation and printer selection and Appendix B covers the various screen elements in WordPerfect 6. If WordPerfect is already installed on your machine and if your system prints when you ask it to, you will be able to skip Appendix A. If you have used the mouse and keyboard to make menu and dialog box selections in other programs, the screen elements described in Appendix B will already seem familiar and can also be skipped.

CONVENTIONS USED IN THIS BOOK

- *Menu Selection Approach* You can use either the mouse or keyboard to make the detailed menu and dialog box selections shown throughout the book. If you need help, you can turn to Appendix B for more details on how to select the various screen elements.

- *User Input* Whenever you are instructed to type text into the computer, the text is shown either in **boldface** or in a different typeface. When entering text, type it continuously, without pressing Enter at the end of each line, and do not insert hyphens. You should press Enter only at the end of a paragraph or a short line, or as otherwise instructed.

- *Keys* Keys are shown in keycap symbols, as in Enter. Keys to be pressed simultaneously are separated by hyphens. For example: Shift-F3 means hold down Shift while you press F3.

- *Review Skills Check, Mastery Skills Check, and Cumulative Skills Check* Skills Checks show the section numbers in brackets that contain information about how to complete the task described.

Teach
Yourself

part one

Essential WordPerfect Features

1

WordPerfect's Basic Components

chapter objectives

After completing this chapter, you should be able to

1.1 Start and end a WordPerfect session

1.2 Clear the screen

1.3 Locate and use special keyboard keys

1.4 Use the Help and Cancel keys

1.5 Control the entry of uppercase and lowercase letters

1.6 Alter the appearance of your screen

BEFORE creating WordPerfect documents, you must master a few basic skills: You need to learn how to begin and end a WordPerfect session. You will want to become acquainted with the keyboard. Even if you have used a typewriter, you will need to learn how WordPerfect uses many of your computer's special keys.

In each example and exercise, the instructions presented first show how you can access a feature by using WordPerfect's menus. You can use either the mouse or the keyboard to make menu selections. Function key alternatives, where available, are presented after the menu selections. You can decide whether to use the keyboard, the mouse, or the function keys by what seems most convenient to you.

1.1 START AND END A WORDPERFECT SESSION

Computer programs make it possible for your computer to perform a specific set of tasks. To use any program, you must load the program into the memory of your computer. WordPerfect is a computer program that provides sophisticated word processing capabilities to your computer. You must load WordPerfect into your computer's memory to make these word processing features available. While WordPerfect is loaded, you can think of everything that you do as part of a WordPerfect session.

Before you can load WordPerfect into your computer's memory, a copy of an operating system, such as DOS 6, must be loaded into memory, and WordPerfect must be installed on the hard disk. You will want to consult Appendix A for instructions if you are uncertain of either condition. If your screen displays a menu selection to begin WordPerfect, you can skip the directions that follow.

TO START A WORDPERFECT 6 SESSION

a. Go to the directory containing the WordPerfect files. If you installed WordPerfect according to the directions in Appendix A or the package documentation, you can type **cd \wp60** and press Enter.
b. Type **wp** to start the WordPerfect program.
c. Press Enter.

When WordPerfect is loaded, the program displays a blank document, as shown in Figure 1-1. A *document* is WordPerfect's basic structure for letters, reports, and other text entries. Everything you type is held in the current document, which you can store on disk.

The screen displays a blinking line called the *cursor.* As you type, WordPerfect places each character at the cursor location and moves the cursor one position to the right. You can determine the current location of the cursor relative to the remainder of the document by looking at the information in the status line. The *status line* indicates the current document, the current page number, and the cursor's distance from the top and left edges of the paper when the document is printed.

When you have finished using WordPerfect, you end the WordPerfect session by exiting the program. Exiting WordPerfect removes the program from the computer's memory, allowing you to use other programs. When you exit, WordPerfect checks to see if you want to save the current document. If you exit WordPerfect without saving the document, the text you have in memory will be lost. In Chapter 2, you will learn how to save a document.

TO EXIT WORDPERFECT

a. Select **File** from the menu bar. The menu bar is the top line of the WordPerfect screen that lists a number of words representing menu options.

FIGURE 1-1

The initial WordPerfect screen

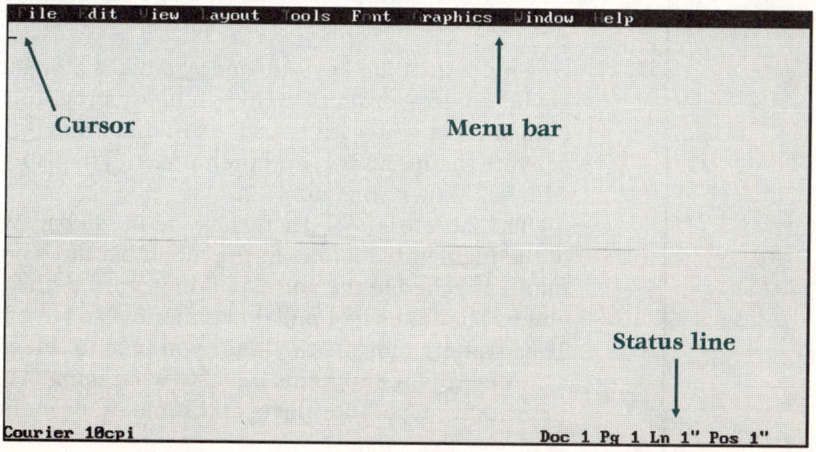

You can press Alt-= to activate the menu bar. Then you can press F to drop down the File menu, or you can click **File** in the menu bar for the same effect.

b. Select E**x**it WP.

Again you have two choices: press X or click E**x**it WP.

c. If an *X* appears in the Save column next to a filename and you do not want to save that document, type the letter next to the *X*. This is explained further in the next section, "Examples."

d. Press Enter to select the Save and Exit button.

When you end a WordPerfect session, you are returned to the DOS prompt. The prompt might appear as C> or C:\WP60>. You can also exit WordPerfect by pressing Home and then F7 in place of steps a and b.

EXAMPLES

1. To start WordPerfect, activate the directory where your WordPerfect files are stored by typing **cd \wp60** and pressing Enter. Then type **wp** and press Enter again to start the program. WordPerfect displays a blank screen like the one shown in Figure 1-1. Note the initial location of the cursor.

2. You can make menu selections from inside WordPerfect. You can try out this feature by exiting WordPerfect. After loading WordPerfect, press the A key seven times. The screen looks like this:

Find one of the keys labeled Alt that is along the bottom of your keyboard. In WordPerfect, like in many programs, you use this key to indicate that you want to use the menu. Press Alt and = together to activate the menu bar, and then press F to display the File menu, which is shown in Figure 1-2.

The keypress Alt-= activates the menu bar. When you press one of the highlighted letters in the menu bar after pressing Alt-=, the menu attached to the corresponding word in the menu bar drops down. The items in a pull-down menu also have highlighted letters. These letters indicate the letter you type to select the menu item.

All of the menu items indicate what happens when you select them. After Open, Retrieve, and some other menu commands are

FIGURE 1-2

The File menu

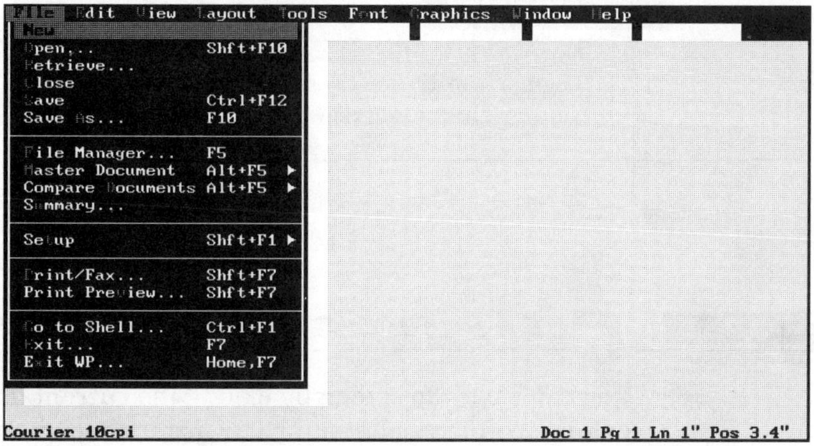

three dots. These ellipses tell you that if you select the command, WordPerfect will display a dialog box. After Master Document, Compare Documents, and Setup are arrows. These arrows tell you that when you select the command, WordPerfect displays a second menu so that you can make another selection that refines your choice. Menu items that do not have ellipses or arrows, such as Save and New, perform their functions as soon as you select them. In addition, function keys and key combinations are listed after many of the commands. These keys and key combinations, when pressed, select the corresponding commands. For example, pressing Home-F7 is the same as selecting E**x**it WP from the File menu.

Press X for E**x**it WP. WordPerfect displays this dialog box:

The *X* under Save tells you that WordPerfect thinks you want to save the document on the screen. Type **a** to remove the *X* from underneath Save. (Un)mark All, Save and Exit, and Cancel are *buttons*. When you select a button, WordPerfect performs the command marked on the button. When you removed the *X* from beneath Save, the Save and Exit button changed to the Exit button. Notice that the Exit button is highlighted. Press Enter. WordPerfect disappears and the DOS prompt appears on your screen. Because the Exit button was highlighted when you pressed Enter, WordPerfect selected this button and completed the Exit command in the File menu.

EXERCISE

Begin a WordPerfect session on your computer. End the WordPerfect session by choosing E**x**it WP from the File menu.

1.2 CLEAR THE SCREEN

You can clear the screen by exiting the current document without exiting WordPerfect. Exiting the current document lets you create more WordPerfect documents during a single WordPerfect session. When you want to remove the document on the screen, you exit it by telling WordPerfect that you do not want to save the file and you do not want to exit WordPerfect.

TO CLEAR THE SCREEN

a. Select **F**ile from the menu bar.

   To use the keyboard, you press Alt-= and then press F. To use the mouse, you click **F**ile in the menu bar.

b. Select **E**xit from the File menu.

   To do this, press E or click **E**xit.

c. Press N to select the **N**o button in response to WordPerfect's prompt about saving the file.

d. Press Enter or press N to select the **N**o button in response to WordPerfect's prompt about exiting WordPerfect.

Pressing F7 provides another option for exiting that only exits the current document. You will get some practice with this approach in the following example. These steps provide you with a blank screen identical to the initial screen that appeared when you started your WordPerfect session. Be sure to clear the screen after each exercise and example throughout this book unless the instructions indicate otherwise. This chapter will include reminders, but after that you're on your own.

EXAMPLE

You can remove the text onscreen quickly if you do not need to save it. Type

this text will be cleared from the screen quickly

Press F7. This has the same effect as selecting **F**ile, **E**xit. WordPerfect displays the following dialog box:

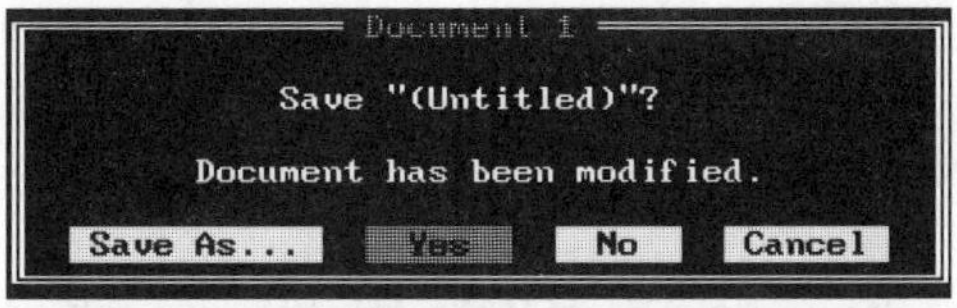

Press N to select the **N**o button. You see the following dialog box:

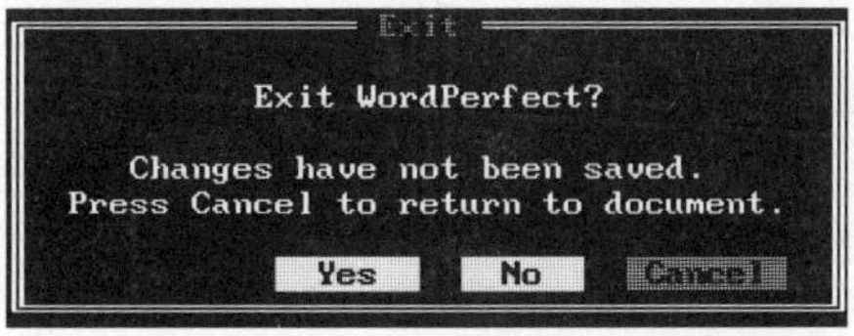

Press N to select the **N**o button. A blank screen results from your entries. If you selected the **Y**es button instead, you would have left WordPerfect and returned to the DOS prompt.

EXERCISES

1. Type **1993 holidays**, and then exit the document.
2. Type **bills, bills, and more bills**, and then clear the screen.

1.3 LOCATE AND USE SPECIAL KEYBOARD KEYS

To use WordPerfect effectively, you must become familiar with some of the special keyboard keys. These keys move the cursor around in a document, provide access to WordPerfect features, and help you make changes to text. Figure 1-3 shows the location of these keys on a popular keyboard. Keyboards can vary, so you might have some keys in different locations. Table 1-1 lists some of the special keys that you will use when working with WordPerfect documents. You will want to find these keys on your keyboard.

NOTE *If you have installed a mouse, you can use it to move around the screen.*

As you move around in a document, WordPerfect indicates the current location in the status line. The **Pg** indicator tells you which page you are on. The **Ln** (line) indicator tells you the position of the cursor from the top of a piece of paper. The **Pos** (position) indicator tells you the position of the cursor from the left edge of the paper. Both line and position are measured in inches in WordPerfect's default setup.

FIGURE 1-3

The IBM enhanced keyboard

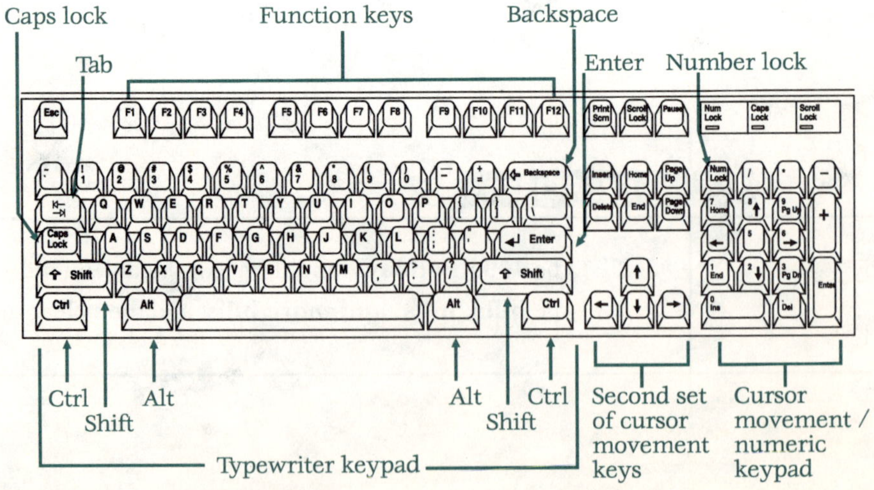

Key Sequence	Action
Enter	Ends a short line or a paragraph
Backspace	Deletes the character to the left of the cursor
↑	Moves the cursor up one line
↓	Moves the cursor down one line
←	Moves the cursor one character to the left
→	Moves the cursor one character to the right
Pg Up	Moves the cursor to the preceding page
Pg Dn	Moves the cursor to the following page
End	Moves the cursor to the end of the line
Home	Moves the cursor in the direction of the arrow key that is pressed next. If you press the Home key once before pressing an arrow key, the cursor moves to the edge of the screen in the direction of the arrow. Using the Home and → key combination moves the cursor to the end of the line rather than to the edge of the screen if the line is not as wide as the screen. Pressing the Home key twice before pressing the ↑ or ↓ key moves the cursor to the top or the bottom of the document.
Tab	Moves the cursor to the next tab stop. The initial setting tabs every 1/2 inch.
Num Lock	Switches the numeric keypad at the side of the keyboard between entering numbers and entering the cursor movement keys
Ctrl-Enter	Inserts a hard page break
Esc	Repeats a keystroke a specified number of times
Ctrl-→	Moves the cursor one word to the right
Ctrl-←	Moves the cursor one word to the left
Screen Up (Grey -)	Moves the cursor to the top of the screen; if pressed again, moves the cursor to the previous screen
Screen Down (Grey +)	Moves the cursor to the bottom of the screen; if pressed again, moves the cursor to the following screen
Ctrl-Home	Moves the cursor to a specified character or page
Function keys	The keys on the side or the top of the keyboard, labeled F1 through F10 or F12. These keys are used alone or combined with the Shift, Ctrl, and Alt keys to access different features. These keys are discussed in the chapters where their features are introduced.
Ctrl-↑	Moves the cursor to the beginning of the current paragraph or to the previous paragraph
Ctrl-↓	Moves the cursor to the beginning of the next paragraph

TABLE 1-1 *WordPerfect's Special Keys*

EXAMPLES

1. You can use the Enter key to create blank lines in the document. Beginning with the initial WordPerfect screen, press Enter three times. The cursor moves down three lines from its original position. The **Ln** indicator in the status line shows **1.5"**. Select **F**ile, **E**xit, and press N twice to clear the document without leaving WordPerfect.
2. You can use the Del and Backspace keys to remove characters from the screen. First type **abc**. Then press the Backspace key to delete the character to the left of the cursor. Next press the ← key twice to position the cursor under the letter *a*. Press the Del key to delete the character above the cursor, leaving only the *b*. Press F7 and press N twice to clear the screen without leaving WordPerfect.
3. You can repeat a keystroke in two ways. This first way is to use Ctrl-R; for example, you can create a line of hyphens by using Ctrl-R to repeat a single hyphen (-). When you press Ctrl-R, a dialog box opens that shows the number of times WordPerfect will repeat the character:

   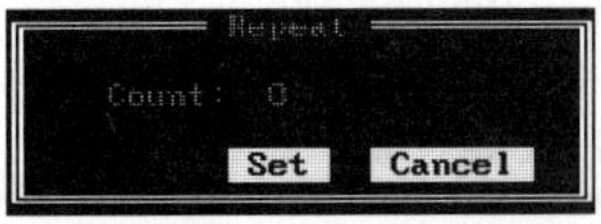

   You can control the number of repeats by typing a new number. For example, type **65** to tell WordPerfect how many times it should repeat the keystroke that follows, and then type a hyphen. The result looks like this:

   The second way to repeat a keystroke is to hold down a key. However, it is more difficult to control the exact number of repeats by using this approach. Press Enter to move to the next line of your document. Create another hyphenated line by holding down the hyphen key. After creating the second line of hyphens, press Enter to move to the next line. Select **F**ile, **E**xit and then press N twice to clear the screen without leaving WordPerfect.
4. You can use the arrow keys to move one position in any direction on the screen. Type **abc** and press Enter. Then type **def** and press Enter. Type **ghi** and press Enter to place text on the third line of the document. The screen looks like this:

When you press the ↑ key once, the cursor moves to the *g*. Then when you press the → key twice, the cursor moves to the *i*. Pressing the ↑ key two more times moves the cursor to the *c*. Pressing the ← key twice moves the cursor to the *a*. Pressing the ↓ key once moves the cursor to the *d*. Select **F**ile, **E**xit and then press N twice to clear the screen without leaving WordPerfect.

5. Special keystroke combinations make it easy to move the cursor quickly within the document. Type

   a stitch in time saves nine.

   Pressing ← while holding down Ctrl moves the cursor one word to the left. Press Ctrl-← five more times to move to the word "a." Move the cursor one word to the right by pressing Ctrl-→. Press Ctrl-→ five more times to move to the end of the line. To move to the end of the line more quickly, press the End key.

   After you have typed a line of text, you can move quickly through it by using the Home key in combination with other keys. Press Home and ← to move the cursor to the first character in the line. Press Home and → to move to the end of the line. Select **F**ile, **E**xit or press F7, and then press N twice to clear the screen without leaving WordPerfect.

6. Special keystrokes can move you quickly through larger sections of the document. You can move from page to page, move from screen to screen, or move directly to the beginning or end of the document.

   You use Pg Up and Pg Dn to move from page to page in a document. Type **1** 24 times, following each entry with Enter. To create a second page, press Ctrl-Enter, which is the shortcut for selecting the **L**ayout menu and the **A**lign and Hard **P**age items. WordPerfect displays the following line to indicate this page break:

   Next type **2** 24 times, following each entry with Enter. Press Pg Up to move from page 2 to page 1. Press Pg Dn to move from page 1 to page 2. WordPerfect displays the first line of a page at the top of the screen.

   Another way to move to a different page is by using Ctrl-Home, the keyboard shortcut for selecting the **G**o To option from the Edit menu. When you press Ctrl and Home together or when you select the command from the menu, WordPerfect displays a dialog box prompting you for the page you want the cursor moved to. Type **1** and press Enter to move the cursor to page 1. Press Ctrl-Home again, type **2**, and then press Enter.

You can move by screens instead of by pages by using the **Screen Down** (Grey +) and **Screen Up** (Grey -) keys. If NUM LOCK is on, press the Num Lock key to turn it off. Press **Screen Up** (Grey -) to move the cursor to the top of the current screen. Press **Screen Up** (Grey -) again to display the preceding screen, which contains the 1's. Press **Screen Down** (Grey +) once to move the cursor to the bottom of the current screen. Press it again to move down to the next screen. Use the entries in this document for the example that follows.

You can use the Home key in combination with other keys to move through the entries in the current document. Press Home then ↑ to move the cursor to the top line of the current screen. Press Home and ↓ to move the cursor to the bottom line of the current screen. When the text does not fill the screen, the cursor moves to the last line of the document. Press Home twice and ↑ once to move the cursor to the beginning of the document. Press Home twice and ↓ once to move the cursor to the end of the document. Select **F**ile, **E**xit and then press N twice to clear the screen without leaving WordPerfect.

7. When you need to enter many numbers, the numeric keypad keys provide an alternative to the number keys in the typewriter keypad. You can use the Num Lock key to switch the numeric keypad between number keys and cursor movement keys. When you press the Num Lock key to turn it on, the **Pos** indicator in the status line changes color. Type **46.73** by using the numeric keypad keys, and press Enter. When you press the Num Lock key again, the **Pos** indicator returns to the same colors as the other indicators. When Num Lock is not on, you can use the numeric keypad keys for the functions that are shown below the numbers. For example, if you press 8 on the numeric keypad, the keypad registers an ↑ to move the cursor back to the line containing "46.73." Press F7 and then press N twice to clear the screen without leaving WordPerfect.
8. Three keys, Alt, Ctrl, and Shift, are used in combination with other keys; they rarely perform actions by themselves. Press Alt, then Shift, then Ctrl. Nothing happens. When used with other keys, these keys provide features not otherwise available. You can press the Ctrl key simultaneously with the Enter key as the shortcut for selecting the **A**lign and Hard **P**age items from the **L**ayout menu. This creates a page break that starts a new page at the cursor location. If you press Alt combined with = and then press one of the letters that appear in a different color in the menu bar, you select the menu that corresponds to that letter.
9. Pressing Tab moves the cursor to the next tab stop to the right. Initially, tab stops are set every 1/2 inch. You can use Tab to indent the beginning of a line. Press Tab and then type **the meeting is scheduled for the 19th**. Next press Enter. Press Tab six times. The

Pos indicator shows that the cursor is now 4 inches from the left edge of the paper. Press ← to move the cursor to the preceding tab stop. If you don't have a mouse, skip the next example; press F7 and then press N twice to clear the screen without leaving WordPerfect. If you do have a mouse, go on to the next example without clearing the screen.

10. If you have installed a mouse or other tracking device, you can use it with WordPerfect. If a mouse is installed, moving it makes the mouse pointer appear on the screen. The mouse pointer is a rectangle that marks your place on the screen. Move the mouse so that it is pointing to the *m* in "meeting." Press the left mouse button. Pressing a mouse button is called *clicking*. Click **F**ile in the menu bar by pointing to File and pressing the left button on the mouse. (If you are left handed, you might later want to switch the mouse buttons' functions so that you will find it easy to use the mouse with your left hand.) Click the 1 in "19th" so that you leave the File menu. Press →. Every time you press a key, WordPerfect hides the mouse pointer. Move the mouse. The pointer reappears so that you are ready to make selections by using the mouse.

NOTE *The instructions in this book will continue to mention the keystrokes you can use to make menu selections, but if you are using a mouse, you can click the indicated menu selections instead.*

EXERCISES

1. Press Enter six times. Use the arrow keys to move to the top of the document and then to the bottom of the document. Clear the screen.
2. Create ten *a*'s by using Ctrl-R. Create another ten *a*'s by holding down the A key. Use the ← and → keys to move through this line. Move to the end of the line and press Enter. Clear the screen.
3. Use the Tab key to move the cursor 3 inches from the left edge of the page. Use the ← key to move back to the left side of the screen. Clear the screen.

4. Press Ctrl-Enter four times. Use the Pg Up and Pg Dn keys to move among the five pages. Use Ctrl-Home [**E**dit, **G**o To] to move to specific pages. Clear the screen.
5. Type

   the early bird gets the worm.

   Press Enter and the ↑ key. Use WordPerfect's cursor movement keys to move from word to word and to the beginning and the end of the line. Clear the screen.
6. Create a six-page document that has four blank lines on each page. Move a screen at a time to the top and the bottom of the document. Use the Home key and the arrow keys to move to the top and the bottom of the document. Check the status line after each move to see where you are. Clear the screen.
7. Use the numeric keypad to enter the following:

   123456789

   Clear the screen.
8. Type the following:

   abc

   Use the Backspace key to delete the *c*. Use the ← key to position the cursor under the *a*, and then delete the *a*.

1.4 USE THE HELP AND CANCEL KEYS

WordPerfect has several function keys and command selections that are useful for all tasks. You can select the **C**ontents command from the Help menu to get help on any topic. You can use the Cancel button to cancel a WordPerfect command or recover deleted text. The function key F1 is the keyboard equivalent of selecting the **C**ontents command from the Help menu and Esc is the equivalent of the Cancel button. You can also select **U**ndelete from the Edit menu or press Esc to restore any of the last three deletions you have made.

If you accidentally press one of the function keys, you will invoke a WordPerfect command. To cancel a WordPerfect command, press Esc until you are returned to your document.

TO USE THE HELP KEY

a. With WordPerfect on the screen, select **H**elp, **C**ontents or press F1.

b. Use the arrow keys to move to the topic that will provide the information you want, and press Enter.

c. Press Esc to return to your document.

You can press F1 to get help when using the menu command is not possible. For example, you can use F1 in the middle of another command to provide help information about the command you are in the middle of.

TO USE THE CANCEL KEY TO CANCEL A COMMAND

Press Esc until your document is displayed on the screen.

TO USE THE CANCEL KEY TO RESTORE TEXT

a. Select **E**dit, **U**ndelete or press Esc. WordPerfect displays the most recently deleted text at the cursor's location.

b. Press 2 or P to restore a previous deletion, or press 1 or R to restore the displayed deletion.

EXAMPLES

1. You can display information about the cursor movement keys. Select **H**elp, **C**ontents or press F1. Each of the topics in a different color is a button you can select to display more information. Press Enter to select the highlighted button, Index. Press the Pg Dn key three times and ↓ until the Counters button is highlighted, and then press Enter. The Help dialog box displays information on counters. You could press any of the cursor movement keys to move to the correct topic. Press Esc to leave Help.

2. You can cancel any command request before it is completed. Select **F**ile, **E**xit or press F7. Press Esc to select the Cancel button. In some

dialog boxes, you will want to press Esc twice to leave the dialog box without completing the dialog box's commands. Just as pressing Enter in a dialog box selects the highlighted button, pressing Esc selects the Cancel button.

3. You can restore deleted characters. Type

   four score and seven years ago

   With the cursor at the end of this phrase, press the Backspace key until all of the text is removed. Select **E**dit, **U**ndelete. This is the same as pressing Esc. WordPerfect displays and highlights the deleted text. Press 1 or R, and the text is returned to the document as if you never deleted it. Press F7 and then press N twice to clear the screen without leaving WordPerfect.

4. You can restore the most recent deletion or either of the prior two deletions. Type **first** and press Enter. Then type **second** and press Enter. Type **third** as the last entry, without pressing Enter. Move to the first line and delete the word "first" by using the Backspace key. Next press the ↓ key, and delete the word "second" by pressing the Del key six times. Press the ↓ key again, and press the Del key five times to delete the word "third." Select **E**dit, **U**ndelete or press Esc. The word "third" is displayed. Press 2. WordPerfect displays the word "second." Press 2 again to display "first." Pressing 1 restores this selection in the current location rather than where "first" appeared when you deleted it. Press F7 and then press N twice to clear the screen without leaving WordPerfect.

EXERCISES

1. Select **C**ontents from the Help menu or press F1, and then use the Help system to determine how to move to the next screen down or up.
2. Type this sentence:

   he suddenly left.

   Delete "suddenly" and select **E**dit, **U**ndelete or press Esc to place it after the word "left." Clear the screen.

3. Select **H**elp, **C**ontents or press F1, and use the Help system to view the template for the function keys.
4. Select **H**elp, **C**ontents or press F1, and use the Help system to look at the keys used to delete characters.
5. Type the following:

   it was a cold, dark, scary evening

   Delete the word "dark" and the comma and space that follow it. Select **E**dit, **U**ndelete or press Esc to place it in front of "cold" as the first adjective in the sentence. Clear the screen.
6. Select the **F**ile Manager command from the File menu. Leave this dialog box without performing the features of this command.

1.5 CONTROL THE ENTRY OF UPPERCASE AND LOWERCASE LETTERS

When you are typing text in WordPerfect, you will want to make some of the letters uppercase and some lowercase. Your keyboard has two types of keys that change the case of letters you type. The Shift key changes the case of any letter that you type when you are pressing it. The Shift key also enables you to type special characters that appear on the number keys and on other keys. The Caps Lock key allows you to switch between typing uppercase and lowercase letters without having to hold down the Shift key.

TO TYPE A CAPITALIZED LETTER OR A SPECIAL CHARACTER BY USING THE SHIFT KEY

a. Press the Shift key and hold it down.
b. Type the letter that you want capitalized, or press the key that displays the special symbol above a number or above another character.
c. Release the Shift key.

TO TYPE CAPITALIZED LETTERS BY USING THE CAPS LOCK KEY

a. Press the Caps Lock key.

b. Type the letters that you want capitalized.

c. Press the Caps Lock key.

Using the Shift key with Caps Lock on causes WordPerfect to enter lowercase characters.

EXAMPLES

1. You can capitalize some letters and enter others in lowercase by selectively pressing the Shift key. Hold down the Shift key and type

   ABC C

   These letters are entered in uppercase. Release the Shift key and type

   orporation

   These letters appear in lowercase. The screen looks like this:

   ```
   File  Edit  View  Layout  Tools  Font  Graphics  Window  Help
   ABC Corporation_
   ```

   Select **F**ile, **E**xit or press F7, and then press N twice to clear the screen without leaving WordPerfect.

2. You can use the Shift key to type special characters. Hold down the Shift key and type

   TO:

   If you hadn't used the Shift key, the last character would have been a semicolon (;). The Shift key causes WordPerfect to produce the symbol at the top of the key. Select **F**ile, **E**xit or press F7, and then press N twice to clear the screen without leaving WordPerfect.

3. You can type capital letters and still type numbers. When CAPS LOCK is on, the keyboard still treats the number keys at the top of keyboard as numbers. Press Caps Lock and type

   SATURDAY 15TH

   Press the key containing the @ above the 2. WordPerfect displays a 2. Even though the letter keys behave as if you are pressing the Shift key, the number keys do not. To type the symbols above the numbers, you still must press the Shift key while you press the number key. Press Backspace to remove the 2, and then hold down Shift while you press @. Release the Shift key and type **PAUL'S PLACE**. Select **F**ile, **E**xit or press F7, and then press N twice to clear the screen without leaving WordPerfect.

EXERCISES

1. Use the Shift key to type these characters:

   JQLYZBEANL

   Clear the screen.
2. Use the Shift key selectively to type

   The ABC Corporation makes Tiger sedans.

   Clear the screen.
3. Without using the numeric keypad, type

   The lending rate is 15%.
   (16*2)+7=39
   Profit & Loss Statement

   Clear the screen.
4. Use the Caps Lock and Shift keys to type

   CAPITALIZATION CAN EMPHASIZE TEXT.
   WORDPERFECT makes typing FUN.

   Clear the screen.
5. Use the Caps Lock key to type

   THE LOCAL CAR DEALERSHIP IS OFFERING 16% APR.
   COMPANY PICNIC 8/19/93

   Clear the screen.

1.6 ALTER THE APPEARANCE OF YOUR SCREEN

When you start WordPerfect, your screen looks like Figure 1-1. This screen is displayed in text mode. You can also display the WordPerfect screen in graphics mode, as shown in Figure 1-4. In addition to changing the mode used to display the document, you can add or remove the Button Bar. The changes you make to the screen display and Button Bar remain in WordPerfect for future WordPerfect sessions. Since the Button Bar can be customized to meet different needs, yours might look different than someone else's.

In text mode, WordPerfect displays all text by using the same font. Text that is formatted differently—for example, italicized text—appears in different colors. Lines might not end in the same positions they will when printed. The advantage of text mode is that WordPerfect runs faster. You will want to use text mode when you are typing a lot of text.

In graphics mode, WordPerfect displays the document as it will appear when you print it. Spacing, character formats, and other

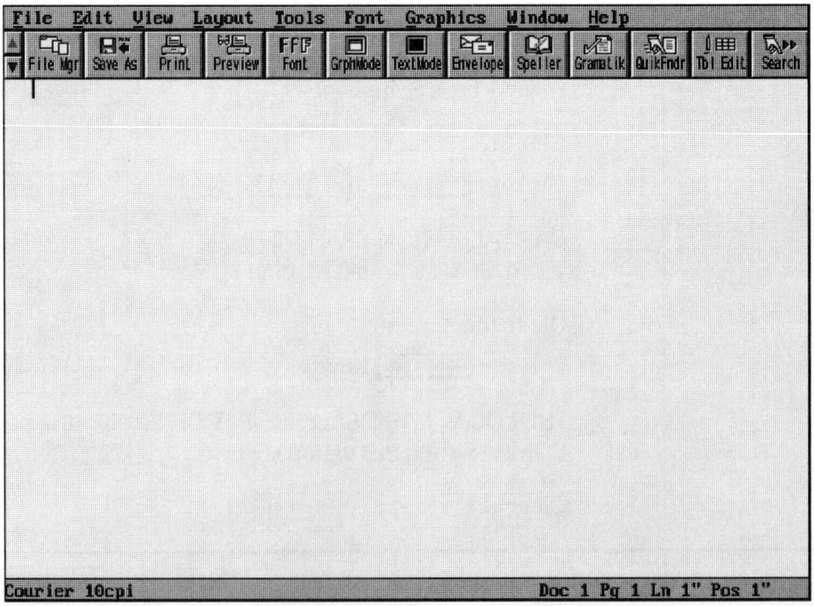

FIGURE 1-4

A screen in graphics mode

features appear on the screen as they will when printed out. Because WordPerfect must use more of your computer's resources to create this display, WordPerfect runs more slowly. Graphics mode lets you know that what you see on the screen is what you get when you print the document.

The Button Bar displays some commonly used commands on buttons. To execute the command a button represents, you select the button by pointing at it with the mouse and clicking the left mouse button. In graphics mode, the buttons use symbols to indicate their purposes; in text mode, the buttons use only text. If you do not have a mouse, you cannot select buttons from the Button Bar.

TO SWITCH TO GRAPHICS MODE

a. Select **V**iew from the menu bar.

b. Select **T**ext Mode.

An alternative method is to press Ctrl-F3 to display the Screen dialog box, press T to select **T**ext item under Display Mode, and press Enter to select OK.

TO SWITCH TO TEXT MODE

a. Select **V**iew from the menu bar.

b. Select **G**raphics Mode.

An alternative method is to press Ctrl-F3 to display the Screen dialog box, press G to select **G**raphics, and press Enter to select OK.

TO DISPLAY OR HIDE THE BUTTON BAR

a. Select **V**iew from the menu bar.

b. Select **B**utton Bar.

Selecting **B**utton Bar is like pressing a toggle switch. Each time you select the menu command, you switch between hiding and displaying the Button Bar. While the Button Bar appears on screen, the View menu will have a mark to the left of Button Bar to indicate that it currently appears. The Button Bar is added separately in text and graphics mode.

NOTE *Most of the figures and illustrations in this book show graphics mode screens. When you are using text mode, your screens will contain the same text, although their position and character appearance might vary. Also, the Button Bar is included in most screens in this book, although yours might be toggled off.*

EXAMPLES

1. By using graphics mode, you can view the document as it will appear when printed. From text mode, select the **V**iew menu and press G for **G**raphics Mode. This is the same as pressing Ctrl-F3, G, and Enter. Type **A new broom sweeps clean**. You can see the effect of the different font. Activate the Button Bar by selecting **V**iew, **B**utton Bar. The top of the screen now looks like this:

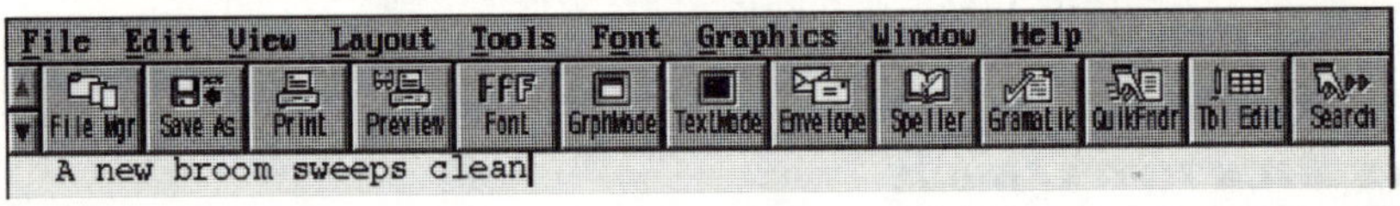

2. If you have a mouse, you can try using the Button Bar. Using the mouse, click any part of the button labeled TextMode. Your screen goes to text mode. Next click any part of the button labeled GrphMode. Your screen goes to graphics mode.
3. Text mode displays a plainer screen, but the screen is sometimes easier to read in text mode. Select **V**iew, **T**ext Mode. This is equivalent to pressing Ctrl-F3, pressing T for Text Mode, and pressing Enter. Active the Button Bar by selecting **V**iew, **B**utton Bar. The Button Bar and the text you have entered look like this:

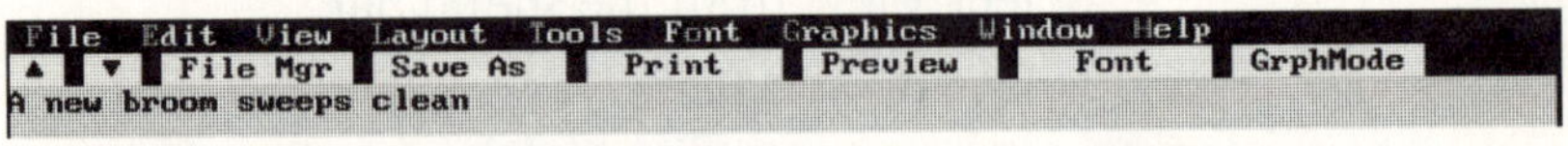

Select **F**ile, **E**xit or press F7, and then press N twice to clear the screen without leaving WordPerfect.

EXERCISES

1. Change to graphics mode and enter **Don't cross the bridge until you come to it.** Then press Ctrl-Enter to start a new page. Clear the screen.
2. Hide the Button Bar.

mastery skills check

1. Exit WordPerfect. [1.1]
2. Load WordPerfect. [1.1]
3. Type the following lines. If you make a mistake, use the Del or Backspace key to erase the mistake. [1.3, 1.5]

   August 15th or SEPTEMBER 3RD
   32+(8*9)

4. Find help on exiting WordPerfect. [1.4]
5. Clear the screen. [1.2]
6. Change to text mode. [1.6]
7. Type the following lines. If you make a mistake, use the Del or Backspace key to erase the mistake. [1.3, 1.5]

   10:34 A.M.
   ACME CORPORATION

8. Exit WordPerfect. [1.1]

2

Creating WordPerfect Documents

chapter objectives

After completing this chapter, you should be able to

2.1 Use WordPerfect's default settings to enter text

2.2 Replace or insert characters

2.3 Delete characters, words, and lines

2.4 Save a document

2.5 Retrieve a document

2.6 Open multiple documents

2.7 Use many documents at once

WORDPERFECT records your every keystroke in a document. You can create a document for a memo, a letter, a list of names and addresses, a report, and so on. As you type, your document is stored in your computer system's memory. WordPerfect places your typed words on the page by using default settings that can be used for all your documents. These settings control many features, such as the amount of white space at the edges of your document. After creating a document, you can save it onto a disk to use later.

The ability to retrieve documents can greatly increase your productivity. No longer do you need to retype an entire document because of a single error. Instead, you can retrieve the document and correct the text. When you have a document stored on disk that is similar to the document you need to create, you can retrieve the document from disk and revise it as necessary. Again, the time required is a fraction of the time required to type a new document. WordPerfect lets you open up to nine documents at a time, and you can easily switch among open documents.

Teach Yourself review skills check

As you complete the following Skills Check exercises, do not clear the screen unless instructed to do so. The numbers in brackets following the instructions indicate the chapter and section in this book to refer to for help.

1. Type the following text. [1.5]

   TO: John Smith
   FROM: Mary Brown
   SUBJECT: 1993 Holiday Schedule

2. Use Ctrl-R to add a line of dashes under the last line you entered in step 1. [1.3]
3. Add three blank lines after the entry you made in step 2. Then type the following text. [1.3, 1.5]

The attached holiday schedule should be circulated to all employees as soon as possible. Note that company holidays have increased to 8.

4. Add a hard page break below your entries, and type the following text on page 2. [1.3, 1.5]

January 1	New Year's Day
January 12	Founders' Day
March 30	Spring holiday
April 3	Easter holiday
May 30	Memorial Day
July 4	Independence Day
November 28	Thanksgiving
December 25	Christmas

5. Move the cursor to page 1 by using the Ctrl-Home option. [1.3]
6. Move to the end of the document. [1.3]
7. Switch to graphics mode and toggle on the Button Bar. [1.6]
8. Clear the screen. [1.2]
9. Toggle off the Button Bar. [1.6]
10. Review the Help screen for exiting WordPerfect. [1.4]
11. Exit WordPerfect. Start WordPerfect. [1.1]

2.1 USE WORDPERFECT'S DEFAULT SETTINGS TO ENTER TEXT

WordPerfect provides a set of default format settings for each new document that are available to you without any work on your part. Because these settings are provided, you can begin typing without having to worry about laying out the format for your document. Later you will learn how to change the basic document format, but for now you need only to understand the settings WordPerfect provides. Figure 2-1 shows a printed copy of a WordPerfect page. The white space at the top, bottom, and sides is referred to as the *margins.* WordPerfect allows for a 1-inch margin on all sides of a document. The lines of the document are single-spaced on the page.

When you type on a typewriter, a bell rings to signal that you are near the end of a line. With WordPerfect, you can type without worrying about the end of the line, because WordPerfect has a feature called *word wrap.* Word wrapping breaks each line to maintain the

FIGURE 2-1

Manuscript printed by using WordPerfect's default settings

Learning To Use WordPerfect

WordPerfect is one of the best word processing packages available today. The short, easy-to-follow lessons in this book are designed to teach you the basic skills. Before long, you will be able to create all types of documents.

This book uses a learning-by-example approach and avoids lengthy discussions of features. The chapters are organized by lessons, each focusing on a learning objective. As you master each learning objective, you will acquire a new WordPerfect skill.

You learned a few basic skills before creating your first document. You learned to begin and end a WordPerfect session. You learned the location of some important keys on the keyboard.

Now that you know a few of the basics, you are ready to create a document. WordPerfect records your every keystroke in a document. You can create a document for a memo, a letter, a list of names and addresses, a report, and so on. As you type, your document is stored in your computer system's memory. WordPerfect places your typed words on the page by using default settings that can be used for all your documents. These settings control many features, such as the amount of white space at the edges of your document. After creating a document, you can save it onto a disk to use later.

You can add emphasis to your text by using WordPerfect's special features. Underlining, boldfacing, and centering help to set off text from the rest of your document. WordPerfect changes the appearance of the text on the screen to indicate these special features. WordPerfect also adds hidden codes to the document for these features.

If you do not add special features to your text as you type it, WordPerfect allows you to add them later. To add a special feature to existing text, you must block the text and then have WordPerfect apply the feature.

WordPerfect also allows you to change the appearance of lines of text. You can change the margin settings to allow more or less white space at the left and right edges of the paper. Lines can also be offset from the left and right edges of the paper, allowing you to set off bulleted items or other important text.

Normally you will want at least one printed copy of every document you create. Some people prefer to proof first drafts of their documents from printed copies. Also, a printed copy is usually the medium used to share the information in your document with others.

WordPerfect offers a considerable amount of flexibility in

right margin. WordPerfect moves text to the next line without requiring you to press Enter. As you edit the text, WordPerfect moves words from line to line in order to keep the same left and right margins, creating a professional appearance, as in the sample output in Figure 2-1.

You can tell WordPerfect exactly where you want a line to end by pressing Enter. The next text you type is placed on a new line. Use Enter to end a paragraph or a short line.

NOTE *Because of typesetting considerations, the length of the lines in this book will not exactly match the length of lines you type. When you enter text, remember to press Enter only at the end of a paragraph or a short line, or as instructed.*

TO ENTER TEXT BY USING WORDPERFECT'S WORD WRAP FEATURE

a. Type the text without pressing Enter at the end of each line.

b. Press Enter at the end of each paragraph.

TO ENTER TEXT WITHOUT USING THE WORD WRAP FEATURE

a. Type the text that you want on the line.

b. Press Enter to end the line.

EXAMPLES

1. WordPerfect's word wrap feature and default margin settings are applied to the text you type. To see how WordPerfect handles text entries that extend for more than one line, type

   ABC's new dryer automatically stops when the clothes are dry. It determines when to stop by checking the humidity inside the dryer. This feature prevents shrinkage that occurs from overdrying clothes.

   Because you did not press Enter, the screen looks like this:

```
ABC's new dryer automatically stops when the clothes are dry. It
determines when to stop by checking the humidity inside the
dryer. This feature prevents shrinkage that occurs from
overdrying clothes.
```

Depending on your initial settings, WordPerfect might wrap your text differently, and your screen might look different than in the examples shown here. Your screen might also look different if you type two spaces, instead of one, after periods. You will use this entry in the next example, so do not clear the screen.

2. Word wrap and margin settings remain in effect when you edit the text entered in example 1. First, press ↑ three times, Ctrl-← twice, and ← once to move the cursor to the space between "dryer" and "automatically." Next, type a comma, press Spacebar, type **Just-Dri** as the dryer's name, and type another comma. Now your entry looks like this:

```
ABC's new dryer, Just-Dri,| automatically stops when the clothes
are dry. It determines when to stop by checking the humidity
inside the dryer. This feature prevents shrinkage that occurs
from overdrying clothes.
```

NOTE *You will want to remove the text on your screen between exercises unless otherwise directed. In the last chapter, you had continual reminders. Now you need to remember to select **E**xit from the File menu and select **N**o twice in between exercises.*

3. Pressing Enter forces WordPerfect to begin a new line even if the first line is not full. Use Enter to type short lines, such as the ones in address labels. First, type

   Carol Gallagan

   Because this is the only text for this line, press Enter. Next, type

   Medical Associates, Inc.

   After you type this, end this line by pressing Enter. Enter the street address by typing

   4511 Valley Street

   To end this line, press Enter. Finally, finish the address information by typing

   New Haven, CT 03421

   Press Enter to end the line. The screen looks like this:

```
Carol Gallagan
Medical Associates, Inc.
4511 Valley Street
New Haven, CT 03421
|
```

4. Enter is also used to end paragraphs. First, press Tab and type

   Enclosed are the insurance forms that Dr. Wilbur must fill out for my insurance claim. I will stop by next Tuesday to pick them up.

   To end the paragraph, press Enter. For the next paragraph, press Tab and type

   I have enclosed a check to cover my August 20th visit. Please note this payment on the insurance form.

   Because you have finished the second paragraph, press Enter. The screen looks like this:

```
     Enclosed are the insurance forms that Dr. Wilbur must fill
out for my insurance claim. I will stop by next Tuesday to pick
them up.
     I have enclosed a check to cover my August 20th visit.
Please note this payment on the insurance form.
|
```

   If you had not used Enter to separate the paragraphs, WordPerfect would have combined them.

EXERCISES

1. Type these lines, using the Enter key to separate them:

   January 21, 1993
   The meeting is next Friday.
   They are planning to have lunch at the Cozy Corner restaurant.
   Johnston Company stock is currently selling at 8 3/8.

2. Type this paragraph by using WordPerfect's word wrap feature:

   The Stone Corporation is merging with the Johnston Company. The new company's name will be Johnston Stone Corporation. The Stone Corporation manufactures jewelry. Johnston's main product line, raw stones, ensures the Stone Corporation a constant supply.

3. Type this list, using Enter at the end of each item in the list. Allow WordPerfect's word wrap feature to wrap the items that extend for more than one line.

Stones and Their Descriptions
Opal–Comes in various colors and varieties, all of which have an iridescent reflection of light
Garnet–Primarily crimson but also can be brown, green, yellow, or black
Topaz–A yellow, white, green, or blue stone that is transparent or translucent
Sapphire–A blue stone that is almost as hard as a diamond

4. Type the following paragraphs:

One frequent cause of problems is the use of an incorrect word or expression. Incorrect word usage can cause readers to lose part of the meaning of your writing.
"Casual" and "causal" are two words that are sometimes interchanged. "Casual" is synonymous with "relaxed" and "low-key." "Causal" relates to involvement with a cause.

2.2 REPLACE OR INSERT CHARACTERS

After typing a document, you can edit it to correct mistakes and omissions. WordPerfect lets you add a missing character, word, or paragraph at any location in a document. You can also replace the characters in a document with other characters. By pressing the Ins key, you can switch between adding new characters in insert mode and replacing old ones in typeover mode.

WordPerfect's default setting is insert mode. When in *insert mode,* WordPerfect places any character you type at the cursor's position, shifting to the right any text after the cursor. When the insertion causes text to extend beyond the right margin, WordPerfect reformats the text to change the word wrap.

Typeover mode lets you replace the character at the current cursor location with another character. Press Ins when WordPerfect is in insert mode to change to typeover mode. Each character that you type replaces a character on the screen until you press the Ins key again to switch back to insert mode. When WordPerfect is in typeover mode, the word "Typeover" appears on the left side of the bottom of the screen.

When you enter text in typeover mode, the word wrapping is not adjusted, because the number of characters in the document does not change. An exception is when you change a space to a character, or vice versa, because this can change the length of a word at the end of a line. In typeover mode, the Backspace key deletes the character to the left of the cursor and replaces it with a space.

TO USE INSERT MODE

a. Look at the left side of the bottom of your screen. If you see "Typeover," press the Ins key to set the keyboard for insert mode.

b. Type the text you want to insert.

TO ENTER REPLACEMENT CHARACTERS IN TYPEOVER MODE

a. Press the Ins key to activate typeover mode. Check for "Typeover" at the bottom of the screen.

b. Type the replacement text.

c. Press Ins again to turn off typeover mode.

EXAMPLES

1. You can use insert mode to add text to the current document. First, type

   The company is releasing a new product that stops kitchen odors.

   Next, move the cursor to the space between "product" and "that." The screen looks like this:

```
The company is releasing a new product| that stops kitchen odors.
```

   Type **, Odor Gone,**. Now the screen looks like this:

```
The company is releasing a new product, Odor Gone,| that stops
kitchen odors.
```

2. You can use typeover mode to replace an entry when the replacement is the same length as the original entry. First, type

   The chairperson of the publicity department is Daryl Smith.

   If Daryl Smith resigns and Donna Jones takes his place, you can change this sentence by moving the cursor to the *D* in "Daryl" and pressing the Ins key. WordPerfect displays "Typeover" along the bottom of your screen. Now type

   Donna Jones

   The screen looks like this:

   ```
   The chairperson of the publicity department is Donna Jones.
   ```

   You will use this entry for the next example.

3. Typeover mode can also be used when the new entry is almost as long as the existing entry. The Del key can remove the extra characters. You can replace the words "Donna Jones" with the words "Jim Lee." Move to the *D* in "Donna" and press Ins if you do not see "Typeover" along the bottom of the screen. Type **Jim Lee**. The screen looks like this:

   ```
   The chairperson of the publicity department is Jim Leehnes.
   ```

   Press the Del key four times to delete the extra four characters.

EXERCISES

1. Type this sentence:

   Company sales reached 1.2 million dollars.

   Insert **ABC** and a space before the word "Company."

2. Type these sentences:

   The company's sales increased to $1,654,834. Net income after taxes was $60,245.

   Insert the following sentence between the two you just typed:

Cost of goods sold was $983,473.

3. Type the following:

   Biography is a region bounded on the north by history, on the south by fiction, and on the west by tedium.
   Philip Guedalla

   Add **on the east by obituary,** in front of "and."

4. Type the following:

   Your current balance is $789.95.

   Change $789.95 to $389.95.

2.3 DELETE CHARACTERS, WORDS, AND LINES

In Chapter 1, you learned to use Del and Backspace to remove characters. WordPerfect provides other speedy deletion options that are useful when you have a number of characters to remove. You can use these options to delete a word or a sentence.

EXAMPLES

1. You can use the Del key to delete the character at the cursor. Type

   Joan Kelley is the Assistant Production Manager.

   After she is promoted, you need to remove the "Assistant" from her title. First, move the cursor to the *A* in "Assistant."

   Next, press Del ten times. You could also hold Del down until the word "Assistant" was deleted. Now the screen looks like this:

```
Joan Kelley is the Production Manager.
```

An alternative to Del is Backspace. First, press End and Enter. Then type

The company's house boat is under repair.

Because "houseboat" is one word, you need to remove the space between the two words. Move the cursor to the *b* in the word "boat." Then press Backspace to remove the space. Now the screen looks like this:

```
Joan Kelley is the Production Manager.
The company's houseboat is under repair.
```

2. When you have to delete several words, you can use Ctrl-Backspace to remove a word at a time. Type

   John is assuming Katie's position until the end of the year.

   If the change becomes permanent, you will want to remove the last six words. Move the cursor to the word "until." Then hold down Ctrl and press Backspace six times.

   Release Ctrl. Finally, press Backspace once and type a period. Now the screen looks like this:

```
John is assuming Katie's position.
```

3. You can use the Ctrl-End key combination to delete several words at one time. Type

   Tasks
   Review Salary Proposals
   Review Budget from Department 439
   Prepare Master Budget

   When you finish the second task, you can delete the entry. First, move the cursor to the beginning of the word "Review" in the second task.

   Next, hold down Ctrl and press End. All of the text in that line disappears. Finally, press Del to delete the hard return that marks where you pressed Enter at the end of the line. You cannot actually see the hard return, but you can see how the line now disappears. The screen looks like this:

```
Tasks
Review Salary Proposals
Prepare Master Budget
```

EXERCISES

1. Type this sentence:

   The ABC Corporation and the XYZ Corporation are merging together to form the Alphabet Corporation next month.

   Use the Del key to remove the word "together." Then use the Backspace key to remove the phrase "next month."

2. Type this paragraph:

   The ABC Corporation manufactures personalized license plates, mugs, name plates, and glassware. The XYZ Corporation produces personalized garment tags, shirts, purses, and pillows.

   Delete the phrase "name plates" and the comma that follows it. Then delete the word "purses" and the comma that follows it.

3. Type the following:

   The major issues to be discussed at the next sales meeting are
   New bonus program
   Smaller sales regions
   Strategies for developing new customers

   Delete the third line.

4. Type the following:

NAME	DEPARTMENT	SALARY
Jan Smith	Biology	25,600
Bill Black	Accounting	29,800
Jeff Jones	Finance	35,400

   Delete the word "SALARY" and all the salary figures.

2.4 SAVE A DOCUMENT

As you type a document, it is stored in the memory of your computer system. You can also save your document to a disk. Saving a document makes it available for another WordPerfect session.

When you save a WordPerfect file, you must follow the rules of the DOS operating system for naming the file. A filename can consist of up to eight letters, numbers, and certain symbols. It cannot contain spaces. You can also use an optional filename extension of up to three characters after the filename. If you use an extension, you must separate it from the filename with a period (.). Each filename on a disk or in a directory must be unique on that disk or in that directory. To make files easier to find, give each document a name that relates to the document's contents.

As a safety measure, WordPerfect saves documents every ten minutes so that you will never lose more than ten minutes of work. Although having this automatic backup is a nice safety net, you should frequently save files that you want to keep.

TO SAVE A DOCUMENT AND CLEAR THE SCREEN OR EXIT WORDPERFECT

a. Select **F**ile, **E**xit. You can press F7 instead.

b. Press Y in response to WordPerfect's prompt for saving the document.

c. Type a filename in the filename text box within the dialog box.

d. Press Enter or click the OK button.

e. Press N to clear the screen, or press Y to exit WordPerfect.

After you have named a file, WordPerfect prompts you with that filename when you try to exit the file. You can press Enter or Y to accept that filename, or you can press S to select **S**ave As and type a new filename before pressing Enter.

TO SAVE A DOCUMENT WITHOUT CLEARING THE DOCUMENT FROM THE SCREEN

a. Select **F**ile, **S**ave.

b. Type a filename.

c. Press Enter or click the OK button.

When you use the **F**ile, **S**ave command, WordPerfect saves the document to the same filename without prompting you.

TO SAVE A DOCUMENT TO ANOTHER NAME

a. Select **F**ile, Save **A**s. You can also press F10.
b. Type a filename.
c. Press Enter or click the OK button.

NOTE *This book assumes that the documents are stored in a directory named \WPDOCS. If you do not have this directory, you can create it following the directions in Appendix A.*

EXAMPLES

1. You can save a document and clear the screen. First, type the following document:

   $456,000
   $400,000
   14%

   To save this file, select **F**ile, **E**xit. You can also press F7. When WordPerfect asks you whether you want to save the document, press Y to select **Y**es. Next, WordPerfect displays this dialog box:

   The area after "Filename" is a *text box*. WordPerfect is waiting for you to make an entry into this text box. Type **sales** and press Enter. Don't worry about the buttons in the dialog box; they are for features you are not using. In most dialog boxes, pressing Enter selects the OK button that completes the command you selected to display the dialog box.

The document is saved on your disk. WordPerfect asks if you want to leave WordPerfect. Press N to select **N**o. The screen is cleared. Use this method of saving a file when you want the document removed from memory as soon as it is saved to disk.

NOTE *WordPerfect uses text boxes within dialog boxes anytime you are expected to make a long entry.*

2. You can save a document without clearing the screen. First, type

   Memo
   To: All Employees
   From: Human Resources
   Re: Christmas Party

   Press Enter and then Tab, and type

   The company Christmas party will be on December 21 at 6:30 p.m.

   Next, select **F**ile, **S**ave. When WordPerfect prompts you for the filename, type **xmas** and press Enter. WordPerfect returns to the document instead of clearing the screen. Also, WordPerfect displays the filename in the bottom of the screen. Use **F**ile, **S**ave to save the document without clearing it from memory. You will use this file in the next example, so do not clear the screen.

3. There is one fewer step when you save a file a second time. Add the following text to the document from example 2:

   Dinner will be served at 8. Dancing will begin at 9:30.

   Next, select **F**ile, **S**ave. WordPerfect saves the updated document by using the same dialog box settings it used when you saved the document the last time.

4. You can create multiple copies of a document on a disk by saving the document under different filenames. This allows you to create a document and modify a copy of it for another purpose. Type

   Jim Allen
   Allen & Associates, CPAs
   412 Oakland
   Tallahassee, FL 31245

   If you need to send two letters to Jim Allen, you can save the name and address under two different filenames to avoid having to type them twice. Select **F**ile, **S**ave.

WordPerfect prompts you for the filename. Type **allen1** and press Enter.

To save the name and address again, select **F**ile, Save **A**s. You can also click the Save As button in the Button Bar. The Save As button looks like this:

WordPerfect displays the same dialog box that you saw before, with "ALLEN1" in the Filename text box. If you press Enter, WordPerfect will save the document again under the same filename. Because you want to save the document under a different filename, type **allen2** and press Enter. Now you have two separate files with the same contents.

EXERCISES

1. Type the following and save it as STITCH:

   A stitch in time saves nine.

2. Type the following and save it as NAME:

   Jim Allen
   1123 Fork Rd.
   Baltimore, Maryland 21237

   Save this document again as NAME2, and clear the screen.

3. Type the following:

   Insanity is hereditary. You can get it from your kids.
   Sam Levenson

   Save the file as KIDS, and clear the screen.

4. Type the following:

   A man who has never gone to school may steal from a freight car; but if he has a university education, he may steal the whole railroad.
   Theodore Roosevelt

Save the file as TEDDY. Save it again as SCHOOL, and clear the screen.

2.5 RETRIEVE A DOCUMENT

Documents saved to a disk can be retrieved. When a document is retrieved when the screen is clear, the only document in memory is the document from the disk. When there is already text on the screen, the text in the document stored on disk is inserted into the text on the screen at the position of the cursor.

NOTE *When a document is already onscreen, retrieving a second document is different from opening a second document. Retrieving a second document inserts the text of the second document into the text of the first document. Opening a second document places a copy of the second document into memory as a new document and keeps it separate from the first document. For more information, see sections 2.6 and 2.7.*

TO RETRIEVE A DOCUMENT

a. Select **F**ile, **R**etrieve.

b. Type the filename of the document that you want.

c. Press Enter or click OK.

After WordPerfect retrieves the file, it displays the filename in the status line. If WordPerfect cannot find the document, it displays a message like this one:

In this case, WordPerfect could not find a file named BUDGRPT.

Press Esc to remove this message, and you return to the Retrieve Document dialog box so that you can reenter the filename.

EXAMPLES

1. You can retrieve a document you created and saved earlier so that you edit it. Select **F**ile, **R**etrieve. WordPerfect displays the Retrieve Document dialog box:

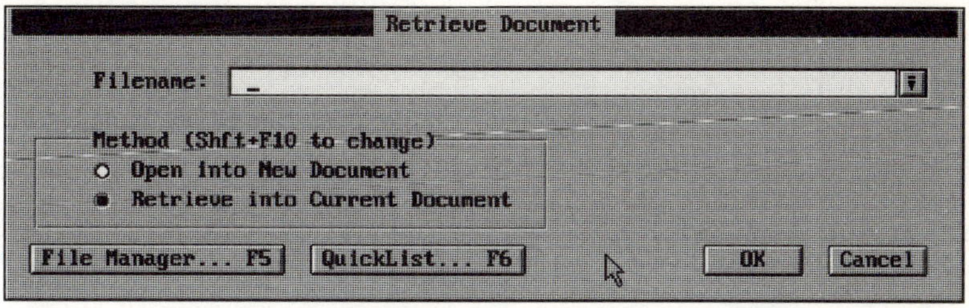

   Type **xmas** and press Enter to select OK. The document saved as XMAS appears on the screen and its filename appears along the bottom of the screen. Do not clear the screen, because you will use this document in the next example.

2. You can retrieve a file with a document already on the screen. Press Enter twice and ↑ twice so that you will have room between the two groups of text. Retrieve the ALLEN1 file you saved in section 2.4 by selecting **F**ile, **R**etrieve. Type **allen1** and press Enter or click OK. The screen looks like this:

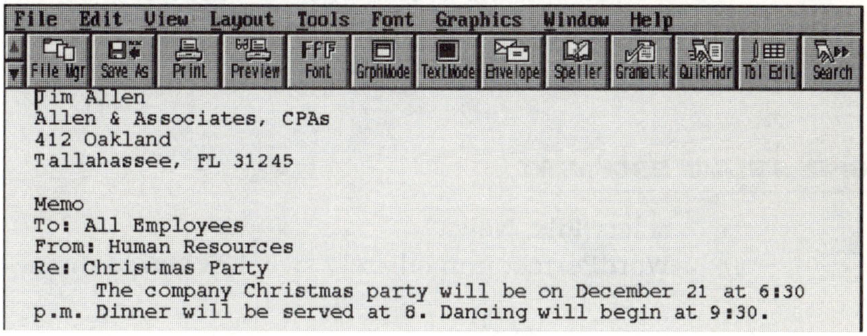

   The document continues to have the filename of the first file retrieved.

EXERCISES

1. Retrieve the file STITCH created in exercise 1 of section 2.4.

2. Retrieve the file NAME created in exercise 2 of section 2.4. Next, retrieve STITCH again without first clearing the screen.
3. Retrieve the file TEDDY created in exercise 4 of section 2.4. Without clearing the screen, retrieve the file a second time. Clear the screen.
4. Type

   Favorite Quotes

   Press Enter and retrieve the file KIDS. Retrieve the file TEDDY. Clear the screen.

2.6 OPEN MULTIPLE DOCUMENTS

So far, you have worked with one document in memory at a time. However, with WordPerfect 6, you can have up to nine documents open in memory at once. Each document is displayed in its own window. The contents of all the documents remain separate.

Because WordPerfect stores each document separately in memory, you must exit each document separately. It does not matter in which order you exit the documents; for example, you can exit document 2 and continue to work in document 1. When you exit the last remaining document, you can also exit WordPerfect.

TO OPEN A BLANK DOCUMENT

Select **F**ile, **N**ew.
WordPerfect immediately switches you to the new document.

TO OPEN A SAVED DOCUMENT

a. Select **F**ile, **O**pen. You can also press Shift-F10.
b. Type the filename of the file that you want to open, including any filename extension.
c. Press Enter to select OK.

EXAMPLES

1. You can create a new document with a document already open. Select **F**ile, **R**etrieve. In the Retrieve Document dialog box, type **xmas**, and press Enter or click OK. At this point, notice how **Doc 1** appears to the right of the filename. **Doc 1** lets you know you are in the window of the first document.

   To create a second document, select **F**ile, **N**ew. The current document disappears from the screen, and the status line looks like this:

   ```
   Courier 10cpi                                Doc 2 Pg 1 Ln 1" Pos 1"
   ```

   Doc 2 indicates that you are in the window of the second document open in memory. For this document, type

   The next meeting of the board of directors is December 14.

   The first document is still intact, because nothing you type in one document affects the other open documents.

   You can exit document 2, which removes it from memory, by selecting **F**ile, **E**xit or by pressing F7. Then press N when Word-Perfect asks you whether to save the document, and press Y when WordPerfect asks you whether to exit document 2. Notice how you are back at the first document. Leave XMAS as document 1 for the next example.

2. You can open a document saved on disk as your second document. Select **F**ile, **O**pen. You can also press Shift-F10 to display the Open Document dialog box. This dialog box looks exactly like the Retrieve Document dialog box except that the black dot is next to Open into New Document rather than Retrieve into Current Document. Type **allen1** and press Enter or click OK. WordPerfect opens ALLEN1 as the second document.

   Exit document 2. Select **F**ile, **E**xit or press F7. When WordPerfect asks if you want to save the file, press N to select the **N**o button. When WordPerfect asks whether you want to exit from the document, press Y to select the **Y**es button. The screen displays the original letter that you typed in example 1. Leave XMAS as the first document for the next example.

3. You can open two copies of the same document. Select **F**ile, **O**pen. Type **xmas**, and press Enter or click OK. Because you already have one copy of the file open, WordPerfect displays a dialog box that tells you that the file can be opened only as a read-only file, which means that you cannot save this document under the same filename. If you

make changes to the second open copy of the file, save this copy under another filename. The second document displays the same document that is displayed in document 1. As a reminder that you cannot save the second version of the file by using the same filename, the filename that appears at the bottom of the screen is enclosed in brackets.

Exit the second document. Select **F**ile, **E**xit or press F7. When WordPerfect asks if you want to save the file, press N to select the **N**o button. When WordPerfect asks whether you want to exit from the document, press Y to select the **Y**es button. The screen displays the original letter that you typed in example 1. Follow the same steps to exit the first document, except press N for the **N**o button when prompted if you want to leave WordPerfect.

EXERCISES

1. Type the following paragraph:

   The company is using a new printer for the current year's financial statements. This allows the company to include pictures of its executive officers and its main office building.

   Save this document as STMT1. Open a second copy of STMT1. Add the following sentence:

   Management felt that the change was necessary, since the company wants to improve its corporate image.

   Save this document as STMT2. Exit from both documents.
2. Open STMT2. Then open STMT1. Exit from both documents.

2.7 USE MANY DOCUMENTS AT ONCE

You can switch back and forth between open document windows or arrange windows so that you can see the contents of more than one. You can use this feature to read one document as you type a response to it in a second document. You can also use this technique to edit text in a number of documents that are open at the same time.

Initially, WordPerfect uses the entire screen to display one document at a time. This is a *maximized document window*. Another possibility is to divide the screen into document windows that evenly display the open documents. This is called *tiling*. In Figure 2-2, two document windows are tiled so that one document can be read while the second is created.

TO SWITCH TO ANOTHER DOCUMENT WINDOW

a. Select **W**indow, S**w**itch To, or press F3.

b. Press the number of the window you want to switch to.

You can press Home and 0 instead of using the menu in step a. This shortcut key combination opens the same dialog box, which lists the open document windows and their contents.

FIGURE 2-2

Tiled windows let you see both documents

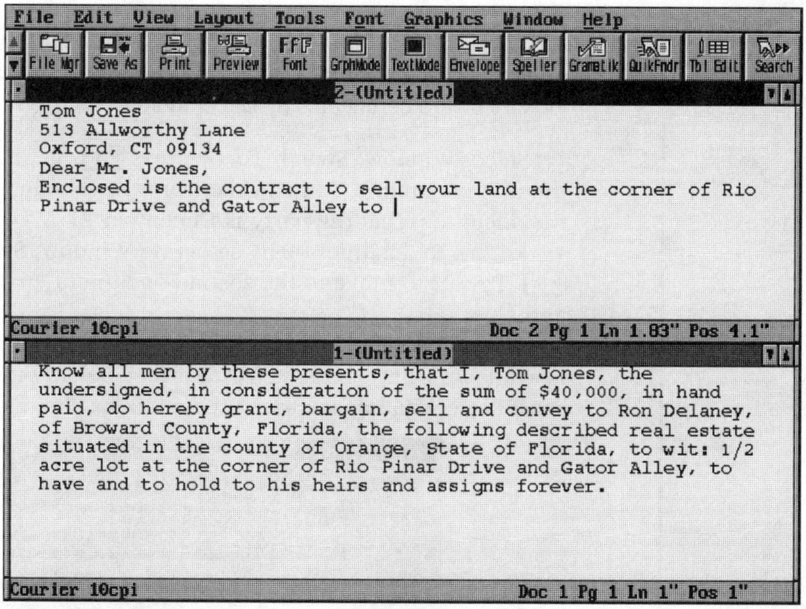

TO SWITCH BETWEEN THE CURRENT AND THE LAST ACTIVE DOCUMENTS

Select **W**indow, **S**witch.

Alternatively, you can press Shift-F3. This feature shifts you between only two document windows, the current one and the last active one.

TO TILE THE OPEN WINDOWS

Select **W**indow, **T**ile.

You can cause a tiled window to be displayed using the full screen by selecting **M**aximize from the Window menu.

EXAMPLES

1. You can switch between two documents when you are creating a document that makes use of information contained in another document. Select **F**ile, **R**etrieve, type **xmas**, and press Enter to select OK.

   Next, open a blank document by selecting **F**ile, **N**ew. In document 2, type

   Reminders for Christmas party
   Pick up award certificates by December

   Select **W**indow, S**w**itch To, or press F3. Type **1** to switch back to the first document. You can see from the schedule at the bottom of the document that the party is December 21.

   Return to document 2 by selecting **W**indow, S**w**itch To or pressing F3. Type **2** to move to the second document window. Then type **21** and a period.

   When you are working with multiple documents, a special feature is available when you exit WordPerfect. Select **F**ile, E**x**it WP. The Exit WordPerfect dialog box that appears looks like this:

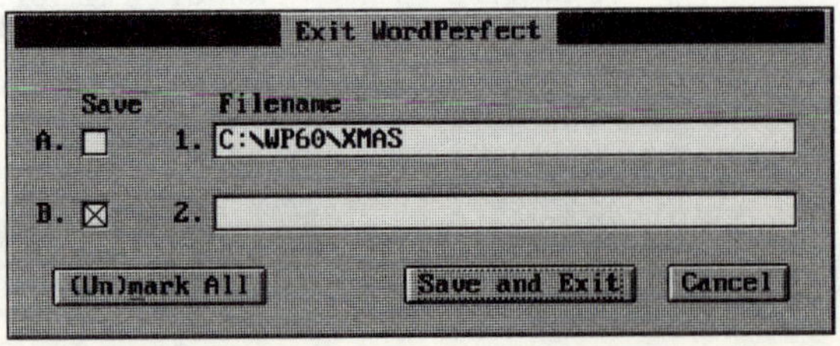

WordPerfect will save every file that has an *X* in the Save check box. You can add or remove the *X* in any check box by typing the letter next to the box or by clicking the box with your right mouse button. WordPerfect puts *X*s in the check boxes for all documents that have unsaved changes.

You can supply filenames for unnamed documents, and you can provide different filenames for documents you have already saved. To enter a filename, press the number next to the adjoining text box or click the text box with the right mouse button. Try this now by pressing 2 to tell WordPerfect you want to supply a filename for the second document. Type **remind** as the filename and press Enter to finish this entry. Press Enter again to select Save and Exit.

NOTE *Check boxes are used to indicate whether an option is selected. An option with an X in the box is a selected option.*

Type **WP** and press Enter to start WordPerfect again.

2. You can tile two documents to create two closely related documents. For example, when you type a summary letter for a contract, you might need to see both the contract and the letter to check that both documents use the same facts. Type

Know all men by these presents, that I, Tom Jones, the undersigned, in consideration of the sum of $40,000, in hand paid, do hereby grant, bargain, sell and convey to Ron Delaney, of Broward County, Florida, the following described real estate situated in the county of Orange, State of Florida, to wit: 1/2 acre lot at the corner of Rio Pinar Drive and Gator Alley, to have and to hold to his heirs and assigns forever.

Now create the summary letter to send with the contract. Select **F**ile, **N**ew. Then type

Tom Jones
513 Allworthy Lane
Oxford, CT 09134
Dear Mr. Jones,
Enclosed is the contract to sell your land at the corner of Rio Pinar Drive and Gator Alley to

To see both documents at once so that you can check the buyer's name and the price, select **W**indow, **T**ile. Your screen looks like Figure 2-2.

The contract states that the buyer is Ron Delaney and the price is $40,000. Type

Ron Delaney for $40,000. Sign the contract, notarize it, and return it to our office as soon as possible.
Sincerely,
Jane Perez, Attorney

By creating both documents at once and tiling the two windows, you can ensure that both documents contain the same information. Later you will learn how you can copy text from one document to another.

Save and close the documents. Select **F**ile, **E**xit. Press Y in the first dialog box. Type **delaney1** as the first filename, and press Enter. Press Y in the next dialog box, to exit the document. Then select **F**ile, **E**xit again. Press Y in the first dialog box. Type **delaney2** as the second filename, and press Enter. Press N in the next dialog box.

To return the first document window to its default size, select **W**indow, **M**aximize.

EXERCISES

1. Type the following paragraph. When you get to the four *X*s, open DELANEY2, tile the two document windows, and find the sales price and new owner. Switch back to document 1, and type this information in place of the four *X*s.

   Contract for sale of property to XXXX for $XXXX–
   3 hours @ $110 per hour $330

2. Type the following sentence:

   The president, Amanda Williams, started with the company as chief production officer fifteen years ago.

   Open a new document, and type

   Ms. Williams' experience includes chief production officer, divisional vice president, production vice president, and president.

   Switch to document 1, and type

   After four years as production officer, she was promoted to divisional vice president of the appliance division.

   Save document 1 as PRESIDNT and document 2 as PRESRESU.ME.

mastery skills check

As you complete the following Mastery Skills Check exercises, do not clear the screen between exercises unless instructed to do so.

1. Type the following paragraph. [2.1]

   At a press conference last Tuesday, XY Graphics Inc. demonstrated its new product, See 'N' Draw. This product is intended for both novices and experts.

2. Insert **June 17** and a comma before "XY Graphics" in the first sentence. [2.2]
3. Delete "Inc." by using the Del key. [2.3]
4. Type **July** over "June." [2.2]
5. Insert a hard return between the two sentences. [2.1]
6. Save the file as SEENDRAW. [2.4]
7. Open the file SEENDRAW so that there are two copies open. [2.6]
8. Switch to the first copy of SEENDRAW. [2.7]
9. Delete the word "both" in the second sentence, and then clear the screen without saving the document. [2.3]
10. Delete the second sentence in the second copy. [2.3]
11. Save the second copy as DRAW. Remove the document from memory. [2.4]

cumulative skills check

As you complete the following Cumulative Skills Check exercises, do not clear the screen between exercises unless instructed to do so.

1. Type the following lines. [2.1]

   CHOCOLATE CHIP COOKIES TASTE GOOD.
   However, they are fattening.

2. Use WordPerfect's Help system to determine which key saves a file. [1.4]
3. Save the file as COOKIE. [2.4]
4. Clear the screen. [1.2]
5. Type the following line. [1.3, 2.1]

   A few of my favorite things:

   Press Enter, add a line of dashes under the entry, and press Enter again.
6. Retrieve the file COOKIE into the current document. [2.5]
7. Insert **AND BUTTERSCOTCH CHIP** between "CHIP" and "COOKIES." [2.2]
8. Delete the last line. [1.3, 2.3]
9. Save the file as LIST. [2.4]
10. Exit WordPerfect. [1.1]

3

Printing a Document

chapter objectives

After completing this chapter, you should be able to

3.1 Print the current document

3.2 Print a selected page from the current document

3.3 Preview before printing

3.4 Print from a file

You will probably want at least one printed copy of each document you create. A printed copy is the usual medium for sharing the information in your documents with others. Some people also like to proof rough drafts of their documents from printed copies.

WordPerfect offers a considerable amount of flexibility in its print features. You can print a document in memory or a document stored on a disk. You can print a document while you are still editing the copy in memory. You can print an entire document or only some of its pages.

To perform any of these tasks, WordPerfect needs an assigned printer. Appendix A covers how to select a printer if one has not already been selected for your system. Chapter 12 covers additional enhancements possible with WordPerfect's print features.

review skills check

As you complete the following Skills Check exercises, do not clear the screen unless instructed to do so.

1. Type the following, including the misspelling. [1.3, 2.1]

   Four score and seven years ago our fathers brought forth on this continent, a new nation, conceived in liberty, and dedicated to the propsition that all men are created equal.

   Gettysburg Address

2. Delete the first four words, and type **87** in their place. [2.3]
3. Restore "Four score and seven" and delete "87." [1.4, 2.3]
4. Change "propsition" to "proposition" by inserting an *o* between the *p* and the *s*. [2.2]

5. Type **Abraham Lincoln** over "Gettysburg Address" by using typeover mode and the Del key. [2.2, 2.3]
6. Save this document as LINCOLN. [2.4]
7. Exit WordPerfect. [1.1]
8. Load WordPerfect, and retrieve the file LINCOLN. [1.1, 2.5]
9. Clear the screen, and display the Button Bar. [1.2]

3.1 PRINT THE CURRENT DOCUMENT

WordPerfect can print the current document without disrupting your work with the document. You can continue to make changes to the document or save it to disk while WordPerfect is printing. These actions will have no effect on the printed document. You can even switch to another document and work with the other document while the first document is printing.

You can use the printed copy of a document to give your eyes a break from the screen as you proof a section of the document, or you can give a printed draft of the document to someone to review while you continue to work.

TO PRINT THE CURRENT DOCUMENT

a. Select **F**ile, **P**rint/Fax to open the Print/Fax dialog box.
b. Press Enter or click P**r**int to print the entire document by using the default settings.

   Pressing Enter has the same effect as clicking the P**r**int button.

You can press Shift-F7 or click the Print button in the Button Bar in place of step a, to open the Print/Fax dialog box.

EXAMPLES

1. You can print a document by executing a single command. Type the following:

   Dear Sir:
   According to our records, your balance is past due. Please send the balance of your account, $150, within 30 days to prevent any legal action.

   Press Enter twice, press Tab five times, and type **Sincerely,**. Press Enter four times, press Tab five times, and type **Ellen Fitzpatrick**.

   When you have finished the letter, you can start printing by selecting **F**ile from the menu bar and then selecting **P**rint/Fax, which opens the Print/Fax dialog box shown in Figure 3-1. Press Enter or click P**r**int to print the document by using the default print settings. The dialog box disappears, and the document is displayed again as printing begins. You can now edit the document without affecting the print output. If you are using WordPerfect's graphics mode display, your printout will match what you see on the screen.

   To save this file as PASTDUE, clear the screen by selecting **F**ile, E**x**it. Then press Enter, type **pastdue**, and press Enter twice more.

2. While WordPerfect is printing a document, you can continue to work on that document or you can work on another document. Type

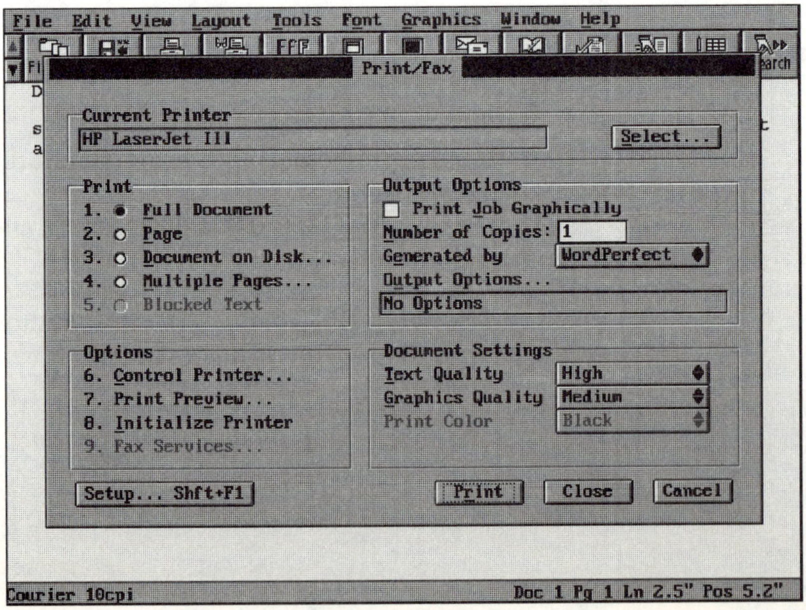

FIGURE 3-1 *Print/Fax dialog box*

Things cannot always go your way. Learn to accept in silence the minor aggravations, cultivate the gift of taciturnity, and consume your own work with an extra draught of hard work, so that those about you may not be annoyed with the dust and soot of your complaints.

Press Shift-F7, the function key equivalent of selecting **F**ile, **P**rint/Fax. If you have a mouse, you can click the Print button in the Button Bar. The Print button looks like this:

Press Enter. While WordPerfect prints your document, press Enter and type

Sir William Osler

Although the ability to edit a document while WordPerfect is printing might appear unimportant now, you will appreciate it when you are printing long documents such as 20-page reports. This ability becomes a crucial aid to your productivity with WordPerfect.

EXERCISES

1. Retrieve and print the file LINCOLN.
2. Type and print the following letter:

12345 Commerce Parkway
Beachwood, OH 44123
December 1, 1993

Samantha Koln
Small Business Administration of Cleveland
1235 Public Square
Cleveland, OH 44115

Dear Ms. Koln,
I am starting a business to manufacture mechanical pencils. Can you

provide information on the services that your organization provides to new companies?

Sincerely,

Tom Lu
President, Various Sundries, Inc.

Save the letter as SBA.

3. Type the following:

   There is hardly anything in the world that some man cannot make a little worse, and sell a little cheaper.

   John Ruskin

   Print a copy of the document. Do not clear the screen.

4. Press Enter twice; then add the following quote:

   It is just as important that business keep out of government as that government keep out of business.

   Herbert Hoover

   Print the document.

3.2 PRINT A SELECTED PAGE FROM THE CURRENT DOCUMENT

When you make corrections to a single page of a document, you do not need to print the pages that are not affected by your changes. WordPerfect allows you to print the current page from a document in memory.

TO SELECTIVELY PRINT A PAGE FROM A DOCUMENT

a. Move the cursor to the page that you want printed.

b. Select **F**ile, **P**rint/Fax. You can also press Shift-F7 or click the Print button in the Button Bar.

c. Select the **P**age radio button.

d. Press Enter to start printing.

EXAMPLES

1. You can print a single page from a document. First, type the following document as shown, using Ctrl-R and the equal sign (=) to draw the dividing line.

MEMORANDUM
To: Fran Stoll, Director, Human Services
From: John Smith, Division Manager
Re: Job Opening

═══════════════════════════════

Fran:
Deborah Winters has accepted a position with another firm. We need someone to fill her vacancy immediately. The following job description can be used for local advertisements.

Next, press Ctrl-Enter to add a hard page break. This places the cursor at the top of the second page of the document. Type the following:

Accountant - Responsibilities include the preparation of budget-analysis and cost-variance data. Must have an MBA or an M.Acct. with 2 years' experience. Salary commensurate with experience.

Select **F**ile, **P**rint/Fax. Press 2 or P to move the circle containing the black dot from the Full Document option to the Page option. These choices with circles next to them are called *radio buttons*. You can select only one radio button from a group of choices. The radio button marked with a black circle is the option currently chosen.

Press Enter to print the second page of the document. Move to the first page of the document by pressing Pg Up. Print this page by selecting **F**ile, **P**rint/Fax and then selecting the **P**age option and the P**r**int button.

2. You can print any page in a multipage document. First, type the following:

THINGS TO DO TODAY
Complete filing
Prepare budget report

Start a new page by pressing Ctrl-Enter. Type

THINGS TO DO NEXT WEEK
Prepare invoices

Order preprinted forms
Complete Part I of Teach Yourself WordPerfect

Press Ctrl-Enter for another page break. Type

END-OF-MONTH ACTIVITIES
Prepare performance reports
Close books

Press Enter to end the last line. Next, select **F**ile, **P**rint/Fax. Press P to select the **P**age radio button, and press Enter or click the P**r**int button to print the current page (page 3). WordPerfect prints only page 3. Save this file as TODO. Select **F**ile, **E**xit. Press Y for Yes to save the file, and type **todo** as the filename. Press Enter twice to use the filename and select the **N**o button in the second dialog box.

EXERCISES

1. Retrieve the file SBA that you created in exercise 2 of section 3.1. Print the document. Add the following paragraph to the end of the letter:

    I have enclosed a notice of our upcoming open house for your monthly newsletter.

    Move to the end of the document, begin a new page, and type

    Attend the Open House Celebration at Various Sundries on May 15 from 7:30 to 9:30 P.M.

    Print a copy of page 2.

2. Assume that you have three salespeople reporting to you. Their names are John Smith, Mary Brown, and Nancy Caster. Create a document that has a page for each employee. Each page should contain "Significant Accomplishments 1993 -" followed by the name of the employee. The first page would look like this:

    ```
    Significant Accomplishments 1993 - John Smith
    ```

    After creating the three pages, print a copy of page 3. Do not clear the screen.

3. Print a copy of page 2 from the document you created in exercise 2. Then print a copy of page 1.
4. Type the following:

   Follow pleasure, and then will pleasure flee;
   Flee pleasure, and pleasure will follow thee.
   John Heywood

   Begin a new page; then type

   But pleasures are like poppies spread—
   you seize the flower, its bloom is shed.
   Robert Burns

   Print a copy of page 1.

3.3 PREVIEW BEFORE PRINTING

You can preview a document to see how it will appear when printed. Previewing a document gives you options that aren't available when you're simply looking at the document in graphics mode. When you preview a document, you will see a preview window that has a different menu and Button Bar.

TO PREVIEW A DOCUMENT BEFORE PRINTING

a. Select **F**ile, Print Pre**v**iew. You can also click the Preview button in the Button Bar.
b. To change the size of the image displayed, select **V**iew and then select one of the options listed.
c. Press Esc or F7 to return to editing the document.

When you do not see the entire page at once, you can use the arrow keys to move around within a page. You can press Pg Up and Pg Dn to move from page to page in the preview image.

EXAMPLES

1. You can use the print preview feature to look at a document close up before you print it. Type

   Ignio Gonzolez
   Italia Buena
   765 Coltman Avenue
   Cleveland, OH 44106

   Dear Ignio,

   Thank you for your assistance with the family reunion. Your excellent foods were delightfully prepared, delivery was punctual, and the service was pleasant. We will think of Italia Buena for our next festive occasion.

   Press Enter twice, press Tab five times, and type **Sincerely,**. Press Enter four times, press Tab five times, and type **Alonzo Benito**.

   Preview the letter to see how it will look when you print it. Select **F**ile from the menu bar and then select Print Pre**v**iew, or click the Preview button in the Button Bar. The Preview button looks like this:

   Assuming that your computer can display graphics, your screen looks like Figure 3-2. You can see the margins at the edges of the document and look at how the text will appear on the printed page. Although you cannot read the text, you can see the general appearance of the letter.

   Select **V**iew from the menu bar and then select **1**00% View to expand the current document to its full size. The document looks much as it looks in graphics mode when you are editing it. Select **V**iew from the menu bar and then select **2**00% View to expand the document even more. Your screen looks like Figure 3-3. Use the arrow keys to move around in the display.

   Press Esc to end this preview. You will use this letter for the next example.

FIGURE 3-2

Full-page print preview

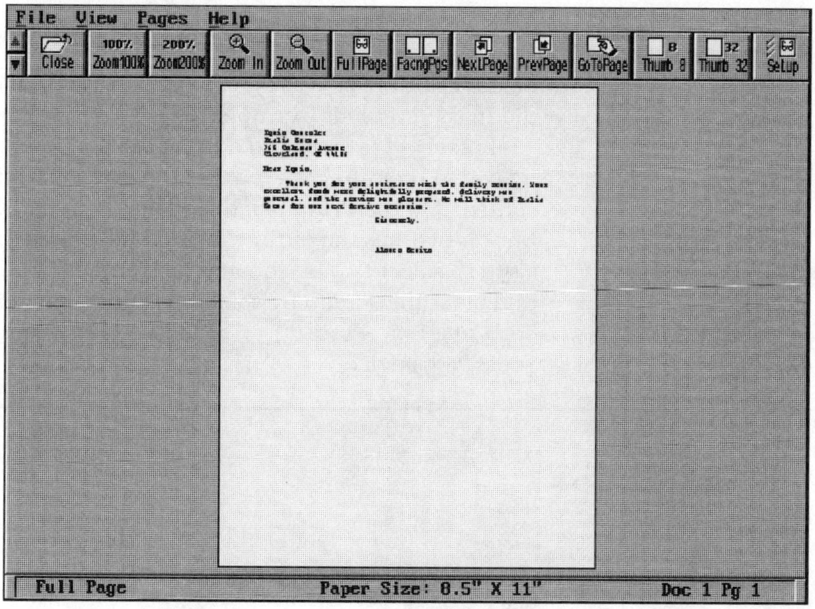

FIGURE 3-3

Print preview at 200%

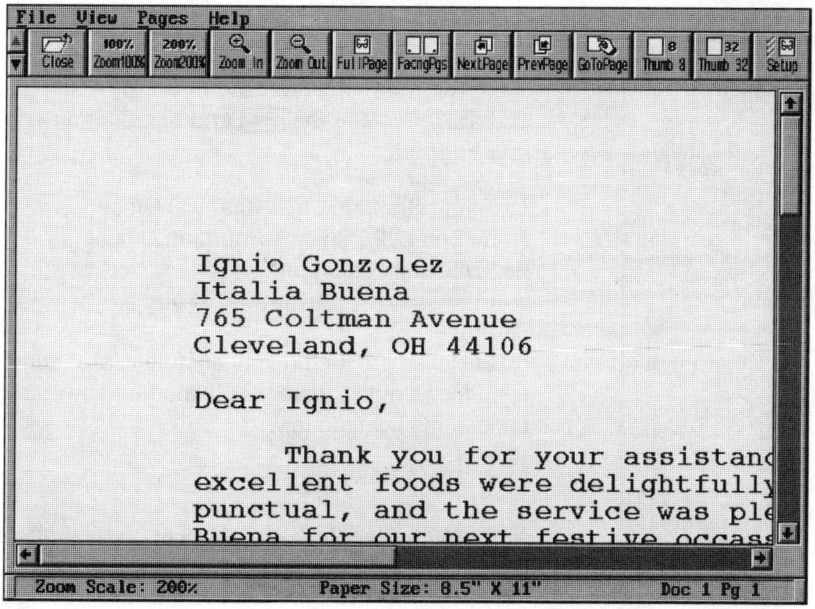

2. You can also preview a document by selecting the **P**rint/Fax command and then selecting Print Pre**v**iew. Select **F**ile, **P**rint/Fax. Select Print Pre**v**iew. You can preview your document exactly as you did in the previous example.

   Press Esc to return to editing the document. Because you activated the preview by using the Print/Fax dialog box, you are returned to the Print/Fax dialog box. The default button, which is the button that has the outline around its text, is the Close button. Press Enter to select this button and close the dialog box. Save the document and clear the screen by selecting **F**ile from the menu bar and then selecting **E**xit. Press Enter, type **ITALIA** as the document name, and press Enter twice.

EXERCISES

1. Retrieve and view the LINCOLN file you created in the Skills Check at the beginning of this chapter. Preview the file at the 100% size. Preview the file at the 200% size.
2. Type the following document and preview it as a full page, at 100%, and at 200%. Use the Esc and equal sign (=) keys to create the dividing line.

   To: Sarah Graham, Chief Financial Officer
   From: Bob Kelly, Chief Accounting Officer
   Re: Financial Statements

   Sarah,
   Enclosed are the preliminary financial statements. The attached text includes all of the footnotes. If you find any corrections or additions, please contact me immediately.

3. Type the following list of entries:

   Meeting on April 20th to discuss new construction.
   Make appointment with Harry to discuss new book series.
   Meet with marketing to discuss new advertising strategies.

   Preview the document. Press Ctrl-Enter at the end of each entry, and preview the document again.

4. Type the following quotations, pressing Ctrl-Enter at the end of each:

   One sees things for the first time only once.
   Theodore White

   Ignorance is never out of style. It was in fashion yesterday, it is the rage today, and will set the pace tomorrow.
   Frank Dane

   Horatio Alger started by shining shoes and within one year made a million dollars. He must have used very little polish.
   Sam Levenson

   Nothing is so good as it seems beforehand.
   George Eliot

   It takes twenty years to become an overnight success.
   Eddie Cantor

   Preview the document, using the facing-pages view to look at two pages at once. Move to the top of the document and then to the bottom while previewing. Save the document as QUOTES.

3.4 PRINT FROM A FILE

Printing from a file is convenient because you do not have to interrupt your current activities to open a copy of the document you want to print. You can print all the pages of a disk file, or you can specify which pages to print. You have greater flexibility in controlling which pages to print when you print from a file than when you print from an open document.

TO PRINT FROM A FILE

a. Select **F**ile, **P**rint/Fax. You can also press Shift-F7 or click the Print button in the Button Bar.
b. Select the **D**ocument on Disk radio button.
c. Type the filename of the document stored on disk that you want to print.
d. Press Enter.

e. To print some pages from the document, select **P**age/Label Range, type the page numbers, and press Enter.

f. Press Enter twice.

You can specify one or more pages to print. Use commas to separate the page numbers you specify. To print a range of pages, you can enter the first page number, a hyphen, and the last page number. You can enter a number preceded by a hyphen to print all pages up to and including that page. Specifying a number followed by a hyphen prints the page specified and all of the pages that follow it. Here are some sample page-number specifications and their results.

Page-Number Specification	Result
1,5–8,12	Prints pages 1, 5, 6, 7, 8, and 12
–5,10–	Prints all pages except 6, 7, 8, and 9
3	Prints page 3

EXAMPLES

1. You can print the file ITALIA that you created in section 3.3. Select **F**ile, **P**rint/Fax, press Shift-F7, or click the Print button in the Button Bar. Next, press D or 3 to select the **D**ocument on Disk radio button. When WordPerfect prompts you for the name of the document, type **italia** and press Enter. WordPerfect displays the Print Multiple Pages dialog box. The default page range is All. Press Enter twice to have WordPerfect print the entire document.
2. You can print a single page from a document stored on disk. First, create a document that consists of short entries on many pages. Type **This is page 1.**, and press Ctrl-Enter to begin a new page. Repeat this process, using consecutive page numbers, until you have entered **This is page 7.** End this line with Enter. Save the document as PAGES by selecting **F**ile from the menu bar and then selecting **E**xit. Press Enter, type **pages**, and press Enter twice. Select **F**ile, **P**rint/Fax. Press D or 3. When WordPerfect prompts you for the name of the document on disk, Type **pages** for the document name, and press Enter. Press 1 or P to select **P**age/Label Range.

Type **4** in the text box, and press Enter. Press Enter twice more. A copy of page 4 is printed.

3. You can print a range of pages from a document stored on disk. First, select **F**ile, **P**rint/Fax. Next, press D or 3 to select **D**ocument on Disk. Type **pages** in the text box, and press Enter. Press 1 or P to select **P**age/Label Range, and then type **2-5** in the text box. Press Enter three times. WordPerfect prints pages 2, 3, 4, and 5.
4. You can exclude a group of pages when printing a document stored on disk. First, select **F**ile, **P**rint/Fax. Next, press D or 3 to select **D**ocument on Disk. Type **pages** in the text box, and press Enter. Press 1 or P to select **P**age/Label Range, and then type **-3,6-** in the text box. The 3 represents the last page printed before the group of pages excluded, and the 6 represents the first page printed after the excluded pages. Press Enter three times. WordPerfect prints pages 1, 2, 3, 6, and 7.

EXERCISES

1. Print the SBA file that you created in exercise 2 of section 3.1.
2. Enter the following:

   RESIDENTS WHO OPPOSE ROAD PAVING
   Black
   Smith
   Campbell
   Gilbert
   Long
   Jackson

   Start a new page, and enter

   RESIDENTS WHO SUPPORT ROAD PAVING
   Wilson
   Boswell
   Dike

   Save the document to disk as ROAD, and clear the screen. Print a copy of the entire document from disk. Print another copy of page 2.

3. Print page 2 of QUOTES, which you created in exercise 4 of section 3.3.
4. Print pages 2 through 4 of QUOTES.
5. Print pages 1 and 4 of QUOTES.

mastery skills check

As you complete the following Mastery Skills Check exercises, do not clear the screen unless instructed to do so.

1. Type this letter:

   To: All Managers
   From: Fred Jones, Director of Human Services
   Subject: Meetings on the New Benefit Package
   The Human Services Department will be conducting one-hour informational meetings on the new benefit package. We have attempted to schedule these meetings at convenient times. Please route the sign-up sheets to your employees and encourage everyone to attend one of these sessions.

   Create four new pages in the same document, with one of the following entries at the top of each page:

   Benefit Package Meeting - April 5, 9:30 A.M.
   Benefit Package Meeting - April 5, 2:30 P.M.
   Benefit Package Meeting - April 6, 8:30 A.M.
   Benefit Package Meeting - April 6, 4:00 P.M.

   Preview the letter. Look first at the full-page view, and then look at facing pages. Finally, look at the two enlarged views. [3.3]
2. Print this letter and the four attachment pages. [3.2]
3. Print another copy of page 1. [3.2]
4. Save the file as BENEFITS, and clear the screen. Print the four attachment pages from disk. [3.4]

Teach Yourself cumulative skills check

As you complete the following exercises, do not clear the screen unless instructed to do so.

1. Type the following paragraphs. [1.3, 1.5, 2.1]

    A meeting is scheduled at 5 P.M. on January 20 to discuss the company's participation in the CLEVELAND CORPORATE OLYMPICS. The meeting will be held in the fourth-floor conference room.

    This year, we need a slogan for the banner and a T-shirt design. We also need a list of the employees participating in each activity. Please encourage your staff members to participate.

    Interested individuals unable to attend the scheduled meeting should contact Steve Spear. His extension is 3963.

2. Delete the second sentence of the third paragraph. [2.3]
3. Change the date to January 25. [2.2]
4. Print the document. [3.1]
5. Go to the end of the document. [1.3]
6. Insert a hard page break at the end of the document. [1.3, 3.2]
7. Type the following list. [1.3, 1.4, 2.1]

Name	Activity
--------	--------
Sue Marianetti	Bike Race
Sharon Campbell	Tug-of-War
John Peterson	Tug-of-War
Tim Smith	5K Race
Ted McGregor	Tug-of-War
Brandon Leidy	Swimming
Marge Thomas	5K Race
Anne Kettlewood	Bike Race

8. Preview the document. [3.3]
9. Print page 2. [3.2]
10. Save this document as OLYMPICS. [1.2, 2.4]

11. Begin typing the following lines in a new document. [2.6, 3.1]

    CORPORATE SLOGAN SUGGESTIONS
    Our Team's the Best

    Print page 1 of OLYMPICS; then continue typing slogans:

    The Best at All We Do
    Scientific Services Employees Have Brains and Brawn
    Sticks and Stones Won't Break Our Bones

4

Using Features to Alter the Appearance of Text

chapter objectives

After completing this chapter, you should be able to

4.1 Underline text as you type

4.2 Boldface text as you type

4.3 Center text as you type

4.4 Reveal the hidden codes for special features

4.5 Delete hidden codes

4.6 Mark and delete blocks of text

4.7 Apply special features to blocks of text

WordPerfect's special features can help you add emphasis to text. Underlining, boldfacing, and centering help to set off text from the rest of your document. WordPerfect changes the appearance of your text on the screen to indicate these special features. WordPerfect also adds hidden codes to the document for each of these features.

If you do not add these special features to your text as you type it, WordPerfect allows you to add them later. To add a special feature to existing text, you must mark the block of text and then have WordPerfect apply the feature to it.

review skills check

As you complete the following Skills Check exercises, do not clear the screen until instructed to do so.

1. Type the following paragraph, including the mistakes. [2.1]

   The next meting of the WordPerfect User Group will be January 5. Each attendeee will receive a free on the use of the new graphics features.

2. Correct the document by changing the spelling of the third word to "meeting," removing the last *e* from "attendeee," and inserting the word "handout" after the word "free." [2.2]
3. Use WordPerfect's Help system to find information about the function key template. Determine the correct key for saving a document. [1.4]
4. Save the document as MEETING. [2.4]
5. Clear the screen. [1.2]
6. Print the document from disk. [3.4]

4.1 UNDERLINE TEXT AS YOU TYPE

You can use underlining to add emphasis to words in a document or to set off book titles. You can also use underlining to represent division in a formula or an equation.

TO UNDERLINE CHARACTERS AS YOU TYPE

a. Select F**o**nt, **U**nderline. You can also press F8.

b. Type the characters to underline.

c. Select F**o**nt, **U**nderline again to turn off the underline feature. You can also press F8 or →.

If you are using text mode, underlined text has a different background shade than normal text. If you are using graphics mode, you can see the underlining as it will appear when printed.

NOTE *Because using the drop-down menus requires four keystrokes, most people prefer to use F8 to underline text. Except in the next example, this book mentions only the F8 method. You can still use the drop-down menus, with the keyboard or the mouse, if you prefer.*

EXAMPLES

1. You can underline text at the beginning of a line. Select F**o**nt, **U**nderline or press F8, and then type

   Project Review

   Select F**o**nt, **U**nderline or press F8 again. You can also press →. The screen looks like this:

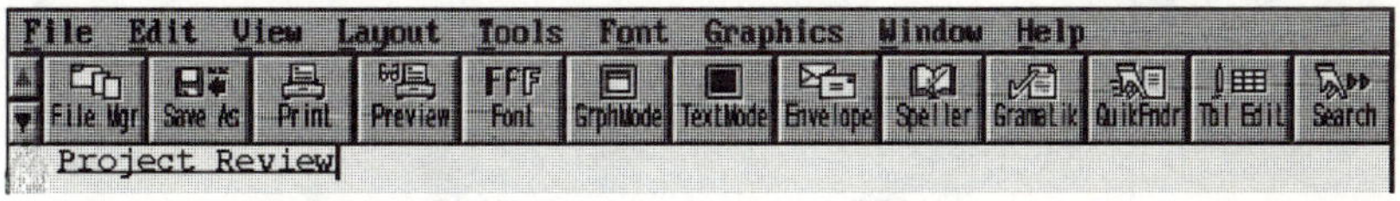

2. You can underline several words in the middle of a sentence. First, type the following words, which do not require underlining, and include a space after the last word:

   The committee will meet on

   Next, press F8 and type

   Monday, April 4,

Finally, press F8 to turn off the underline feature, and type

at 3 PM.

The display looks like the following:

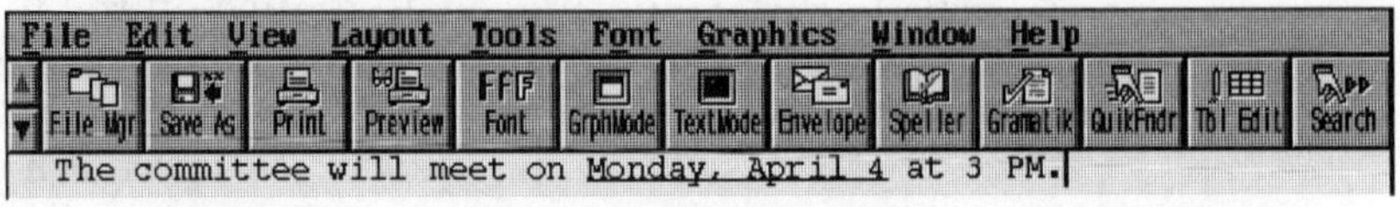

EXERCISES

1. Create the following bibliography:

   Campbell, Mary, Best WordPerfect Tips Ever, Osborne/McGraw-Hill, 1993.
   Mincberg, Mella, WordPerfect 6 Made Easy, Osborne/McGraw-Hill, 1993.

2. Type the following document:

   We will honor employees who have more than twenty-five years of service at the annual appreciation dinner. The following employees are honorees at this year's dinner:

EMPLOYEE	YEARS OF SERVICE
J. Smith	25
R. Taylor	35
P. Volker	31

3. Type the following formula:

   $$\text{Cost per square foot} = \frac{\text{Total cost}}{\text{Square feet}}$$

4. Type the following exactly as shown:

   There are many interesting tales in mythology. The gods, goddesses, and heroes in these stories have unusual names and adventures. The names of the gods and other special characters in the following passage are underlined to highlight them.

Aconteus looked at Medusa's head and turned into stone. Medusa was a monster whose hair was made of serpents. Perseus, the son of Danae and Jupiter, killed Medusa. To make himself invisible to Medusa, he wore Pluto's helmet and a pair of winged shoes.

4.2 BOLDFACE TEXT AS YOU TYPE

Bold text is text that is darker than the surrounding text. You can use the bold feature to add emphasis to text.

TO BOLDFACE CHARACTERS AS YOU TYPE

a. Select F**o**nt, **B**old or press F6.

b. Type the characters you want to show in boldface.

c. Select F**o**nt, **B**old again, press F6, or press →.

NOTE *Because using F6 requires one keystroke and using the drop-down menus requires more, most people use F6 to boldface text. Except in the next example, this book uses the F6 key exclusively. You can still use the drop-down menus, with the keyboard or the mouse, if you prefer.*

In text mode, the bold text is shown with increased intensity or in a different color. In graphics mode, you can see the letters boldfaced, as they will appear when you print the document.

EXAMPLES

1. You can use the bold feature to highlight a date and time in an entry. First, type the following text, which does not require boldface:

   The next meeting is scheduled for

Next, add a space after the last word. Select F**o**nt, **B**old or press F6, and type

11 P.M. on Friday, January 14

End the bold text by selecting F**o**nt, **B**old again or pressing F6. You can also press →. Then type a period to end the sentence. The boldfacing makes the text look like this:

The next meeting is scheduled for **11 P.M. on Friday, January 14**.

2. You can invoke the bold feature once and continue to type bold text until you turn off the feature. To enter a list of bulleted items in boldface, turn on the bold feature before typing the first bulleted item, and turn off the bold feature after typing the last item. Type the following text, which does not require boldface:

   We will discuss the following topics at the next meeting:

   Next, press Enter and press F6. Then, for each bulleted item, press Tab, type the text, and press Enter:

   * Part-time versus full-time benefits
   * Training opportunities
   * Stock option plan eligibility

   Press F6 to turn off the bold feature. The text looks like this:

   We will discuss the following topics at the next meeting:
   *** Part-time versus full-time benefits**
   *** Training opportunities**
   *** Stock option plan eligibility**

3. You can combine the bold and underline features to add extra emphasis to text. To begin an entry that uses both the bold and the underline features, press F6 and then press F8. Type

   ANNUAL REPORT

   If you are using text mode, the text should look different than both underlined text and bold text. Next, press F8 and F6 or press → twice to turn off both features. The printed text looks like this:

   <u>ANNUAL REPORT</u>

EXERCISES

1. Type the following accounts and their balances. Use boldface for all negative balances (shown in parentheses).

ACCOUNT	BALANCE
Rent	$5,125
Utilities	**(1,250)**
Phone	**(950)**

2. Type the following sentences. Use boldface for "more than 90 days' past due" and "immediately."

Your account balance is **more than 90 days' past due**. Unless you contact us **immediately**, we will begin legal action to collect the balance of your account.

3. Type the following. Use boldface and underlining for the label at the top of each column:

DEPT	**HEAD COUNT**
ACCT	14
FIN	10
MFG	84

4. Type the following, using boldface for the foreign phrases.

Foreign words can add variety to your writing. When you select foreign phrases, you will want to be certain that both you and your readers understand their meaning. **Deo gratias** means thanks to God. **Dei gratia** means by the grace of God. **Deo volente** means by God's will. **Dieu vous garde** means God protect you.

5. Type the following quotations. Use boldface for the author of each quote, and use boldface and underlining for the source of each quote:

Noble by birth, yet nobler by great deeds.
Henry Wadsworth Longfellow, **Tales of a Wayside Inn**
Who fears t'offend takes the first step to please.
Colley Cibber, **Love in a Riddle**
The art of praising is the beginning of the art of pleasing.
Voltaire, **La Pucelle**

4.3 CENTER TEXT AS YOU TYPE

You can use centering to place words in the center of a line in your document. You might want to use this feature to center a report tile, a company name, or a department name.

TO CENTER CHARACTERS ON A LINE AS YOU TYPE THEM

a. Select **L**ayout, **A**lignment, **C**enter or press Shift-F6.

b. Type the characters you want to center on the line.

c. Press Enter to turn off the centering feature. WordPerfect displays the text centered on the line.

NOTE *Again, because using the shortcut key takes so much less effort than using the drop-down menu, most users prefer to use Shift-F6. Except in the first example, this book uses Shift-F6 exclusively. You can still use the drop-down menus, with the keyboard or the mouse, if you prefer.*

EXAMPLES

1. You can use centering to create a heading. Select **L**ayout, **A**lignment, and then select **C**enter. Next, type the following company name:

   ABC COMPANY

   Press Enter to indicate the end of the entry. Your screen looks like this:

   You must reselect this command to center the next line of text. Only the text typed on this line is centered. Press Shift-F6 and type

   111 North Avenue

Press Enter to end the line, press Shift-F6, and type

Chicago, IL 30211

The screen looks like this:

2. You can enter text at the left margin on the same line as centered text. First, type

   Roger Smith

   Next, press Shift-F6, and type

   ABC Company

   The results look like this:

3. You can use the centering feature with the underline and bold features. Press F6, press F8, and press Shift-F6. Type

   ABC Company

   Press F6, F8, and Enter. If you print the page, the line looks like this:

ABC Company

EXERCISES

1. Type your name, street address, and city and state on three separate lines, using the centering feature for each line.

2. Using the centering and bold features, type **Tinsel Company** on a line.
3. Turn on the centering feature and type the following text. Watch the screen as you type.

   This text is too long for one line. WordPerfect cannot fit the entire entry on one line. When you print the text, you will notice that WordPerfect centers only the text in the first line.

   As you type this text, you cannot see the centering on the screen, because of the length of the lines. Initially, the first characters of the first sentence seem to disappear.
4. Center the following lines as you type them:

   ABC COMPANY
   PERFORMANCE REPORT
   FOR THE QUARTER ENDING JUNE 30, 1993

4.4 REVEAL THE HIDDEN CODES FOR SPECIAL FEATURES

WordPerfect marks special features, such as the end of a line, the end of a page, and boldface text, with hidden codes. The codes provide specific information about each feature used and its exact location within the document. Although some features might be obvious as you look at the screen, others are not apparent unless you reveal the codes within the document. WordPerfect splits the screen to display the codes, using the top window for the normal display and showing the text and codes in the bottom window. You cannot type a new code over an existing code to make a change. You must delete the existing code or insert a new one after it in the document.

TO REVEAL HIDDEN CODES IN A DOCUMENT

a. Select **V**iew, Reveal **C**odes, press Alt-F3, or press F11.
b. Use the arrow keys to move around the Reveal Codes screen.
c. Select **V**iew, Reveal **C**odes, press Alt-F3, or press F11 again to return to the normal display.

EXAMPLES

1. Even without using special attributes (such as boldface and underlining), your document contains special codes. To see them, use the reveal codes feature. Type

   ABC Company

   Press Enter. This adds a hidden code for a hard return. Select **V**iew, Reveal **C**odes or press Alt-F3 to produce the split screen display shown in Figure 4-1. The [HRt] code represents the hard return that was inserted where you pressed Enter. WordPerfect inserts a soft return code [SRt] when it uses its word wrap feature to begin another line. A soft page break is generated when WordPerfect fills a page. The code for a soft page break is [SPg]. When you force WordPerfect to end a page by selecting **L**ayout, **A**lignment, Hard **P**age or pressing Ctrl-Enter, a hard page break code, [HPg], is inserted. The code [Open Style:InitialCodes] at the beginning of the document indicates that the document picks up any initial codes that you can assign to all new documents. Press Alt-F3 to hide the codes again.

2. You can use the reveal codes feature to look at the special attributes in your documents. Press F6, and type

   BUDGET SUMMARY

   Press F6 to turn off the bold feature. Next, press Enter twice and F8 once. Type

   ACCOUNTING DEPARTMENT

   Press F8 to turn off the underline feature. To look at the codes for these features, select **V**iew, Reveal **C**odes or press Alt-F3. Press ↑ twice so that you can see more of the codes. As you examine the Reveal Codes screen, you will notice that each attribute uses a code at the beginning and at the end of the affected text, as shown here:

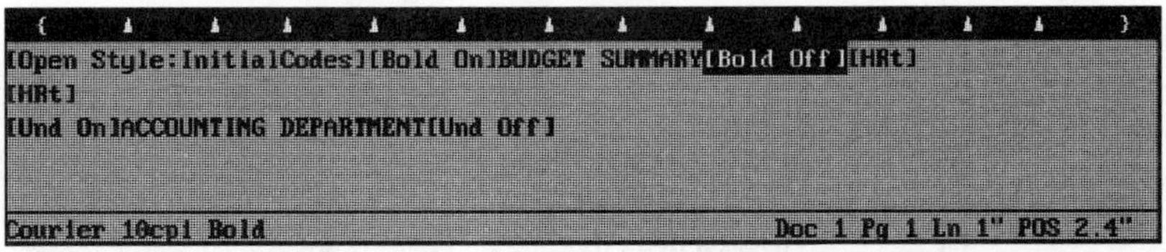

FIGURE 4-1

WordPerfect Reveal Codes screen

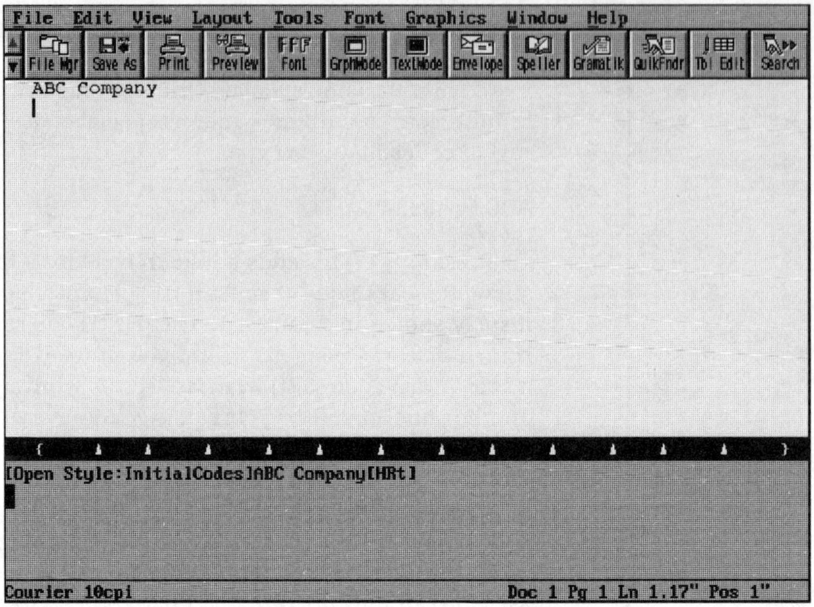

WordPerfect places [Bold On] and [Bold Off] codes around bold text. It uses [Und On] and [Und Off] for underlined text. In each case, a pair of codes surrounds the text that is affected by the feature.

Press ↓ twice, → once, and Enter once. Then press Shift-F6 to center text. WordPerfect inserts a [Cntr on Mar] code to indicate that the entry is to be centered. Type **ABC Company**, and press Enter.

You can remove the Reveal Codes display from the screen by selecting **V**iew, Reveal **C**odes or by pressing Alt-F3 again.

EXERCISES

1. Type the following lines, using the centering feature for each line:

   ABC COMPANY
   BUDGET REPORT
   FISCAL 1993

Use the reveal codes feature to find the codes for centering at the beginning and end of each entry.

2. Type the following, using boldface where indicated:

   New Sunday store hours are **Noon to 5 P.M.**

   Use the reveal codes feature to locate the codes for boldface.

3. Open the reveal codes screen. Type the following, using boldface and underlining:

   Overdue Accounts

   Note the addition of the codes to the document.

4. Center the following lines:

   I think, therefore I am.
   Rene Descartes

   Reveal the hidden codes to see the codes added for centering the lines. Save the file as THINK. Hide the codes.

4.5 DELETE HIDDEN CODES

If you used special features on text, you do not need to delete the text to remove the special features. You can remove a special feature by deleting the code for the special feature from the Reveal Codes display. To remove underline or boldface codes, you can remove either of the pair of special codes that mark the attribute.

TO DELETE A CODE IN THE REVEAL CODES DISPLAY

a. Select **V**iew, Reveal **C**odes. If you prefer, you can press Alt-F3 or press F11 to display the Reveal Codes screen.
b. Use the arrow keys to move the cursor to the code you want to remove.
c. Press Del.

You can also delete a code by moving the cursor to the right of the code and pressing Backspace.

d. Select **V**iew, Reveal **C**odes, press Alt-F3, or press F11 again to return to the normal display.

NOTE *Most codes can be deleted only by displaying the hidden codes first. When you press Del or Backspace without the hidden codes revealed, you will skip over the codes in the document and delete characters that you see in the document.*

EXAMPLES

1. You can enter text with a special attribute and later remove the attribute. First, press F6 and type

   BUDGET REPORT

   Next, press F6 to turn off the bold feature. To look at the hidden codes, select **V**iew, Reveal **C**odes or press Alt-F3. If you position the cursor in the Reveal Codes screen on either the [Bold On] or [Bold Off] code and press Del, WordPerfect deletes both codes. The text remains on the screen.

   Select **V**iew, Reveal **C**odes or press Alt-F3 again to return to the normal display.

2. You can assign multiple attributes to text and delete any of the attributes without affecting the remaining codes or the text. Press F6 and then F8. Next, type

   Expenses

   Press F6 and then press F8 to turn off both features. After displaying the Reveal Codes screen by selecting **V**iew, Reveal **C**odes or pressing Alt-F3, use the arrow keys to highlight [Und On], and press Del. This action removes the underlining but retains the text and the boldface. Select **V**iew, Reveal **C**odes or press Alt-F3 to return to the normal display.

EXERCISES

As you complete the following exercises, do not clear the screen between exercises unless instructed to do so.

1. Enter the following text exactly as shown, but center the indented lines.

   Quality Corporation is pleased to announce the following Christmas bonus structures:

   Less than 2 years of service - 2% bonus

   2 years or more of service - 5% bonus

   Checks will be available for distribution on December 23.

   Find the codes for the bold, underline, and centering features in the Reveal Codes screen. Delete the code for centering.
2. Retrieve the file THINK that you created in the fourth exercise of the last section, and delete the code for centering.

4.6 MARK AND DELETE BLOCKS OF TEXT

Normally, the Del and Backspace keys affect only a single character or code, or one pair of codes, at a time. You can use the block feature to mark adjacent characters and codes to perform an action on all the marked material at one time.

NOTE *If you prefer you can skip the block procedure and just use the Backspace key to delete adjacent codes. Blocking can be quicker when you have large blocks of codes and text to remove.*

TO MARK A BLOCK OF TEXT

a. Use the cursor movement keys to position the cursor on the first character or code in the block you want to mark.

b. Select **E**dit, **B**lock, press Alt-F4, or press F12.

c. Use the arrow keys to move the cursor one position past the last character in the block.

The text within the block is highlighted. The colors used to highlight your text depend on whether you are in graphics or text mode and on what kind of monitor you have. If you want to remove the highlighting without taking an action, press Esc, select **E**dit, **B**lock, or press Alt-F4 or F12 again.

Mouse users can block text by placing the mouse pointer at the beginning of the text to be blocked, holding down the left mouse button, moving the pointer one position past the last character of the block, and releasing the mouse button.

EXAMPLES

1. You can block a word in a document and delete it. First, type the following sentence:

   The next loan payment is due January 14.

   Use the arrow keys to move to the *p* in "payment." Next, select **E**dit, **B**lock or press Alt-F4. WordPerfect changes the background display of the position number on the bottom of the screen to indicate that the block feature has been activated. Press Ctrl-→ to place the cursor on the *i* in "is." WordPerfect changes the display of the blocked text. The screen looks like this:

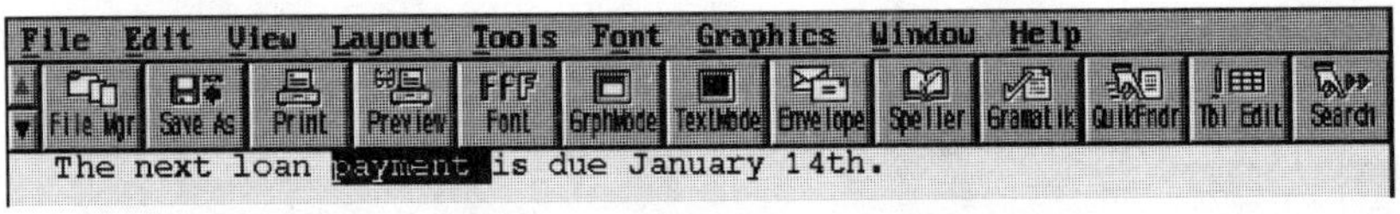

   To delete the blocked text, press Del or Backspace.

2. You can block larger portions of a document by using the same method or by using shortcuts. For example, when the block feature is activated, typing any character causes everything up to and including the next occurrence of that character to be included within the block. First, type the following:

   The first Advanced WordPerfect seminar is scheduled for November 22, 1993. Employees must complete the exercises in Teach Yourself WordPerfect to be eligible for enrollment.

Next, use the arrow keys to move to the *E* at the beginning of the second sentence. Select **E**dit, **B**lock or press Alt-F4 to activate the block feature. To block the entire sentence, press [.]. Press Del to remove the sentence.

EXERCISES

1. Type the following:

   An excuse uncalled for becomes an obvious accusation.
   Law Maxim

   Block the word "excuse." Turn off the block feature, and save the file as EXCUSE.

2. Type the following text:

   You must submit expense reports by the 15th of the month following travel.

   Use the block feature to block "15th." Turn off the block feature. Do not clear the screen.

3. Insert the word "previous" before the word "month." Block the new word and delete it.
4. Retrieve the file named THINK. Block and delete "Rene Descartes."

4.7 APPLY SPECIAL FEATURES TO BLOCKS OF TEXT

Using special features such as boldface, underlining, and centering is simplest if you turn on the feature before typing the text. However, if you forget, or if you want to change the appearance of text that has already been typed, you can still add these features. You block the text that you want to change and then you turn on the feature.

TO APPLY SPECIAL FEATURES TO A GROUP OF CHARACTERS

a. Block the text.

b. Activate the special feature by using the drop-down menu or the function key shortcut. For example, select F**o**nt, **B**old or press F6.

EXAMPLES

1. You can underline text without retyping it. First, complete these entries, pressing Enter at the end of each line:

   A few box office hits are
   Aladdin
   A Few Good Men
   Unforgiven
   Howards End

   Press Enter after typing the last title. Although you did not underline the movie titles when typing them, you can do so now. Move the cursor to the *A* in the first title, and select **E**dit, **B**lock or press Alt-F4. Use ↓ to move the cursor to the line below the last title. Next, select F**o**nt, **U**nderline or press F8. WordPerfect underlines the titles.

2. You can add more than one attribute to existing text. Type the following:

   The last date for renewing your membership at this year's rate
   is December 31.

   You can add both bold and underlining to "last date" and "December 31" by blocking the entries. First, move the cursor to the *l* in "last." Select **E**dit, **B**lock or press Alt-F4, and then move the cursor to the *e* in "date." Press F8. To add bold, block the data again by pressing Alt-F4. To quickly return to the first character of the block, hold down Ctrl and press Home twice. Press F6 to add the second attribute. You can repeat this procedure for "December 31." The sentence looks like this:

   The **last date** for renewing your membership at this year's rate is **December 31**.

EXERCISES

1. Type the following:

   After completing this book, you can continue to build your skills with WordPerfect 6 Made Easy. Soon you will be your company's WordPerfect expert.

   Use the block feature to underline "WordPerfect 6 Made Easy." Do not clear the screen.
2. Use the block feature to make "WordPerfect expert" bold.
3. Retrieve the file EXCUSE. Add the following quotation at the end of the document:

   A bad excuse is better, they say, than none at all.
   Stephen Gosson

   Block the word "excuse" in each quotation and make it boldface.
4. Type the following:

   A cruel story runs on wheels, and every hand oils the wheels as they run.
   Ouida

   Underline and boldface both occurrences of "wheels" after completing the entry.

mastery skills check

As you complete the following Mastery Skills Check exercises, do not clear the screen between exercises unless instructed to do so.

1. Underline the following text as you type it:

   Bylaws of the WordPerfect User Group

   Clear the screen. [4.1]

2. Enter the following sentence, using boldface for the company name, location, and date. [4.2]

   ABC Company will hold its annual picnic at the **Loch Raven Pavilion** on **July 17th**.

3. Use the reveal codes feature to look at the hidden codes for boldface. Delete the bold codes for "Loch Raven Pavilion." Deactivate the reveal codes feature. [4.4, 4.5]
4. Move to the top of the document. With the reveal codes feature activated, type the following line, using the centering and underline features. [4.1, 4.2, 4.4]

   COMPANY PICNIC ANNOUNCEMENT

5. Add two blank lines. Reveal the codes to see the codes added for the text you entered in the last exercise. Hide the codes. Print the document, and clear the screen. [3.1, 4.4]
6. Type the following memo as shown:

   ABC COMPANY
   INTERNAL MEMORANDUM

   TO: All staff
   FROM: John Smith
   SUBJECT: Completion of parking lot resurfacing
   DATE: February 15, 1994

   The resurfacing of parking lots A and B is complete. Resurfacing of parking lot C is scheduled to begin Monday, February 21.

   Your continued cooperation is appreciated.

   Use the reveal codes feature to remove the hard return before the last line. Save the memo as PARKING. [2.4, 4.2, 4.4]

7. Add boldface to the word "complete" in the first sentence. Use the block feature to mark the second sentence and delete it. Clear the screen. [4.2, 4.6]
8. Type the following:

ACCT NO	BALANCE
1204	$12,350
1567	$17,865
2569	$23,789

Use the block feature to add boldface and underlining to the heading at the top of each column. [4.6, 4.7]

cumulative skills check

As you work through the following exercises, do not clear the screen between exercises unless instructed to do so.

1. Type the following document as shown. [1.3, 4.3]

    ABC BOOKS
    1115 Warren Avenue
    Cleveland, OH 44017

    Mr. John Myers
    Winsom Corporation
    111 North St.
    Akron, OH 43124

    Dear Mr. Myers:

    We are holding a copy of Successful Office Management for you. We will hold this book for you until October 12.

    Sincerely,

    Ralph Jones
    Customer Service

2. Save the document as MYERS, and clear the screen. Print a copy of the letter from disk. [2.4, 3.4]
3. Retrieve the file twice, and make the following changes to the second copy: Use typeover mode to change "North" to "South." Add

underlining to "Successful Office Management." Add boldface to the date in the last sentence. [2.2, 2.5, 4.6, 4.7]

4. Activate the block feature, and block the main part of the letter. Then turn off the block feature. [4.6]
5. Save the second document to disk, with the name MYERS2. Preview the document on the screen. Print a copy. [2.4, 3.1, 3.3]
6. Clear both documents from the screen. [1.2]

5

Changing the Appearance of Lines and Paragraphs in a Document

chapter objectives

After completing this chapter, you should be able to

5.1 Use indentation

5.2 Use the back tab feature

5.3 Set tabs

5.4 Use the flush right feature

5.5 Change line spacing

5.6 Alter justification

WordPerfect's line-formatting features allow you to change the appearance of one or more lines of text. Lines can be indented from the sides of the paper, which lets you offset bulleted items or other important text. You can change tab settings to match how you want to make entries. WordPerfect lets you change line spacing to provide extra space between lines.

The flush right feature allows you to align text, such as the date or a letter heading, with the right margin of a document. Justification affects entire paragraphs of text. It lets you align text with either the left or the right margin, center text between the margins, or align text with both margins at the same time.

Each of these options affects the text of a document beginning at the line or paragraph in which it is invoked. If you want a formatting change to affect the entire document, you must invoke the feature at the top of the document.

review
skills check

As you complete the following Skills Check exercises, do not clear the screen until you are instructed to do so.

1. Type the following bibliography, centering the heading and underlining the book titles as you type them. [4.1, 4.3]

    Bibliography

    Mincberg, Mella, WordPerfect 6 Made Easy,
    Osborne/McGraw-Hill, 832 pages.
    Campbell, Mary, 1-2-3 Release 2.4 Made Easy,
    Osborne/McGraw-Hill, 475 pages.

2. Insert the copyright date for each book—1993 and 1992, respectively—between the publisher and the page count. [2.2.]
3. Save the document as BIBLIO. [2.4]
4. Reveal hidden codes, and then locate the codes for underlining and delete them in the Reveal Codes screen. [4.5]

5. Clear the screen. [1.3]
6. Print the file BIBLIO. [3.4]

5.1 USE INDENTATION

WordPerfect lets you indent a paragraph of text from the left margin. Each time you enter an indentation, WordPerfect moves the beginning of each line in the current paragraph one tab stop to the right and establishes a temporary margin at that position. This feature lets you set off bulleted items and special text from regular text. The hidden code inserted for an indentation is [Lft Indent]. If you delete this code, the indentation is removed.

TO INDENT A PARAGRAPH FROM THE LEFT MARGIN

a. Move the cursor to the beginning of the paragraph that you want to indent.
b. Select **L**ayout, **A**lignment, **I**ndent →.
   You can also press F4 to indent a paragraph.
c. Repeat step b until the paragraph is indented at the tab stop you want.

A similar feature allows you to indent text from both the left and right margins at the same time. WordPerfect's left and right indent feature creates temporary margins for the current paragraph. When you indent a paragraph from both sides, the margins move in one tab stop from both the left and right edges of the document. Indentation from both sides is used to indicate a long quotation within the body of a letter or report. The hidden code that is added to a document when this feature is used is [Lft/Rgt Indent].

TO INDENT A PARAGRAPH FROM BOTH MARGINS

a. Move the cursor to the beginning of the paragraph that you want to indent.
b. Select **L**ayout, **A**lignment, I**n**dent → ←.
   Pressing Shift-F4 is another way of accomplishing step b.

c. Repeat step b one or more times to indent the paragraph to the tab settings you want.

You can perform these steps before or after you type the text.

EXAMPLES

1. You can indent text from the left margin to create professional-looking lists. First, type **1**. Next, select **L**ayout, **A**lignment, **I**ndent → or press F4, and type

   Type the text of the document you are creating, including simple character formatting.

   Press Enter, type **2**, press F4, and type

   Check the grammar and spelling of the text in your document, remembering to use the thesaurus to find words that can improve your document.

   Press Enter, type **3**, press F4, and type

   Add the formatting, such as margins, columns, and graphics, that you will use to enhance the appearance of your document.

   The document looks like this:

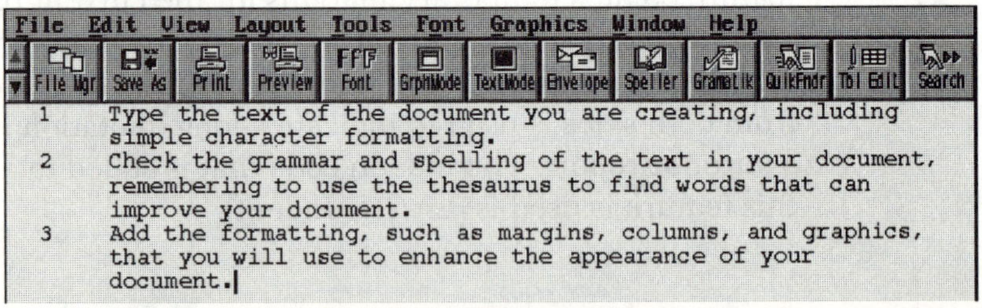

   You can display the hidden code for the indent feature by selecting **V**iew, Reveal **C**odes or pressing Alt-F3. Notice that because the numbers appear before the indent codes, they are not indented, although all the other text in the paragraphs is. If you delete these codes, the indentations are removed.

2. You can indent both sides of a paragraph. This is customary when typing a long quotation. To indent both sides of a paragraph, type

Isaac Newton, a mathematician, philosopher, and scientist, said

Press Enter to end the paragraph. Then select **L**ayout, **A**lignment, I**n**dent →← or press Shift-F4, and type

I do not know what I may appear to the world, but to myself I seem to have been only like a boy playing on the seashore, and diverting myself in now and then finding a smoother pebble, or a prettier shell than ordinary, whilst the great ocean of truth lay all undiscovered before me.

After you type the text, the screen looks like this:

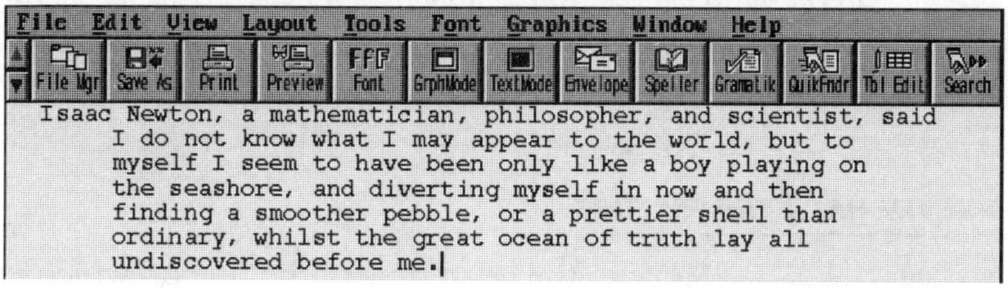

EXERCISES

1. Type the following paragraph after entering the left and right indent code four times:

   Next Monday, the executive officers are meeting to discuss five-year growth projections for the firm. The agenda for this meeting will include these topics: financial planning and new debt issues, new product lines, the competition, and foreign market opportunities.

   Reveal the codes, and delete two of the left and right indent codes from the paragraph.

2. Type the following paragraph, entering the left indent and the left and right indent codes where indicated.

   [Lft/Rgt Indent][Lft Indent]Frequently saving work in progress is a good habit that all computer users should acquire. It avoids the potential for loss of large amounts of work due to power outages, someone tripping over a power cord, etc.

5.2 USE THE BACK TAB FEATURE

WordPerfect's back tab feature allows you to type text to the left of the left margin. If the text fills more than one line, WordPerfect wraps subsequent lines to the left margin. You can also use this feature to start the first line of an indented paragraph at the left margin; the other lines will wrap to the designated tab stop. The hidden code for the back tab feature is [Back Tab].

NOTE *Those familiar with WordPerfect 5.1 will quickly recognize that the back tab feature is the same as WordPerfect 5.1's margin release feature. Only the name has changed.*

TO USE THE BACK TAB FEATURE

a. Move to the beginning of the line on which you want to use the back tab feature.

b. Select **L**ayout, **A**lignment, **B**ack Tab ← or press Shift-Tab. WordPerfect moves the cursor one tab stop to the left.

c. Repeat step b until the cursor is correctly placed.

You can use the back tab feature only when there are tab stops to the left of the cursor. If there are no tab stops to the left of the cursor, or if the **Pos** indicator on the status line shows that the cursor is at 0 inches, the cursor stays in its current location.

EXAMPLES

1. When you create forms, you can use the back tab feature to put the labels for the data to the left of the left margin. Select **L**ayout, **A**lignment, **B**ack Tab ← or press Shift-Tab, and type

   Name:

Press Enter and then press Shift-Tab. Type

Dept:

Press Enter and Shift-Tab again. Type

ID #:

The screen looks like this:

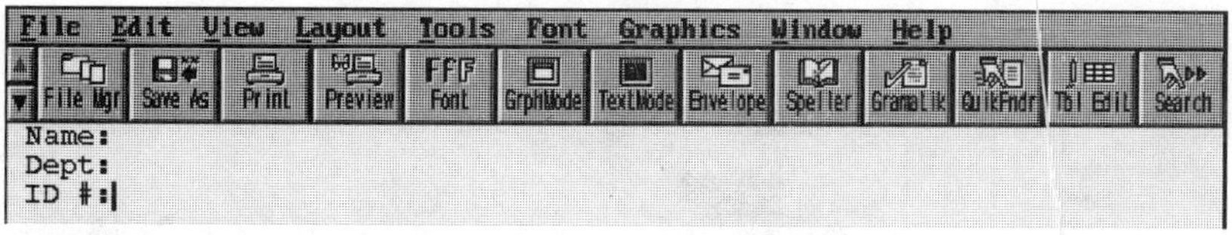

NOTE *If you use a laser printer, be careful when using the back tab feature. Many laser printers have a thin margin around the page that cannot be printed on, and WordPerfect will not let you use the back tab feature to place text in that area. For example, with the Hewlett-Packard LaserJet III, if you pressed Shift-Tab twice, instead of moving to the tab stop set at 0 inches the cursor would move to a tab stop set at .29 inch, which is the closest this printer can get to the edge of the paper.*

2. You can use the back tab feature to remove indentation from the first line of an indented paragraph. Select **L**ayout, **A**lignment, **I**ndent → or press F4 for indentation. To move the first line back to the margin, select **L**ayout, **A**lignment, **B**ack Tab ← or press Shift-Tab. Then type

   When you have an indented paragraph, you might want the first line to align with paragraphs that are not indented. The back tab feature lets you do this.

   The paragraph looks like this:

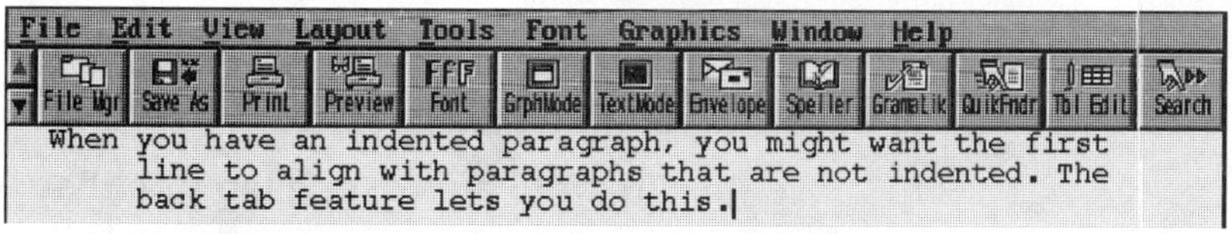

EXERCISES

1. Invoke the back tab feature until you cannot move the first line any farther to the left, and then type the following paragraph:

   You can use the back tab feature to make an indented paragraph begin at the left margin. You can also use it to fit additional characters on a line.

2. Create an employment application form like the one shown here:

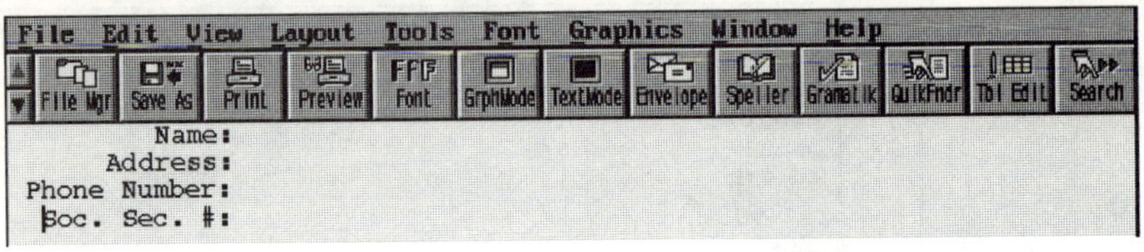

   "Name:" starts one space from the left margin. Use the back tab feature on the next three lines so the colons align with the one after "Name."

5.3 SET TABS

When you press the Tab key, WordPerfect inserts the hidden code [Lft Tab] in your document and moves the cursor to the next tab stop. Tab stops provide an easy way to align text at locations other than the left margin. Initially, WordPerfect has tab stops set at every half inch. You can change the tab stops to any positions you want. You can use the first tab stop for paragraph indentation.

You might change the tab stops when you want to align columns of entries or when you want to place a column of entries near the middle or right edge of the page. Eliminating unnecessary tab stops allows you to press the Tab key once to position the cursor correctly.

TO CHANGE TAB STOPS

a. Select **L**ayout, **T**ab Set.
b. Move the cursor to an existing tab stop that you want to move.
c. Use Ctrl-← or Ctrl-→ to move the tab stop.
d. Move the cursor to an existing tab stop that you want to remove.
e. Select Clear **O**ne or press Del.
f. Select Clear **A**ll to delete all current tab stops.

g. Use the cursor control keys to move the cursor to where you want to insert a tab stop.

h. Select the **L**eft, **R**ight, **C**enter, or **D**ecimal option button.

i. Select OK.

When you select **L**ayout, **T**ab Set in step a, the Tab Set dialog box opens, as shown in Figure 5-1. During steps b through g, you press ← or → to move the cursor one position to the left or right. Press Home and ← or → to first move to the edge of the screen and then move 2.7 inches left or right. Press Home twice and press ← or → once to move to the beginning or end of the paper.

The option button you select in step h determines how text is aligned at the tab stop. The Left option button left-aligns text at the tab stop, the Right option button right-aligns text at the tab stop, and the Center option button centers text on the tab stop. The Decimal option button right-aligns all characters typed before a decimal point or period. The different tab alignments produce these results:

Left	Center	Right	Decimal
Text and	Text and	Text and	Text is
numbers	numbers	numbers	left-aligned
left-aligned	centered	right-aligned	55
55	55	55	7891.42
7891.42	7891.42	7891.42	.45731

FIGURE 5-1

Tab Set dialog box

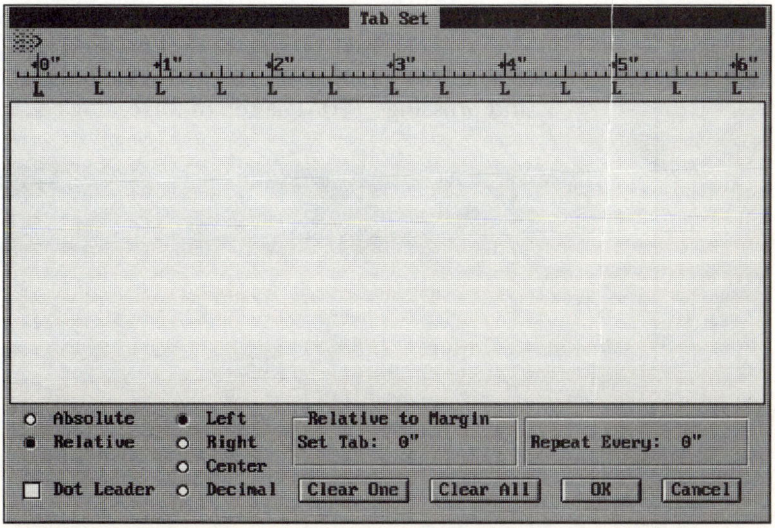

An alternative to steps g and h is typing the number of the desired tab stop position (for example, **2.5**) in the **S**et Tab text box and pressing Enter. This inserts a left-aligned tab stop at the specified location and places the cursor there. You can press R, C, or D to change the type of tab stop at that position, and you can press Del or O to delete the tab stop at that position.

When you select OK after changing tab settings, the hidden code [Tab Set] is inserted to indicate the change. When you move the cursor to highlight the hidden code on the Reveal Codes screen, the code expands to indicate the locations and alignment of the tabs you set. For example, the expanded code might look like this: [Tab Set:Rel: 1"L,1.5"L,2.5"R,3"D].

EXAMPLES

1. For letters, you usually need only two tab stops: one for indenting paragraphs and one for aligning the address, date, and closing. Extra tab stops get in your way and make it easy to misalign the address, date, and closing. You can remove extra tab stops by selecting **L**ayout, **T**ab Set to open the Tab Set dialog box.

   Select Clear **A**ll to remove all the tab stops. Move the cursor to a position on the ruler .5 inch from the left margin, and press Spacebar. You can also create this tab by pressing S to move to the **S**et Tab text box, typing **.5**, and pressing Enter. Move the cursor to the 3-inch position, and press Spacebar to set a tab stop. You could also create this second tab stop by pressing S to move to the **S**et Tab text box, typing **3**, and pressing Enter. The top of the dialog box now looks like this:

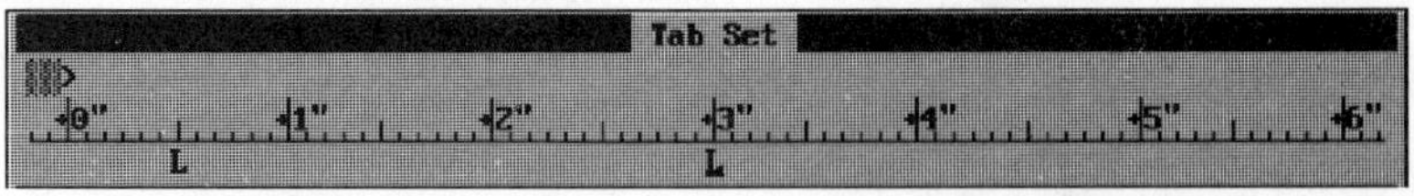

Press F7 to select the OK button. Then begin typing the letter. Press Tab twice to align each line of first address, the date, and the closing. Press Tab once to start each paragraph.

2. When you create reports, you often want numbers or text to appear in columns. Use tab stops to ensure that information aligns properly. First, select **L**ayout, **T**ab Set to open the Tab Set dialog box. Select Clear **A**ll to delete all current tab stops. Press S to move to the **S**et Tab text box, type **.5**, and press Enter. This creates a left-aligned tab stop for text at .5 inches from the left edge of the paper. You could also move the cursor to the .5-inch position and press Spacebar. Next, because you will align numbers with decimals in a column to the right, type **3**, press Enter, and then type **D**; or move to the 3-inch position and type **D**. This will cause text entered at the 3-inch tab stop to align at the decimal points. Select the OK button to return to the document. Type the following, pressing the Tab key where indicated:

   ExpensesTabAmount

   TabInsuranceTab5,600

   TabRentTab2,135.50

   TabSalariesTab128,937.13

   The document looks like this:

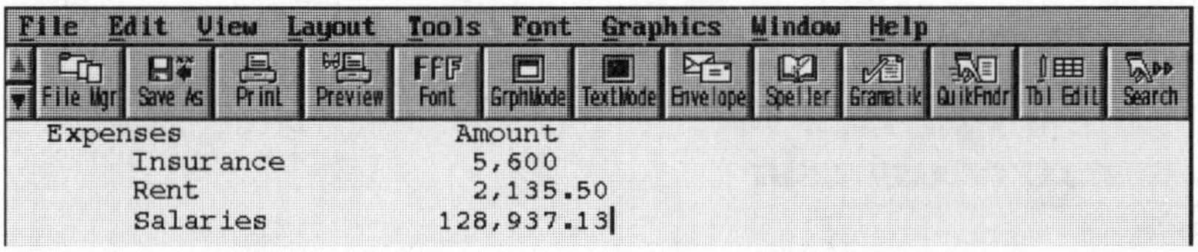

3. You can set tab stops to any regular interval. Select **L**ayout, **T**ab Set to display the Tab Set dialog box. Select Clear **A**ll to remove the existing tab stops. Next, select the **S**et Tab text box, type **0**, and press Enter. Select the Re**p**eat Every text box, type **.6**, and press Enter. Word-Perfect sets left-aligned tab stops every .6 inch, starting at thc lcft margin. If you select one of the alignment option buttons before setting the first tab stop, all the tab stops have that alignment. Select the OK button to return to the document.

EXERCISES

1. Create a decimal-aligned tab stop at 2.5 inches and a right-aligned tab stop at 4 inches.
2. Remove all existing tab stops and set left-aligned tab stops at 2 inches and 4.5 inches. Type the following entries, using the Tab key to place the names at the 2-inch position and the salaries at the 4.5-inch position:

   Jones 17,850

   Culver 23,489

   Walker 32,500

   Clear the screen.
3. Change the tab stops to every .75 inch, starting at 2 inches.

5.4 USE THE FLUSH RIGHT FEATURE

WordPerfect's flush right feature allows you to align a line of text at the right margin. It is normally used for short entries, such as company names, dates, or addresses.

TO ENTER TEXT FLUSH RIGHT

a. Move to the line on which you want to place the flush-right text.
b. Select **L**ayout, **A**lignment, **F**lush Right or press Alt-F6.
c. Type the text you want aligned at the right margin.
d. Press Enter.

   WordPerfect 6 inserts the hidden code [Flsh Rgt].

NOTE *If you insert the [Flsh Rgt] code twice without moving the cursor, WordPerfect changes the code to read [Flsh Rgt (Dot)]. This code still aligns the text that follows with the right margin, but it also adds a dot leader. A dot leader is a line of dots between the last text on the line before the [Flsh Rgt] code, and the beginning of the text after it.*

EXAMPLES

1. You can use the flush right feature when you add a date to a document. A special WordPerfect feature can be used to enter the current date. First, select **L**ayout, **A**lignment, **F**lush Right or press Alt-F6. Next, select **T**ools, **D**ate, **T**ext. You can also press Shift-F5 and select Insert Date **T**ext. Your screen shows the current date aligned at the right margin, as shown here:

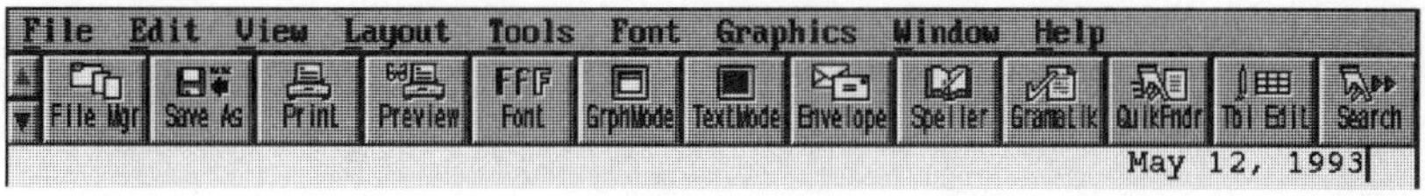

If the date is not correct, exit WordPerfect, type **date**, press Enter, type the correct date by using the format indicated at the prompt, press Enter, and reload WordPerfect.

2. You can enter text on the same line as right-aligned text. Type **Date:**, press Spacebar, and select **T**ools, **D**ate, **T**ext. Next, select **L**ayout, **A**lignment, **F**lush Right or press Alt-F6. Type **ABC Company**, and press Enter. The text looks like this:

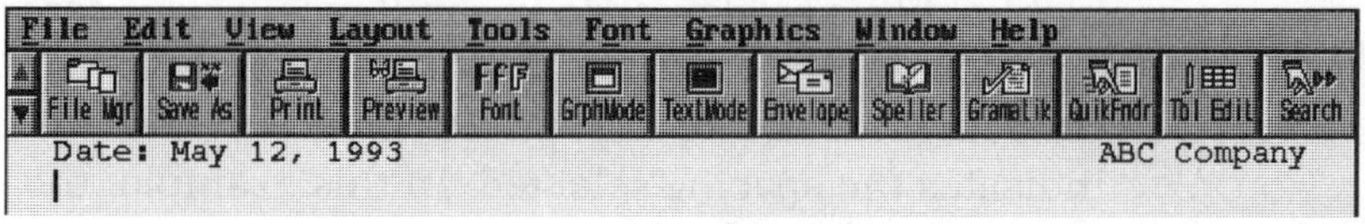

EXERCISES

1. Use the date feature to enter the current date flush right in the top line of a new document.
2. Type the following memo, using the date feature to provide the current date.

MEMO
To: All Employees   Date: September 10, 1993
From: Bea Smith   Re: Cleaning Computer Screens

Do not use alcohol-based window cleaners to clean your computer screen. Use the special cleaner that is stored with the blank disks.

5.5 CHANGE LINE SPACING

Many letters and other correspondence are single-spaced. Long reports or documents are often double-spaced to make them easier to read. You can set the spacing in WordPerfect for an entire document or for a portion of a document. WordPerfect's default is to use single line spacing.

When you change line spacing, WordPerfect inserts a hidden code into the document that looks like this: [Ln Spacing]. When you highlight this hidden code in the Reveal Codes screen, WordPerfect expands the code to show the line spacing setting. For example, the code might look like this: [Ln Spacing:2]. The number after the colon indicates the spacing selected. In this example, the 2 means the text will be double-spaced.

TO SET LINE SPACING

a. Select **L**ayout, **L**ine, or press Shift-F8 and select **L**ine.

b. Select the Line **S**pacing text box.

c. Type the number of spaces you want between lines.

d. Press Enter twice to return to the document. If you used Shift-F8, you need to press Enter a third time.

The line spacing selected by using these steps begins at the cursor location, where the hidden code is inserted. WordPerfect uses the new spacing up to the end of the document unless it encounters a new line-spacing code. The change does not affect the text before the location of the hidden code.

EXAMPLE

A lengthy quotation can be single-spaced and indented from both sides to set it off from the rest of the text. First, select **L**ayout, **L**ine, or press Shift-F8 and select **L**ine. Select the Line **S**pacing text box, and type **2**. Press Enter twice (or three times if you used Shift-F8) to return to the document. WordPerfect inserts a code to change the text to double-spaced. Type

> Quotes from famous people can be fun to read. The language is often a little different from English as we know it today.

Press Enter. Before typing the quotation on the next line, select **L**ayout, **L**ine, or press Shift-F8 and select **L**ine. Select the Line **S**pacing text box, and type **1**. Press Enter twice (or three times if you used Shift-F8) to return to the document and change the line spacing. All of the text after this point is single-spaced. Next, select **L**ayout, **A**lignment, I**n**dent →← or press Shift-F4, and type

> I do not know what I may appear to the world, but to myself I seem to have been only like a boy playing on the seashore, and diverting myself in now and then finding a smoother pebble, or a prettier shell than ordinary, whilst the great ocean of truth lay all undiscovered before me.
> Isaac Newton

Select **L**ayout, **L**ine, or press Shift-F8 and select **L**ine. Select the Line **S**pacing text box, type **2**, and press Enter twice (or three times if you used Shift-F8) to return the document to double spacing after the quote. Press Enter, and type

> The diverse interests of some famous individuals may seem surprising. The quote from Isaac Newton is very simplistic when contrasted with some of his scientific theorems.

This last paragraph is double-spaced.

EXERCISES

1. Type the following paragraph:

A sense of humor sharp enough to show a man his own absurdities will keep him from the commission of all sins, or nearly all, except those that are worth committing. (Samuel Butler from Life and Habit)

Move to the first character in the paragraph. Change the spacing to double spacing. Next, try triple spacing. Then set the spacing back to single spacing.

2. Type the following paragraphs. Use the default of single spacing for the first paragraph. Change the line spacing to double spacing before typing the second paragraph. Set the line spacing to triple spacing before typing the third paragraph.

The new Widget maker will expand our current capacity to meet expected demand levels for the next five to ten years. It has a net present value of $25,687.

The manufacturer gives a 10% trade-in value on its old Widget maker. This is a slightly lower price than expected in the open market. The capital budgeting plan contains the lower trade-in value, but the company will probably sell the used machine in the second-hand market.

The new Widget maker has many new features. One of these, a free one-year service contract, will save the company $50,000 in the first year.

Make the first and third paragraphs double-spaced and the second paragraph triple-spaced.

5.6 ALTER JUSTIFICATION

Initially, WordPerfect is set to left justify text when you print it. You can change the setting to full justification, which causes WordPerfect to add spaces between words so that all full lines end at the right margin. You can also format your text with center justification so that each line is centered between the margins, or you can format your text with right justification so that it has a smooth right margin and a ragged left margin. A new setting is available in WordPerfect 6: full, all lines justification. This setting is the same as full justification, but it affects the jusification of the last line of paragraphs.

NOTE *Although there are other methods you can use to change justification, selecting **L**ayout, **J**ustification or pressing Shift-F8 and selecting **J**ustification are the quickest methods.*

TO CHANGE JUSTIFICATION

a. Select **L**ayout, **J**ustification.

b. Select **L**eft for left justification, **C**enter for center justification, **R**ight for right justification, **F**ull for full justification, or Full, **A**ll Lines for full justification of all lines.

EXAMPLE

You can change justification to change the appearance of printed lines. Type

The company's financial position is improving. The company retired a million dollars of debt this year and will retire another million next year. The company is retiring the debt by buying stock on the open market and retiring the certificates. Also, the lag between invoice dates and payment dates has decreased by 3 days.

Move the cursor to the beginning of the paragraph. Select **L**ayout, **J**ustification, **F**ull. The paragraph looks like this in graphics mode and when you preview how it will print:

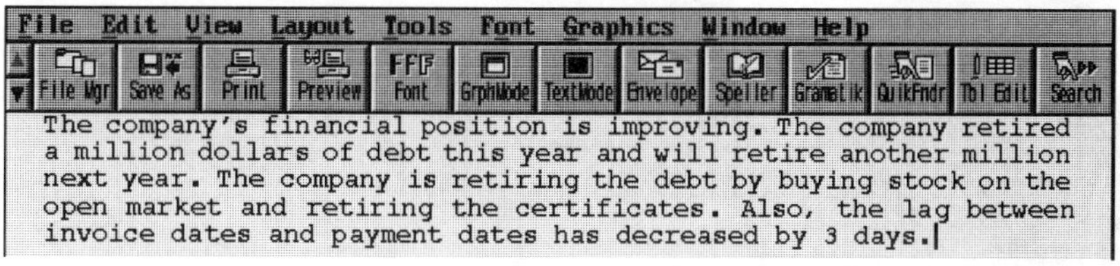

EXERCISES

1. Type the following paragraph. View the document in graphics mode, or preview the document by using the print preview feature. Change

to full, all lines justification, and view the document again. Return the document to left justification.

The Accounts Receivable computer system was installed last January. Due to this new system, the average daily accounts receivable amount dropped by $50. Also, the percentage of bad accounts has dropped from 4% to 2%, mostly due to quicker action on overdue accounts.

2. Type the first of the following paragraphs. Change to full justification, and type the second paragraph. Use graphics mode or the print preview feature to view how WordPerfect will print the document.

When a paragraph is left justified, WordPerfect does not change the space between words. The right margin has a ragged appearance, because lines are different lengths.

When a paragraph is fully justified, WordPerfect inserts additional space into the lines of the printed copy of the document. This creates even left and right margins, since every line is made the same length.

mastery skills check

1. Type the following paragraph, indenting it 1 inch from the left margin.

   A disk drive reads information from a disk. The disk drive spins the disk quickly. A read/write head above the disk reads the information as it spins past the head.

   Save this file as DISKREAD. [5.1]

2. Remove all tab stops. Set one tab stop at 4 inches, and use the Tab key to create the following letter heading. [5.3]

   Acme Corporation

496 Prospect Road
Cleveland, Ohio 44115
January 3, 1994

3. Type the following paragraph after changing the line spacing to double spacing. Save the file as DISK. [5.5]

   Disks store information by using magnetized material to hold information. The basic unit of storage is a byte. A byte stores one character of information.

4. Open DISKREAD, and change to right justification. Save the file. [5.6]
5. Enter the following account numbers flush right, with one account number per line. [5.4]

   ACC-9876

   HDG-3218

   CRC-9873

6. Duplicate the following title by using the back tab and indent features. [5.1, 5.2]

   Campbell, Mary, Teach Yourself WordPerfect 6,
   Osborne/McGraw-Hill, 1993.

cumulative skills check

1. Type the following bibliography. Indent all of the entries. Use the back tab feature to make the first line of each entry begin one tab stop to the left of the indent position. [5.1, 5.2]

   Crosby, Samuel, "Mergers and Acquisitions," Business Yearly, (OMB Publishing, 1983), June, pp. 46-49.

Lee, Jane and Lifeson, Tom, "Effectively Combining Companies," Journal of Business Results, (AMBA, 1987), vol 36, Fall, pp. 101-9.

2. Use formatting features to create a heading that has the following information on a single line. [4.1, 4.3, 5.5]

   Acme Corporation
   1560 Main Street
   Cleveland, Ohio 44103

   Place the company name at the left edge of the page. Center the street address. Right align the city, state, and ZIP code. Underline the entire line.

3. Type the following letter:

   Joan Smith
   President, Widgets Inc.
   7946 Madison Avenue
   New York, New York 10061

   Dear Ms. Smith:

   Enclosed is the pamphlet you requested, Wrapping Consumer Goods. Our products can shrink-wrap any product. If you send the dimensions of the products that you want to shrink-wrap, one of our representatives will prepare a list of the materials and equipment you will need.

   Sincerely,

   Larry Kennedy

   Plastic Covering Co.

   Change to full justification for the letter. Underline the pamphlet name. Reveal the codes, and delete the underline code. Print the document. [3.1, 4.1, 5.6]

4. Match the following codes with the features they represent. [4.1, 4.2, 4.3, 4.4, 5.1, 5.2, 5.3, 5.4, 5.5, 5.6]

1.	Soft return	a.	[Ln Spacing:3]
2.	Underlined text	b.	[Back Tab]
3.	Flush right	c.	[Lft Indent]
4.	Back tab	d.	[Bold On][Bold Off]

5.	Indent	e.	[Und On][Und Off]
6.	Hard return	f.	[Center]
7.	Hard page break	g.	[Flsh Rgt]
8.	Triple line spacing	h.	[Lft/Rgt Indent]
9.	Bold text	i.	[HRt]
10.	Full justification	j.	[SRt]
11.	Set tabs	k.	[Just:Full]
12.	Left and right indent	l.	[HPg]
13.	Center text on line	m.	[Tab Set:Rel:0",0.5",2.5"]

5. Enter the current date flush right. Reveal codes and delete the flush right code. [4.4, 5.4]

6

Changing the Format of a Page

chapter objectives

After completing this chapter, you should be able to

6.1 Center text on a page

6.2 Change the margins

6.3 Add page numbers

6.4 Change the paper size and type

USING a pleasing page format can help you create a document with a professional appearance. Rather than continuing to use the default features, you can enhance the presentation quality of your output with page format changes.

Such options as centering the text between the top and bottom of the page allow you to create a short document that still presents a professional image. You can alter the margin settings for the four sides of the page, add page numbers, and adjust the page length to make additional appearance enhancements.

review skills check

As you complete the following exercises, do not clear the screen unless you are told to do so.

1. Type the following text, using bold for "Education:". [4.2]

   John Doe
   23405 Lander Road
   Cleveland, Ohio 44130
   (216)229-8976

   Education: Cleveland State University, Cleveland, Ohio
   Business Administration, August 1983
   Dean's List 7 Quarters, GPA 3.75

2. Center the name, address, and phone number. [4.3, 4.7]
3. Boldface the name. [4.2, 4.7]
4. Underline the word "Education." [4.1, 4.7]
5. At the beginning of the document, create a tab stop at 1.2 inches and remove the ones at .5 and 1 inch. [5.3]
6. Indent the three lines containing educational information. [5.1]
7. Move the first line containing educational information back to the left margin using the Back Tab feature. [5.2]
8. Print the document. [3.1]

6.1 CENTER TEXT ON A PAGE

A short memo or letter can present a strong impression if it is centered vertically on the page. Other text, such as the title page of a report, is also most effectively presented centered between the top and bottom of the page. This feature is different from the line centering option covered in Chapter 4 because this option centers the text between the top and bottom margins instead of the left and right margins. It can be used separately or in combination with line centering features.

The page centering command adds the hidden code [Cntr Cur Pg] or [Cntr Pgs] to your document at the beginning of the current page. To remove the feature, you must delete the code.

TO CENTER TEXT ON A PAGE

a. Select **L**ayout, **P**age, or press Shift-F8 and select **P**age.
b. Select **C**enter Current Page to center only the current page.
c. Press Enter or click OK to return to the document. If you use Shift-F8 in step a, you will need to press Enter or click OK a second time.
d. Type the text if it is not already in the document.
e. Select **L**ayout, **A**lignment, Hard **P**age or press Ctrl-Enter to end the page.

In step b, you could select Center **P**ages if you want all of the pages from that point on to have their contents vertically centered.

EXAMPLES

1. When you create a title page for a report, you often want the title to be in the middle of the page. Rather than pressing Enter until the cursor is in the middle of the page, you can have WordPerfect automatically center the text for you. First, select **L**ayout, **P**age to display the Page Format dialog box shown in Figure 6-1. Next to

Center Current Page and Center **P**ages are check boxes. These *check boxes* are for features that are turned on and off. When the feature is turned on, the check box is marked with an X. When the feature is turned off, the check box is empty. Press C to select the **C**enter Current Page check box. Press Enter or click OK to close this dialog box and return to the document.

Press Shift-F6 to center text on a line, then type

Horton Corporation Financial Statements

Press Enter to move to the next line. Press Shift-F6 to center text and then type

As of July 30, 1994

Vertically centering the contents of a page does not change how the document appears on the screen, although you will see the difference when you print the document or preview how the document will print. When you select **F**ile, Print Pre**v**iew and **V**iew, **F**ull Page, your screen looks like Figure 6-2. Press Esc to return to the document.

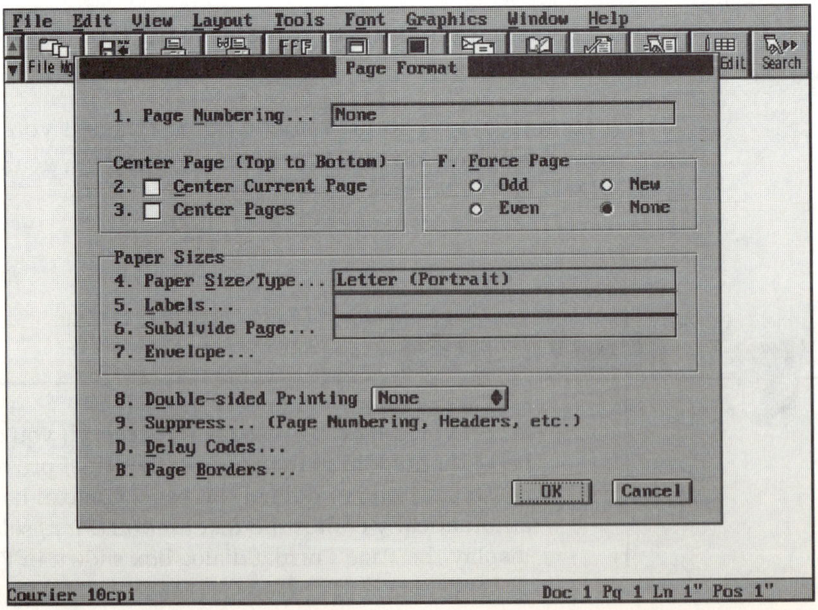

FIGURE 6-1

Page Format dialog box

FIGURE 6-2

Print preview of lines centered on a page

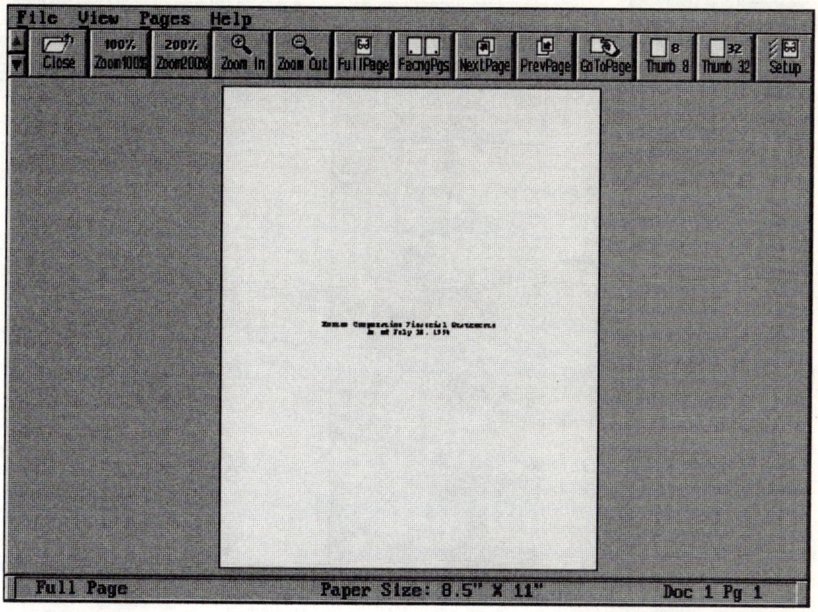

2. You can improve the appearance of short business letters by centering them vertically on the page. To center a short letter, select **L**ayout, **P**age, and **C**enter Current Page. Press Enter or click OK to return to the document and type

Tracy Smith
2647 Chillecothe Road
Kirkland, Ohio 44296

Dear Tracy,
I have enclosed the information you requested. Please contact me at (212) 555-5931 if you have any questions.

Sincerely,

Darren Jeck

When you preview this letter before printing, it looks like Figure 6-3. Press Esc to return to the document.

FIGURE 6-3

Print preview of a short letter centered on a page

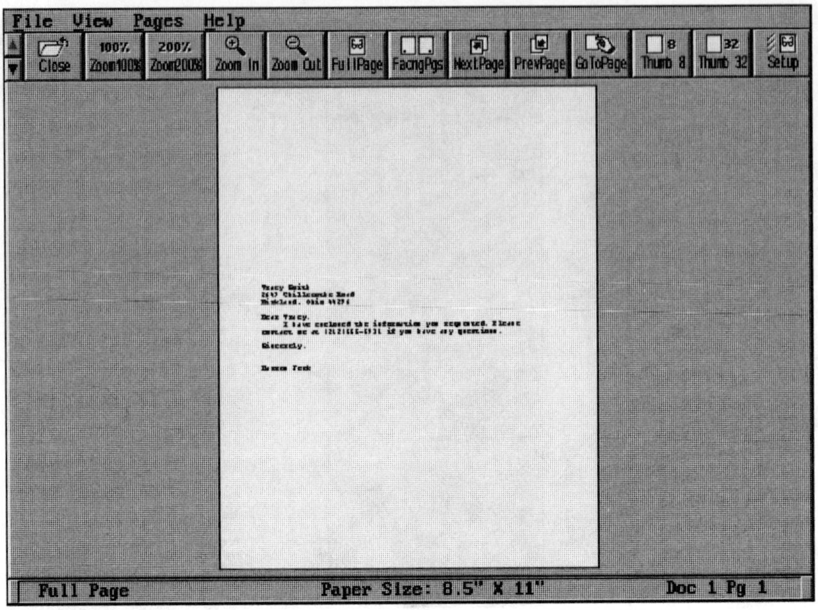

EXERCISES

1. Create a title page with the following three lines centered horizontally and vertically:

   Investigation into the Physical Properties of Rust
   Dissertation
   Angus McPhearson

   Preview the document to see how it will appear when printed.

2. Create a short thank-you letter to Jules McBride at 234 Main Street, Lawrence, PA 28634, thanking him for promptly sending the information you have requested. Center the letter on the page.

3. Create a title page with the following lines centered horizontally and vertically. Preview how WordPerfect will print it.

   1994 Financial Statements
   Acme Corporation

6.2 CHANGE THE MARGINS

Margins are the white areas between the edge of the paper and the edge of the area WordPerfect uses to print your document. A page has four margins—top, bottom, left, and right. Increasing the size of the margins lessens the amount of text that can be shown on a page. Decreasing the size of the margins increases the amount of text that can be shown on a page.

WordPerfect measures each margin as the number of inches from the text to the edge of the paper. WordPerfect initially has 1-inch margins on each side. WordPerfect uses the default margin settings unless it finds a hidden code representing another margin specification. When you change the margins, WordPerfect inserts a hidden code and adjusts the number of lines that print on each page.

TO CHANGE THE MARGINS

a. Move the cursor to the point where you want the margins to change.

b. Select **L**ayout, **M**argins. You can also press Shift-F8 and select **M**argins.

c. Select **L**eft Margin, **R**ight Margin, **T**op Margin, or **B**ottom Margin to change that margin setting.

d. Type the number of inches WordPerfect should leave between the top of the paper and the printed text and press Enter.

e. Repeat steps c and d for each margin you want to change.

f. **S**elect OK to leave the dialog box. When you use Shift-F8 in step b, you need to select **C**lose also.

WordPerfect inserts [Lft Mar], [Rgt Mar], [Top Mar], or [Bot Mar] as a hidden code to represent the altered margins at the cursor location. To see the hidden code, press Alt-F3 or select **V**iew, Reveal **C**odes. When you highlight a code, the code expands to show the current margin setting. For example [Lft Mar] may expand to [Lft Mar:2"] to indicate a left margin of 2 inches.

EXAMPLES

1. You can increase the margins to decrease the amount of text that fits on a page. For example, you can increase the margins to 2 inches. First, select **L**ayout, **M**argins. The top of the dialog box looks like this:

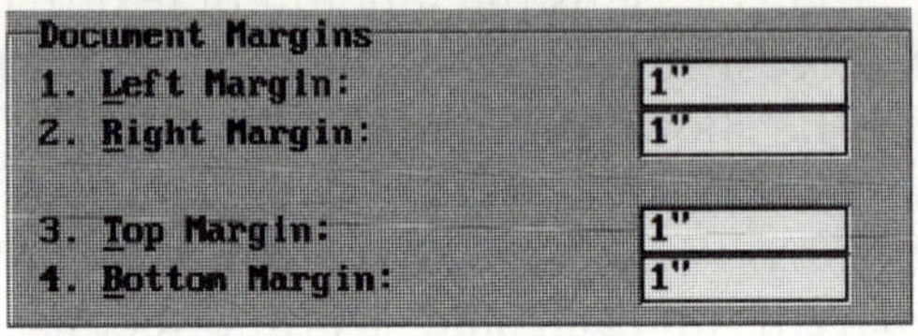

   Select **L**eft Margin, type **2"** for the new margin setting, and press Enter. Select **R**ight Margin, type **2"** for the new margin setting, and press Enter. Select **T**op Margin, type **2"** for the new margin setting, and press Enter. Select **B**ottom Margin, type **2"** for the new margin setting, and press Enter. Press Enter or click OK to leave the dialog box.

   Next, to use these new margins, type the following:

   A presentation on WordPerfect's exciting new graphics features is scheduled for the next meeting of the WordPerfect User Group. This meeting will be held at noon on April 28th.

   You can see how WordPerfect leaves more space on the left and right sides. Select **F**ile, Print Pre**v**iew to see how the document also has more room at the top because of the larger top margin. Press Esc to return to the document.

   Press Alt-F3 to reveal the document's hidden codes, then move to the beginning of the document. You can see the [Lft Mar], [Rgt Mar], [Top Mar], and [Bot Mar] codes. If you deleted these codes, the margin for the code you deleted would return to the default, since the document does not have prior codes for its margins. Press Alt-F3 again to hide the codes.

   Do not clear the screen; you will use it in the next example.

2. You can alter margin settings within a document. First, move to the end of the document and select **L**ayout, **M**argins. Press 1 or L for **L**eft Margin, type **.5"** for the new margin setting, and press Enter. Press 2 or R for **R**ight Margin, type **.5"** for the new margin setting, and press Enter. Press Enter or click OK to leave the dialog box. To use these new margins, type the following:

   April's meeting will focus on enhancements made to WordPerfect's interface. This includes the Button Bar, the WYSIWYG (what-you-see-is-what-you-get) display, and the ribbon to add styles.

The text using the two different styles of margins looks like this:

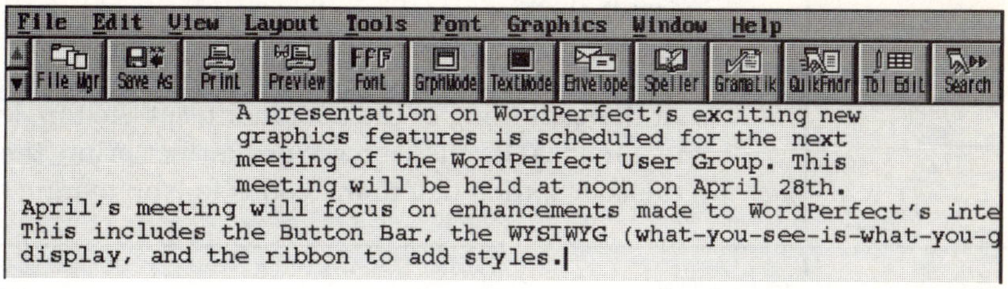

EXERCISES

1. Set the top margin to 9.5 inches, leaving the bottom margin at 1 inch. Type the following paragraphs. Preview how WordPerfect will print the document.

   The top margin determines the space WordPerfect skips on a page when printing a document. You must specify this measurement in inches.

   The bottom margin determines the space WordPerfect leaves on a page when printing a document. As WordPerfect prints a document, it determines how much room is left on the page. When the amount of remaining space equals the size of the bottom margin, WordPerfect inserts a soft page break.

2. Type the following:

   Some are born great, some achieve greatness, others have greatness thrust upon 'em.

   William Shakespeare

   What makes us discontented with our condition is the absurdly exaggerated idea we have of the happiness of others.

   Proverb

   Change the left margin to 2 inches and the right margin to 1.5 inches.

3. Type the following lines:

   ABC COMPANY - MEMO
   Date: Monday, Sept 12, 1994

When using the copier by the coffee machine, only use the paper stacked next to the machine. Since the machine is old, if you use different paper (envelopes, letterheads, and so forth), the machine jams.

At the beginning of the document, set the top, left, and right margins to 3 inches. Preview how WordPerfect prints the document. Reveal the codes, then delete the codes for the margin settings.

6.3 ADD PAGE NUMBERS

WordPerfect does not print page numbers in a document automatically. This is convenient, since you probably do not want page numbers on letters, memos, and similar documents. However, you can have WordPerfect add page numbers in a number of locations on a page. You can also have text appear next to the page number.

TO NUMBER THE PAGES

a. Select **L**ayout, **P**age or press Shift-F8 and select **P**age.
b. Select Page **N**umbering.
c. Select Page Number **P**osition.
d. Select the radio button that corresponds to where you want WordPerfect to place the page numbers and select OK.
e. Select Page Number **F**ormat to change the text around the page number.
f. Type an entry around the [page #] code for the text you want to appear next to the page number and press Enter.
g. Select OK twice to return to the document. If you used Shift-F8 in step a, you need to select **C**lose also.

EXAMPLES

1. You can instruct WordPerfect where to place page numbers in a printed document. First, select **L**ayout, **P**age and then select Page **N**umbering to open the Page Numbering dialog box. This dialog box lets you select a location on the page for page numbers as well as

change the style of page numbers and start with a number other than 1. Next, select Page Number **P**osition to display the page numbering format options, as shown in Figure 6-4. Each number represents a specific location for page numbers. For example, 4 and 8 put the page numbers at the left on even-numbered pages and at the right on odd-numbered pages. Select the Bottom **R**ight radio button. Select OK three times to return to the document. When you print the document, WordPerfect will place page numbers in the lower-right corner on every page.

2. You can add text around the page numbers. You can use this feature to make the first page number look like "Page - 1," for example. First, select **L**ayout, **P**age, then Page **N**umbering, and Page Number **F**ormat. In the text box, you can type the text to appear with the page number. The [page #] represents the page number. Type **Page** and a space, press Home, and type a hyphen, and another space. Press Enter. Select Page Number **P**osition and the Alternating, **T**op radio button to place the page numbers in the upper-left corner on even-numbered pages and in the upper-right corner on odd-numbered pages. Select OK three times to return to the document.

   Next, type

   This page will contain text in front of the page number because you changed the page number format.

FIGURE 6-4

Page Number Position dialog box

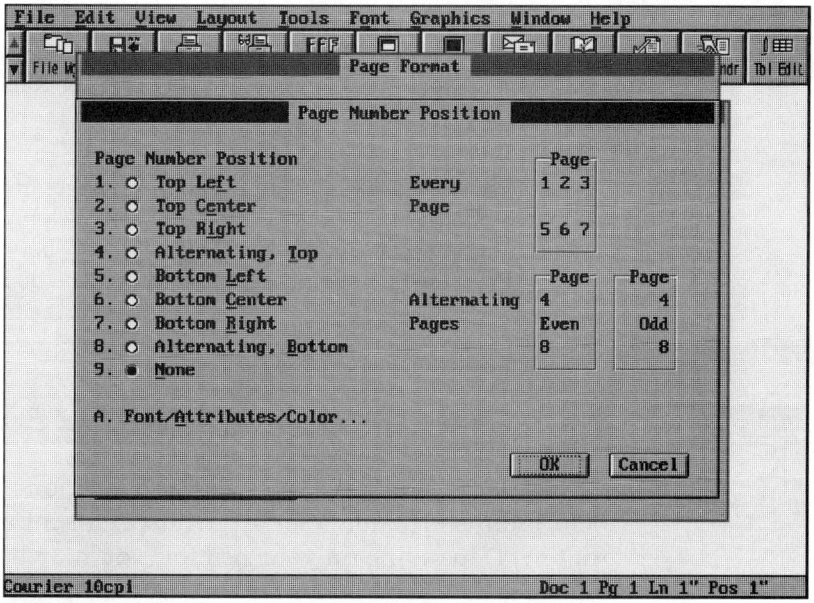

Then select **F**ile, Print Pre**v**iew. Select **V**iew, **1**00% View to see the document the same size as it is printed. The top of the preview looks like this:

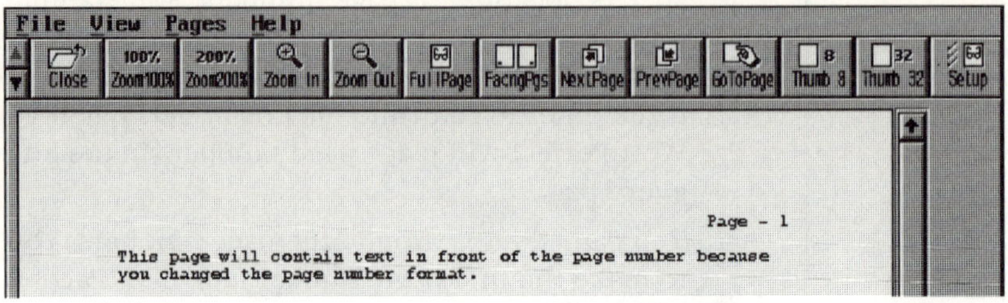

Press Esc to return to the document. Press Alt-F3 to see the hidden codes. At the beginning of the document, you can see the codes [Pg Num Pos] and [Pg Num Fmt] for the page number position and formatting you have added. Press Alt-F3 again to remove the codes from view.

EXERCISES

1. Instruct WordPerfect to place page numbers in the center at the bottom of each page. Type **Travel Expenses** and press Ctrl-Enter. Type **Benefits** and press Ctrl-Enter. Type **Salary Expense** and press Enter. Preview the document to see where the page numbers will appear.
2. Instruct WordPerfect to number the pages at the bottom center with hyphens and spaces on either side of the page number. Next, type the numbers 1 through 5, pressing Ctrl-Enter between numbers to place each one on a separate page. Preview the document.

6.4 CHANGE THE PAPER SIZE AND TYPE

WordPerfect's standard paper size and location are determined when the printer is installed. (See Appendix A for information on installing a printer.) Depending on your printer, you may have a variety of other options available for printing documents.

For example, your printer may be able to print on various sizes of paper, such as legal-sized sheets and envelopes. Your printer may have more than one paper bin, or location, from which different forms are pulled. These forms could include letterhead, bond paper, card stock, or mailing labels. Some types of paper may be continuously fed through the printer, while others may have to be manually fed. Usually you will want your documents to be printed in *portrait orientation,* which prints text across the narrower side of the paper. At other times you'll want the printer to use the paper in *landscape orientation,* which prints sideways, across the wider side of the paper. Using 8-1/2-by-11-inch paper, portrait mode prints across the 8-1/2-inch side, and landscape prints across the 11-inch side of the sheet. Using WordPerfect, you can select the size, location, and orientation for printing your documents.

TO CHANGE THE PAPER FORMAT

a. Select **L**ayout, **P**age or press Shift-F8 and select **P**age.
b. Select Paper **S**ize/Type.
c. Highlight the paper selection you want to use and press Enter.
d. Select OK to return to the document. If you use Shift-F8 in step a, you will need to select **C**lose also.

EXAMPLES

1. You can set the page size and style to print addresses on envelopes. First, select **L**ayout, **P**age, and Paper **S**ize/Type. The Paper Size/Type dialog box that appears, as shown in Figure 6-5, lists the available paper sizes. Since the available paper sizes depend on the selected printer, your list may look different. Next, highlight the first Envelope selection. (You may have many sizes available.) Press Enter to select this paper and size type. Finally, press Enter to return to the document. Now you can type addresses on separate pages of a document and have WordPerfect print each address on an envelope. If you press Alt-F3 to reveal hidden codes, you can see the code [Paper Sz/Typ] that expands to [Paper Sz/Typ:9.5" x 4.13",Envelope (Com 10)] when highlighted. Your code may look different depending on the printer you are using.

FIGURE 6-5

Paper Size/Type dialog box

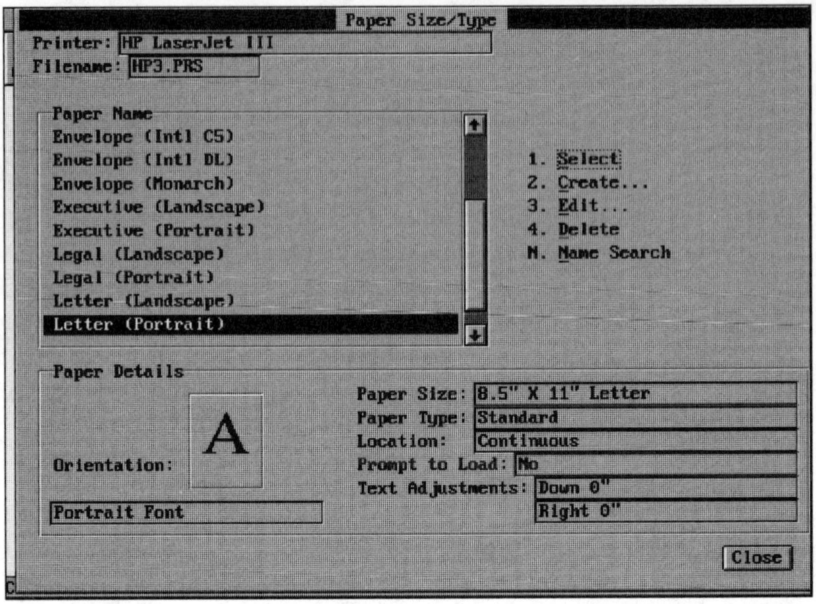

2. When you change the paper size and type, it affects all pages after the code. You can use multiple codes to have pages of a document print on different sizes or types of paper. First, type

   Dear Jim,

   Here is the information that you wanted.

   To create an envelope for this message, press Ctrl-Enter to start a new page. Select **L**ayout, **P**age, and Paper **S**ize/Type. Next, highlight the first Envelope selection and press Enter to select it. Press Enter again to return to the document. Type

   Jim Adler
   514 Washington Avenue
   Columbus, OH 43213

   To see how WordPerfect has changed the paper size, select **F**ile, Print Pre**v**iew. WordPerfect shows the name and address on an envelope-shaped page. When you press Pg Up, WordPerfect shows the letter on a normal page. Press Esc to return to the document.

EXERCISES

1. Set the paper size and type for standard legal-sized paper (8 1/2 by 14 inches), assuming that your printer supports this size paper. Type **Legal-Sized Paper** and create a hard page break. For the second page, return the paper size and type to standard (8 1/2 by 11 inches). Type **Standard-Sized Paper**. Preview how WordPerfect will print the pages.
2. Type the address from the second example in this section in a document set for a Carta-sized piece of paper. Preview how WordPerfect will print it.

Teach Yourself mastery skills check

As you complete the exercises, do not clear the screen unless you are told to do so.

1. Type the following, centering each line as well as centering the document on the page:

   Wilbur Horse Supplies
   Financial Statements
   For the Year Ending December 31, 1993

   Preview the document as WordPerfect will print it. [6.1]
2. Set the top margin to 3 inches. Preview the document again. [6.2]
3. Set WordPerfect to print page numbers in the center at the top of each page. [6.3]
4. Move to the bottom of the document and enter a hard page break. Set WordPerfect to put the word "Page" in front of the page number. [6.3]
5. Change the paper size to Envelope (Intl C4). [6.4]

cumulative skills check

Do not clear the screen until you have completed the last exercise.

1. Center the following lines as you type them: [4.3]

   Archie's California Grapes
   Production Records
   For the season ending September 30, 1994

2. Center the three lines vertically on the page. [6.1]
3. Boldface the first line and underline the second line. [4.1, 4.2]
4. Move to the bottom of the document and insert a hard page break. Set the page numbers to appear in the upper-right corner. [1.3, 6.3]
5. Change the spacing to double spacing and type the following paragraph: [5.5]

   This year's crop is the largest in the last 20 years. It is primarily due to improved fertilization methods and increased rainfall. The plants damaged by last year's drought were replaced.

6. Change the paragraph so that it is right justified. [5.6]
7. Print the document. [3.1]

7

Search and Replace Options

chapter objectives

After completing this chapter, you should be able to

7.1 Search for a word or phrase from the beginning of a document

7.2 Use special search options

7.3 Use the replace feature

WORDPERFECT can search through your document to pinpoint the exact location of a word or phrase. This feature provides a significant time savings over visually searching the document and is usually more accurate as well. WordPerfect begins its search at the location of the cursor when you start the search operation, and searches toward the end of the document.

WordPerfect provides a number of options that refine the search operation. You can search backward through the document, toward the beginning. You can also perform a case-sensitive search or look for whole word matches.

In addition to finding an entry, WordPerfect's replace feature lets you replace the entry with a new entry. This feature helps you make corrections in several places with ease. Tasks such as correcting the spelling of a name used throughout a document can be handled quickly with this feature.

WordPerfect can find text, numbers, special characters, hidden codes, and any combination of them. You will find that searching for text follows a similar pattern for all types of searches.

review
skills check

As you perform the Skills Check, do not clear the screen until you have completed the last exercise.

1. Type the following paragraphs. [1.3, 2.1]

   Product Announcement

   The XY Graphics Company has announced the release of its new product, See 'N' Draw. This package creates custom pictures by combining existing drawings and advanced graphics features. Since each new feature added to an image is considered a unique layer, you can edit one layer without affecting the others. The print options offer features unavailable in any competing product.

2. Boldface the title. [4.2]
3. Center the title. [4.3]
4. Remove the boldfacing in the title by removing the hidden codes. [4.5]
5. Indent the text paragraph on both sides. [5.2]
6. Double-space the paragraph. [5.6]
7. Center the text vertically on the page. [6.1]
8. Print the page. [3.1]

7.1 SEARCH FOR A WORD OR PHRASE FROM THE BEGINNING OF A DOCUMENT

WordPerfect's search feature can find a match for a *string,* or series of characters or codes. You can place from 1 to 80 characters (including spaces) in the search string. Since you will be searching forward (from the beginning to the end), it is important to begin with the cursor in front of all the text that you want to include in the search.

WordPerfect ignores case when searching for a match. If WordPerfect finds a match, it positions the cursor immediately past the matching letter, word, or phrase. If WordPerfect cannot find a match, the message "Not found" appears on the screen until you select the OK button, and the cursor remains where it was.

TO HAVE WORDPERFECT SEARCH FOR A WORD OR PHRASE

a. Select **E**dit, Searc**h** or press F2.
b. Type the word or phrase that WordPerfect should find in the text box.
c. Select the S**e**arch button.

To search for the same word or phrase a second time, select **E**dit, Searc**h** or press F2 again. If you have already used the search command, WordPerfect displays the last string that you searched for. You can edit this text rather than typing the new search text. Select the S**e**arch button to start the search.

EXAMPLES

1. WordPerfect ignores the case of the text you type unless you give it special instructions. You can have WordPerfect search for a word in a document until you find the occurrence you want. You may add other words to refine the search operation before repeating it. First, type the following:

   There are many stores that sell computer software. Discount stores, office supply houses, full-service computer stores, and specialized software stores are all options. I prefer to shop at Upgrade Computer.

   Next, move the cursor to the beginning by pressing Home, Home, ↑. To find the word "Computer" in "Upgrade Computer," select **E**dit, Searc**h** or press F2, and type **Computer** in the text box shown in Figure 7-1. Press F2 to select the S**e**arch button. WordPerfect moves the cursor to the space preceding "software." Since this is not the occurrence you are looking for, you can provide additional information in the text box with the next search.

   Select **E**dit, Searc**h** or press F2. Press ←, then type **upgrade** and press Spacebar to add a space after "upgrade." Select the S**e**arch button.

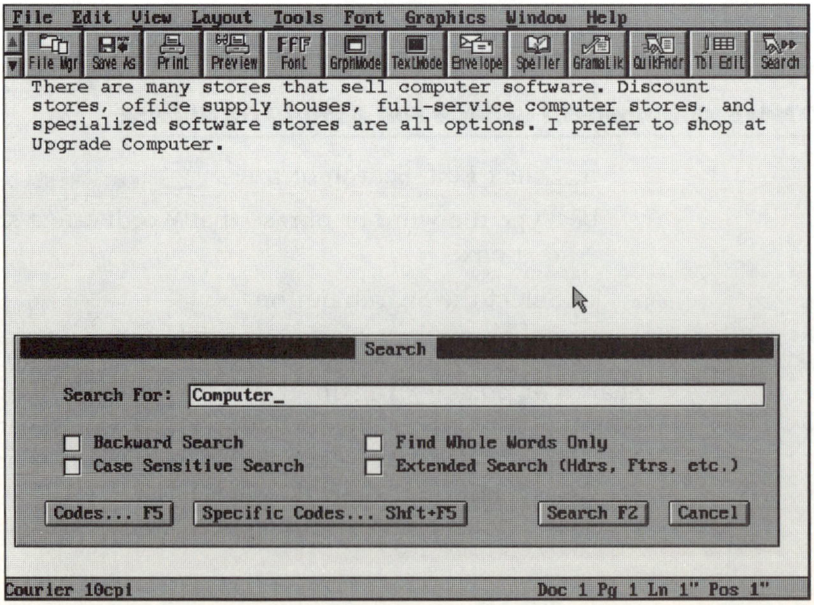

FIGURE 7-1

Dialog box for a search request

WordPerfect places the cursor before the period following "Upgrade Computer." Use this paragraph to look at the other search features in the next two examples.

NOTE *In the next objective you will learn how to perform a case-sensitive search and find "Computer" with only one search request.*

2. You can use the search feature to help locate a word or phrase you wish to delete. To find and delete the phrase "office supply houses," in the paragraph, move to the top of the paragraph by pressing Home, Home, ↑. Select **Edit**, **Search** or press F2, and type

   office supply houses,

   When you press F2 to select the Search button, WordPerfect positions the cursor at the end of this phrase. Press Backspace until you eliminate the phrase.

3. You can use the search feature to find a combination of text and hidden codes. This can help you pinpoint a specific location of a word that may occur many times in a document. First, type the following quote from Shakespeare, adding an underline to the word "His" in the last line:

   His words are bonds, his oaths are oracles;
   His love sincere, his thoughts immaculate;
   His tears, pure messengers sent from his heart;
   His heart as far from fraud as heaven from earth.

   Move to the top of the entry by pressing Home, Home, ↑. Select **Edit**, **Search** or press F2. Then press F8 for underline, type **his**, and press F8 again. The search entry looks like this:

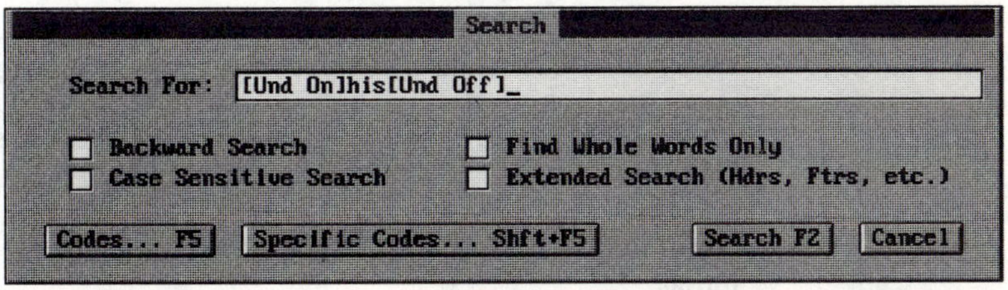

   The [Und On] and [Und Off] symbols are part of the hidden codes for the document. When you press F2 to select the Search button, WordPerfect finds the entry "His" in the last line.

NOTE *You can also select the Codes button at the bottom of the dialog box to select the underline code from the list provided. Choose whichever option seems easier. With a frequently used code option such as underline, where you know the keypress needed, it may save time to press F8 for underline.*

4. You can use the search feature to look for part of a word. If you know that you are searching for a name that begins with "Smith" but are not certain if it is "Smithson," "Smithsonian," or "Smithfield," you can search for "Smith" to find all words that begin with "Smith." First, type

   We have invited the Smithfields and the Harpers for dinner on Friday.

   Press Home, Home, ↑ to move to the beginning of the document. Select **E**dit, Searc**h** or press F2, type **Smith**, and press F2 to select the S**e**arch button. WordPerfect places the cursor on the *f* in "Smithfields."

   If you want to find "Smith" alone in the middle of a sentence, you can type **Smith** for the search string and press Spacebar. To find "Smith" at the end of a sentence, type **Smith** and a period for the search string. In the next objective you will learn about a special option that looks for whole word matches only.

EXERCISES

1. Type the following paragraph. Use the search feature to locate the name "Jill Smith."

   On Saturday, May 16, XY Graphics is holding a press conference for their new product, See 'N' Draw. At this conference, the public relations director, Jill Smith, will reveal the company's marketing strategy for the product.

2. Type the following text. Then find all occurrences of the word "forgive."

   "I can forgive but I cannot forget," is only another way of saying, "I cannot forgive."
   Henry Ward Beecher

   Forgive! How many will say "Forgive" and find
   A sort of absolution in the sound
   To hate a little longer.
   Alfred, Lord Tennyson

7.2 USE SPECIAL SEARCH OPTIONS

WordPerfect provides a number of special search options as check box options in the Search dialog box. After you supply the search text, you can select the **B**ackward Search check box to look at the text above the cursor for a match. When the **C**ase Sensitive check box is selected, WordPerfect only considers the text as a match when its case is identical to the search text entry. When Find **W**hole Words Only is checked, the search text will not match with part of a word. You can check more than one box when you want to combine features such as case sensitivity and searching backwards.

TO USE A SPECIAL SEARCH FEATURE

a. Select **E**dit, Searc**h** or press F2.
b. Type the word or phrase that you want WordPerfect to find and press Enter.
c. Select the check box for the feature you want to use.
d. Select the S**e**arch button.

NOTE *WordPerfect provides a shortcut for a backward search. You can press Shift-F2. This is equivalent to selecting **E**dit, **S**earch and selecting the **B**ackward Search check box.*

EXAMPLES

1. You can use the **B**ackward Search check box to perform a search through a document you have just finished typing without first moving to the beginning of the document. First, type the following paragraph:

   The See 'N' Draw package is easy to install. The installation program creates a subdirectory and copies the files to it. After running the installation program, the See 'N' Draw program is ready to run.

   To find where the text mentions "subdirectories," select **E**dit, Searc**h** or press F2, and type

   subdirector

Because you did not include the suffix, WordPerfect can find either "subdirectory" or "subdirectories." Press Enter. Select **B**ackward Search, then the S**e**arch button. WordPerfect moves the cursor to the "y" in "subdirectory" in the second sentence.

2. You can also use the **B**ackward Search option to find hidden codes. For example, when you type a paragraph, you might keep WordPerfect from wrapping the lines correctly by pressing Enter at the end of a line that is not the end of the paragraph. You can locate the [HRt] symbol by pressing F5 when prompted for the search string and selecting [HRT]. You can locate other attributes, such as centering, boldface, and underlining, just as easily. First, type the following, without pressing Enter:

   A strong feature of See 'N' Draw is the

   Continue the entry on the same line by pressing Spacebar and F6, for bold, and typing

   automatic detection of the hardware components.

   Press F6 again to end bold, press Spacebar twice, and type the following without pressing Enter:

   When you initially load See 'N' Draw, the program prompts you for information about the equipment you are using. The program determines the proper settings to use for your equipment. You can change these assumptions during installation or later through the menu.

   To find the code representing the end of boldfacing, press F2 or select **E**dit, Searc**h**. Since you want the [Bold Off] code, press F6 twice and use ← and Backspace to remove the first bold code. Press Enter. Next, select the **B**ackward Search check box, then the S**e**arch button. WordPerfect moves the cursor to the end of the first sentence.

   NOTE *You can use the Codes button to select the bold option from the list provided.*

3. You can look for a match where the text box entry only matches full words. Type the following:

   Yellow cat, black cat, as long as it catches mice, it is a good cat.
   Deng Xiaoping

   To find the word "cat" that follows "black," without finding a match for "catches," select **E**dit, Searc**h** and type **cat** in the text box, then press Enter. Select the **B**ackward Search and Find **W**hole Words Only check boxes. WordPerfect positions the cursor on the period. Repeat the search by selecting **E**dit, Searc**h**. There is no need to reenter the text, but you will need to reselect the **B**ackward Search check box. Find **W**hole Words Only remains checked. You can select the S**e**arch button.

NOTE *If you use Shift-F2 to invoke a backward search each time, the* ***B****ackward Search check box will automatically be checked.*

4. You can perform a case-sensitive search with a special search check box option. If the word that you are looking for precedes the cursor, you can combine the case-sensitive option with a backward search. Type the following:

   Fool me once, shame on you; fool me twice, shame on me.
   Chinese Proverb

   To find "Fool" in the entry you just made, select **E**dit, Searc**h** or press F2. Next, type **Fool** and press Enter. Select the **B**ackward Search and **C**ase Sensitive Search check boxes. Select the S**e**arch button. WordPerfect skips "fool" and places the cursor immediately following the word "Fool" that starts the quote.

EXERCISES

1. Type the following sentence:

   The entire project was moved to Tobler Hall under the direction of John Tomita.

   Use **B**ackward Search to find all occurrences of the string "to."

2. Type the following sentences:

   The meeting is Friday, August 11th. All must attend. Discuss previous commitments with Carol Stevens.

   Use **B**ackward Search to find the ending underline code.

3. Type the following paragraph:

   The next forum for the Secretary's Association is in Buffalo. Since it is close to the Canadian border, they are expecting an increased number of foreigners. The cost, including dinner, is forty dollars.

   Use **B**ackward Search to find all occurrences of the string "for." Use **B**ackward Search again, but this time find all occurrences of the word "for," without finding other words that have that letter combination in them.

4. Type the following:

   To travel hopefully is a better thing than to arrive.
   Robert Louis Stevenson

   Use the **B**ackward Search option and search for the word "To," matching only the uppercase occurrence.

7.3 USE THE REPLACE FEATURE

In addition to searching for text, WordPerfect can replace a string of characters with another string of characters. Further, this feature provides *global* replacement, meaning that WordPerfect searches the entire document and changes each occurrence of the search string to the replacement string. You can choose to confirm every replacement or allow WordPerfect to make the replacements without waiting for confirmation. To restrict the text affected by the replace operation, you can use the block feature to mark the text to be searched.

The replace feature provides a convenient method for correcting names or product numbers entered incorrectly, or any other information you wish to change. You must supply both the original search string and its replacement.

TO HAVE WORDPERFECT FIND AND REPLACE A WORD OR PHRASE

a. Select **E**dit, Rep**l**ace or press Alt-F2.

b. Type the text you want to replace in the Search For text box that is active and press Enter.

c. Type the text you want to insert in place of the search text and press Enter.

   If you want to delete the text you are searching for, leave the Replace With text box set at <Nothing> and skip to step d.

d. Select the Con**f**irm Replacement, **B**ackward Search, **C**ase Sensitive Search, or Find **W**hole Words Only check boxes to activate those features.

e. Select the R**e**place button.

If you have already performed a search or replace during the current WordPerfect session, you need to remove the previous search string. If you begin typing the new search string, WordPerfect deletes the first search string automatically. You can also delete the old entry with Del.

WordPerfect 6 automatically reformats the document as it replaces text and codes. You can press Esc at any time during the replace procedure if you make a mistake or change your mind.

EXAMPLES

1. You can use the replace feature to change every occurrence of a word or phrase to another word or phrase. First, type the following text:

   See 'N' Draw is a product designed for first-time users and artists who want to push the limits of a graphics package. Compared with competitors' products, See 'N' Draw has the easiest user interface to learn. See 'N' Draw is available at most retail software dealers.

   Next, to change the package name to "Scene Draw," select **E**dit, Rep**l**ace or press Alt-F2. WordPerfect displays the dialog box shown in Figure 7-2. Type this text in the Search For text box:

   See 'N'

   Press Enter. Move to the Replace With text box and type

   Scene

   Press Enter. Clear the Con**f**irm Replacement and Case Sensitive Search check boxes if they contain an X from a previous search request. Select the **B**ackward Search check box to have the search

FIGURE 7-2

Dialog box for a search and replace operation

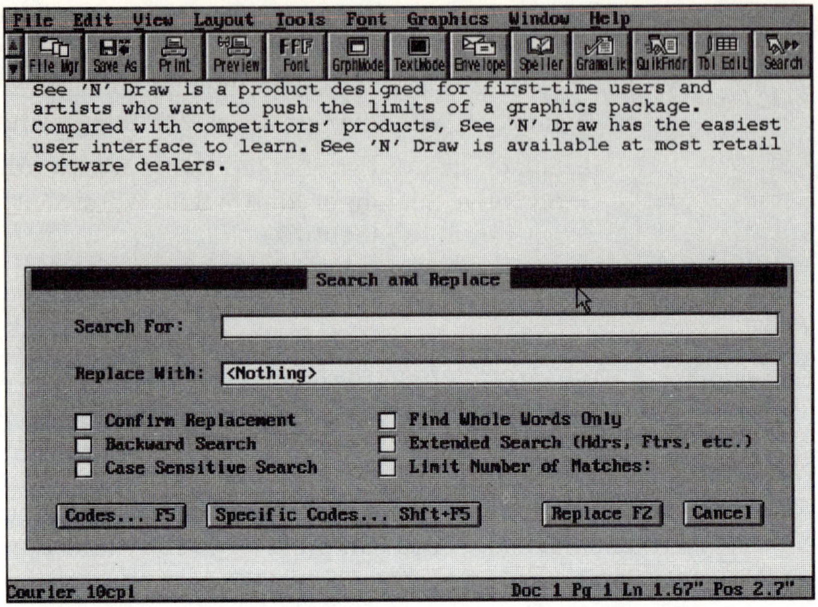

conducted from the cursor toward the beginning of the document. The dialog box should look like this before you start the next step:

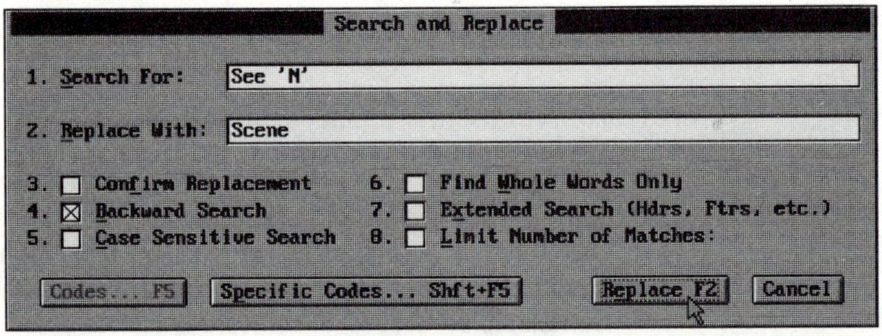

Select the Replace button and OK. WordPerfect displays a box showing that three replacements were made. Select OK. The paragraph now looks like this:

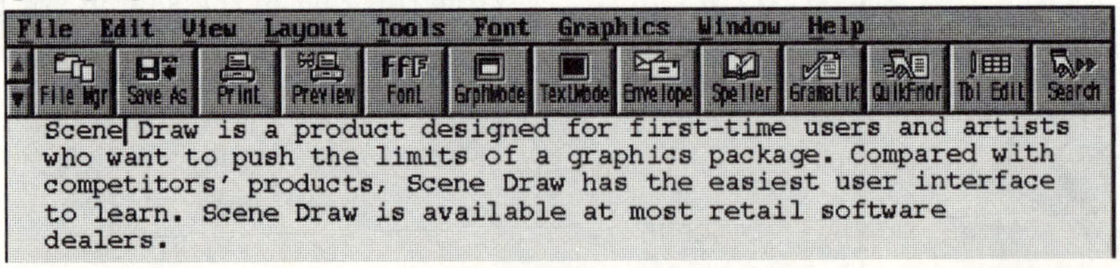

2. You can use search and replace to selectively replace text or codes. If you have a document in which you have pressed Enter at the end of each line, changing the margins might cause the lines to display incorrectly. To correct the problem, you need to remove all the hard

returns that do not end a paragraph. This allows WordPerfect to adjust the text correctly within any margin settings you select.

First, type the following lines, pressing e at the end of each sentence:

The product will be released on August 17th.
The initial press conference is on August 11th.
The distributors will have the package on August 14th.
A product review in a monthly newsletter was excellent.
The newsletter is considering another article for a later issue.

Next, select **E**dit, Rep**l**ace or press Alt-F2. Press F5 to select the Codes button, and select HRt from the list by highlighting it and selecting the Select button. WordPerfect displays the [HRt] code in the Search For text box. Move to the Replace With text box. Since you want the hard returns replaced with spaces, press the Spacebar and press Enter. Select the Con**f**irm Replacement and **B**ackward Search check boxes. The dialog box looks like this:

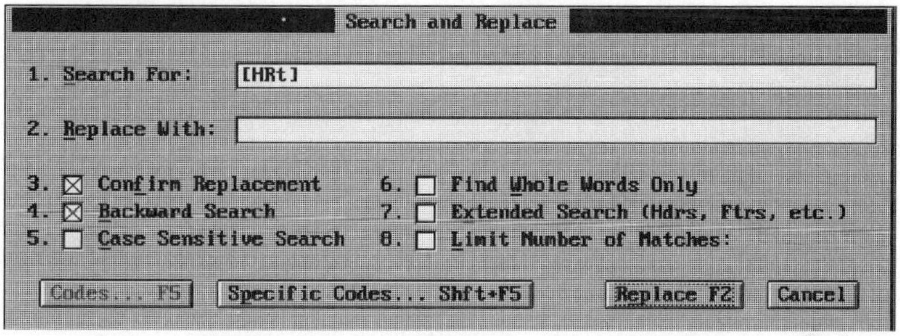

Select the Replace button. The area to the right of the period after "excellent" and to the left of "The" in the last line is highlighted to mark the location of the hidden [HRt] code, and WordPerfect displays this prompt:

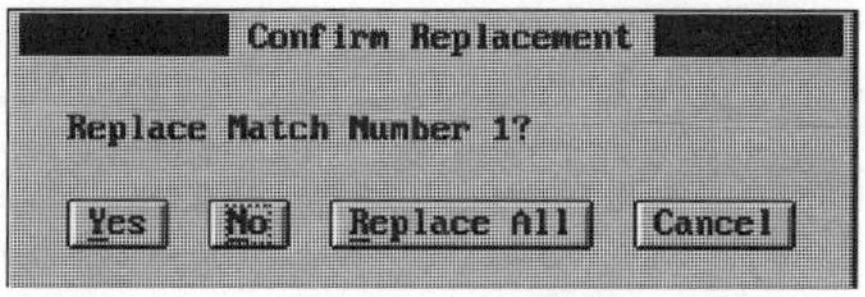

Since you want this replacement made, select Yes. For each of the successive prompts, select Yes again, and then OK. After the last replacement is made, select OK again. The paragraph now looks like this:

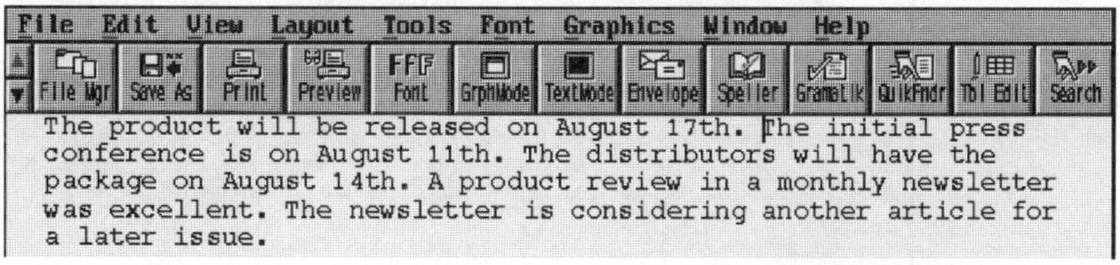

3. You can find an exact match for a word by selecting the Find **W**hole Words Only check box. In this example, if you want WordPerfect to replace the name "Green" with "Lime" and skip "Greenly," "Greensen," Greenfield," and "Greene," this option will allow you to make the change without confirming each change.

   First, type

   He invited John Greenly, Howard Greensen, Mary Greenfield, Beth Greene, and Paul Green to his St. Patrick's Day party.

   Move to the top of the document by pressing Home, Home, ↑. Select **E**dit, R**e**place or press Alt-F2. Next, type

   Green

   Press Enter to move to the Replace With text box and type

   Lime

   Press Enter. Clear the *X* from the Con**f**irm Replacement check box, if necessary, to make the replacement without confirmation. Select the Find **W**hole Words Only check box. Select the R**e**place button. When you select the R**e**place button, WordPerfect performs the replacement.

4. You can restrict the scope of the replacement by blocking the text you wish to be affected. Type

   ABC Company had a very profitable year. Five successful new products helped to make 1993 the best year ever for ABC Company. ABC Company performed poorly this year. A record 90 million dollar loss for ABC Company was recorded.

   Press Enter to end the paragraph. Next, move to the beginning of the third sentence. Block the last two sentences. Select **E**dit, Rep**l**ace or press Alt-F2. Type **ABC** in the Search For text box and press Enter. Move to the Replace With text box, type **XYZ** and press Enter. Clear the *X* from the Confirm Replacement check box if necessary. When you select the R**e**place button and select OK, WordPerfect changes the text to look like this:

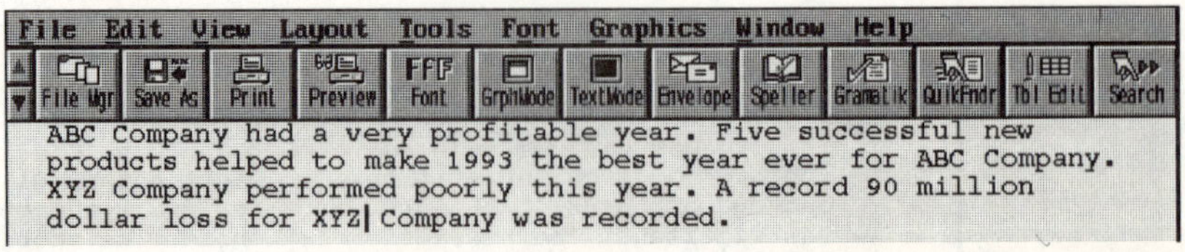

EXERCISES

1. Type the following paragraph:

   Sam Cook is the production manager. He has five years' experience in this position. Prior to this position, Sam Cook was a sergeant in the army. Sam Cook succeeded Thomas MacNamara in his current position.

   Replace all occurrences of "Sam Cook" with **Daniel Jones**.

2. Type the following text:

   WordPerfect's replace feature allows you to selectively replace one string of characters with another character string. You can have WordPerfect prompt you before completing each replacement, or you can have it make the changes automatically.

   Use the replace feature to change all occurrences of "WordPerfect" to **WordPerfect 6**.

3. Type the following paragraph:

   The Public Relations Director for your area is XX. XX has been with the company for many years and can answer your questions.

   Replace "XX" with **Nancy Clark**. Then replace "Nancy Clark" with **Martin Smith**.

4. Type the following paragraph:

   You can use WP's replace feature to shorten typing in a ms or doc. In a ms or doc, you type the abbreviations in place of the words and have WP replace the abbreviations with the words they represent.

   Replace "ms" with **manuscript**. Replace "doc" with **document**. Replace "WP" with **WordPerfect**.

mastery skills check

As you perform the skills check, do not clear the screen between exercises unless instructed to do so.

1. Type the following paragraph:

   WordPerfect lets you search for text. You can search either backward or forward. This means that you do not have to move the cursor to a specific location before you can use this feature.

   Go to the top of the paragraph and use the search feature to locate each occurrence of the word "search." [7.1]

2. Go back to the top of the paragraph and use the search feature to look at each use of the word "you." [7.1]
3. Go to the bottom of the paragraph and use **B**ackward Search to look at each occurrence of "for." Clear the screen. [7.2]
4. Type the following:

   Aeneades was a Trojan prince. He was the son of Diomedes and Achilles. Aeneades married Lavinia.

   Replace all occurrences of "Aeneades" with **Aeneas**. [7.3]

cumulative skills check

Do not clear the screen until you have completed the last exercise.

1. Type the following paragraph:

Proposal

The Quick Time division of New Men's Look, Inc., would like to expand their product line to include pocket watches. Adding pocket watches would fit into the division's current production capacity. The plant is operating 30% below capacity. The technology required is already available. This product would also complement the suits produced by another subsidiary, the Taylor division.

Use search to move the cursor to the hidden code for underlining. Use Reveal Codes to determine the cursor's location in relation to the hidden code. [4.1, 4.4, 7.1]

2. Use the replace feature to change "Quick Time" to uppercase. [7.2]
3. Replace "Taylor" with **Tailor**. [7.3]
4. Center the text on the page. [6.1]
5. Preview the document as WordPerfect would print it. [3.3]

8

Restructuring Your Document

chapter objectives

After completing this chapter, you should be able to

8.1 Move or copy a sentence, a paragraph, or a page

8.2 Move or copy a block of text

8.3 Move or copy text to many locations

ONE of the greatest advantages of using WordPerfect over using a typewriter is that you can restructure documents without retyping them. Moving and copying words, sentences, paragraphs, and pages is easy with WordPerfect's convenient features. You can move or copy phrases, multiple sentences, or multiple pages of text by first blocking them. You have mastered the first step in this process already, because you have used the block feature to mark text to be underlined and boldfaced. You can move or copy a section of text to more than one location by using another useful WordPerfect feature. This lets you create two similar sections of text by copying the original text and modifying the copy.

review skills check

As you work through the following Skills Check exercises, do not clear the screen until you have completed the last exercise.

1. Set all four margins to 2 inches. [6.1]
2. Set the page numbers to appear in the upper-left corner when you print the document. [6.3]
3. Remove all of the tab stops, and set new ones every inch. [5.3]
4. Type the following letter:

   Dale Thompson
   Birds of a Feather
   2398 Manzanita Park
   Stanford, CA 94321

   Dear Dale,

   According to your advertisement in Feathered Friends, you are interested in purchasing two white cockatoos. I own several and would like to sell them. Please contact me at (813) 212-2634.

Sincerely,

Byron Wilson

Underline "Feathered Friends." [2.1, 4,1, 4.7]

5. Use the replace feature to change "cockatoos" to "parakeets." [7.3]
6. Print the document. Center the document on the page and reprint it. [3.1]
7. Reset all four margins to 1 inch, and set tab stops every .5 inch. Eliminate page numbering. [4.3, 6.1, 6.3]

8.1 MOVE OR COPY A SENTENCE, A PARAGRAPH, OR A PAGE

Polishing initial drafts of a document can improve the quality and clarity of the writing. Rearranging text is often part of the revision process, because it enables you to place text in the most effective order. WordPerfect provides options for copying or moving a sentence, a paragraph, or a page, to make it easy to rearrange text.

NOTE *Although you can use the menus to move or copy a sentence, paragraph, or page, the method presented in this book is much more direct and involves fewer selections.*

TO MOVE OR COPY TEXT

a. Move the cursor so that it is within the text you want to move or copy.
b. Press Ctrl-F4.
c. Select **S**entence, Pa**r**agraph, or P**a**ge to block the sentence, paragraph, or page in which the cursor is positioned.
d. Select Cu**t** and Paste to move the text to a new location, or select **C**opy and Paste to make a copy of the text in a new location.
e. Move the cursor to where you want the text placed.
f. Press Enter.

In step d, WordPerfect reads the text to a special file called the Clipboard. If you selected Cut and Paste, WordPerfect deletes the original copy of the text after reading it to the Clipboard. If you selected Copy and Paste, WordPerfect does not delete the original text. When you press Enter in step f, WordPerfect reads the contents of the Clipboard back into the document at the cursor's current location.

If you select Sentence in step c, WordPerfect copies or moves text from the beginning of the current sentence through the space that follows the period, question mark, or exclamation point that ends the sentence. Select Paragraph to move or copy text from the beginning of the paragraph through the hard return at the end. Select Page to move or copy text from the top of the page through the page break at the end.

EXAMPLES

1. You can move one sentence at a time. Type

   Please return the books immediately! According to our records, Dave, you were the last one to borrow the department's tax reference books.

   This paragraph makes more sense if you reverse the sentence order. Move the cursor to any character in the first sentence, and press Ctrl-F4. WordPerfect displays this dialog box:

   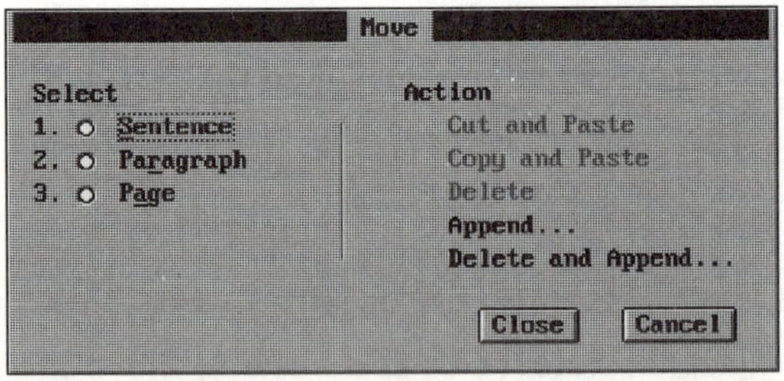

   Select Sentence. WordPerfect highlights the sentence and activates the other dialog box elements. Select Cut and Paste to move the sentence. The sentence disappears. WordPerfect displays a reminder on the bottom of the screen that tells you to press Enter where you want the text to be placed. Move the cursor to the end of the remaining sentence. If you did not include a space at the end of the second sentence when you typed it, press the Spacebar. Press Enter. The sentence that was originally first is placed after the other sentence, and the screen looks like this:

2. Because WordPerfect recognizes a period as the end of a sentence, you can get unexpected results when trying to copy a sentence that contains abbreviations or numbers that include decimals. Type

   Dr. and Mrs. Jones bought a St. Bernard puppy.

   Press Home and ← to move to the beginning of the sentence. Press Ctrl-F4, and select **S**entence. Instead of highlighting the entire sentence, WordPerfect highlights only "Dr." Because the abbreviations in this sentence require periods, the sentence needs to be copied by using the procedures covered later in this chapter. Press Esc to leave the dialog box without copying.

3. You can create a second copy of a paragraph. To copy a paragraph, first type

   The MIS department retains a copy of the manuals for all of the company's software. To borrow a manual, check it out from one of the reference librarians. You may borrow a manual for up to three days.

   After pressing Enter, move the cursor to any character in the paragraph. Press Ctrl-F4, and select Pa**r**agraph. WordPerfect highlights the entire paragraph. Select **C**opy and Paste. WordPerfect places the cursor at the beginning of the next paragraph. Press Enter to create the second copy of the paragraph.

4. You can move a page of text to a new location in a document. First, type the following text, entering a hard page break between each line by selecting **L**ayout, **A**lignment, Hard **P**age or pressing Ctrl-Enter.

   Preparation and Approval of Building Plans
   Construction of the Building Exterior
   Interior Finishing Tasks
   Site Excavation

   Enter another hard page break after the last entry. Let's say that as you review the pages, you notice that page 4 should be the second

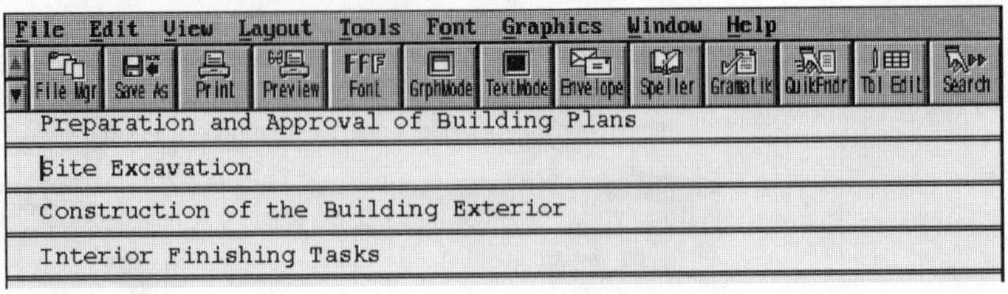

FIGURE 8-1 *The effect of moving a page*

page in the document. Position the cursor on page 4, press Ctrl-F4, and select P**a**ge . All of the text on the page is highlighted. Next, select Cu**t** and Paste. Finally, move the cursor to the first character on page 2. When you press Enter, WordPerfect inserts the page, and the screen looks like that shown in Figure 8-1.

EXERCISES

1. Type the following paragraph:

   A complex sentence consists of an independent clause, which can stand alone, and one or more dependent clauses. A compound sentence is two or more simple sentences joined by a conjunction, such as "and," "or," "but," or "for." A simple sentence expresses a single action or thought.

   Change the sentence order so that the first sentence is third and the third sentence is first.

2. Type the following paragraph:

   First, put the correct pens in the plotter. This is an important step. Next, put the paper or transparency in the plotter.

   Copy the second sentence, placing the copy after the third sentence.

3. Type the following lines, inserting a hard page break after each line. Move the first page to after the third page.

   A nebula is a mass of gas in space.
   A meteoroid is a small object in space.
   A constellation is a group of stars.

8.2 MOVE OR COPY A BLOCK OF TEXT

You can move or copy blocks of text that do not fit WordPerfect's definition of a sentence, a paragraph, or a page. For example, you will need to block text when you want to move or copy groups of words, several sentences, half of a page, a sentence that contains periods, or a paragraph that has [HRt] codes to end short lines.

WordPerfect 6 offers the new drag and drop capability that lets you move or copy text using only your mouse. This drag and drop ability makes moving or copying text even quicker than using the menu commands.

TO MOVE OR COPY A BLOCK OF TEXT WITH THE MOUSE

a. Drag the mouse across the text you want to move or copy.

   To do this, move the mouse pointer to the beginning of the text you want to move or copy. Then press the mouse button, and move the pointer to the end of the text before releasing the mouse button.

b. Drag the blocked text to where you want it, pressing Ctrl if you want to copy it.

To do this, point the mouse pointer on the blocked text and press the mouse button, then move the mouse pointer to where you want the text to appear before releasing the mouse button. The cursor appears at the location you are pointing to so that you can be sure the mouse pointer is correctly positioned. When the cursor is at the location where you want to move the text, release the mouse button.

TO MOVE OR COPY A BLOCK OF TEXT WITH THE KEYBOARD

a. Move the cursor to the first character or code in the text you want to move or copy.

b. Select **E**dit, **B**lock or press Alt-F4 or F12.

c. Move the cursor to highlight all of the text and codes you want to move or copy.

d. Press Ctrl-F4 or select **E**dit.

e. Select Cut and Paste to move the text, or select Copy and Paste to copy it.

f. Move the cursor to where you want the block of text placed.

g. Press Enter.

NOTE *The highlighted characters are not marked in step e, because different letters are highlighted in the menu and the dialog box. However, the commands have the same names, and they work in the same way.*

EXAMPLES

1. You can use the mouse to move part of a sentence. Type

   In order to complete your request, we need the following information: your address, the date of the purchase, your name, and the name of the salesperson who handled the order.

   To move the words "your name" to precede the words "your address," move the mouse pointer to the *y* in "your name," and press the mouse button. Next, move the mouse pointer to before the *a* in "and" and release the button. The screen looks like this:

   Point the mouse at the blocked text, and press the mouse button. Move the pointer to the *y* in "your address," and release the mouse button. You probably noticed that as you moved the mouse to a new location, the mouse pointer had a box attached to it to remind you that you are moving a block of text. The screen looks like this:

2. You can copy a block of text using the mouse. First, type

   You, Nancy Collins, have been chosen the employee of the month for the Dallas branch of Widget-For-All on the basis of the many customer remarks we have received about your service. Please call the Human Resources department to select your prize.

   Press Enter at the end of this paragraph. You will want to copy this entire block of text so that you can quickly create the notice for this month's employee. Next, block the text by pointing the mouse at the *Y* in "You," pressing the mouse button, dragging the mouse to the period after "prize," and releasing the mouse button. Next, you want to copy this text by pointing the mouse on the block you have selected. Press and hold down the Ctrl key. With the Ctrl key depressed, press and hold down the mouse button. Move the pointer to the line beneath the current copy of the paragraph. Release the mouse button, then release Ctrl.

   Notice that when you press Ctrl the mouse pointer changes slightly, indicating that when you release the mouse button, the text is copied instead of moved. You can press Ctrl at any time, so long as it is still pressed when you release the mouse button.

3. You can copy a block of any size. Type the following lines, pressing Enter at the end of each line.

   The policy that applies to borrowing the company's 35mm camera is
   The borrower must return the camera within 24 hours.
   The borrower is responsible for film and development.
   The borrower is responsible for damage or loss.

   To copy the policy, select **E**dit, **B**lock or press Alt-F4, and press Pg Up to move the cursor to the *T* in the first line. Next, press Ctrl-F4 or select **E**dit, and select Copy and Paste.

   Finally, move the cursor to the bottom of the document by pressing Pg Dn. Press Enter to insert a copy of the text. You can modify the copy to produce a policy for borrowing the company's new video camera.

EXERCISES

1. Type this sentence:

   See 'N' Draw, XY Graphics' new product, should capture a large part of the graphics market for first-time users.

   Move the product name and the comma and space that follow it to after the comma and space that follow "product." The restructured sentence should read

   XY Graphics' new product, See 'N' Draw, should capture a large part of the graphics market for first-time users.

2. Type the following partial paragraph:

   Directions to Cloverleaf Hall: Take the interstate to the Bay Street exit. At the exit, turn right, and take the next left after the light. Stay on this road until you pass the shopping mall on the right. After passing the shopping mall,

   Complete the last sentence by blocking and copying "take the next left after the light."

3. Type these lines:

   Review meeting agenda.
   Nominate potential candidates for new director position.
   Review financial statements.
   Review minutes from the last meeting.
   Introduce new corporate treasurer to board.

   Move the last two lines so that they follow the first line.

4. Type the following lines. Block them, copy them, and make three additional copies.

   Current Month:
   Sales:
   Cost of Goods Sold:

8.3 MOVE OR COPY TEXT TO MANY LOCATIONS

You have learned to move and copy text from one location to another. If you want multiple copies of text, you can copy it multiple times, but WordPerfect offers an easier way. This feature uses the Clipboard. When you cut or copy text, WordPerfect reads the text to the Clipboard. When you cut text, WordPerfect deletes the original copy of the text. When you copy text, WordPerfect leaves the original text in the document. After the text is read to the Clipboard, you can move to any position within the document and paste the contents of the Clipboard into the document at that location. The text is inserted as if you had typed it at the cursor's location. The Clipboard is not emptied when you paste its contents into the document, so you can repeatedly paste text into a document.

TO MOVE OR COPY TEXT TO MANY LOCATIONS

a. Move the cursor to the first character or code in the text you want to move or copy.

b. Select **E**dit, **B**lock or press Alt-F4 or F12.

c. Move the cursor to highlight all of the text and codes that you want to move or copy.

d. Select **E**dit, Cu**t** or press Ctrl-X to move the text; or select **E**dit, **C**opy or press Ctrl-C to copy the text.

e. Move the cursor to where you want the block of text placed.

f. Select **E**dit, **P**aste or press Ctrl-V.

g. Repeat steps e and f for each copy you want.

EXAMPLE

You can create multiple copies of text. Type

The MIS department retains a copy of the manuals for all of the company's database software. To borrow a manual, check it out from one of the reference librarians. You may borrow a manual for up to three days.

Press Enter, select **E**dit, **B**lock or press Alt-F4, and then press Pg Up to move the cursor to the beginning of the paragraph, where you want the text to appear. Select **E**dit, **C**opy or press Ctrl-C. Move the cursor to after the paragraph. Select **E**dit, **P**aste or press Ctrl-V to insert a copy of the paragraph at the cursor location.

Delete "database" in the second copy of the paragraph and insert "spreadsheet" in its place.

To make an additional copy of the paragraph, move the cursor to between the two paragraphs. Select **E**dit, **P**aste or press Ctrl-V to insert another copy of the original text. You can then edit this paragraph to give different instructions for borrowing manuals.

EXERCISES

1. Type

   Gayle Fein received a 92 efficiency score on the Efficiency Test.

   Copy this paragraph and paste it into the document three times. Change the names and scores in the three new copies as follows:

   Howard Otlowski 93
   Carla Holbinko 95
   Steven Lash 96

2. Type

   George Herbert
   "The lion is not so fierce as they paint him."
   "One father is more than a hundred schoolmasters."
   "Poverty is no sin."
   "One hour's sleep before midnight is worth three after."
   "Half the world knows not how the other half lives."
   "His bark is worse than his bite."

   Cut the first line and paste it beneath each of the quotations.

3. Type the following lines, and then place a copy of the lines below the originals.

   Name: Patrick Rabbit
   Address: 777 Carrot Lane

   Modify the copy to change the second "Patrick" to "Nancy" and the second street number to "515." Make an additional copy of the original two lines.

mastery skills check

1. Type the following sentences. Move the first sentence to between the second and third sentences. [8.1]

   The cost of goods sold is $2,363,782. The beginning inventory is $689,578. The ending inventory is $234,245.

2. Type

   Benjamin Franklin originally wrote a great many now common sayings.
   "Three may keep a secret, if two of them are dead."
   "Don't throw stones at your neighbors' if your own windows are glass."
   "Early to bed and early to rise, makes a man healthy wealthy and wise."
   These were written in Poor Richard's Almanac.

   Copy the last sentence to the end of the first sentence. [8.1, 8.2]

3. Type the following paragraph:

   Today's weather will be lovely. The temperature will rise to 82 and will cool to an evening low of 70. The low humidity will contribute to the day's pleasant weather.

   Make three copies of the paragraph. [8.3]

cumulative skills check

As you complete the following exercises, do not clear the screen between exercises unless instructed to do so.

1. Type the following paragraph:

The ABC widget uses point-of-sale displays as its primary marketing strategy. The new point-of-sale displays are designed to fit at the end of an aisle. As an incentive to the retailer, we are selling the widgets in the aisle pre-packs at a slightly lower cost. Each retailer can choose whether to pass the lower cost on to the customer or to increase profits.

Insert a hard page break, and move the paragraph to the second page. [1.3, 8.1]

2. Indent the paragraph. Clear the screen. [1.2, 5.1]
3. Type the following lines:

   Marketing Strategy
   ABC WIDGETS
   Prepared on July 7, 1993

   Delete the first two words in the last line. Center this information on the page. Preview how WordPerfect will print the document. Clear the screen. [1.2, 2.3, 3.3, 4.3]
4. Create a receipt form by typing

   Date:
   Name:
   Amount:
   Explanation:
   Signature:

   Insert a hard page break. Block the lines and the page break, and place a copy below the original. [1.3, 8.2, 8.3]
5. Make three additional copies of the page. [8.3]
6. Add page numbers in the center at the top of each page, and print the receipt forms. [3.1, 6.3]
7. Replace all occurrences of "Explanation" with "For." [7.3]

part two

Building on the Basics

9

Using WordPerfect's Writing Tools

chapter objectives

After completing this chapter, you should be able to

9.1 Check the spelling of a word

9.2 Check the spelling of an entire document

9.3 Find double words

9.4 Add a word to the supplemental dictionary

9.5 Replace correctly spelled words that are misused

9.6 Look up a word in the thesaurus

9.7 Replace a word with a word from the thesaurus

9.8 Use the grammar checker for an overview of your document

WHEN you create a document, you hope that it will convey your message in a clear, concise way. Another objective may be to present a professional image of yourself and your firm.

Part of creating a professional image is creating a document that is flawless in spelling and grammar. WordPerfect's spell feature lets you check the spelling of a word, a page, or the entire document. It lets you create personal dictionaries for specialized terminology. WordPerfect's spelling checker also finds occurrences of double words.

In addition to spelling the words correctly, to convey your message effectively, you must use the right words to express the meaning you intend. WordPerfect has a thesaurus feature to help you find the right words easily.

WordPerfect 6 has a new grammar checking feature that helps you to improve your writing and to target your audience. Although this chapter does not cover all the details of the grammar checker, it gives you a start with it by looking at the statistics it provides for your document.

review
skills check

As you perform the Skills Check, do not clear the screen until you have completed the last exercise.

1. Change the left and right margins to 2 inches. [6.2]
2. Add page numbers in the upper-left corner of the document. [6.3]
3. Type the following paragraph:

   WordPerfect's spell feature can find your spelling and typing mistakes. WordPerfect prompts you with suggested alternatives when it finds a word that is not in one of its dictionaries.

   Find all occurrences of "spell" in the text you just typed. [7.1]

4. Replace all occurrences of the word "it" with **WordPerfect**. [7.3]
5. Add the following sentence to the end of the paragraph:

   WordPerfect's thesaurus feature can help you find a word that has the exact meaning you need.

   Copy the second sentence in the paragraph to the end of the paragraph. From the copied sentence, delete "when it finds a word that is not in one of its dictionaries" and add **for the word that you look up in its thesaurus**. The completed paragraph should read as shown below. [1.3, 2.3, 8.1]

   WordPerfect's spell feature can find your spelling and typing mistakes. WordPerfect prompts you with suggested alternatives when it finds a word that is not in one of its dictionaries. WordPerfect's thesaurus feature can help you find a word that has the exact meaning you need. WordPerfect prompts you with suggested alternatives for the word that you look up in its thesaurus.

9.1 CHECK THE SPELLING OF A WORD

If you are uncertain of the correct spelling of a word, you can have WordPerfect check it for you. The ability to check the spelling of a single word is a time-saving feature. Once you have verified it, you can stop questioning the spelling and focus on finishing the document.

TO HAVE WORDPERFECT CHECK THE SPELLING OF A WORD

a. Move the cursor to the word that you want to check.

b. Select **T**ools, **W**riting Tools, **S**peller or press Ctrl-F2.

c. Select **W**ord.

   If you spelled the word correctly, WordPerfect moves the cursor to the next word. If WordPerfect does not find the word in its dictionaries, it displays the Word Not Found dialog box with a list of similarly spelled or pronounced words. The choices are labeled with letters for your selection.

d. Select the correct word or one of the dialog box options, if WordPerfect did not move the cursor to the next word.

e. Press F7 to select Close to return to the document.

EXAMPLES

1. You can use WordPerfect's spell feature to check the spelling of a few individual words. To illustrate how the spelling checker works, type the following sentence, including the misspelling of "strategy."

   Next Tuesday, the marketing department will present their promotional straegy for the See 'N' Draw package.

   To check the spelling of the words "promotional" and "straegy," first move the cursor to the word "promotional." Next, select **T**ools, **W**riting Tools, **S**peller or press Ctrl-F2. WordPerfect displays this dialog box:

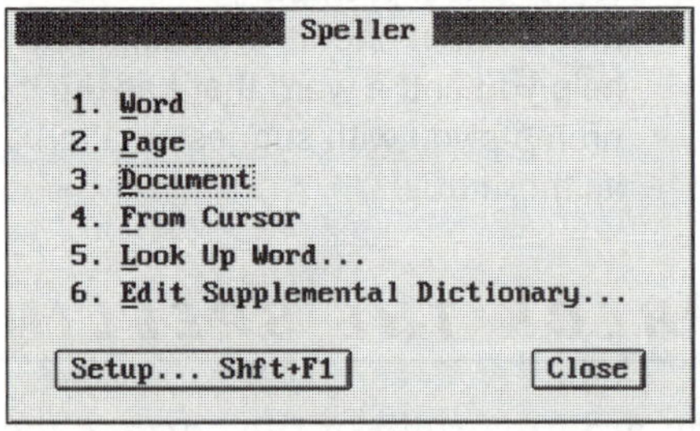

   Select **W**ord to check a word at a time. WordPerfect checks the spelling of "promotional." Because "promotional" is spelled correctly, WordPerfect moves the cursor over to the next word, "straegy," and returns you to the Speller dialog box. Select **W**ord again to check the spelling of this word. Because it cannot find that word in its dictionary, WordPerfect displays a dialog box that looks like this:

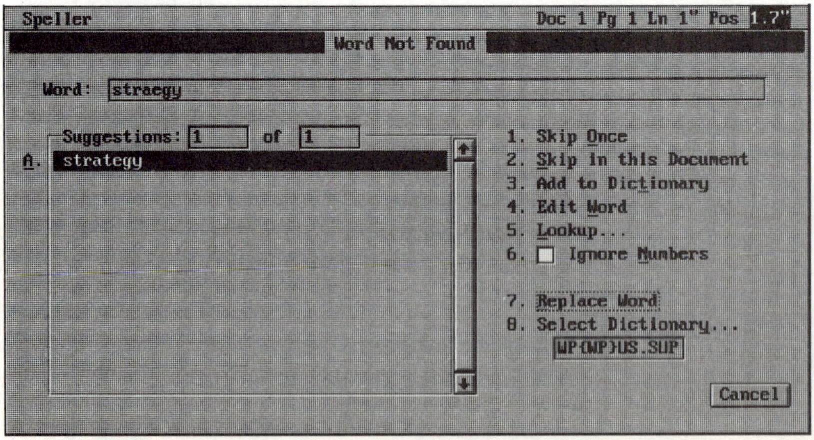

WordPerfect displays a suggestion for the correct spelling of the word. Since the suggestion is correct, you can make the replacement by selecting **R**eplace Word. Select the Close button to leave the spell feature.

2. When you use the spell feature on words that are spelled correctly but are not in WordPerfect's dictionary, WordPerfect still suggests replacements and offers a menu of correction alternatives. You can tell WordPerfect to ignore correctly spelled words it does not recognize. First, type

   Adele Stein is representing the European divisions at the stockholders' meeting.

   You can check the spelling of this sentence word by word by moving the cursor to the beginning of the sentence and selecting **T**ools, **W**riting Tools, **S**peller or pressing Ctrl-F2. Next, select **W**ord. WordPerfect highlights "Adele," which it doesn't recognize, and offers suggestions for other spellings. Since you have spelled the name properly, you want WordPerfect to skip this word within the document; select **S**kip in this Document. By selecting this option, you instruct WordPerfect to ignore "Adele" whenever it finds that word. If you select Skip **O**nce, WordPerfect would skip only this occurrence of the word. Select the Close button to leave the spell feature.

3. WordPerfect's spell feature may offer many alternatives for a word that it does not find in its dictionary. First, type

   Lake Erie usualy freezes in November or December.

   Next, move the cursor to the word "usualy," select **T**ools, **W**riting Tools, **S**peller or press Ctrl-F2, then select **W**ord. Since you misspelled this word, the screen looks like Figure 9-1. Each of WordPerfect's suggestions has a different letter next to it. Since the replacement word that you want is "usually," press B to have WordPerfect substitute the correctly spelled word. After checking other words in the sentence, select the Close button to exit from the spell feature.

4. When WordPerfect checks spelling, you may need to modify, rather than replace, a word that it does not recognize. First, type

   For some misspellings, WordPerfect maynot give appropriate suggestions.

   Press Enter. Then press the ↑ key twice to move to the word "For." Press Ctrl-F2 or use the menu to activate the spelling checker. Select **W**ord five times. WordPerfect does not recognize "maynot." You can easily fix this typographical mistake by editing it. Select Edit **W**ord.

FIGURE 9-1

Suggested spelling corrections supplied by the spelling checker

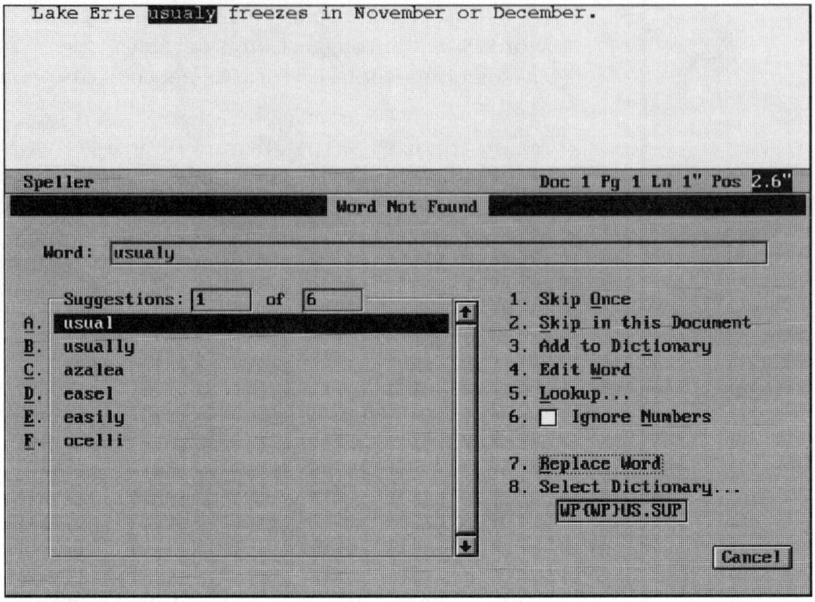

Press the → key three times and the Spacebar once. Then press F7 or Enter to end editing. WordPerfect checks the modified text. Since the edited words are correctly spelled, WordPerfect moves to the next word. Continue selecting **W**ord to check the rest of the sentence. Then select OK to return to the document.

EXERCISES

1. Type the following words:

   Regrdless
   Disinterested
   Paradox
   Momento
   Subsequential
   Torturous

   Use the spell feature to correct the misspelled words.

2. Type the following sentence as it appears:

   WordPerfecty can chek a word at a thime, a blok, or an entear document.

   Move to the beginning of the sentence and check the spelling a word at a time.
3. Type the following sentence as it appears:

   Arwena McClellan is th product managr.

   Move to the beginning of the sentence and check the spelling a word at a time. Assume that "Arwena McClellan" is spelled correctly.
4. Type the following:

   Ofthe eople, bythe oeople, andfor thepeople.

   Move to the beginning and check the spelling a word at a time. Use the Edit option of the spell feature to modify the words so that the final result looks like this:

   Of the people, by the people, and for the people.

9.2 CHECK THE SPELLING OF AN ENTIRE DOCUMENT

For long documents, pressing keys to check the spelling of every word you are unsure of would be a tedious process. Also, it is likely that you would overlook errors. WordPerfect can check the spelling for the entire document for you with one easy command.

TO HAVE WORDPERFECT CHECK THE SPELLING OF A DOCUMENT

a. Select **T**ools, **W**riting Tools, **S**peller or press Ctrl-F2.

b. Select **D**ocument.

WordPerfect reviews the entire document. When it finds a word that is not in its dictionaries, WordPerfect displays its suggestions. After you have instructed WordPerfect how to handle the word it flags as misspelled, it searches for the next misspelled word.

NOTE *If you want to check the document from the cursor to the end of the document you can select **F**rom **C**ursor instead of **D**ocument in step b.*

EXAMPLES

1. WordPerfect's spell feature may find a number of words that are not in its dictionaries when you check a document. If you elect to make a replacement for any of these words, WordPerfect makes the correction wherever it finds the misspelling throughout the document. First, type

   The factory's new heeting system uses natural gas. Solar panels assist the heeting system by prividing 20% of the power.

   Next, select **T**ools**, W**riting Tools, **S**peller or press Ctrl-F2, then select **D**ocument. The first word WordPerfect flags as misspelled is "heeting." Press A to replace it with WordPerfect's first suggestion, "heating." Since the spell feature replaces the misspelling wherever it finds the word, WordPerfect automatically corrects "heeting" in the second sentence.

   The next misspelling that WordPerfect brings to your attention is "prividing." Press A to accept WordPerfect's first suggestion, "providing." WordPerfect finishes checking the document. Select OK to exit from the spell feature.

2. When you check a document's spelling, WordPerfect may question correctly spelled words. Most of the correctly spelled words that WordPerfect questions will be names or technical terms. To see an example of this, type

   Jim Wright
   2209 Sunrise Boulevard
   Ft. Lauderdale, Florida 33304

   Dear Mr. Wright,

   We have shipped the supplies that you ordered. You will receive them in a few days. The paper that you ordered is out of stock. We will shipped it once we receive it.

   Sincerely,

   Adele Stein

To check the spelling of this document, select **T**ools, **W**riting Tools, **S**peller or press Ctrl-F2, then select **D**ocument. Because WordPerfect does not have the word "Adele" in its dictionaries, it prompts you with alternate spellings. Since you spelled the name correctly, select **S**kip in this Document. When WordPerfect finishes checking the document, select OK to leave the spell feature. Notice that WordPerfect does not flag the second occurrence of "shipped" as an incorrect word; although it is grammatically incorrect, the spelling is not wrong. The spell feature is a valuable aid, but it is not a replacement for proofreading your documents.

EXERCISES

1. Type the following paragraph:

   The biologicl lab reports that it has created a new hybrid plant called the Panophile. This plant tolerates extreem differences in humidity and temperature provided that it is adequately watered during its first yeer. Its flowers can be red, yellow, white, or purple.

   Use the spell feature to check the paragraph for spelling errors. Assume "Panophile" is correct.

2. Type the following paragraph:

   As part of the city's 100-year celabration, thei are having a fiar, the first since before World War II. The fair will emphsize how the city looked 100 years ago.

   Use the spell feature to correct the misspelled words.

3. Type the following paragraph:

   Last Tuesday, Markum Products anounced a dividend of $.30 per share. Thes dividend changes its dividend policy, since the lattest dividend equals the total dividends of the last two years.

   Use the spell feature to make necessary spelling corrections. Assume "Markum" is spelled correctly.

4. Type the following paragraph:

When you use the spell feature, it finds two types of words. The first type is mispelled words. These words are typographical errors or words that you do not know how to spell. The second type is corectly spelled words that the spel feature does not recognize. Most of thees words are names or technical terms.

Use the spell feature to find and correct misspellings.

9.3 FIND DOUBLE WORDS

As you type, you may unintentionally type a word twice. WordPerfect is able to scan your document for occurrences of repeated, or double, words. Checking for double words is an automatic function of WordPerfect's spell feature.

WordPerfect lets you approve the occurrence of a double word or delete the second occurrence of the word. It also lets you edit the document, in case one of the words should be changed. As a final option, it lets you disable further checking for double words in documents in which double words are intended.

TO HAVE WORDPERFECT FIND DOUBLE WORDS

a. Select **T**ools, **W**riting Tools, then select **S**peller.

b. Select **D**ocument.

When WordPerfect finds a double word, it provides a different dialog box than the one for misspelled words. You can choose **S**kip Duplicate Word to ignore it, **D**elete Duplicate Word to eliminate the double entry, **E**dit Word to change one occurrence to another word, or Disable Duplicate **C**hecking to stop WordPerfect's checking in this document.

EXAMPLES

1. Double words are easy to overlook. Type the following paragraph, making sure to include the repeated words "a" and "the":

As part of the city's 100 year celebration, the city is having a a fair, the first since before World War II. The fair will emphasize how the the city looked 100 years ago.

To find the double words, select **T**ools, **W**riting Tools, **S**peller or press Ctrl-F2, then select **D**ocument. WordPerfect highlights the second "a" before "fair." You can select from the following dialog box options:

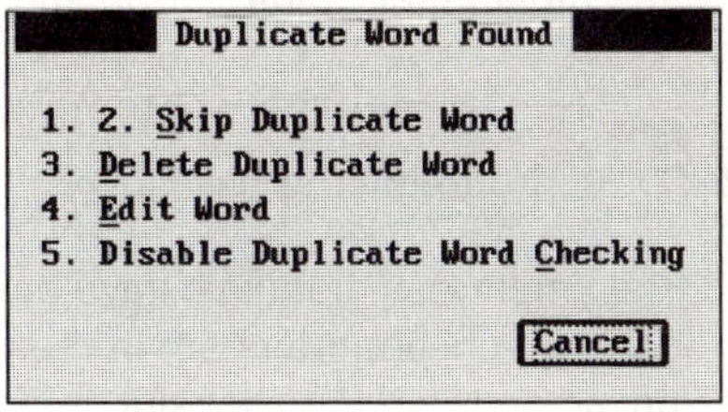

To remove one of the words, select **D**elete Duplicate Word. Next, WordPerfect highlights the repeated "the" in the second sentence. Since you want to remove one of them, select **D**elete Duplicate Word.

Finally, since that was the last spelling error or double word occurrence, select OK to return to the document.

2. WordPerfect's spell feature automatically searches for double words. When your document contains misspelled words and double words, WordPerfect prompts you for the desired actions for misspellings and double words in the order that WordPerfect finds them. Type the following paragraph, making sure to include the misspellings and repeated words:

The company is redirecting its resources, while remaining in the the personalized items business. This is due to demigraphic changes in its customer base. Its demigraphic base is aging and and has more disposable income.

Select **T**ools, **W**riting Tools, **S**peller or press Ctrl-F2 to activate the spell check feature. Then select **D**ocument. WordPerfect highlights the double "the" in the first sentence. Select **D**elete Duplicate Word to remove the extra word. Next, WordPerfect highlights "demigraphic" as a misspelled word. Press A to substitute WordPerfect's only suggestion. WordPerfect corrects both occurrences of the misspelling and highlights the double "and" in the last sentence. Select **D**elete Duplicate Word again to remove the second "and." When WordPerfect finishes checking the document, select OK to exit from the spell feature.

EXERCISES

1. Type the following paragraph:

   When ABC Corporation combines its corporate offices into a a central location, they expect to to reduce their staff by 30%. Most of the reduction of personnel costs for the first year will be be consumed by severance pay and other employment termination costs.

   Use the spell feature to remove double words.

2. Type the following paragraph:

   The employees that have have been invited to to move to the new new corporate headqurters are in the process of moving. Human Resourses is is providing temporary housing and and moving services. Some of of the staff who are not moving to the new new headquarters have already found new jobs.

   Use the spell feature to remove double words and correct spelling mistakes.

3. Type the following paragraph:

   Double words often occur with edited text. When you edit text text, you may add a a word to the end of of a phrase you are are adding, not realizing that it it is already there. Double words often happen with with short words.

   Use the spell feature to remove double words.

4. Type the following lines, pressing Enter after the first, second, third, and fifth lines:

   WordPerfect does
   does not
   not check to see if the
   the last word of one paragraph is the same word as the first word word of the next paragraph.

   Use the spell feature to remove double words.

9.4 ADD A WORD TO THE SUPPLEMENTAL DICTIONARY

WordPerfect's main dictionary contains more than 100,000 words. The words in WordPerfect's dictionary have been identified as the words most commonly used in business writing. Despite the extensiveness of this dictionary, it cannot contain all the properly spelled words that you use in your documents. Because of this, WordPerfect occasionally flags correctly spelled words as potential misspellings. You can circumvent this situation by asking WordPerfect to skip the word.

On a one-time basis, this solution works. However, when you use the word frequently in your writing, you soon become frustrated by having to tell WordPerfect to skip the word. WordPerfect offers you a supplemental dictionary to overcome this problem. You can use the supplemental dictionary to expand WordPerfect's dictionary with your own customized additions. You might want to add proper names (names of persons, company names, geographical names, and so on) or technical terms. Rather than skipping such words every time WordPerfect prompts you for an action, you can add them to your dictionary. WordPerfect maintains a supplemental dictionary file, named WP{WP}US.SUP, for these entries.

NOTE *You can purchase supplemental dictionaries to provide a dictionary of legal or other specialized terms without having to add them one by one.*

TO ADD A WORD TO THE SUPPLEMENTAL DICTIONARY

a. Check the spelling of the word by selecting **T**ools, **W**riting Tools, **S**peller or pressing Ctrl-F2, then selecting **W**ord or **D**ocument.

b. Select Add to Dic**t**ionary when WordPerfect prompts you for action on a properly spelled word.

EXAMPLES

1. While WordPerfect's dictionary contains many words, it is missing most technical terms. In certain areas of business, you might use some of these terms frequently. If you add these words to the supplemental dictionary the first time you encounter them,

WordPerfect will recognize the words when checking subsequent documents. First, type

To assemble the vambrace, align the holes on the largest piece with the holes in the shorter end of the smallest piece. Attach a 2-piece rivet in each hole.

When you select **T**ools, **W**riting Tools, **S**peller or press Ctrl-F2, and then select **D**ocument, WordPerfect does not find "vambrace" in its dictionary. Since this word, which describes a type of arm protection, is spelled correctly, you can add it to the supplemental dictionary. To do this, select Add to Dic**t**ionary. As you create other documents that mention "vambrace," WordPerfect will not stop at that word when checking spelling.

2. You will want to add frequently used names to the supplemental dictionary. WordPerfect recognizes many common names such as John, Nancy, Smith, and Jones. Many other, less common names, are not recognized as correctly spelled words. To see an example of this, type the following letter:

Jim Johansen
1209 Sunrise Boulevard
Ft. Lauderdale, Florida 33304

Dear Mr. Johansen,

We have shipped the supplies that you ordered. You will receive them in a few days. The paper that you ordered is out of stock. We will ship it once our inventory is restocked.

Sincerely,

Adele Stein

When you check the spelling, WordPerfect does not recognize the name "Johansen." If Mr. Johansen is one of your regular customers and you spelled his name correctly, you can add his name to the supplemental dictionary by selecting Add to Dic**t**ionary. When WordPerfect finds "Johansen" in other documents, it will recognize it as a correctly spelled word.

Next, WordPerfect suggests that you have misspelled "Adele." Since it is spelled correctly, add it to the dictionary by selecting Add to Dic**t**ionary. WordPerfect finishes checking the document. Select OK to end spell checking.

EXERCISES

1. Type the following names and addresses:

   Ann Slater
   2573 Curtiswood
   Plantation, Florida 33145

   Timothy McKee
   8964 Lorain Avenue
   Lakewood, Ohio 44106

   Check the spelling. If WordPerfect flags a proper name as misspelled, add it to your supplemental dictionary.
2. Type your full name. Use the spell feature to determine if each part of it is in WordPerfect's dictionary. If it is not, add it to your supplemental dictionary.
3. Type the following lines, pressing Enter at the end of each one:

   Abbreviations
   ATMOS - Atmosphere
   IDP - Integrated Data Processing
   OCS - Officer Candidate School
   SWAZ - Swaziland

   Check the spelling. If WordPerfect flags a proper name or abbreviation as misspelled, add it to your supplemental dictionary.
4. Type the following paragraph:

   Pygmalion was a sculptor who created a beautiful statue called Galatea, which Aphrodite brought to life. George Bernard Shaw wrote a play, called Pygmalion, that relied on this myth for some ideas. The film version of the musical, called "My Fair Lady," starred Audrey Hepburn.

   Check the spelling. Add any proper names that WordPerfect suggests to your supplemental dictionary.

9.5 REPLACE CORRECTLY SPELLED WORDS THAT ARE MISUSED

WordPerfect's spell feature checks the spelling in a document; however, it does not check usage. You can have a document with correctly spelled words that are incorrect in usage. Typically, each person makes a mistake or two like this repeatedly. Such habitual mistakes might be caused by a typographical error, for example, typing "form" instead of "from." They might also be caused by the mistaken use of homonyms, as in the use of "their" for "there" or "to" for "too." If you are able to identify any mistakes that you tend to make on a regular basis, you will want to use the replace feature as part of your document correction process, to check for these potential errors.

EXAMPLES

1. One common mistake that you can make is typing "form" when you want "from" and vice versa. First, type

   Enclosed is the order from received form your department.

   The "form" and "from" are in the wrong places. Since both words are spelled correctly, the spell feature will not detect the error. To correct this error, select **E**dit, Rep**l**ace or press Alt-F2. Type **from** in the **S**earch For text box, move to the **R**eplace With text box, and type **form**. Make sure there is an *X* in the **B**ackward Search and Conf**i**rm Replacement check boxes. If they do not contain an *X*, select them. Select the R**e**place command button to start the replace operation. WordPerfect asks if you want to replace "from" with "form" as the fifth word in the sentence. Select **Y**es to confirm the replacement. Then, select OK when told the replacement process is complete.

   To make the second correction, press Home, Home, ↑ to move to the top of the document. Select **E**dit, Rep**l**ace or press Alt-F2. Type **form** in the **S**earch For text box, press Tab, and type **from** in the **R**eplace With text box. Remove the *X* from the **B**ackward Search check box by selecting it. Select R**e**place to start the search and replace operation. WordPerfect prompts you to replace the first "form" with "from." Select **N**o. WordPerfect checks to see if you want the second "form" in the sentence replaced. Select **Y**es to confirm that you want this replaced. Select OK when prompted that the process is done.

2. Homonyms present a problem that WordPerfect's spell feature cannot solve. *Homonyms* are words that sound the same but have different

meanings. Examples are "to," "too," and "two." Whenever these words are used in a document, WordPerfect accepts the spelling, although the usage may not be correct. To illustrate the problem, type

Since the dinner had too speakers, the guests were encouraged not two ask to many questions.

This sentence has three occurrences of the homonyms, but none is used correctly: "Too" should have been "two," "two" should have been "to," and "to" should have been "too." Checking the spelling does not correct these errors. Since "to" is such a common word, searching a document for every occurrence of the word may require a significant investment of time. You probably would not want to do this unless you made this type of mistake on a regular basis; proofreading each document carefully would be a better solution.

EXERCISES

1. Type the following sentence:

   The fair four the bridge to get to the fare is for dollars.

   Replace "fair" and "fare" so that each word is in the correct place. Replace "for" and "four" so that each word is in the correct place.
2. Type the following sentence:

   Their demonstrating there new product over they're.

   Use the replace feature to place "their," "there," and "they're" in their proper contexts.

9.6 LOOK UP A WORD IN THE THESAURUS

One important aspect of communicating effectively is using words that convey your exact meaning. WordPerfect assists you in finding the right words with its online thesaurus feature.

WordPerfect's thesaurus is similar to *Roget's Thesaurus,* with which you may be familiar. Although its function is the same, WordPerfect's thesaurus feature is much easier to use. When you ask WordPerfect to find a word in its thesaurus, it provides a listing of synonyms, organized by parts of speech, such as noun, verb, and adjective. Some of the words listed will have synonym lists of their own, which you can review to expand the potential replacement options. The thesaurus feature provides a handy check for words used infrequently. By looking at the list of synonyms for a word you have used, you can verify its correct usage in your sentence.

TO FIND A WORD IN WORDPERFECT'S THESAURUS

a. Move the cursor to a word that you want to find a synonym for.

b. Select **T**ools, **W**riting Tools or press Alt-F1.

c. Select **T**hesaurus.

d. Scroll up and down in the list provided, choose an option from the buttons at the bottom of the box, or highlight a word with a dot in front of it, and press Enter to display an additional list of alternative words.

e. Select Cancel until your document is displayed on the screen again.

If the cursor is not on a word, WordPerfect normally uses the next word in the document. If you are at the end of the document or in a blank one, WordPerfect prompts you for the word you want to look up. If it cannot find a word in its thesaurus, WordPerfect prompts you for another word.

NOTE *Instead of highlighting a word with a dot in front of it and pressing Enter, you can highlight the word and select **L**ookup. However, since selecting **L**ookup takes more keypresses, pressing Enter is the method presented in this book.*

EXAMPLES

1. You can use the thesaurus feature to find a word that you want as you are typing a document. For example, to find words that are similar in meaning to "meet," select **T**ools, **W**riting Tools or press Alt-F1, then

FIGURE 9-2

Thesaurus entries for "meet"

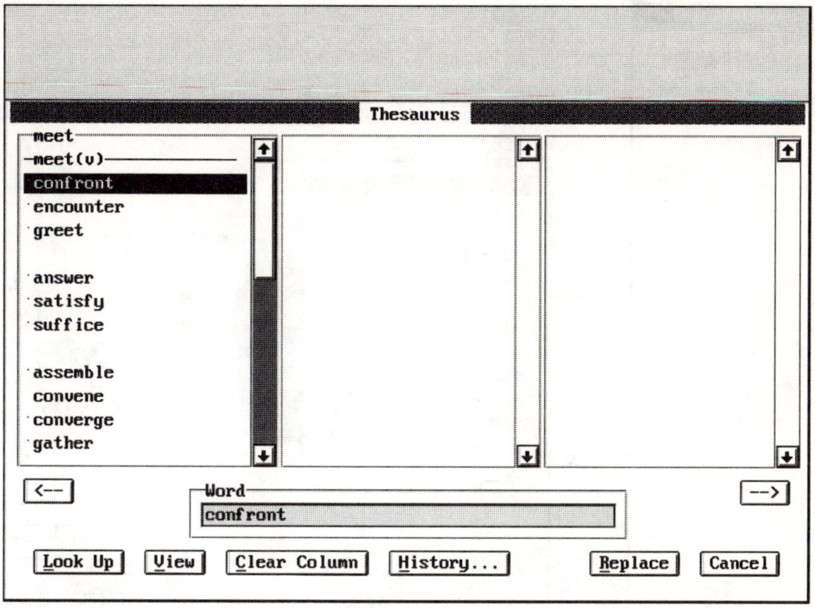

choose **T**hesaurus. Since the document is blank, WordPerfect prompts you for a word to look up. Type **meet** and press Enter.

Now the screen looks like Figure 9-2. If you scroll through the choices with ↑ and ↓, or click the arrows on the scroll bars to the right of the options, you can see that WordPerfect separates the different parts of speech. Each word with a dot before it has its own entry in the thesaurus. You can look at that entry if you highlight the word and press Enter. Some entries also list antonyms.

Once you have looked over the synonyms for the word, select Cancel to return to the document and type the word that you want to use.

2. You can use a word already in a document to find an entry in the thesaurus. For example, type **use**. Although the cursor is to the right of the word, WordPerfect looks for "use" in its thesaurus when you select **T**ools, **W**riting Tools or press Alt-F1, then select **T**hesaurus. The screen looks like Figure 9-3. Select Cancel to return to the document.

3. You can use synonyms in the thesaurus to find other synonyms. First, type **associate**. Then, select **T**ools, **W**riting Tools or press Alt-F1, and select **T**hesaurus. The screen looks like Figure 9-4. Several of the words have dots next to them. You can find synonyms for any of those words by highlighting them and pressing Enter.

FIGURE 9-3

Thesaurus entries for "use"

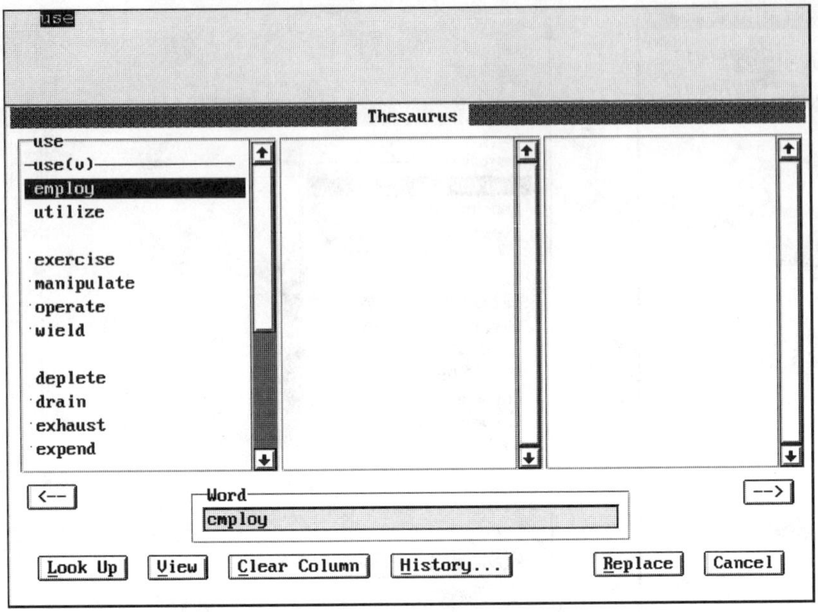

To find other synonyms for "relate," highlight the word and press Enter. Now, the screen looks like Figure 9-5. When you look up a synonym's thesaurus entry, WordPerfect puts the word's entry in the

FIGURE 9-4

Thesaurus entries for "associate"

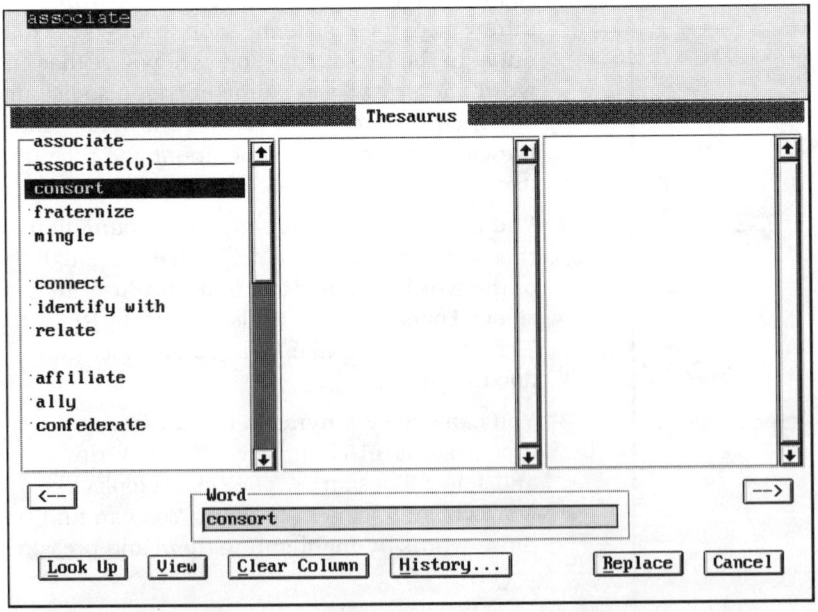

next blank column, or in the rightmost column if all three are full. Only the current column words can be used as replacement options, and you can select words to look up only from the current column. To change the current column, use the → or the ← key. To remove the current column, select **C**lear Column. As a column is emptied, WordPerfect moves any remaining columns to the left to fill the emptied one. Press Esc twice or click Cancel to return to the document.

4. You can also look up synonyms for a word that is not listed in the current thesaurus entry. You can do this when you find synonyms for one word to be unsatisfactory and want to see synonyms for another word. With this approach, you do not have to exit the thesaurus, move to the other word, and activate the feature again. To see how this works, type **business**. Then, select **T**ools, **W**riting Tools or press Alt-F1, then select **T**hesaurus to display the entries for "business."

   Next, to find the entries for "product," select **L**ook Up, type **product** in the Word text box, and press Enter. Now the screen shows entries for both "business" and "product." Select Cancel to return to the document.

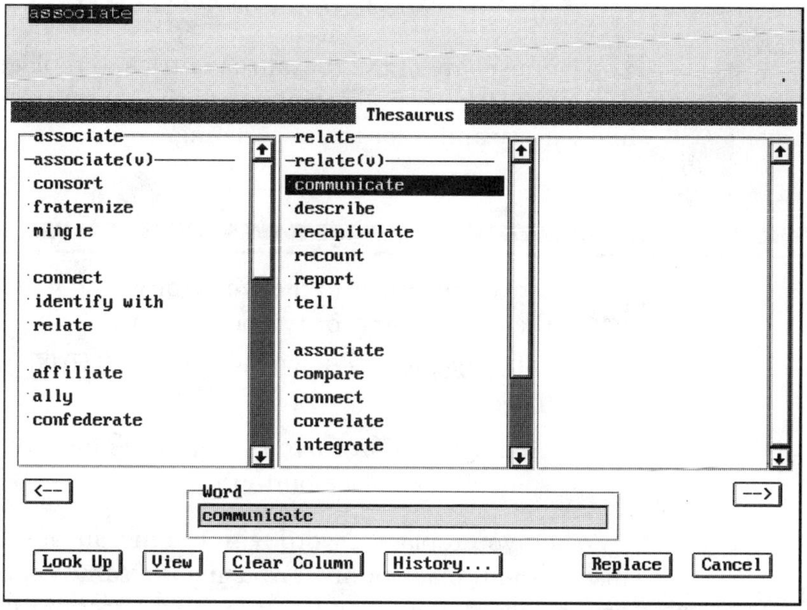

FIGURE 9-5

Using a thesaurus entry to look up another thesaurus entry

EXERCISES

1. Find the thesaurus entry for "table."
2. Find the thesaurus entry for "adjoining."
3. Type **rich** and find the thesaurus entry for that word. Use that entry to find the thesaurus entry for "prosperous."
4. Activate the thesaurus feature and find the entry for "limit." Use this entry to find the entry for "bar." Use this entry to find the entry for "board." Use this entry to find the entry for "cabinet." Use this entry to find the entry for "cupboard." Use this entry to find the entry for "press." Remove the "limit" and "bar" entries from the screen.

9.7 REPLACE A WORD WITH A WORD FROM THE THESAURUS

You can use any of the thesaurus entries to replace a word in your document. The options available in the thesaurus entries allow you to add variety and color to your writing.

TO REPLACE A WORD WITH WORDPERFECT'S THESAURUS FEATURE

a. Move the cursor to the word for which you want to find the thesaurus entry, or type the word.
b. Select **T**ools, **W**riting Tools or press Alt-F1, then select **T**hesaurus.
c. Highlight the word you want to use for the replacement and select the **R**eplace button.

When you replace a word with the thesaurus feature, WordPerfect inserts the replacement word using the same capitalization as the original word. For example, if the first letter of the original word is capitalized, the first letter of the replacement word is capitalized. After replacing a word, WordPerfect exits the thesaurus feature.

EXAMPLES

1. You can use the replace word feature of the thesaurus when you are editing a document. For example, type

   Jim Stevens is the newest associate at Stevens & Stevens.

   You can find a replacement word for "associate" by consulting the thesaurus. First, press Ctrl-← five times to move the cursor to the word "associate." Then select **T**ools, **W**riting Tools or press Alt-F1, and select **T**hesaurus. Highlight "partner" and select the **R**eplace button. WordPerfect exits the thesaurus feature, and the sentence now looks like this:

   ```
   Jim Stevens is the newest partner at Stevens & Stevens.
   ```

2. Although WordPerfect supplies lettered choices for only the active column, you can change the active column. Type

   At the end of the day, the store manager totals the daily sales.

   To find another word to use in place of "totals," press Ctrl-← four times to move the cursor to the word "totals." Next, select **T**ools, **W**riting Tools or press Alt-F1, then select **T**hesaurus. Looking through the entries, you can see the verb "add." Before you can replace "totals" with "add," you must highlight "add," then select the **R**eplace button. Type an **s** to change "add" to "adds," and the replacement is complete. Now, the sentence looks like this:

EXERCISES

1. Type the following sentence:

   The report includes a three-page insert.

Use the thesaurus feature to find another word for "insert." Replace it.

2. Type the following sentence:

   The nylon division reported a 13% increase in sales.

   Use the thesaurus feature to find synonyms for "division." Replace "division" with "branch."

3. Type the following sentence:

   The Bargain Business is having a 30% sale.

   Use the thesaurus feature to find synonyms for "business." Replace "business" with "company."

4. Type the following paragraph:

   The land holdings include land for raising cattle, land for growing corn, and some land with a high resale value.

   Use the thesaurus feature to replace the four occurrences of "land" with "estate," "ranch," "farm," and "property," respectively. (Naturally, you would also want to add articles to make the sentence read correctly.)

9.8 USE THE GRAMMAR CHECKER FOR AN OVERVIEW OF YOUR DOCUMENT

WordPerfect 6 includes a grammar checking package, Grammatik. You can use this package to help improve your writing. One of the things that it can do for you is to provide overview statistics for a document. The package assesses the readability level of the document to help you determine if it is at the correct level for your audience. It allows you to see how many words, sentences, and paragraphs the document contains. It also tells you the average length of each word, sentence, and paragraph, and provides an interpretation of the readability statistics.

TO LOOK AT THE SUMMARY STATISTICS FOR A DOCUMENT

a. Select **T**ools, **W**riting Tools or press Alt-F1, then select **G**rammatik.

b. Type a **T** to see a statistics check of the current document.

c. Press Enter to move to the screen that interprets the statistics.

d. Press Esc to return to the main screen, then type **Q** to quit Grammatik and return to your document.

EXAMPLES

1. If you use short words and sentences, anyone will be able to read your material. However, choosing a level which is too low may make it boring. Type this paragraph

   Bill and Jane went to the store. They bought food. They came home and put the food away. They will go to the store again in two weeks.

   Select **T**ools, **W**riting Tools or press Alt-F1, then select **G**rammatik. Type **T** to look at the readability statistics. You can see that the sentences, as well as the words within them, are short. For example, the words average 3.67 letters and 1.21 syllables long, as shown in Figure 9-6. The writing level is so low some readers would

FIGURE 9-6

Grammatik statistics for a simplistic paragraph

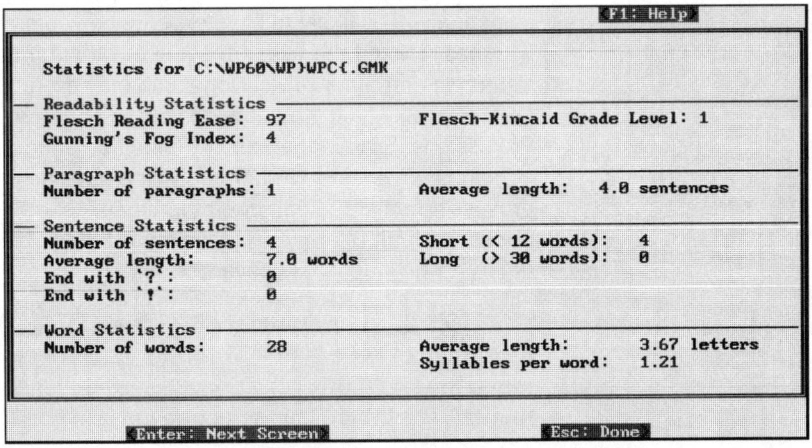

FIGURE 9-7

Grammatik interpretation of statistics for a more complex paragraph

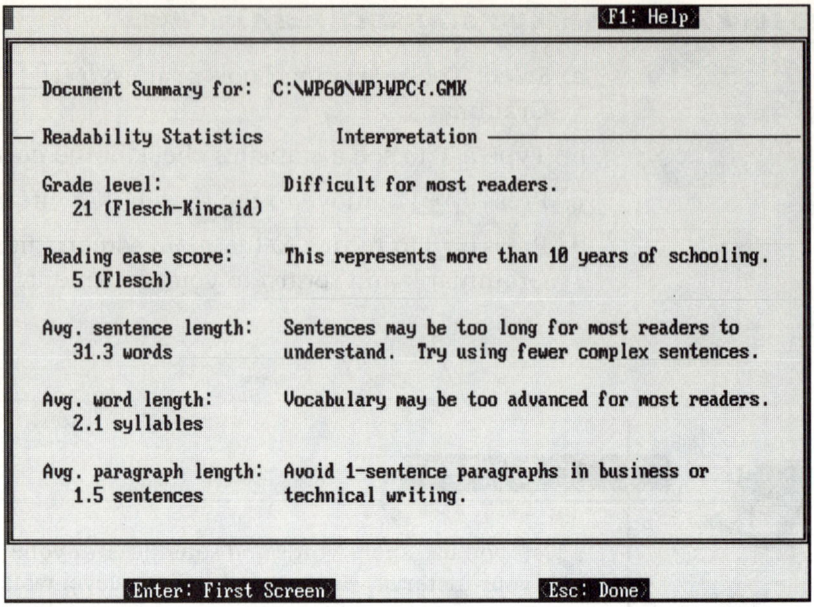

feel as if you were not giving them credit for being able to read more interesting and higher level material. Press Enter when you are ready for an interpretation of the readability statistics. Press Esc, then type **Q** to return to your document.

2. If you use long words and sentences, only other experts in the field you are writing about are likely to understand what you are writing. Type this paragraph:

   If you are a computer specialist or computer programmer, you are not someone who is likely to have experienced computer phobia nor someone who has resisted the use of the latest computer hardware and software. You are a computer professional and may even be a Certified Systems Professional, which would mean that you passed the Certified Systems Professional Examination and attended an adequate number of continuing education programs. Undoubtedly, you have heard terms such as central processing unit, Boolean operator, binary coded decimal, high-persistence phosphor, fault tolerance, erasable programmable read-only memory, and binary-to-hexadecimal conversion.

   Select **T**ools, **W**riting Tools or press Alt-F1, then choose **G**rammatik. Type **T** to look at the statistics. Sentences and words are much longer in this selection. The grade level is much higher than in the first selection. This selection could be rewritten to shorten sentences and make them less complex, which would bring the reading level within the range of the average reader. Press Enter when you are ready for an interpretation of thc statistics, as shown in Figure 9-7. Press Esc, then type **Q** to return to your document.

EXERCISES

1. Type a paragraph that describes your use of the computer in short, childlike sentences. Check the statistics for this paragraph with Grammatik.
2. Type a paragraph on a technical subject such as computers or medicine using technical terms that are part of the subject matter. Use Grammatik to look at the statistics for this paragraph.

mastery skills check

1. Type the following words as they appear:

   Infomation
   Capitalisation
   Iregardless
   Nevertheless

Use the spell feature to check the spelling and correct any mistakes. [9.2]

2. Type the following paragraph, including the errors:

   Based on the results of a market study, the XYZ Corporation woll market its its personalized hubcaps nationaly. According to the survey, men are four times more likely to to buy them than women. Also, the product appeals primarily to buyers in the 19- to 34year-old age group.

   Use the spell feature to correct errors. [9.2]

3. Type the following letter as it appears:

   Ingram Scott
   536 S. Green Road
   Cleveland Heights, Ohio 44108

   Dear Iggy,

   Here is the information that you requested. Please return it when you complete your project.

   Sincerely,

   Tabitha Marletti

   Use the spell feature to check the spelling. Add the proper names that WordPerfect does not recognize to your supplemental dictionary. Look at the grammar checker's statistics for this document. [9.1, 9.4, 9.8]

4. Type the following paragraph:

   Because of the market study, the XYZ Corporation will market it's personalized hubcaps nationally. According to the survey, men are for times moor likely to buy them than women. Also, the product appeals primarily too individuals 19 two 34 years old.

   Several words in the paragraph are homonyms. Use the replace feature to correct the improper usage. [7.3, 9.5]

5. Copy a paragraph from your local newspaper, typing it into WordPerfect. Use Grammatik to check the statistics for it. [9.8]
6. Use the thesaurus feature to find synonyms for "bar," "block," and "light." [9.6]
7. Type the following sentence:

Reviewing the data revealed that people thought that the product was overpriced.

Use the thesaurus feature to find synonyms for "data." Replace "data" with "statistics." [9.7]

cumulative skills check

As you perform the Skills Check, do not clear the screen until you have completed the last exercise.

1. Set all margins to 3 inches. [6.2]
2. Type the following paragraph, including the errors:

   The company is reducing its products aimed at the do-it-youself market. It is applying these resources towards manufaturing more higher-proced items. The company expects to increace sales by 15% with this stratagy.

   Use the spell feature to correct errors. Use Grammatik to check the statistics for the paragraph. [9.2, 9.8]
3. Type the following paragraph, including the errors:

   Howard Moore designed an instant-strip wallpaper removr. The product can be used by inexperienced home owners. It removes wallpaper in half the time required for conventonal methods. The trade name for the product is Wall-Off.

   Check the spelling. Add the proper names to the supplemental dictionary if WordPerfect does not recognize them. [9.2, 9.4]
4. Move the paragraph created in exercise 3 to precede the paragraph created in exercise 2. [8.1]
5. Block and copy the paragraph created in exercise 2. Place two additional copies in the document. [8.3]

6. Type the following sentence:

   All of the McGregors had light complexions.

   Use the thesaurus feature to find synonyms for "light." Replace "light" with "fair." [9.7]

7. Print the document. [3.1]
8. Save the file as WORDS. [2.4]
9. Type a paragraph from one of the most technical references you can find into WordPerfect. Check the statistics for it with Grammatik. See if you can rewrite the paragraph to make it easier for the average reader to understand. Check the statistics again. [9.8]

10

Page Breaks, Paragraph Breaks, and Other Options

chapter objectives

After completing this chapter, you should be able to

10.1 Control widow and orphan lines

10.2 Use headers and footers on pages

10.3 Add footnotes

THE appearance of a document can help convey its message to the reader. This chapter covers some features that provide additional options for controlling the appearance of the text on a page. Widow and orphan protection features prevent single lines of a paragraph from appearing at the top or bottom of a page. This helps the clarity of your documents because the reader does not have to turn the page in the middle of a thought.

In addition, this chapter introduces headers and footers, which allow you to add fixed lines of text at the top and bottom of every page. You can use headers and footers to include, for example, your name or a report name and number on each page of a document. Footnotes provide the opportunity for removing technical data, equations, and bibliographic references from the main text. WordPerfect's features allow you to automatically number footnotes and print them at the bottom of the page.

review
skills check

As you go through the skills check, do not clear the screen until you have completed the last exercise.

1. Type the following paragraph, including the errors:

   Cash dividents distribute earnings to the shareholders. Cash dividends have several important dates. The declaraction date is the date the board of directors declares the dividend. The date of record is the date that decides which stockholders are paid the dividend. The date of record is the day used to establish stock ownership. The payment date is the date that the company pays its dividents.

   Use the spell feature to check and correct the spelling. [9.2]
2. Use the thesaurus feature to replace "decides" with "determines." [9.7]
3. Move the first sentence to the end of the paragraph. [8.1]
4. Use the search feature to find each occurrence of "date." [7.1]
5. Delete the last sentence. [4.6]

10.1 CONTROL WIDOW AND ORPHAN LINES

When you work on a document, the first or last line of a paragraph may appear by itself on a page with the rest of the paragraph on the next or preceding page. The first line of a paragraph placed alone at the bottom of a page is called a *widow*. The last line of a paragraph placed alone at the top of a page is called an *orphan*. Both can cause the reader to lose the line of thought of the paragraph. Widows and orphans also detract from the appearance of a document. WordPerfect lets you prevent widows and orphans from appearing in a document.

TO PREVENT WIDOWS AND ORPHANS

a. Select **L**ayout, **O**ther or press Shift-F8 and select **O**ther.

b. Select **W**idow/Orphan Protect.

c. Select OK to return to the document. If you used Shift-F8 in step a, you need to select Close also.

When you enable Widow/Orphan Protection, WordPerfect adds the hidden code [Delay] to the beginning of the current page.

EXAMPLES

1. WordPerfect's widow/orphan protection feature prevents the last line of a paragraph from appearing as an orphan at the top of a page. To see the effect of orphans while minimizing typing, you can increase the top and bottom margins to limit the amount of text on a page. If you set the top and bottom margins to 5 inches, only six lines will display on each page. First, select **L**ayout, **M**argins to display the Margin Format dialog box. Select **T**op Margin, type **5"**, and press Enter. Select **B**ottom Margin, type **5"**, and press Enter. Select OK to leave the dialog box.

   Next, type

   The company picnic is scheduled for July 15 at Waverly Park. A full day of activities is planned for employees and their families. Food, games, clowns, bingo, and prizes are a few of the attractions. This year's food selections

FIGURE 10-1

Orphan line at the top of a page

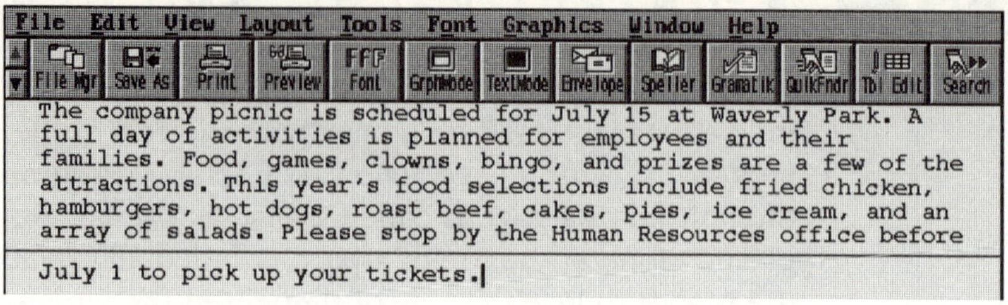

include fried chicken, hamburgers, hot dogs, roast beef, cakes, pies, ice cream, and an array of salads. Please stop by the Human Resources office before July 1 to pick up your tickets.

Now, the screen looks like Figure 10-1. The last line of the paragraph is an orphan at the top of a new page.

Select **L**ayout, **O**ther to display the Other Format dialog box. Select **W**idow/Orphan Protect. Select OK to return to the document. Now the page break changes, as shown in Figure 10-2, to include two lines from the paragraph on the next page.

2. Preventing widows also makes documents easier to read. You can obtain protection from widows with the same procedure. First, set the top and bottom margins to 5 inches by selecting **L**ayout, **M**argins. Select **T**op Margin, type **5"**, and press Enter. Select **B**ottom Margin, type **5"**, and press Enter. Select OK to leave the dialog box. Type

The company picnic is scheduled for July 15 at Waverly Hills Park. A full day of activities is planned for employees and their families. This year's special activities include softball, bingo, horseshoes, an executive dunk tank, carnival rides, and a puppet show.

FIGURE 10-2

Orphan eliminated with widow/orphan protection feature

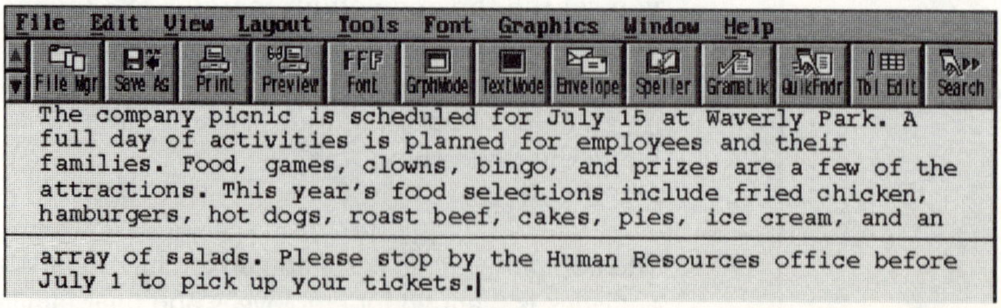

FIGURE 10-3
Widow line at the bottom of a page

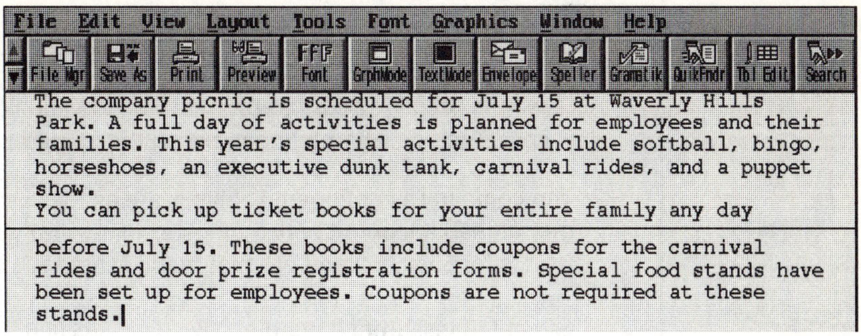

You can pick up ticket books for your entire family any day before July 15. These books include coupons for the carnival rides and door prize registration forms. Special food stands have been set up for employees. Coupons are not required at these stands.

The screen looks like Figure 10-3. The first line of the second paragraph displays as a widow at the bottom of page 1.

NOTE *It is possible that the lines in your entry will not break in the same place if you use a different printer or default font.*

Move to the top of the document by pressing Home, Home, ↑. Invoke widow and orphan protection by selecting **L**ayout, **O**ther, and **W**idow/Orphan Protect. Select OK to return to the document. The text is rearranged as in Figure 10-4. The widow line now appears on the second page along with the rest of the paragraph.

FIGURE 10-4
Widow eliminated with widow/orphan protection feature

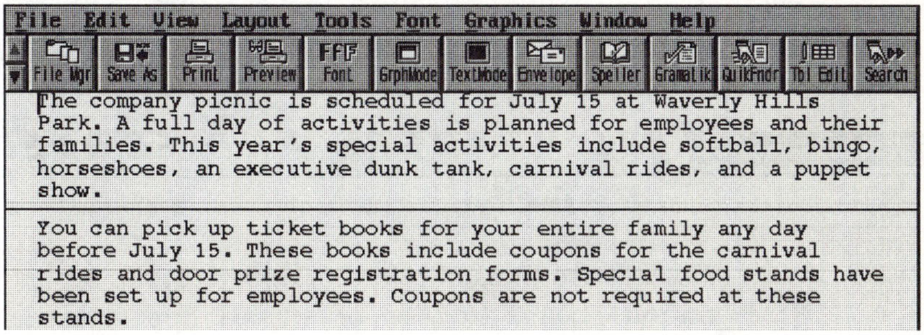

EXERCISES

1. Type the following paragraphs with the top and bottom margins set to 5 inches. Include a blank line between the paragraphs when you type them.

   The company's contingent liabilities are as follows: The company has guaranteed a loan on behalf of a subsidiary that was recently spun off. The loan is for $500,000 and will mature on March 30, 1994.

   Estimated loss from a pending lawsuit is $65,000. The suit should be concluded within the next two months.

   Prevent widows and orphans.
2. Type the following paragraph with the top and bottom margins set to 5 inches:

   Cost-flow assumptions affect inventory valuation. If a company uses the LIFO method, it assumes that the last inventory items purchased are the first ones sold. This assumption makes the cost of goods sold closely reflect the current cost of the inventory sold. On the other hand, the ending inventory is valued at prior-period purchase costs. This method is best used when purchase costs are rising and the inventory turnover is low.

   Prevent widows and orphans. Save the document as LIFO and clear the screen.
3. Retrieve LIFO. Remove the top and bottom margin settings. Set the margins to 1 inch on top and 9 inches at the bottom. Save the document and clear the screen.
4. Retrieve LIFO. Leaving the top and bottom margins intact, reset the left and right margins to 3 inches on each side. Save the document and clear the screen.

10.2 USE HEADERS AND FOOTERS ON PAGES

Headers are lines of text that appear at the top of every page of printed output. *Footers* are lines of text that appear at the bottom of every printed page. Header and footer lines are handy options for displaying information identifying a document. WordPerfect provides two headers and footers so that you can use one header or footer on even-numbered pages and another on odd-numbered pages. The first header or footer you create is referred to as header or footer A. The second is referred to as header or footer B. WordPerfect supports many formatting features (for example, bold and centering) in headers and footers.

Neither headers nor footers display on the screen with the text. To keep a header or footer from printing, or to make changes to either, you need to issue a command.

TO INCLUDE A HEADER OR FOOTER ON EVERY PAGE

a. Move the cursor to the first page on which you want a header or footer.

b. Select **L**ayout, **H**eader/Footer/Watermark. You can also press Shift-F8 and select **H**eader/Footer/Watermark.

c. Select **H**eaders or **F**ooters.

d. Select Header or Footer **A** or Header or Footer **B**.

e. Select **C**reate to have the header or footer appear on every page.

f. Type the header or footer text.

g. Press F7 to return to the Header/Footer/Watermark dialog box.

h. Select OK to leave the dialog box. If you used Shift-F8 in step b, you need to select Close.

Headers and footers do not appear on your screen with the document; they appear when you print or preview the document. WordPerfect puts the header on the first line after the top margin. It adds a blank line between the header and the main part of the document. For a footer, WordPerfect stops printing the body of the document two lines before the bottom margin, skips a line, and prints the footer.

To stop printing a header or footer, move to the first page that will not have the header or footer. Perform steps b through d, as you did to create the header or footer, then select the O**f**f button and select OK to return to the document.

You can also remove a header or footer for an entire document by deleting the hidden code for it. The hidden code for a header is [Header X:Y;Z]. The letter *X* is replaced by A or B, depending on which header the code represents. The *Y* is replaced by All Pages, Even

Pages, or Odd Pages, depending on where the header will appear. The *Z* represents the text in the header. It ends with an ellipsis if the header contains more than 50 characters. Footers use the same hidden code, but with the word "Footer" in place of "Header."

EXAMPLES

1. You can use headers to place a repeating line at the top of each page of a document. First, select **L**ayout, **H**eader/Footer/Watermark, **H**eaders, and Header **A**. The **A**ll Pages radio button is selected to put the header on every page. Select the **C**reate button and type

   1993 Financial Report

   Press F7 to return to the dialog box and Enter to return to the document. The header does not appear on the screen. Type the following lines of text in the document:

   Consolidated Changes in Financial Position
   Limestone Corporation
   Sources of Funds:
    Operations:

   When you select **F**ile, Print Pre**v**iew, the screen looks like Figure 10-5. (You may need to select **V**iew **1**00%.) The header that appears on this page will appear on every page in the document. Press Esc to return to the document.

2. You can use WordPerfect's formatting features in headers and footers, and you can include page numbers in headers and footers. First, select **L**ayout, **H**eader/Footer/Watermark, **F**ooters, and Footer **A**. With the **A**ll Pages radio button selected, select the **C**reate button.

   Type **Page** and press Spacebar. To have WordPerfect automatically place page numbers on the line, press Ctrl-P. WordPerfect adds a formatted page number that looks like a 1. Press Shift-F6 to center text and F8 to underline text, and type

   Prepared on 7/1/93

FIGURE 10-5
View showing header and text

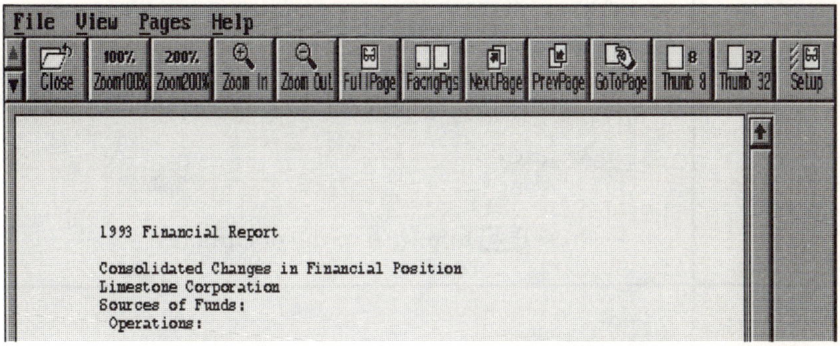

Press F7 to return to the dialog box and Enter to return to the document. The footer does not appear on the screen. Select **F**ile, Print Pre**v**iew. Press ↓ until you can see the bottom of the page. The screen looks like this:

The footer line on this page will appear at the bottom of each page of the document. On subsequent pages, the 1 will be replaced by the correct page number. Press Esc to return to the document.

3. You can define two headers or footers for a document. For example, you may want one header on even pages and another on odd pages. First, select **L**ayout, **H**eader/Footer/Watermark, **H**eaders, and Header **A**. Next, select the **O**dd Pages radio button, to have the header appear on odd-numbered pages, and select the **C**reate button. Press Alt-F6 to right-align text, and type **1993 Financial Report**. Then press F7 to return to the Header/Footer/Watermark dialog box. Select **H**eader and Header **B**. Select the E**v**en Pages radio button, to have the header appear on even-numbered pages, and select the **C**reate button. Type **Ace Corporation**, and press F7 to create the second header. Press Enter to return to the document. Press Ctrl-Enter twice to create additional pages in the document. Press Home, Home, and ↑ to move to the beginning of the document. When you select **F**ile, Print Pre**v**iew and then select **V**iew, Fa**c**ing Pages, you can press Pg Dn to show pages 2 and 3 with the two headers that look like those shown in the following illustration.

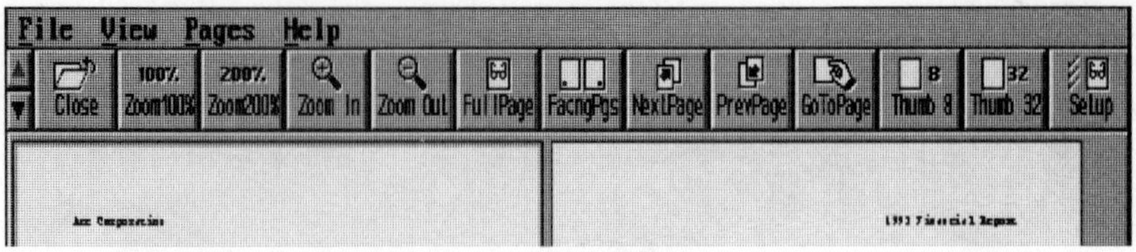

Press Esc to return to the document.

EXERCISES

1. Create a header that says "Acme Inc. Income Statement." Preview how WordPerfect will print it.
2. Create a footer that displays your name in boldface. Preview how WordPerfect will print it.
3. Create a header consisting of the page number encased in hyphens and centered on the page. Preview how WordPerfect will print it.
4. Create a header that prints the page numbers on odd-numbered pages and your name on even-numbered pages. Preview how WordPerfect will print it.

10.3 ADD FOOTNOTES

Footnotes allow you to store supplemental information in notes at the bottom of each page. Financial reports, legal documents, and academic research papers normally contain footnoted text. Footnotes may contain explanatory information or a reference to a source for a specific piece of information in the document.

WordPerfect automatically inserts sequential reference numbers for footnotes. Each footnote number is printed as a *superscript*; that is, it appears slightly smaller and higher than the other text on the line. WordPerfect prints each footnote at the bottom of the page containing the footnote reference. If a footnote is long or near the bottom of a page, WordPerfect allows space for a minimum of three lines of footnote text on the page and continues the footnote at the bottom of the next page. A single footnote can contain as many as 16,000 lines.

TO CREATE A FOOTNOTE

a. Select **L**ayout, or press Ctrl-F7, and select **F**ootnote.

b. Select **C**reate.

c. Type the footnote text.

d. Press F7 to finish the footnote text and return to the document.

A [Footnote] code is inserted in the document at the location of each footnote. When you move the cursor to highlight this code, it expands to show you many details about the footnote, including some of its text. You can delete a footnote by removing the hidden code or by deleting the footnote number that displays on the screen.

EXAMPLES

1. You can use a footnote to identify the source of a quote. Type

   Getting over the hurdle of learning something new can feel uncomfortable and takes both time and practice, so you must be patient with yourself as you learn WordPerfect. Work at your own pace. Tackle a chapter or two a day, whatever is appropriate for you. And make sure that you don't just read the chapters, but that you follow along on the computer, step by step. Pretty soon you'll be using WordPerfect like a pro.

   Once you have typed this quote, select **L**ayout, **F**ootnote, and **C**reate to create a footnote. The screen looks like this:

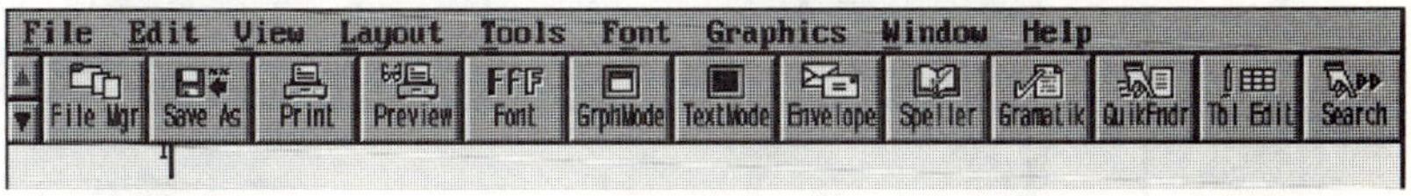

   Next, type a space and the following footnote text, remembering to press F8 to underline the book title:

   Mella Mincberg, WordPerfect 6 Made Easy, Osborne/McGraw-Hill, 1993, pp. xiii-xiv.

Now, the screen looks like this:

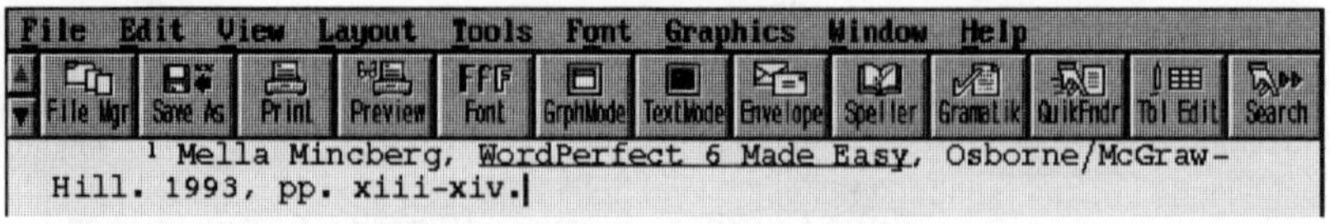

Press F7 to finish the footnote and return to the document. In text mode, WordPerfect may display the footnote number with a different color to indicate that it is superscript.

2. WordPerfect keeps track of the footnote numbers as you add or delete footnotes. To illustrate this, you need at least two footnotes. First, increase the bottom margin so that you will be able to see the text and the footnotes together in a print preview. Select **L**ayout, **M**argins; then select **B**ottom Margin, type **8.5**, and press Enter twice to leave the dialog box. Next, type

   The company's EPS is 3.48. The dividend date is August 15.

   Move the cursor to the end of the first sentence. Select **L**ayout, **F**ootnote, and **C**reate. Press Spacebar and type the footnote text:

   $1,169,280 1993 income/336,000 shares

   Press F7 to return to the document. For the second footnote, move to the end of the second sentence, select **L**ayout, **F**ootnote, and **C**reate. Press Spacebar and type

   The date of record is August 1.

   Press F7 to return to the document. When you select **F**ile, Print Pre**v**iew and then select **V**iew, **1**00% View, the text and the footnotes look like this:

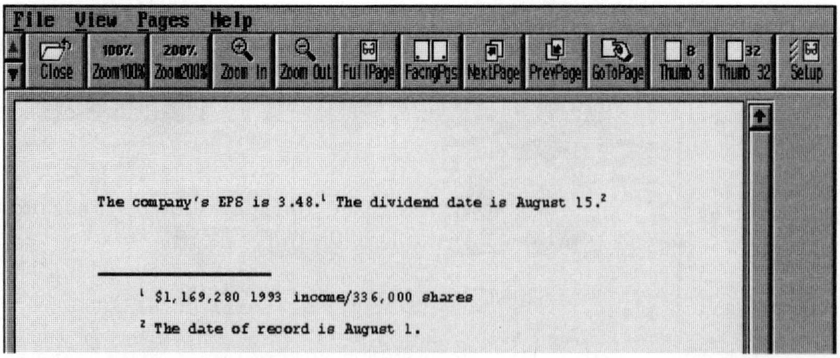

Press Esc to return to the document. Do not clear the screen; you will use these entries in the next example.

3. You can delete a footnote without invoking the menu. When you move or delete a footnote, WordPerfect automatically adjusts the footnote numbering. To remove a footnote, move the cursor to the footnote number that you want to eliminate and press Del. Using the footnotes from example 2, move to the 1 for the first footnote and press Del. WordPerfect reformats the other footnote number. Now, the screen looks like this:

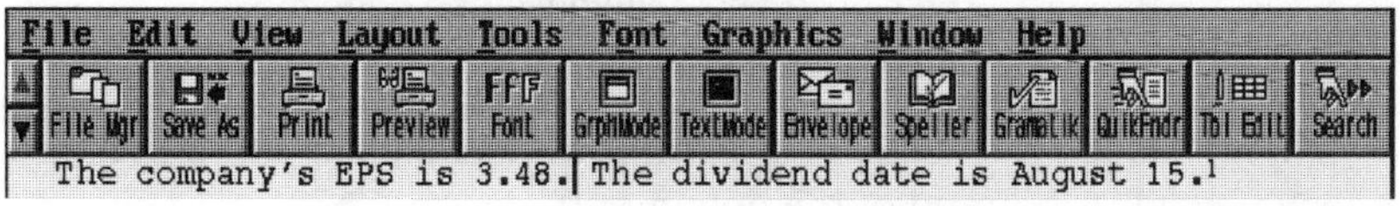

Do not clear the screen. You use these entries in the next example.

4. You can edit footnote text. Select **L**ayout, **F**ootnote, and **E**dit. WordPerfect prompts for the footnote number to edit. Press 1 and select OK. Next, move the cursor to the *A* in "August 1," press Ctrl-End, and type **July 31** and a period. The screen looks like this:

Press F7 to return to the document.

EXERCISES

Do not clear the screen between exercises unless instructed to do so.

1. Type the following:

   <u>WordPerfect 6 Made Easy</u> is written for beginning and intermediate users.

   Add a footnote using the following information:

   Mella Mincberg, <u>WordPerfect 6 Made Easy</u>, Osborne/McGraw-Hill, 1993, pp. xiii-xiv.

Clear the screen.

2. Type the first line from each of the following pairs of lines and use the second line in each pair as a footnote:

   Once upon a time, . . .
   Fairy Tales by the Brothers Grimm

   Mary had a little lamb
   Mother Goose

   The Goose That Laid a Golden Egg
   Aesop's Fables

3. Block the first line and its footnote number and move the line to the end of the document.
4. Edit the footnote for the Grimm Brothers to read "Grimm's Fairy Tales."

mastery skills check

As you perform the skills check, do not clear the screen until you have completed the last exercise.

1. Set the bottom margin to 9 inches. Type the following:

   Preparing a Trial Balance
   When you prepare a trial balance, you must make several adjusting entries to properly reflect your income and expenses. You must include prepaid expenses as an asset rather than as an expense. You must include unearned revenue, such as unredeemed gift certificates, as a liability. You must include accrued expenses as expenses.

   Invoke the widow/orphan protection feature. [10.1]
2. Insert a page break between the title and the paragraph. Add the following footnote at the end of the paragraph. [10.3]

For example, if half of the period between pay days has elapsed, you must include half of the expected salaries and wages.

3. Add the following footnote to the end of the second sentence. [10.3]

   For example, if you pay an insurance premium for two years at the beginning of this year, half of what you paid is classified as an expense for this year, and half is a prepaid expense and classified as an asset.

4. Edit the footnote that you created in exercise 3 so that it says [10.3]

   For example, if you pay a $600 insurance premium for two years at the beginning of this year, $300 is classified as an expense for last year, and $300 is a prepaid expense and classified as an asset.

5. Create a header for every page that consists of the title you typed in exercise 1. Remove the title from the body of the text. [10.2]
6. Create a footer with your name in it to appear on odd pages. Preview the document. Page through it. [10.2]

cumulative skills check

Do not clear the screen until you have completed the last exercise.

1. Type the following addresses:

   Johann Sebastian
   390 Market Street
   Newport, Rhode Island 01307
   Karl Davis
   7439 Coral Drive
   Stanford, CA 94237
   Angus Fuller
   764 Ovine Trail
   Kansas City, Missouri 12305

   Insert a hard page break after each address. [1.3]
2. Go to the bottom of the first page and type the following letter.

According to our records, we have not received your subscription renewal for our newsletter. To continue to receive this publication, send the enclosed order blank and a check for $35.00.

Sincerely,

Elsie Brown
Secretary, United Dairy Farmers

Use the thesaurus feature to review synonyms for "continue" and "receive." [9.6]

3. Use the spell feature to check the spelling of the letter. [9.2]
4. Insert the following footnote after the word "publication." [10.3]

   United Dairy Farmers, Dairy Moo-ving

5. Edit the footnote you just typed to include the publisher, Angus Magazines. [10.3]
6. Block and copy the letter to follow the other addresses on the other pages. [8.3]
7. Add a right-justified header that contains your name. [10.2]

11

Managing Files

chapter objectives

After completing this chapter, you should be able to

11.1 Create backup copies

11.2 Create directories

11.3 Change directories

11.4 Delete files and directories

11.5 Rename files

11.6 Create document summaries

11.7 Search for a word within a document on disk

11.8 Look at files on disk

YOU have already learned that saving a document to disk protects your investment in the document. After a document is stored on a disk, you can retrieve it even if the system goes down and you lose the copy of the document in memory. WordPerfect offers file options that increase your control over the documents you store on disk. Understanding these options gives you the power to manage your resources effectively.

In this chapter, you will learn how to create backup copies. You will learn how to create and manage directories for organizing the documents you create. You will learn how to rename files on disk and how to delete those you no longer need. You will learn how to create a document summary to provide an overview of a document. You will learn how to search for a file based on text stored within the file. Finally, you will see how displaying the contents of a file without retrieving it provides a quick way to verify a file selection.

Because this chapter covers so many file options, it is a little longer than some of the other chapters. Your investment of time will prove worthwhile, however, because you will learn a whole tool kit of skills that can be applied to every WordPerfect document you create.

review skills check

As you work through these Skills Check exercises, do not clear the screen until you have completed the last exercise.

1. Type the following lines exactly as shown:

   Companies often issue these types of equity:
   Common stock - This stock closely reflects the value of the company. Stockholders receive a return in value by an increase in price and dividends. Common stockholders have voting control of the company.
   Preferred stock - This stock must pay a required dividend before the common stockholders receive dividends. Preferred stockholders frequently do not have voting rights.
   Convertible bonds - These are bonds that the bond holders may redeem for other stock.

Move the paragraph about bonds between the two stock paragraphs. [2.1, 8.1]

2. Use WordPerfect's spell feature to check for spelling errors. [9.2]
3. Use the thesaurus feature to replace "redeem" with "exchange." [9.7]
4. Set the top and bottom margins to 5 inches. [6.2]
5. Prevent widow and orphan lines. [10.1]
6. Add the following footnote at the end of the convertible bonds paragraph. [10.3]

   Usually in exchange for common stock

7. Save the document as STOCKS, and clear the screen. [1.2, 2.4]

11.1 CREATE BACKUP COPIES

A *backup copy* is a second or third copy of a document that you can use if something happens to the original document. Whenever you have a document that would take a lot of time to re-create, you should make a backup copy of it. Create the backup copy of your document on another disk so that you can use it in the event the disk that contains the original is damaged. This might mean backing up the document during a full hard disk backup or simply making a copy of the document on another floppy disk.

TO CREATE A BACKUP COPY OF A DOCUMENT

a. Select **F**ile, **F**ile Manager, or click the File Mgr button in the Button Bar, or press F5.
b. Type the pathname for the directory of the document you want to back up, if it is different from the one displayed.
c. Press Enter.
d. Move the highlight to the file that you want to back up.
e. Select **C**opy.
f. Type the drive, directory, and filename under which you want to store the backup of the file.
g. Press Enter.
h. Press Esc to return to the document.

You can also create a backup copy by opening a file and saving it under a different filename or in a different directory.

NOTE *As a reminder, this chapter assumes your WordPerfect documents are in the \WPDOCS directory.*

EXAMPLES

1. You can back up a file to a disk and place the backup where it is safe from harm. First, type

   The company is expanding its product line to include more products for the older generation.

   Next, save this document as OLDER by selecting **F**ile, **S**ave, typing **older**, and pressing Enter.

   To back up the file, place a disk in drive A, and select **F**ile, **F**ile Manager, or click the File Mgr button in the Button Bar, or press F5. The Specify File Manager List dialog box opens, as shown here:

   Because the directory that you want already appears in the dialog box, press Enter. The File Manager dialog box shown in Figure 11-1 appears.

   Move the highlight to the file named OLDER. Select **C**opy. WordPerfect displays this Copy dialog box:

   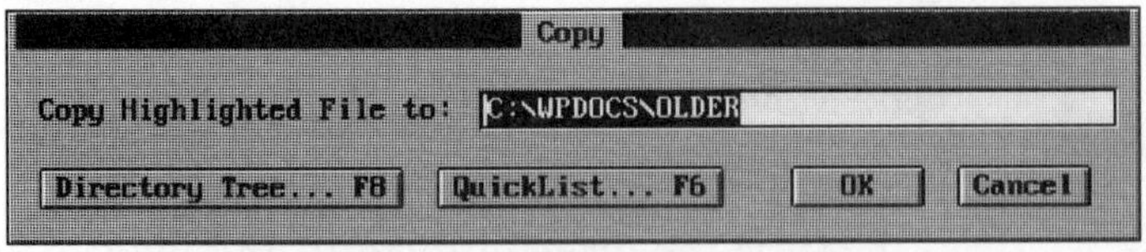

   Type **a:\older** for the drive and filename of the backup file, and press Enter. You can use the same filename because you are copying the file to another disk. If you were storing the backup file in the same directory on the hard disk, you would have to use a different filename.

FIGURE 11-1

File Manager dialog box

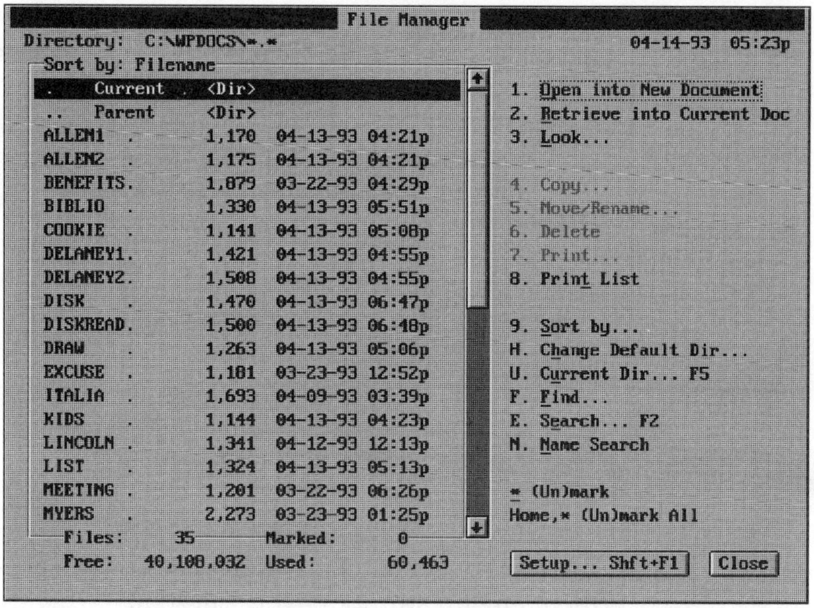

Press Esc to return to the document. Store the backup floppy disk in a safe location. You might want to store it somewhere away from your computer so that if anything happens to your system, such as a flood, fire, tornado, or theft, the backup will still be safe.

2. You can create a backup copy on the same disk as the original by using a different filename. You might create this type of backup when you want to make changes to a document yet retain a copy of the original. First, type

   The company is instituting a pension plan for all salaried employees. This pension plan will be operated by a trust fund created for this purpose. The pension plan is a defined-contribution plan. The company's contribution is a percentage of each employee's yearly salary. The contract came into effect April 30, 1993.

   Save this document as PENSIONS by selecting **F**ile, **S**ave, typing **pensions**, and pressing Enter. Select **F**ile, **F**ile Manager or press F5. Because you want to back up a file from the directory that WordPerfect displays in the prompt, press Enter.

   Next, move the highlight to the PENSIONS filename. Select **C**opy, type **pensions**, and press Enter. Press Esc to return to the document.

EXERCISES

1. Type the following paragraph:

   The pension plan is expected to earn 6% per year. New employees become vested in the plan after five years with the company.

   Save it as PLAN. Clear the screen. Back up the file as EARN.
2. Back up PLAN to another disk.
3. Back up EARN as PENPLAN.

11.2 CREATE DIRECTORIES

Directories are logical disk divisions that you can create and use to organize files. If you place all of your documents on your hard disk without any organization, you will soon have difficulty finding specific documents, because you will need to read through a list of all the files on the disk. To make it easier to find files, you can place related documents or specific types of documents in directories.

You can create just a few directories or many, depending on how you categorize the documents that you create. If you installed WordPerfect as instructed in Appendix A of this book or your WordPerfect manual, you already have your first three directories, WP60, WPCDOS60, and WPDOCS. You can create additional directories on this level, or you can create directories beneath the WPDOCS directory.

TO CREATE A DIRECTORY

a. Select **F**ile, **F**ile Manager, or click the File Mgr button in the Button Bar, or press F5.
b. Press Enter.
c. Select C**h**ange Default Dir.
d. Type a name for the new directory.
e. Press Enter.
f. Select **Y**es to create the directory.

Subdirectories are defined as directories within an existing directory. The first-level directory is the root directory, which is always indicated by a backslash. For example, to indicate the root directory on drive C, you would type **C:**.

You use a *pathname* to tell the computer which directory to find a file in. A full pathname includes the drive letter, the root directory, and any subdirectories. You use backslashes to separate subdirectories in the pathname. To indicate a subdirectory named LEGAL in the root directory on drive C, you would type **C:\LEGAL**. If LEGAL were a subdirectory within the WPDOCS subdirectory instead, you would type **C:\WPDOCS\LEGAL**.

NOTE *Often the terms "subdirectory" and "directory" are used interchangeably. This book will generally use "directory" as a generic term to mean "subdirectory" or "directory."*

EXAMPLES

1. You can create a directory on the same level as the WordPerfect directory. You might want one directory to contain all the budget files you use with different software packages. Select **F**ile, **F**ile Manager or press F5, and press Enter. Next, select C**h**ange Default Dir, type **C:\BUDGET**, and press Enter. The screen displays this prompt:

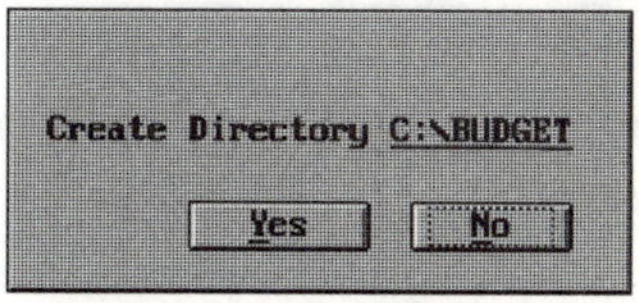

Select **Y**es to create the directory. The structure of the disk now looks like Figure 11-2.

2. You can create a directory within the WordPerfect directory. For example, you can create a directory for all of the form letters that you use in WordPerfect. First, select **F**ile, **F**ile Manager and press Enter. Select C**h**ange Default Dir, type **C:\WPDOCS\FORMLETT** for the directory name, and press Enter. Select **Y**es when WordPerfect prompts you to confirm that you want to create the directory.

FIGURE 11-2

Creating a directory at the same level as WPDOCS

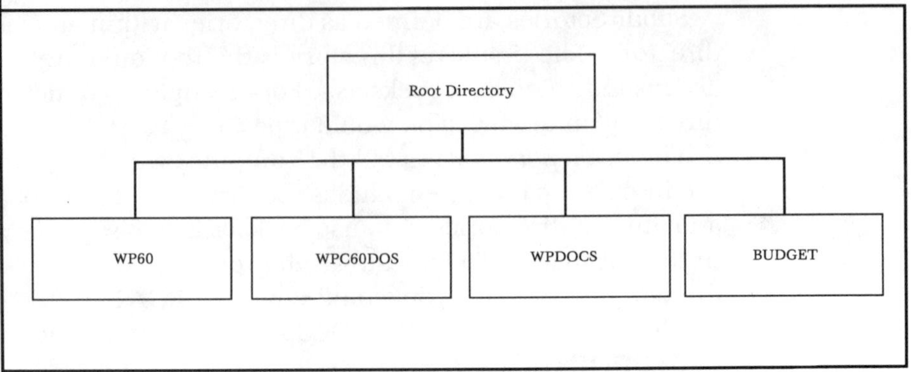

WordPerfect places the new directory within the current directory. The screen looks like this:

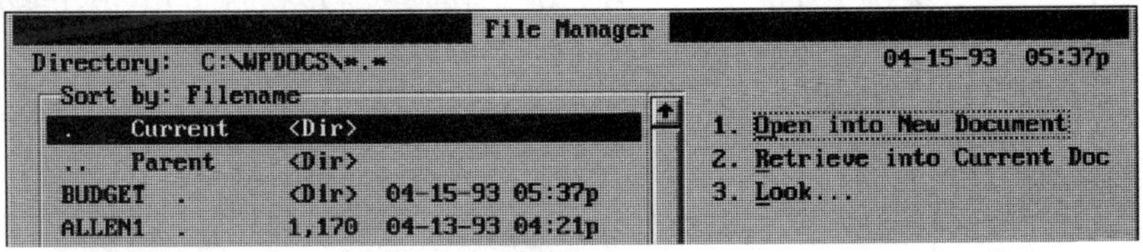

The structure of the disk now looks like Figure 11-3. Press Esc to return to the document.

FIGURE 11-3

Creating a directory within WPDOCS

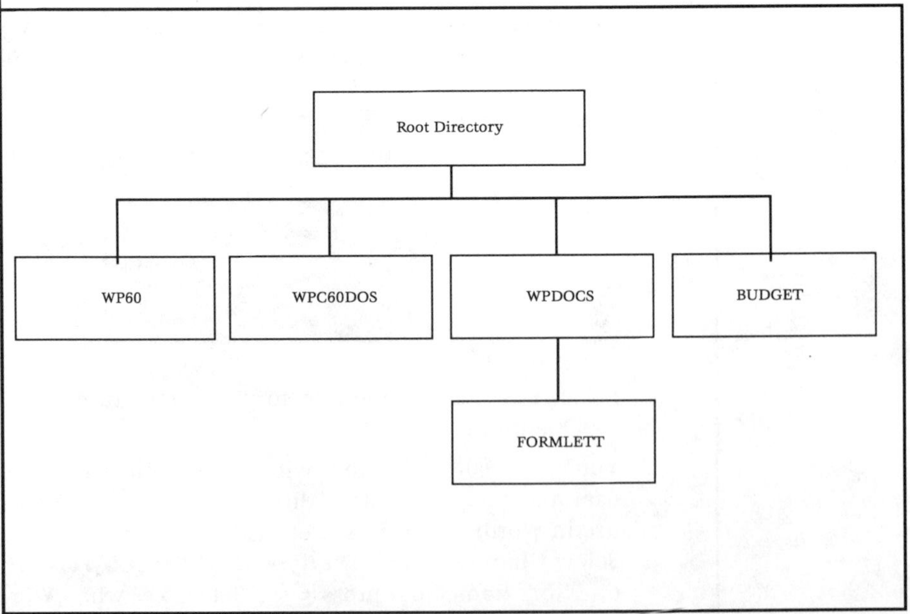

EXERCISES

1. Create a directory called FINANCE on the same level as the WordPerfect document directory.
2. Create a directory called LETTERS within the WordPerfect document directory.
3. Create a subdirectory of FINANCE called FINC1993.
4. Create a subdirectory of FINANCE called FINC1994.

11.3 CHANGE DIRECTORIES

It is not necessary to work in one directory for an entire WordPerfect session. To access a file in a different directory without changing directories, type the full pathname for the file when you open it. If you plan to work within a different directory for a while, however, it is easier to make that directory active. You can then save, open, and retrieve files in the directory without having to provide the pathname each time.

TO CHANGE THE DIRECTORY

a. Select **F**ile, **F**ile Manager, or click the File Mgr button in the Button Bar, or press F5.

c. Press Enter.

b. Select C**h**ange Default Dir.

d. Enter the pathname for the directory you want to use.

e. Press Enter.

f. When WordPerfect displays the Specify File Manager List dialog box again, press Enter.

EXAMPLES

1. You can use the directory tree to locate the directory you want to use. This approach is actually the simplest. To change to the FORMLETT directory that you created in example 2 of section 11.2, first select **F**ile, **F**ile Manager or press F5, and press Enter. Select C**h**ange Default Dir. Select Directory Tree by clicking on it or pressing F8. The Directory Tree dialog box opens, as shown in Figure 11-4.

   Move the highlight to the directory that you want to use. In this case, move the highlight to the FORMLETT directory within the WPDOCS directory, and press Enter. WordPerfect returns the Change Default Directory dialog box, which displays the directory you have chosen. Press Enter twice to change to this directory and display its contents in the File Manager dialog box. Press Esc to return to the document and close the File Manager dialog box. When you later save, open, or retrieve a file, WordPerfect uses the FORMLETT directory unless you provide a different pathname.

2. You can change directories when you know the pathname of the directory you want to change to. For practice, let's use the BUDGET directory that you created in example 1 of section 11.2. Select **F**ile, **F**ile Manager or press F5, and then press Enter. Select C**h**ange Default Dir, type **C:\BUDGET**, and press Enter twice. Press Esc in the

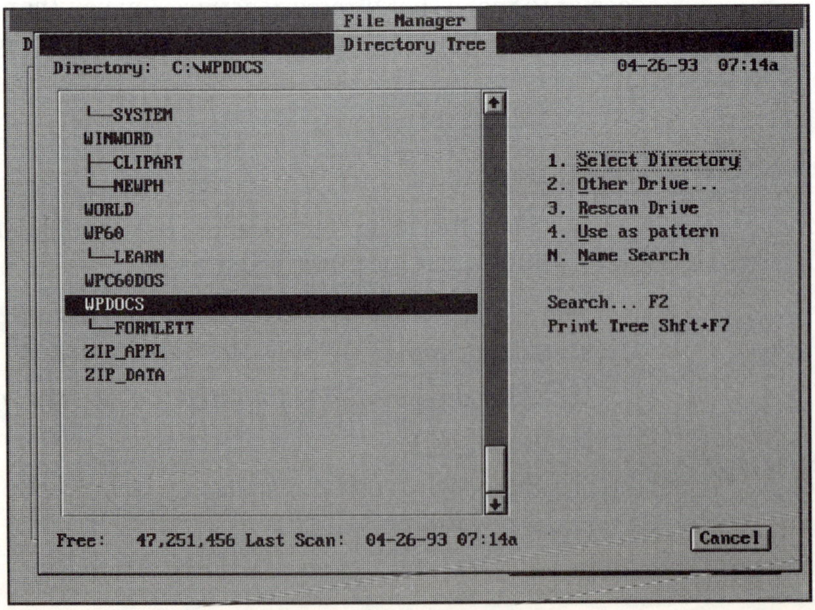

FIGURE 11-4

Directory Tree dialog box

File Manager dialog box to return to the document. When you subsequently save, open, or retrieve a file, WordPerfect uses the BUDGET directory unless you provide a different pathname.

EXERCISES

1. Change to the FINANCE directory that you created in exercise 1 of section 11.2.
2. Change to the LETTERS directory that you created in exercise 2 of section 11.2.
3. Change to the FINC1993 directory that you created in exercise 3 of section 11.2.
4. Change to the FINC1994 directory that you created in exercise 4 of section 11.2.
5. Change to the WPDOCS directory.

11.4 DELETE FILES AND DIRECTORIES

Even when you create a document for one-time use, you should save it just in case you find a need for it later. Periodically, you should review your disk's contents to ensure that you are not cluttering it with unneeded files. Unneeded files waste disk space and slow access time to the disk. WordPerfect provides an easy-to-use option for removing unneeded files.

NOTE *You should back up all the files on your hard disk periodically. You should delete files from your hard disk only after you have backed up all those files to floppy disks. That way, if you accidentally remove a file that you need, you have a backup.*

TO DELETE A FILE FROM DISK

a. Select **F**ile, **F**ile Manager, or click the File Mgr button in the Button Bar, or press F5.

b. Type the pathname if the file is in a different directory.
c. Press Enter.
d. Move the highlight to the file that you want to delete.
e. Select **D**elete.
f. Select **Y**es to confirm that you want to delete the file.
g. Press Esc to return to the document.

EXAMPLES

1. You can delete a backup file that you no longer need. To delete the backup file PENSIONS that you created in example 2 of section 11.1, first select **F**ile, **F**ile Manager or press F5.

   Next, press Enter, because WordPerfect displays the directory that you want to use. Move the highlight to the file PENSIONS. When you select **D**elete, WordPerfect displays this prompt:

   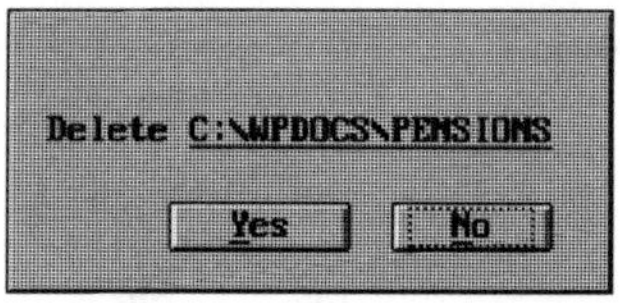

   Select **Y**es to confirm that you want to delete this file. Press Esc to return to the document.

2. You can delete a directory in the same way you delete a file. For example, you can delete the FORMLETT directory you created in example 2 of section 11.2. Select **F**ile, **F**ile Manager or press F5. Then press Enter, because WordPerfect displays the directory that you want to use. Move the highlight to the FORMLETT directory. When you select **D**elete, WordPerfect displays this prompt:

   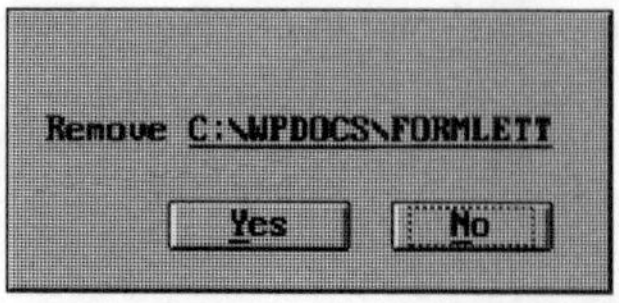

Select **Y**es to confirm that you want to delete this directory. Press Esc to return to the document. A directory must be empty before you can delete it. If the FORMLETT directory had contained any files, you would have had to delete all the files in it before you could delete the directory.

EXERCISES

1. Delete the file PLAN that you created in exercise 2 of section 11.1 from the disk in drive A.
2. Delete the directory LETTERS that you created in exercise 2 of section 11.2.
3. Delete the directory FINC1993 that you created in exercise 3 of section 11.2.
4. Delete the directory FINC1994 that you created in exercise 4 of section 11.2.

11.5 RENAME FILES

You should always give files filenames that are meaningful. Setting standard ways of creating filenames gives you consistent filenames. You can rename files on disk that do not conform to the rules that you establish. This renaming process does not require you to re-create the files; you simply change the filenames. When you choose a new filename, you need to use a filename that is unique for the current disk or directory.

TO RENAME A FILE

a. Select **F**ile, **F**ile Manager, or click the File Mgr button in the Button Bar, or press F5.
b. Type the pathname if the file you want to rename is in a different directory.

c. Press Enter.

d. Move the highlight to the file that you want to rename.

e. Select **M**ove/Rename.

f. Type a new filename for the file.

g. Press Enter.

h. Press Esc to leave the File Manager dialog box.

You can edit the filename in step f instead of retyping it. Press the → or End key to begin the editing process.

EXAMPLES

1. You can rename the OLDER file that you created in example 1 of section 11.1. First, select **F**ile, **F**ile Manager or press F5. Press Enter to accept the default directory, move the highlight to the file named OLDER, and select **M**ove/Rename. Type the new filename, **PENSION1**, and press Enter. Notice how the file appears as PENSION1 in the list of files. Press Esc.
2. You can move a file to a different directory by renaming it. Let's move the PENSION1 file used in the last example to the BUDGET directory you created in example 1 of section 11.2. Select **F**ile, **F**ile Manager or press F5, and press Enter to accept the current directory. Move the highlight to the file PENSION1, and select **M**ove/Rename. Type **C:\BUDGET\PENSION1**, which gives the file a different pathname but the same filename. Press Enter. Press Esc to return to the document.

EXERCISES

1. Rename the file PLAN that you created in exercise 1 of section 11.1. Use PENSION3 as the new filename.

2. Rename the file EARN that you created in exercise 1 of section 11.1. Use EARNED as the new filename.
3. Retrieve the file EARNED. Save it as ERN_INC, and clear the screen. Rename ERN_INC as EARN_INC.

11.6 CREATE DOCUMENT SUMMARIES

A document summary is a WordPerfect feature that helps you manage files. Document summaries let you store descriptive information about every document file you create. In a document summary, you can provide a descriptive name to supplement the information conveyed by the filename. You can also enter a descriptive type, the name of the author, and the name of the typist. You can enter information in the Subject, Account, and Keywords fields. In the Keywords field, you can enter words and phrases that you can use to search for the document. The Abstract field can contain information that summarizes the document; later, you can use this information to provide an overview of the file's contents and use the overview to make decisions concerning the disposition of the file.

NOTE *Previous releases of WordPerfect impose limits on the number of characters that can be entered in these fields. Now the limits are so high that they are irrelevant. Even so, you will want to be concise in the document summary, or you will find it of little use.*

TO CREATE A DOCUMENT SUMMARY

a. Select **F**ile, S**u**mmary.
b. Select the desired field, type the entry, and press Enter.
c. Select OK to return to the document.

Although completing a document summary requires many steps, WordPerfect provides a number of shortcuts to reduce the amount of typing required. First of all, you are not required to fill in all entries of the document summary. Also, by selecting Extract (Shift-F10), you can have WordPerfect insert the last entered author and typist in the Author and Typist fields and the beginning text from the document in the Abstract field. If you choose, you can then edit the text in the Abstract field.

EXAMPLES

1. You can create a document summary before creating a document. With a clear screen, select **F**ile, S**u**mmary. The Document Summary dialog box appears, as shown in Figure 11-5.

   Press Enter twice to move to the Descriptive Name field, and type

   Pension Plan

   Press Enter to move to the Descriptive Type field, and type

   Trust

   Press Enter. In the Author field, type

   Allen Jones

   Press Enter. In the Typist field, type

FIGURE 11-5

Blank document summary screen

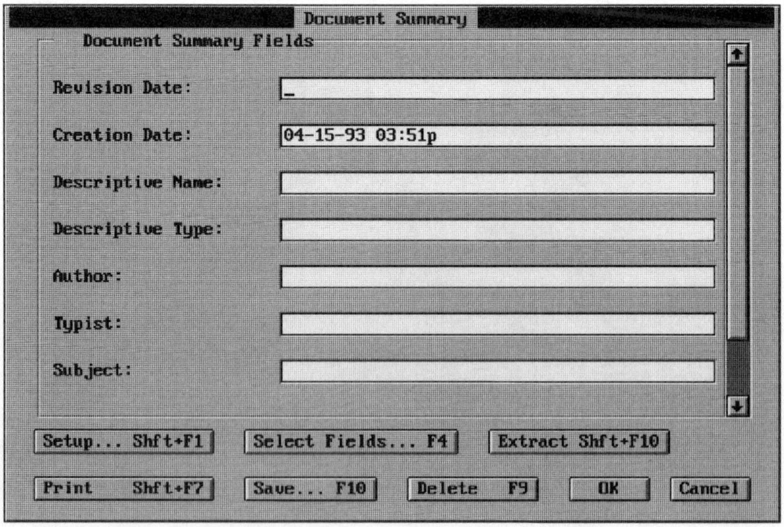

Jim Smith

Press Enter to move to the Subject field. Type

Acme Corporation

Press Enter to move to the Account field, and type

10023

Press Enter. In the Keywords field, type

contract Acme pension plan

Press Enter. In the Abstract field, type

This document contains the original contract on pages 1 through 17. Pages 18 and 19 contain the addendum passed June 30, 1993.

Press F7 to complete the abstract. The dialog box looks like Figure 11-6. Select OK to return to the document. Save and exit this document by selecting **F**ile, **S**ave, typing **penscont**, and pressing Enter.

2. After you have created one document summary, creating others is easy, especially if the other documents already contain text. Select File, Open or press Shift-F10, type **pension**, and press Enter. Select **F**ile, S**u**mmary.

FIGURE 11-6

Completed document summary

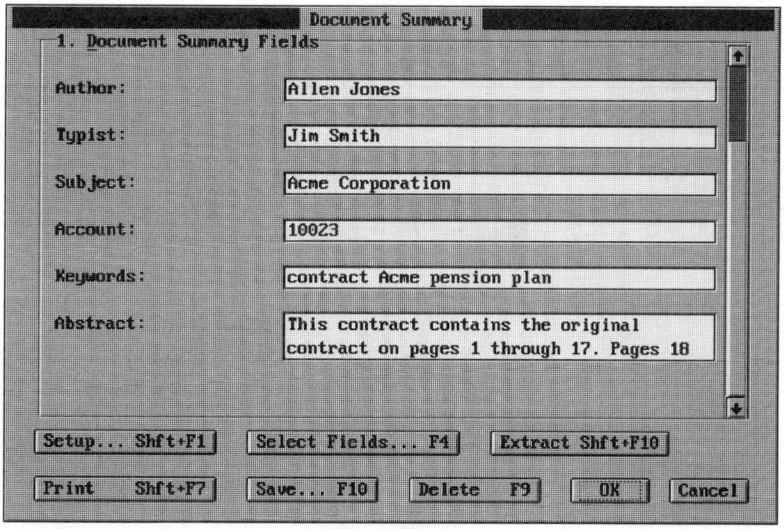

Press Tab twice to move to the Descriptive Name field, and type

Acme Corp - Pension Plan

Press Enter, and type

Press Release

Press Enter twice to move to the Subject field, and type

Public Announcement 7/1/93

Press Enter, and type

10023

Press Enter. Type

Pension plan announcement press release

Press Enter. Select the Extract command button by pressing Shift-F10, and then select **Y**es to accept the previous author and typist names and incorporate text from the document into the abstract. Select OK to return to the document. Select **F**ile, **S**ave to save this file.

EXERCISES

1. Create a document summary that contains this information:

   Descriptive Name: Blank Quit Claim Sales Contract
   Descriptive Type: Contract
   Author: Jonas Smith
   Typist: Karen Polk
   Subject: Undeveloped Real Estate
   Keywords: Form Contract Quit Claim
   Abstract: This blank contract covers most undeveloped land sales in the state of Florida. This contract has four Xs where you must fill in information. Paragraphs contained in braces are optional. Remove them if they are unnecessary for a particular contract.

   Save the document as CONTRACT.

2. Type the following new document:

   The August 17th meeting discussed the following issues:
   Installation of new parking lot lights
   Hiring of security personnel to patrol the parking lots after dark
   Completion of new research and development building
   Improved insurance benefits

   Create a document summary that has the following descriptive name:

   August 17th meeting notes

   Use the entries from the Author and Typist fields in exercise 1, and use text from the document for the abstract. Save the document as ISSUES.

3. Enter the following paragraph:

   WordPerfect's graphics features are among the most advanced in the industry. Investing some time in mastering these features could offer a significant payoff for our company. Outside service costs for creating newsletters and brochures can be reduced significantly.

   Create a document summary that contains this information:

   Descriptive Name: Cut costs with WordPerfect's graphics
   Descriptive Type: Product Comment
   Abstract: Reduce newsletter and brochure development costs with graphics features. We can recover the cost of the upgrade to WordPerfect 6 with the first job.
   Incorporate the Author and Typist entries from the previous document summary.

   Save the document as SAVING.

4. Retrieve the ISSUES file. In the document summary, change the name of the typist to Martha King. Save the document again.

11.7 SEARCH FOR A WORD WITHIN A DOCUMENT ON DISK

WordPerfect provides a document-search feature that examines the contents of files on disk. You enter a word or phrase to use as a search string, and WordPerfect marks the files that contain that word or phrase. You can have WordPerfect look for the search string in the document summaries, the first page of every document, or the entire text of every document. After WordPerfect has marked the files that contain your entry, you can use the look feature to examine the files more closely, or you can use other options in the File Manager dialog box.

TO SEARCH FOR A WORD OR A PHRASE IN DOCUMENTS

a. Select **F**ile, **F**ile Manager, or click the File Mgr in the Button Bar, or press F5.

b. Type the pathname containing the files you wish to check, if they are in a different directory.

c. Press Enter.

d. Select **F**ind.

e. Select the option for where you want to search. You can select **N**ame to search for a filename, **D**ocument Summary to search the document summaries, First **P**age to search the first pages, or **E**ntire Document to search the entire documents.

f. Type the text for which WordPerfect should search.

g. Press Enter.

WordPerfect searches the files and lists those that contain the specified word or phrase. You can then highlight a file and open it, or you can press Esc to return to your current document.

EXAMPLES

1. You can search files in the current directory to find all of the document summaries that contain the word "contract." First, select **F**ile, **F**ile Manager or press F5. Next, press Enter to select the default directory.

   Select **F**ind, **D**ocument Summary, type **contract**, and press Enter. After WordPerfect completes its search, it displays the files that have the word "contract" within their document summaries. The files

WordPerfect displays should include PENSIONS, CONTRACT, and PENSCONT. Press Esc to return to the current document.

2. You can search for a phrase in the first page of every file in the current directory. For example, you can find all of the documents that contain the phrase "pension plan" on the first page. First, select **F**ile, **F**ile Manager or press F5. Press Enter to select the default directory.

   Select **F**ind, First **P**age. When WordPerfect prompts you for a search string, type a quotation mark ("), the phrase **pension plan**, and another quotation mark. Enclosing the phrase in quotation marks tells WordPerfect to treat the words in the phrase as a single unit. Press Enter. After WordPerfect completes its search, it lists the filenames that meet the search criterion. Press Esc to return to the document.

3. You can search for a specific word in all the text of the documents in the current directory. For example, you can search for the name Jones. Select **F**ile, **F**ile Manager or press F5. Then press Enter to select the default directory. Select **F**ind, **E**ntire Document, and type **Jones**. When you press Enter, WordPerfect searches the documents and lists the filenames that meet the search criterion. Each of these files contains the name Jones somewhere in the document. Press Esc to return to the current document.

4. You can search for more than one word or phrase at a time. You can have WordPerfect mark all documents that contain both of the search strings, or you can elect to have WordPerfect mark all files that contain either of the search strings.

   You use what WordPerfect refers to as *logical operators* to specify multiple search criteria. The semicolon (;) and the comma (,) are the two logical operators that you use to join multiple search strings. The semicolon is used to indicate a logical "and." If you join two words by using a semicolon, WordPerfect searches for files that contain both words. The comma is used to indicate a logical "or." If you join two words by using a comma, WordPerfect searches for files containing *either* word.

   To practice, find all the documents that contain the word "pension" or the word "Mary." Select **F**ind, **F**ile Manager or press F5, and press Enter when WordPerfect prompts you for the current directory. Then, select **F**ind, **E**ntire Document. When WordPerfect prompts you for the search string, type **pension, Mary**, and press Enter. After marking the files, WordPerfect lists the filenames that meet the search criteria. Each listed file contains the word "pension" or the word "Mary," or both. Press Esc to return to the current document.

EXERCISES

1. Find all documents that contain the word "August" in the document summary.
2. Find all documents that contain the phrase "Acme Corporation" in the first page.
3. Find all documents that contain the word "plan."
4. Find all documents that contain your first name.
5. Find all documents that contain the words "company" and "product" in the document summary.
6. Find all documents that contain either the word "pension" or the word "contract."

11.8 LOOK AT FILES ON DISK

Sometimes when you are looking for a particular file, you might narrow down the choice to a few files but still be uncertain of the one that you want. A quick way to find the correct file is to use WordPerfect's look feature. With this feature, you can see a document's contents on the screen without having to retrieve the file. After you have identified the correct file, you can print it, rename it, delete it, copy it, or retrieve it for editing.

TO USE THE LOOK FEATURE

a. Select **F**ile, **F**ile Manager, or click the File Mgr button in the Button Bar, or press F5.
b. Type the pathname if you want to look at files in a different directory.
c. Press Enter.
d. Move the highlight to the file that you want to view.
e. Select **L**ook.
f. Read the document summary (if there is one).
g. Toggle between viewing the document summary and the text of the document by selecting **L**ook at Text/Summary.

h. Select OK to return to the list of files.

i. Press Esc to return to the current document.

EXAMPLES

1. You can use the look feature to display a document without opening or retrieving it. Select **F**ile, **F**ile Manager or press F5. Then press Enter to select the default directory. Highlight the filename PENSION3, select **L**ook, and then select **L**ook at Text/Summary. You can use ↑, ↓, Pg Up, and Pg Dn to view the document.
   WordPerfect does not let you edit the document. When you finish viewing the document, select OK and press Esc to return to the current document.
2. You can use the look feature to review document summaries. Select **F**ile, **F**ile Manager or press F5, and press Enter. Highlight the filename PENSIONS, and select **L**ook. WordPerfect displays the document summary. When you finish viewing the document and document summary, select OK and press Esc to return to the current document.

EXERCISES

1. Use the look feature to view the EARNED file that you used in exercise 2 of section 11.5.
2. Use the look feature to view the document summary of the CONTRACT file that you created in exercise 1 of section 11.6.
3. Use the look feature to view the document summary of the ISSUES file that you created in exercise 2 of section 11.6.
4. Use the look feature to view the PENPLAN file that you created in exercise 3 of section 11.1.
5. Use the look feature to view the STOCKS file that you created in the Skills Check in this chapter.

mastery skills check

As you complete the following Mastery Skills Check exercises, do not clear the screen between exercises unless instructed to do so.

1. Create a directory named BUDGET94 within the WPDOCS directory. [11.2]
2. Type the following lines:

Acme Corporation - 1994 Budget	
Estimated Sales	$1,000,000
Fixed Costs	$400,000
Variable Costs	$400,000
Gross Profit	$200,000

   Save the document as BUDGET. Clear the screen. Copy the BUDGET file to the BUDGET94 directory within the WPDOCS directory. [11.2]
3. Make the BUDGET94 directory the current directory. [11.3]
4. Back up the BUDGET file in the BUDGET94 directory to a file named BDGT1994. [11.1]
5. Delete the BUDGET file in the BUDGET94 directory. [11.4]
6. Change the filename of BDGT1994 to BDGT94. [11.5]
7. Retrieve BDGT94, and create a document summary that contains the following information. [11.6]

   Descriptive Name: Budget 1994
   Descriptive Type: Budget
   Author: Jane Smith
   Typist: John Dow
   Subject: Acme Corporation
   Account: 10023
   Abstract: Michael McCormick must have this report by September 30, 1993.
8. Save the file.
9. Search through document summaries for the word "budget." [11.7]

10. Clear the screen. View the BDGT94 file. [11.8]
11. Make the WPDOCS directory the current directory. [11.3]

Teach Yourself cumulative skills check

As you work through the following exercises, do not clear the screen between exercises unless instructed to do so.

1. Type the following paragraphs:

   Discussions about preferred stock use the following descriptive terms:

   Participation - This feature determines if the preferred stock can receive an additional dividend after the common stock receives a dividend at the same rate of the preferred stock dividend. The additional dividend is determined by whether the stock is fully or partially participating stock.

   Callable - This feature allows the corporation to buy back the preferred stock at a specific price. This feature often places a ceiling on the preferred stock's price.

   Cumulative - This feature determines whether dividends that were not declared in prior years must be paid before current dividends are paid.

   Conversion - This feature allows the stockholder to convert the preferred stock into common stock. If preferred stock has this feature, the stock often fluctuates with the common stock, although not to the same extent.

   Use WordPerfect's spell feature to determine if you have introduced any spelling errors. [2.1, 9.2]
2. Save the document as PREFER. [2.4]
3. Back up the file as PREFERRD. [11.1]
4. Create a directory named STOCK within the WPDOCS directory. [11.2]
5. Clear the screen. [1.2]
6. Back up the PREFERRD file to the STOCK directory. [11.1]
7. Make the STOCK directory current, and retrieve the PREFERRD file. [2.6, 11.3]

8. Rearrange the paragraphs so that the four features are in alphabetical order. [8.1]
9. Change the top and bottom margins to 5 inches. [6.2]
10. Prevent widow and orphan lines. [10.1]
11. Save the file. [2.4]
12. Delete the PREFER file from the WPDOCS directory. [11.4]
13. Use the search feature to locate the first occurrence of "dividend." [7.2]
14. Use the thesaurus to find synonyms for "fluctuates" and "extent." [9.7]

12

Changing Print Options

chapter objectives

After completing this chapter, you should be able to

12.1 Print multiple copies

12.2 Display the print queue

12.3 Cancel a print request

12.4 Rush a print request

12.5 Affect the print quality

12.6 Change fonts

WORDPERFECT'S print features allow you to do more than simply print a copy of your document. You can request printed copies of many documents at a time. WordPerfect keeps track of print priorities and sends jobs to the printer in the proper order.

WordPerfect maintains a print queue to manage print requests that have not yet been fulfilled. You can display the jobs in this queue and cancel a job or specify a rush print job.

Another print option allows you to print multiple copies of a document with one print request. You can select from draft-quality to high-quality print output, if your printer supports multiple quality options.

WordPerfect provides options for changing the font, size, and style of your printed text. (Naturally, to use these features, your printer must support these options.) WordPerfect's font support allows you to use different character sets. It also supports changes that affect the size of the characters.

review skills check

Do not clear the screen until you have completed the last Skills Check exercise.

1. Type the following paragraph as shown, including the misspellings and repeated words.

   In Chapter 3, you learned the basic skills for printiing your your document. This chapter covers other printer feetures that allow you to customize your document's appearence.

   Use the spell feature to correct spelling errors and eliminate double words. [9.2]

2. Use the thesaurus feature to find synonyms for "customize." Replace "customize" with "tailor." [9.7]
3. Add a header that will print **WordPerfect Print Features**. Add a centered footer that will print **Page** followed by the page number. Preview how WordPerfect will print this document. [10.2]
4. Create a document summary that contains the following information. [11.6]

   Descriptive Name: Describing WordPerfect's print features

   Descriptive Type: DOCUMENTATION

   Author: [your name]

   Typist: [your name]

   Subject: Teach Yourself WordPerfect

   Abstract: [Incorporate beginning of document]

5. Save the document as ADVPRINT. Save a copy of this file as PRINTADV. Rename ADVPRINT to PRNTFEAT. Delete PRINTADV. [11.1, 11.4, 11.5]

12.1 PRINT MULTIPLE COPIES

With one print request, you can specify that WordPerfect print more than one copy of a document. For a short document, printing two copies is usually quicker than a trip to the copy machine.

You can request multiple copies by using the Print menu. The number of copies you select remains in effect for the current WordPerfect session.

TO PRINT MULTIPLE COPIES

a. Select **F**ile, **P**rint/Fax or press Shift-F7.
b. Select **N**umber of Copies.
c. Type the number of copies you want.
d. Press Enter.
e. Press Enter or click P**r**int to start printing.

EXAMPLES

1. You can have WordPerfect print two copies of a document. First, type

   The print options allow you to customize your printer output.

   Next, select **F**ile, **P**rint/Fax or press Shift-F7, press N, type **2**, and press Enter. To start printing, press Enter to select the P**r**int button. WordPerfect returns to the document and prints two copies. Press F7 or select **F**ile, E**x**it, press Enter, type **printopt**, press Enter, and press N to save the file and clear the screen.

2. WordPerfect returns the multiple-copy setting for the current WordPerfect session to one copy. First, type

   WordPerfect retains some settings for all documents used in the current session. Other settings are saved with a document and do not apply to other documents.

   Next, select **F**ile, **P**rint/Fax or press Shift-F7. The setting that you selected in the first example is returned to the default. To print two copies of this new document, press N, type **2**, and press Enter. Press Enter again to print the two copies. Press F7 or select **F**ile, E**x**it, press Enter, type **wpset**, press Enter, and press N to save the file and clear the screen.

EXERCISES

1. Type the following paragraph:

   You should delete files when you no longer need them. Deleting files frees up needed space on your hard disk or floppy disks.

   Print three copies of the document. Save it as FILEDEL.

2. Type the following paragraph:

   When you save a file, you should use a name that describes the document's purpose. If you do not select meaningful names, you will have difficulty remembering what each document contains. You can rename a file if you wish to change its filename.

Print two copies of the document. Save it as RENAME.

3. Print three copies of the file PRINTOPT.
4. Print two copies of WPSET.
5. Print two copies of FILEDEL. Print one copy of WPSET.

12.2 DISPLAY THE PRINT QUEUE

WordPerfect permits you to display the print queue. The *print queue* shows the status of the current print job as well as that of jobs waiting to print. From the display of print jobs, you can make an assessment of how long it will take to complete the print jobs that you have requested.

TO DISPLAY THE PRINT QUEUE

a. Select **F**ile, **P**rint/Fax or press Shift-F7.
b. Press C or **6** to select **C**ontrol Printer.
c. Press Enter or click the Close button to return to the current document.

Each job that is displayed in the print queue has a number. WordPerfect assigns the number 1 to the first print request it receives in each session and assigns each subsequent print request the next number. As you will learn in later sections, viewing the print queue allows you to use other WordPerfect print options.

EXAMPLES

1. When you tell WordPerfect to print a document, it creates a print job for the task. When you display the print queue, you can look at the status of every print request that has not yet been fulfilled. First, select **F**ile, **P**rint/Fax or press Shift-F7.

Select **D**ocument on Disk, type **printopt**, and press Enter three times. You will need to make several additional print requests quickly to create a backlog. Select **F**ile, **P**rint/Fax, select **D**ocument on Disk, type **printopt**, and press Enter three times again. Repeat this request one more time. If you proceed quickly to the print queue display, at least one of the print requests should still be in the queue.

Select **F**ile, **P**rint/Fax and select **C**ontrol Printer from the Print dialog box. The screen looks like Figure 12-1 if you manage to display the Control Printer dialog box while all three print jobs are still in the queue. Print jobs usually disappear from the queue quickly, depending on the speed of your computer and printer and on the sizes of your print requests. The list of print jobs shows the filenames to be printed, or it shows (Screen) when the print job is for the document on screen.

2. The queue display shows the printer backlog. You can use this display to help you estimate the time it will take to print the jobs in the queue. Even though WordPerfect does not estimate the time requirements for you, if you are familiar with the documents in the queue, you will have a good idea of their length and the required time for printing.

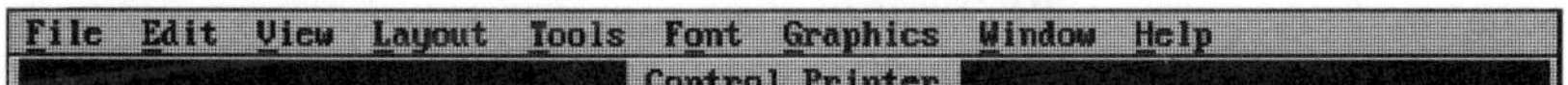

FIGURE 12-1

Control Printer dialog box

Temporarily stopping the print process allows you to look at print requests in the print queue. First, take the printer offline. (A button on your printer allows you to do this.) Taking the printer offline stops the printing process until you switch the printer back online. Select **F**ile, **P**rint/Fax. Then select **D**ocument on Disk, type **printopt**, and press Enter three times. Select **F**ile, **P**rint/Fax, select **N**umber of Copies, type **2**, and press Enter. Select **D**ocument on Disk, type **wpset**, and press Enter three times.

Next, select **F**ile, **P**rint/Fax and press C to select **C**ontrol Printer from the Print/Fax dialog box. The queue displays both print jobs. Because the printer is offline, the status message indicates that the printer is not accepting the information that WordPerfect is sending. Notice how the box at the bottom of the dialog box shows the text quality, graphics quality, number of copies, and priority level of the highlighted print job. Press ↓ to highlight the second print job. WordPerfect updates the box of information to match the second print job.

Switch the printer online to make it accept and print the information the computer sends it. As WordPerfect finishes the first job, it removes the job from the queue and changes the information in the top half of the screen to display the print information for the second document. Press Enter to return to the document.

EXERCISES

1. Print three copies of the file RENAME that you created in exercise 2 of section 12.1. Display the print queue while the job is printing.
2. Print three copies of the file RENAME. Print two copies of FILEDEL, which you created in exercise 1 of section 12.1. Print one copy of the file WPSET. Display the print queue and watch how it changes as WordPerfect prints each job.

12.3 CANCEL A PRINT REQUEST

If you change your mind about printing a document, you can cancel your print request. If the job has already started printing, your printer will continue to print for a page or two: WordPerfect stops transmitting data to the printer when you cancel a job, but it does not clear the printer's memory. The printer continues to print until all the data in its memory has been printed.

TO CANCEL A PRINT REQUEST

a. Select **F**ile, **P**rint/Fax or press Shift-F7.
b. Select **C**ontrol Printer.
c. Highlight the print job you want to cancel.
d. Select **C**ancel Job.
e. Press Y to confirm that you want to cancel the print job.
f. Press F7 to return to the current document.

To cancel all print jobs, select (Un)mark All before step d.

EXAMPLES

1. You can cancel a print job that is currently printing. First, type

   WordPerfect lets you perform several DOS commands by using the file manager, which is available by pressing F5.

   Then press Ctrl-Enter to insert a hard page break. On the second page, type

   Using the file manager, you can select commands that are equivalent to DOS's COPY, ERASE, RENAME, CD, and TYPE commands.

   To print three copies of this document, select **F**ile, **P**rint/Fax or press Shift-F7, select **N**umber of Copies, type **3**, and press Enter twice. To cancel this request, select **F**ile, **P**rint/Fax or press Shift-F7, select **C**ontrol Printer, and select **C**ancel Job. WordPerfect prompts you to confirm that you want to cancel the highlighted print job. Press Enter to select **Y**es. Your printer might continue to print the information the computer has already sent. To return to the document, press F7 to select the Close button. Press F7 or select **F**ile, **E**xit, press Enter, type **listfile**, press Enter, and select **N**o to save the document and clear the screen.

2. You can cancel all the print requests in the print queue at once. First, you must enter several print requests. Select **F**ile, **P**rint/Fax or press Shift-F7. Select **D**ocument on Disk, type **printopt**, and press Enter three times. To print another document, select **F**ile, **P**rint/Fax or press Shift-F7, select **D**ocument on Disk, type **wpset**, and press Enter three times. To print a third document, select **F**ile, **P**rint/Fax or press Shift-F7, select **D**ocument on Disk, type **listfile**, and press Enter three times.

   To cancel all the print requests, select **F**ile, **P**rint/Fax or press Shift-F7, and press C to select **C**ontrol Printer. Select (Un)mark All to mark each print job with an asterisk. Select **C**ancel Job. WordPerfect prompts you to confirm whether you want to cancel all print jobs. Press Y to select **Y**es. To return to the document, press F7 to select the Close button.

EXERCISES

1. Start printing five copies of the RENAME file, which you created in exercise 2 of section 12.1. Cancel the print job.
2. Start printing three copies of RENAME, FILEDEL, and WPSET, which you created in section 12.1. Cancel all print jobs.
3. Switch the printer offline to temporarily disable WordPerfect from printing. Request one copy of FILEDEL. Cancel the print job.
4. With the printer offline, request printouts of WPSET, FILEDEL, and RENAME. Cancel the WPSET and RENAME print requests. Turn the printer on.

12.4 RUSH A PRINT REQUEST

Because WordPerfect allows you to create many print requests at one time, you can accumulate a backlog of print requests. WordPerfect provides a way to expedite a print request so that the entire backlog does not have to finish printing before an important job is printed. After requesting a job in the normal fashion, you use an option on the Print menu to specify that the job is a "rush" job. When the current job finishes printing, the rush job is printed before any other jobs in the print queue.

TO RUSH A PRINT REQUEST

a. Select **F**ile, **P**rint/Fax or press Shift-F7.

b. Select **C**ontrol Printer.

c. Highlight the print job you want to expedite.

d. Select **R**ush Job.

e. Press Y to confirm that you want to rush the print job.

f. Press Y if you want to interrupt the current print job or N if you do not want to interrupt it.

g. Press Tab twice and Enter once to return to the current document.

If you interrupt the current print job, WordPerfect finishes the page it is printing, prints the rush job, and then continues printing the interrupted job. If you do not interrupt the current print job, WordPerfect finishes printing it, prints the rush job, and then prints the other jobs in the queue.

EXAMPLES

1. You can use the Rush Job option to change the order of the print jobs. Select **F**ile, **P**rint/Fax or press Shift-F7. Select **N**umber of Copies, type **2**, and press Enter. Select **D**ocument on Disk, type **printopt**, and press Enter three times. Select **F**ile, **P**rint/Fax or press Shift-F7.

Select **N**umber of Copies, type **2**, and press Enter. Select **D**ocument on Disk, type **wpset**, and press Enter three times. Select **F**ile, **P**rint/Fax or press Shift-F7. Select **N**umber of Copies, type **2**, and press Enter. Select **D**ocument on Disk, type **listfile**, and press Enter three times.

To rush the LISTFILE print job, select **F**ile, **P**rint/Fax or press Shift-F7, and select **C**ontrol Printer. Press ↓ until you highlight the LISTFILE print job. Select **R**ush Job and press Y to confirm that you want to rush the highlighted job. When WordPerfect asks you whether to interrupt the current job, press Y. Finally, press F7.

2. When you rush a print request, you can direct WordPerfect not to print the rush job until it finishes the current job. Press Ctrl-Enter six times to create a multiple-page document. Then select **F**ile, **P**rint/Fax or press Shift-F7, and press Enter or click **P**rint to print the full document. Switch the printer offline to temporarily halt the printing process. To print a file from disk, select **F**ile, **P**rint/Fax or press Shift-F7, select **D**ocument on Disk, type **listfile**, and press Enter three times.

   To rush the LISTFILE print request, select **F**ile, **P**rint/Fax or press Shift-F7, and then press C. Press ↓ to highlight the LISTFILE print job. Select **R**ush Job and press Y to confirm that you want to rush the print job. When WordPerfect asks whether you want to interrupt the current job, press N. WordPerfect will not print LISTFILE immediately, even though it is a rush request. WordPerfect must finish printing the seven blank pages of the current document. Switch the printer back online.

EXERCISES

1. Create a print request for RENAME. Create a print request for FILEDEL. Create a print request for PRINTOPT. Rush the PRINTOPT request, interrupting the current print job.
2. Turn the printer off, and request printouts of WPSET, FILEDEL, and RENAME. Rush the RENAME print request. Turn the printer on.

12.5 AFFECT THE PRINT QUALITY

Many printers support more than one quality of print output. Some printers have a draft mode that prints quickly but is not so high in quality as other modes. WordPerfect supports draft-, medium-, and high-quality print output. It provides separate print quality selections for text and graphics. These settings also provide a Do Not Print option that allows you to print text and graphics in separate print jobs.

TO AFFECT THE PRINT QUALITY

a. Select **F**ile, **P**rint/Fax or press Shift-F7.
b. Select **T**ext Quality or **G**raphics Quality.
c. Select Do **N**ot Print, **D**raft, **M**edium, or **H**igh.
d. Press Enter or click the **P**rint button to start printing.

With some printers, the higher the quality, the longer it takes the printer to print. The Do Not Print option in step c can be used for printing text and graphics on a printer that can print one or the other but not both at the same time. The options available for graphics are identical to the options for text. They are not discussed here, because they use skills that you will develop in Chapter 17. Text and graphics quality settings are saved with a document file.

EXAMPLES

1. You can set the text quality to draft when you need a quick printed copy. Retrieve PRINTOPT by selecting **F**ile, **R**etrieve, typing **printopt**, and pressing Enter. Select **F**ile, **P**rint/Fax or press Shift-F7, and then select **T**ext Quality, **D**raft. To see how draft-quality print appears, press Enter to select the Print button and print the current document. Do not clear the screen; you will use this document in the next example.
2. You can use high text quality when you are printing your document for presentation to others. Select **F**ile, **P**rint or press Shift-F7, and select **T**ext Quality, **H**igh. To see how high-quality text prints, press Enter.

EXERCISES

Do not clear the screen until you have completed the last exercise.

1. Retrieve WPSET. Set the text quality to medium. Print the document.
2. Set the text quality to high. Print the document.
3. Set the text quality to draft. Print the document.

12.6 CHANGE FONTS

You can incorporate different fonts into your documents. Fonts are character sets that are created in different styles. Some fonts are proportional; that is, different characters take up different amounts of space on a line. The fonts available to you in WordPerfect vary according to your printer and software. WordPerfect includes software fonts called Speedo and Type 1 that you can include in your documents. When setting a font in a document, you can set its size and attributes, such as bold and underline, which you learned about in Chapter 4.

You can change fonts within a document, a paragraph, or a line. WordPerfect adjusts the text and the word wrapping on the screen to reflect the new font. When you change fonts, you can still use other WordPerfect features, such as boldfacing, underlining, and centering. Figure 12-2 shows how WordPerfect will print different fonts.

NOTE *WordPerfect 6 has a ribbon that you can add to the screen by selecting **V**iew, **R**ibbon. When you display this ribbon, you can use your mouse to change the font style by clicking the font name and then selecting a font from the list. You can also change the font size by clicking the font size in the ribbon and then selecting a new size.*

FIGURE 12-2
Sample fonts

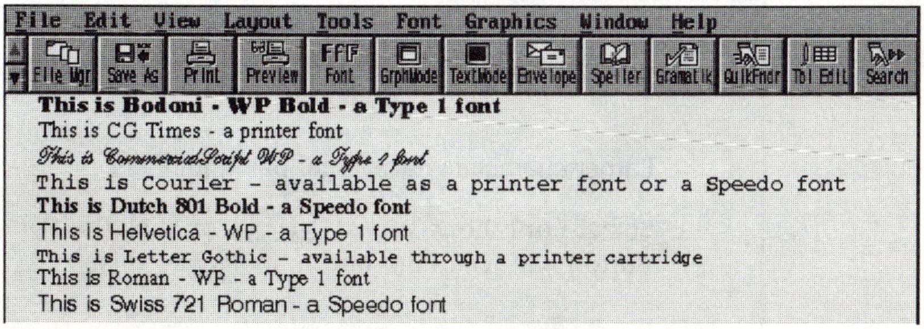

TO CHANGE THE FONT

a. Select F**o**nt, F**o**nt, press Ctrl-F8, or click the Font button in the Button Bar.

b. Select **F**ont.

c. Use the cursor movement keys to move the highlight to the font that you want, and press Enter.

d. Select **S**ize.

e. Type the size for the font, or press ↓ and highlight one of the listed sizes.

f. Press Enter.

g. Select **A**ppearance and then select **B**old, **U**nderline, **D**bl Undline, **I**talics, **O**utline, Sh**a**dow, Small **C**aps, **R**edline, or **S**trikeout if you want to add any of these effects to the text.

h. Select **P**osition and then select **N**ormal, **S**uperscript, or Su**b**script if you want to add any of these effects to the text.

i. Press Enter or click OK to select the font you have chosen.

Another method of changing the size is to select **R**elative Size and then select **N**ormal (12), **F**ine (7), **S**mall (10), **L**arge (14), **V**ery Large (18), or **E**xtra Large (24). The number in parentheses is the point size that the selection is equivalent to. When you change the font, Word-Perfect inserts the code [Font:*font name*] or [Font Size:*font size*]. *Font name* and *font size* are replaced by the font description and font size that you selected.

EXAMPLES

1. You can change the font to try different fonts in a single document. Type

   Larger characters have larger point numbers.

   Select F**o**nt, F**o**nt, press Ctrl-F8, or click the Font button in the Button Bar. The Font button looks like this:

The Font dialog box appears, as shown in Figure 12-3. Notice the Resulting Font box. This box shows sample text using the current font selections. As you make changes in the dialog box, WordPerfect adjusts the text to show how your selections will make text appear. Press F for **F**ont. WordPerfect displays the available fonts, like these:

In the list shown here, the CG Times fonts are created by the printer, a Hewlett-Packard LaserJet Series III. The Type 1 and Speedo fonts are available for most printers. Your list will be slightly different.

FIGURE 12-3

Font dialog box

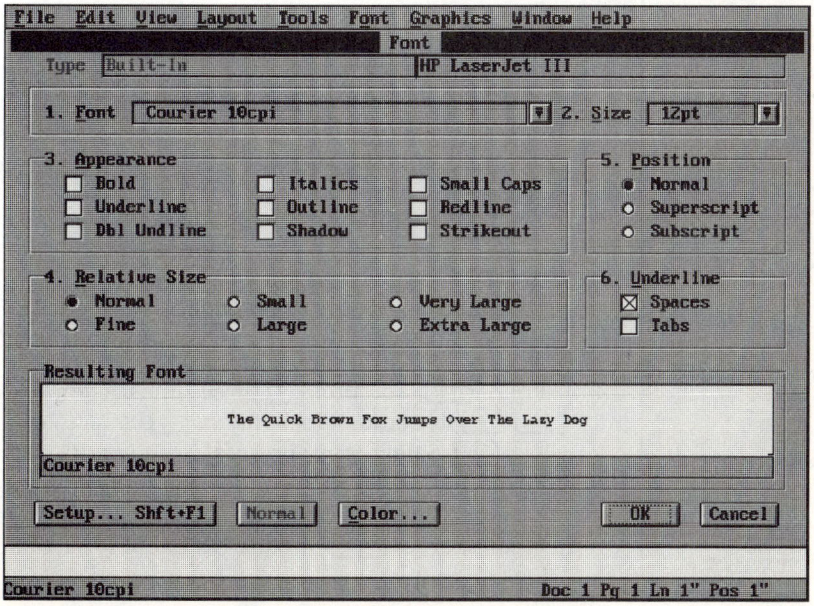

Press ↑ or ↓ to move the highlight to the Helve-WP (Type 1) font, and press Enter to select this font. Select **S**ize. Some fonts are available only in predefined sizes, but not the Helve-WP font. Type **10** for the font size, and press Enter. Press Enter again to finish with this dialog box. Next, type

Smaller characters have smaller point numbers. WordPerfect automatically adjusts for the different sizes of characters.

Notice how the bottom of the screen displays Helve-WP (Type 1). Your document looks like this:

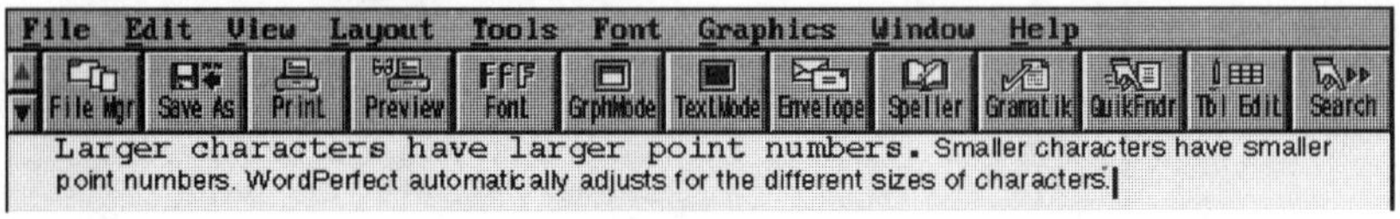

2. Some of the font selections provide other attributes. Type

   A point equals 1/72 of an inch.

   Press Enter to start a new line. Select F**o**nt, F**o**nt or press Ctrl-F8, and press F for **F**ont. Press ↓ to move the highlight to Dutch 801 Bold Italic (Speedo), and press Enter. Press S for **S**ize, type **18**, and press Enter twice. Next, type

   Therefore, an 18-point font is 1/4 of an inch high.

   Because the characters are larger, WordPerfect fits fewer characters on each line. The screen looks like this:

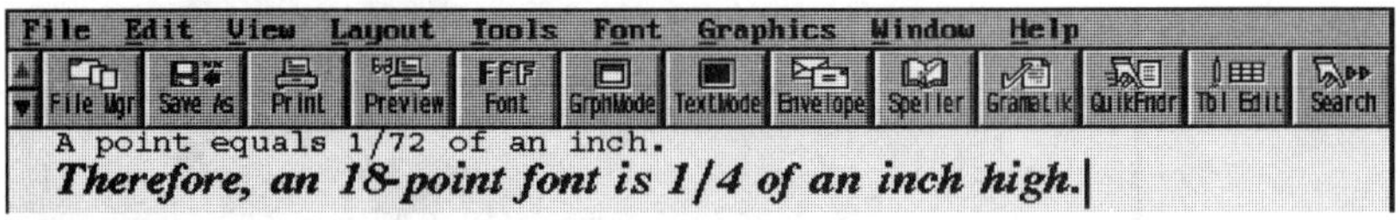

3. You can use different fonts to make a heading stand out. First, type

   ATTENTION:
   The auditors will arrive on Monday. Please provide any assistance and/or answers they require.

   Press Enter, and press ↑ three times. Then select **E**dit, **B**lock or press Alt-F4 to mark a block. Press End. Select F**o**nt, F**o**nt or press Ctrl-F8. Select **F**ont, press ↑ until you highlight Bodoni-WP Bold (Type 1), and press Enter. Select **R**elative Size and press E, for **E**xtra Large, to have the blocked text print as extra large (24-point) letters. Finally, press Enter or click OK to close the dialog box. The document looks like this:

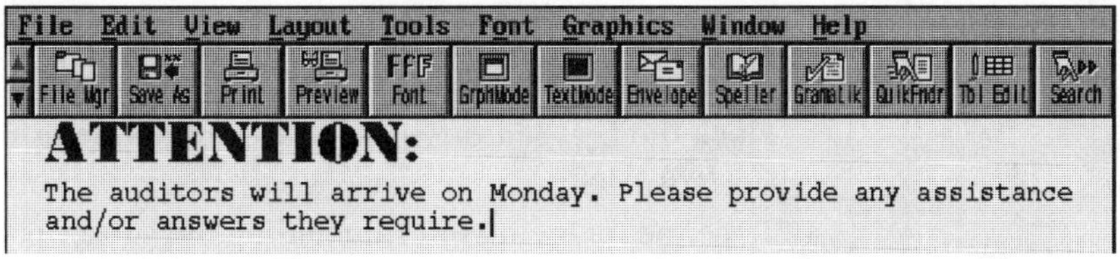

4. You can use superscripts and subscripts to type formulas. First, type **a**. Select F**o**nt, F**o**nt or press Ctrl-F8, press P for **P**osition, press S for Superscript text, and press Enter. Then type **2**, select F**o**nt, F**o**nt or press Ctrl-F8, select **P**osition, select **N**ormal, and press Enter. Next, press Spacebar, type a plus sign (+), press Spacebar, and type **b**. Select F**o**nt, F**o**nt or press Ctrl-F8, select **P**osition, select **S**uperscript, and press Enter. Then type **2**. Select F**o**nt, F**o**nt or press Ctrl-F8, select **P**osition, select **N**ormal, and press Enter. Then press Spacebar, type an equal sign (=), press Spacebar, and type **x**. Select F**o**nt, F**o**nt or press Ctrl-F8, select **P**osition, select **S**uperscript, and press Enter. Then type **2** to complete the Pythagorean theorem, which states that the square of the longest side of a right triangle is equal to the sum of the squares of the other two sides. The formula looks like this:

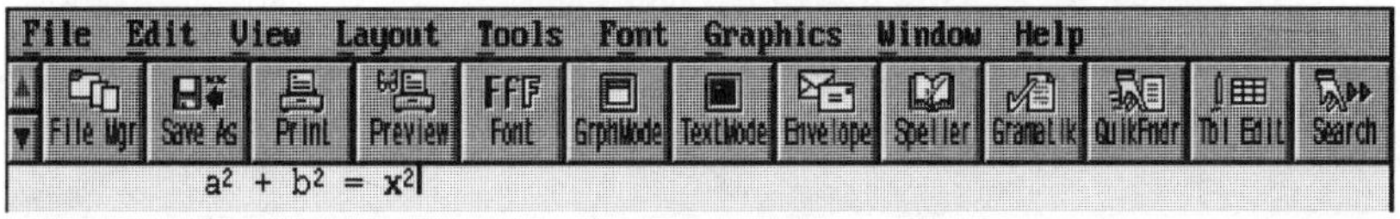

EXERCISES

1. Type the first sentence of the following paragraph. Change the font to Swiss 721 Bold (Speedo) 14 point, and type the second sentence.

   When you change the font, all characters after the font change are affected. Characters before the font change use the initial font setting.

2. Type the first sentence of the following paragraph. Change the font to Helve-WP (Type 1). Type the last two sentences of the paragraph.

   Fonts can be proportionally spaced. In proportionally spaced fonts, each character uses a different amount of space. For example, an I takes less space than an m.

3. Type the following paragraph:

Always make sure to read the fine print. It may contain information not found in other parts of the document.

Block the first sentence and change it to fine print by changing its relative size.

4. Type the following lines, including the subscript and superscript information, as shown. Press Enter twice at the end of each line.

   H_2O
   $E=mc^2$
   Subscripted text appears $_{\text{below the normal text.}}$
   Superscripted text appears $^{\text{above the normal text.}}$

5. Type the following sentences, setting the size of the characters in each line to the size described in the sentence:

   Extra large text prints like this.
   Very large text prints like this.
   Large text prints like this.
   Small text prints like this.
   Fine text prints like this.

   Block the text and change the font, without changing the size, to Roman-WP (Type 1).

mastery skills check

Do not clear the screen until you have completed the last Mastery Skills Check exercise.

1. Type the following paragraph.

   WordPerfect uses points to measure character size. A point is 1/72 of an inch. Common character sizes are 10, 12, 16, and 18 points. You can use the larger point sizes for headings.

Select this text and change the font to Swiss 721 Roman (Speedo). [12.6]

2. Change the size of the word "points" wherever it appears to 16 points. [12.6]
3. Print four copies of the document by using draft print quality. [12.1, 12.5]
4. Cancel the print request. [12.3]
5. Print two copies of the document by using high print quality. Print four copies by using draft print quality. Rush the draft print job. [12.1, 12.4, 12.5]

Teach Yourself cumulative skills check

Do not clear the screen until you have completed the last exercise.

1. Type the following paragraph:

   When you change the size and style of the characters, you change the number of characters that WordPerfect fits on each line. WordPerfect adjusts word wrapping for different font sizes, such as fine, small, and extra large. WordPerfect also adjusts word wrapping for different font styles that might use different character widths.

   Check the document for spelling errors. [9.2]
2. Save the document as WORDWRAP. Create a backup called FONTADJ. Delete the WORDWRAP file. [11.1, 11.4]
3. Change the size of the words "fine," "extra large," and "small" so that the words will print in the sizes they describe. Include the punctuation for the words when you change the sizes. [12.6]
4. Select the text and change the font to Bodoni-WP Bold (Type 1). [12.6]
5. Add the following footnote at the end of the first sentence. [10.3]

Changing the font does not change WordPerfect's other default settings, such as margins and page size.

6. Print four copies of the document by using high print quality. Print three copies. Set the text quality to draft, and print two copies. Rush the draft print request. [12.1, 12.4, 12.5]
7. Look at the file FONTADJ on disk. [11.8]

13

Working with Multiple Documents

chapter objectives

After completing this chapter, you should be able to

13.1 Change the size of a document window

13.2 Move document windows

13.3 Copy and move text between documents

WORDPERFECT permits you to have up to nine documents open at once. This allows you to refer to one document while working on another. You can copy or move information from one document to another document. You can split the screen to allow multiple documents to be visible at once.

WordPerfect maintains each document separately; changes to one document do not affect the others. You can switch between documents to edit any one, and you can save the documents in separate files.

review
skills check

As you complete the following Skills Check exercises, do not clear the screen between exercises unless instructed to do so.

1. Type the following paragraph. [2.1, 10.3]

   In March, the company exchanged 30,000 shares of newly issued common stock for $500,000 principal value of its 6% bonds. It recognized a $145,000 extraordinary gain.

   Add the following footnote at the end of the first sentence.

   These bonds were originally issued to upgrade production facilities.

2. Create a footer containing your name. [10.2]
3. Create a header that will print the word "Page" followed by a space and the page number. [6.3, 10.2]
4. Set the text quality to draft. [12.5]
5. Set the font for the document to Courier 10 Italic (Speedo). Save the file as XTRAGAIN, and clear the screen. [1.2, 2.4, 12.6]
6. Create a directory called NOTES within the WP60 directory. [11.2]
7. Back up the file XTRAGAIN to the NOTES directory by using the same filename. [11.1]
8. Print the file XTRAGAIN that is in the NOTES directory. [3.4]
9. Delete the file XTRAGAIN from the NOTES directory. [11.4]
10. Delete the NOTES directory. [11.4]

13.1 CHANGE THE SIZE OF A DOCUMENT WINDOW

WordPerfect normally displays each document window *maximized*, which means that the document window uses all of the available screen space. You can change the size of a document window so that you can see another open document window. You can review the contents of a document in one window while you work on a document in another window.

TO CHANGE THE SIZE OF A DOCUMENT WINDOW

a. Select **W**indow, **F**rame to frame the window so that it can be sized.

b. Press Ctrl-F3.

c. Select **W**indow.

d. Select **S**ize.

e. Use the arrow keys to change the size of the window frame until it is the size you want the window to be.

f. Press Enter.

You must frame the window because you use the frame to set the window's size. You can use the arrow keys to move the right side and the bottom side of the window. The upper-left corner remains anchored in one location.

You can also change the size of a window by framing it and then dragging the left, right, and bottom sides with the mouse.

EXAMPLES

1. You can change the size of a window. Open XTRAGAIN by selecting **F**ile, **O**pen or pressing Shift-F10, typing **xtragain**, and pressing Enter.

Select **W**indow, **F**rame. Notice that the filename does not appear at the top of the window until you add the frame. Press Ctrl-F3, and select **W**indow. WordPerfect displays this dialog box:

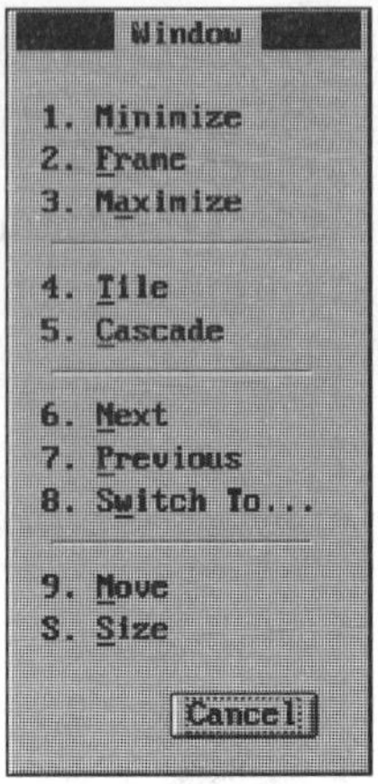

Select **S**ize, use the arrow keys to change the size of the window, and press Enter. Your screen might now look like that shown in Figure 13-1. As you can see, the window has its own filename and status line.

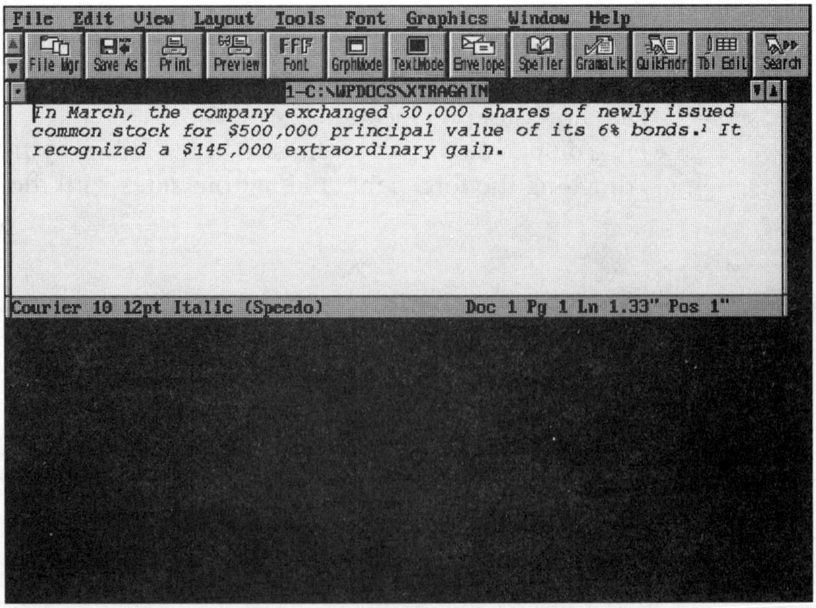

FIGURE 13-1

A sized document window

2. You can reset the window to use the full screen by maximizing the window. Select **W**indow, **M**aximize. The document window returns to its full size.

EXERCISES

1. Set the document 1 window to the full screen width but only half a screen long. Maximize the window.
2. Set the document 1 window a full screen long but only half a screen wide. Maximize the window again.

13.2 MOVE DOCUMENT WINDOWS

If you open more than one document, the documents appear directly on top of one another, and you will be able to see only one at a time. When you size the windows, their upper-left corners remain anchored in one position, so the documents still overlap. WordPerfect lets you move your document windows so that you can see all of them. You can use this feature when you want to review text in one document while typing another document.

TO MOVE A DOCUMENT WINDOW

a. Make sure the document has a frame and is sized as you want it.
b. Press Ctrl-F3.
c. Select **W**indows.
d. Select **M**ove.
e. Use the arrow keys to move the border of the window to the appropriate location.
f. Press Enter.

You can also use the mouse to move the window by dragging the document name at the top of the window to the window's new location.

EXAMPLES

1. You can move document windows so that you can see more than one window at once. First, type

   Life is made up, not of great sacrifices or duties, but of little things, in which smiles and kindness, and small obligations given habitually, are what preserve the heart and secure comfort. William Davey

   Select **W**indow, **F**rame, press Ctrl-F3, and select **W**indow. Select **S**ize. Use the arrow keys to change the size of the window so that it is the full width of the screen but only a third of the screen long. Because of the differences between monitors and the differences between text mode and graphics mode, the number of times you press ↑ will vary.

   Select **F**ile, **N**ew. Type

   The time men spend in trying to impress others they could spend in doing the things by which others would be impressed. Frank Romer

   Select **W**indow, **F**rame, press Ctrl-F3, and select **W**indow. Select **S**ize. Use the arrow keys to change the size of the window so that it is the full width of the screen but only a half of the screen long. Because of the differences between monitors and the differences between text mode and graphics mode, the number of keypresses will vary. Press Enter.

   Now you need to move the second window so that you can see the first window. In the second window, press Ctrl-F3, select **W**indow, and select **M**ove. Use the arrow keys to move the outline of the window down until the entire first window can be seen. Press Enter. Your screen should look like that shown in Figure 13-2.

   You can restore these windows to their full size. Select **W**indow, **M**aximize to maximize the second document window. Switch to the first document window by selecting **W**indow, **S**witch or pressing Shift-F3. Select **W**indow, **M**aximize again to maximize the first document window.

   Do not clear the screen, because you will use these documents in the next example.

2. You can have WordPerfect size and move your open windows automatically to let you see all of them. With the two documents created in example 1 open and maximized, select **W**indow, **T**ile. Your screen will look like that shown in Figure 13-3.

FIGURE 13-2

Two document windows on the screen

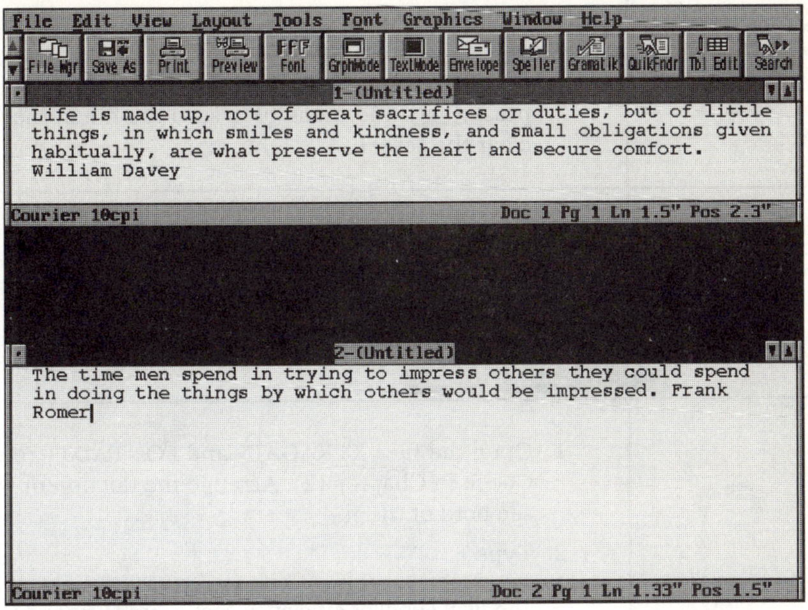

FIGURE 13-3

Two tiled document windows on the screen

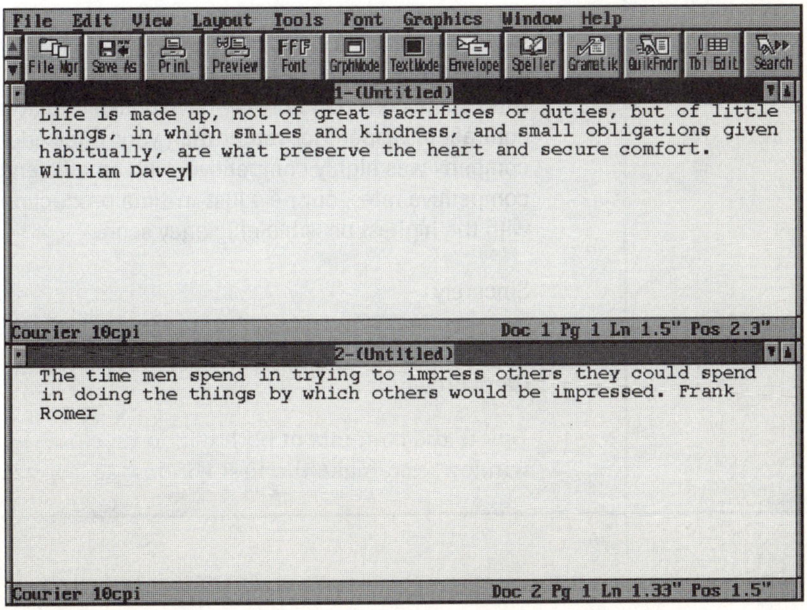

Press F7 or select **F**ile, **E**xit, press Enter, type **saying1**, press Enter, and press Y to save the file in the first window and exit the document. Press F7 or select **F**ile, **E**xit, press Enter, type **saying2**, press Enter, and press N to save the file in the second window and clear the screen.

EXERCISES

1. Open the files XTRAGAIN and FONTADJ (from the Cumulative Skills Check in Chapter 12). Arrange the document windows so that you can see both of them.
2. Type

   The final supplier efficiency scores are Diamond Corp., 92, Chalcedony Bros., 93, and Jasper Inc., 95. The committee recommends awarding the contract to Jasper Inc.

   Open a new document window. Size and arrange the two document windows so that you can see the first while working in the second. Type

   Dear John Smith:

   After some consideration, we have decided to award our purchasing contract to Jasper Inc., rather than your Chalcedony Bros. Although your company was highly competitive, with an efficiency score of 93 and competitive rates, our new just-in-time production plan requires that we go with the highest possible efficiency score.

   Sincerely,

   Carol Brown

   Delete the contents of both windows, close the second document window, and make the first window as large as possible.

13.3 COPY AND MOVE TEXT BETWEEN DOCUMENTS

You can use the techniques for copying and moving text in one document to copy and move text between documents. By using these techniques, you can recall a file from disk and use all or part of it in another document. When you move data between documents, the data from the current document is removed and placed in the other document. When you copy text, the text is left in its original location and a copy of it is placed in the other document.

TO COPY OR MOVE TEXT BETWEEN DOCUMENTS

a. Move the cursor to a character in the sentence, paragraph, or page that you want to copy or move.

b. Press Ctrl-F4.

c. Select **S**entence to copy or move a sentence, Pa**r**agraph to copy or move a paragraph, or P**a**ge to copy or move a page.

d. Select Cu**t** and Paste to move the text, or select **C**opy and Paste to copy it.

e. Switch to the other document by selecting **W**indow, **S**witch or pressing Shift-F3.

f. Move the cursor to the point at which you want the text to be placed.

g. Press Enter.

TO COPY OR MOVE BLOCKED TEXT BETWEEN DOCUMENTS

a. Move the cursor to the beginning of the text that you want to move or copy.

b. Select **E**dit, **B**lock or press Alt-F4.

c. Move the cursor to the end of the text that you want to move or copy.

d. Select **E**dit or press Ctrl-F4.

e. Select Cu**t** and Paste to move the text, or select **C**opy and Paste to copy it.

f. Select **W**indow, **S**witch or press Shift-F3 to switch to the other document.

g. Place the cursor where you want the blocked text to be copied or moved to.

h. Press Enter.

EXAMPLES

1. You can move text from one document to another. Select **F**ile, **R**etrieve, type **saying1**, and press Enter. Select **F**ile, **O**pen or press Shift-F10, type **saying2**, and press Enter.

   To move the paragraph in SAYING2 to SAYING1, press Ctrl-F4, select Pa**r**agraph, and select Cu**t** and Paste. The paragraph is removed from SAYING2.

   Next, select **W**indow, **S**witch or press Shift-F3 to return to SAYING1. Press Home twice and ↓ once to place the cursor at the end of the document. Press Enter twice. WordPerfect inserts the paragraph from SAYING2 into SAYING1 and adds a hard return.

   Do not clear the screen. You will use these documents in the next example.

2. You can copy a block of text from one document to another. To copy the two paragraphs in SAYING1 to a new document, first press Home twice and ↑ once. Select **E**dit, **B**lock or press Alt-F4, and move the cursor to the end of the second saying. Select **E**dit, Cop**y** and Paste. The highlight disappears, and the block remains in SAYING1.

   Next, select **F**ile, **N**ew to create a new document. Press Enter to place a copy of the block in the new document. Select **W**indow, **T**ile so that you can see all three of the documents you have open.

EXERCISES

1. Type the following paragraphs:

   Peter Sullivan is production vice president. He has held this position for the past three years.

Paula Atchinson is the financial vice president. She has held this position for the past two years.

Move the first paragraph to a second document, and then clear both documents.

2. Type the following name and address:

   Terry Kesley
   Kesley Associates
   496 Berry Avenue
   Newport, Rhode Island 03563

   Copy them to a second document.

mastery skills check

Do not clear the screen until you have completed the last Mastery Skills Check exercise.

1. Type the following paragraphs:

   The company has made the following accounting changes:

   Inventory valuation now uses the FIFO method instead of the LIFO method. The change to this year's income is $40,000, and the change to last year's income is $48,000. The total effect on income from prior years is $88,000.

   Contracts are now accounted for by using the percentage-of-completion method rather than the completed-contract method. This increased last year's net income by $40,000 and this year's by $60,000.

Size this document so that it is about one-fourth the length of the screen. Create a new document and switch to it. [13.1]

2. Size the second window so that it is about half a screen long, and move it to the bottom half of the screen. [13.1, 13.2]
3. Copy the first accounting change paragraph to document 2. [13.3]
4. Move the second accounting change paragraph to the beginning of document 2. [13.3]

Teach Yourself cumulative skills check

Do not clear the screen until you have completed the last exercise.

1. Type the following paragraphs:

   The company leases most of its office space and mainframe computer equipment. It owns all of its production facilities.

   Total rental expense was $1,709,000 for the current year, $998,000 for 1992, and $923,000 for 1991.

   Save these paragraphs as LEASES. Back up the file as LEASES.BAK. [2.4, 11.1]
2. Open LEASES.BAK. [2.6]
3. Add the following paragraph at the bottom of the document:

   The company's minimum lease obligations are $503,000 for 1994, $432,000 for 1995, $401,000 for 1996, $352,000 for 1997, $318,000 for 1998, and $1,293,000 for later years.

   Copy the last paragraph to the bottom of document 1. [2.1, 8.1]
4. Save document 1 as LEASES.NEW, and switch to document 2. [2.4, 2.7]

5. Create a document summary that contains the following information. [11.6]

   Descriptive Name: Notes for financial statements

   Author: [your name]

   Typist: [your name]

   Subject: For 1993 financial statements

6. Delete the file LEASES.BAK. [11.4]
7. Add the following header. [10.3]

   Financial Statement Notes

8. Create a footer that will print your name. [10.2]
9. Switch your printer offline. (If you attempted this exercise with your printer online, it is likely that the print job would finish before you could activate the Control Printer screen.) Start a print job to create two copies of the current document. Cancel the print job. Switch your printer online. [12.1, 12.3]

part three

Special Features

14

Merging Variable Information into a Standard Letter

chapter objectives

After completing this chapter, you should be able to

14.1 Create a data file

14.2 Create a form file

14.3 Produce the merge document

14.4 Print the merge document

SOMETIMES you need to create many documents that are almost identical. The only difference in the documents may be individualized information, such as a customer name and address or an account balance. Such documents are referred to as *form letters* since each of them follows an identical format. You probably receive form letters every day that have your name, address, and other personal data worked into the document. WordPerfect supports the creation of form letters with its merge features. The merge features let you integrate variable information with a document that is fixed in content and format. This capability lets you create letters, invoices, and other documents that are similar without having to type each document from scratch.

You can create a base document with special markers entered where variable information will be inserted. You can create a second document containing the variable information, such as names, addresses, and account balances. At your command, WordPerfect merges the variable information into the base document to create individualized documents.

To merge files in WordPerfect, you must have form and data document files. The *form file* contains the form letter or other nonchanging text. It also tells WordPerfect the specific locations at which information should be inserted. The *data file* contains the variable information that WordPerfect places into the form document. When the merge operation is complete, you will have individualized documents for the information in the data file. These documents will all be stored in one file in memory.

Teach Yourself
review
skills check

As you perform the Skills Check, do not clear the screen between exercises unless instructed to do so.

1. Delete the default tab stops and set tabs stops at 1.5 inches and 4 inches. Type the following letter:

Highland Graphics, Inc.
24257 N.W. 5th Street
Sunrise, FL 33146
305-331-2473

Mark Scheimer
Chairman, Education and Development
Association of Computer Graphic Artists
1347 S.W. 14 Ave.
Davie, FL 33136

Dear Mr. Scheimer,

Since my company is having a display at your upcoming forum, I need the dimensions for the display space. I also need the number of electrical outlets available for use in my display and the distance from the display to these outlets.

Sincerely,

Ann Slater
President, Highland Graphics, Inc.

Use WordPerfect's spell feature to check the spelling. [5.3, 9.2]

2. Block the name and address information for Mark Scheimer, then place a copy of the block in a new document. Tile the windows to see the contents of both documents. [2.7, 8.3, 13.2, 13.3]
3. Return to the first document. Save the document as REQUEST, then print two copies of the letter. [2.2, 12.1]
4. Print two more copies. Then cancel all print jobs. [12.1, 12.3]
5. Add the following paragraph to the letter:

   I have enclosed a list of the sales representatives who will be attending the forum.

   Add a hard page break at the end of the letter. Type the following list of names on the new page:

   Jim Styverson
   Karen Acermann
   Julie Greenlowe
   Paul Hatterfield

   Copy the list of names from the first document to the end of the second. [1.3, 13.3]

6. Add the following header to the second page of the first document. [10.2]

   Forum Attendees

7. Make a backup of the REQUEST file named LETTER.BK. [11.1]

14.1 CREATE A DATA FILE

Data files contain the information that you want WordPerfect to substitute in place of markers in a form file. Each unit of information that WordPerfect substitutes is called a *field.* WordPerfect has no limit on the amount of text that a field can contain; different fields may contain one word, one line, multiple lines, or they may be blank.

WordPerfect refers to each field by a number; for example, the second field is field 2. The set of fields that WordPerfect uses for each part of a merge document is called a *record.* WordPerfect has no limit on the number of records that your data file can contain.

TO CREATE A DATA FILE

a. Type the information for the first field.
b. Press F9 to end the field.
c. Type the information for the additional fields of a record, pressing F9 each time you finish a field.
d. Select **T**ools, M**e**rge, **D**efine. You can also press Shift-F9.
e. Select **E**nd Record and OK.
f. Repeat steps a through e for each record.
g. Save the file.

The first time you perform step d, you must first select OK from the Merge Codes dialog box. This dialog box lets WordPerfect know that you are creating a data file rather than a form file. Once WordPerfect knows you are creating a data file, you will not see the dialog box again. As you perform these steps, WordPerfect adds codes to the file. The default for WordPerfect is to display these codes as ENDFIELD and ENDRECORD. If you look at the hidden codes, ENDFIELD will appear as [MRG:ENDFIELD] and ENDRECORD will appear as [MRG:ENDRECORD].

EXAMPLES

1. You can create a record containing different fields of data in a data file. The record can contain fields for a person's name, title, company, the first line of the address, the second line of the address, the phone number, and a salutation to use in a form letter to the person. First, type **Mary Ann Kelley**. Next, press F9. The screen looks like this:

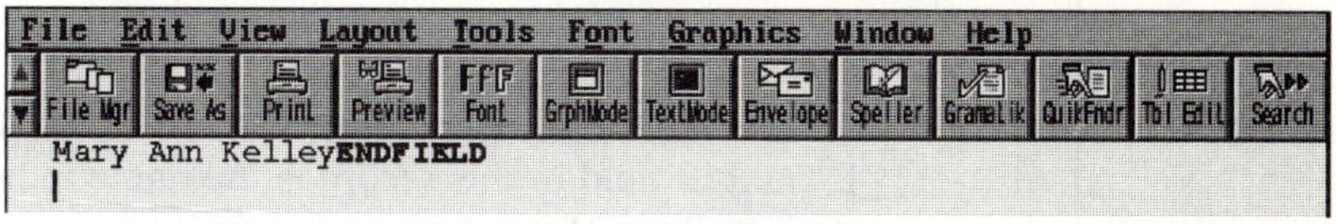

Next, enter the field for the title by typing **President** and pressing F9. Enter the field for the company by typing **Kelley Graphics** and pressing F9. The screen now looks like this:

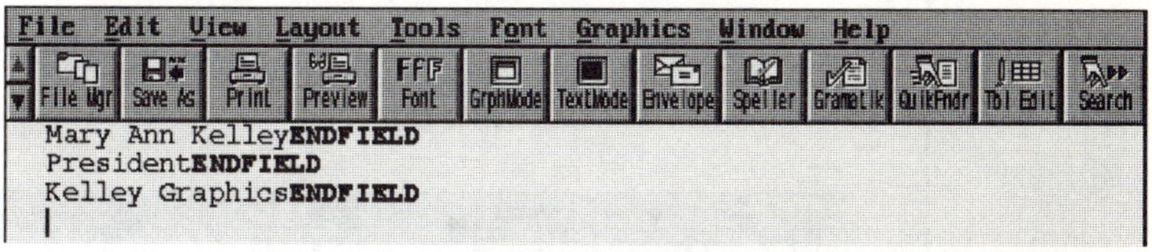

You can complete the address fields by typing **6035 N.E. 25th Avenue**, pressing F9, typing **Lighthouse Point, FL 33041**, and pressing F9 again. Next, type **(305)275-6582** and press F9 to add the phone number field to the record. Add the name to be used in a salutation by typing **Mary Ann** and pressing F9 to mark the end of that field.

Finally, select **T**ools, M**e**rge, **D**efine or press Shift-F9. From the Merge Codes dialog box, select OK, since WordPerfect has correctly chosen the **D**ata [Text] option button for the type of file you are creating. Select **E**nd Record. This ends the record you have just entered. The record now looks like this:

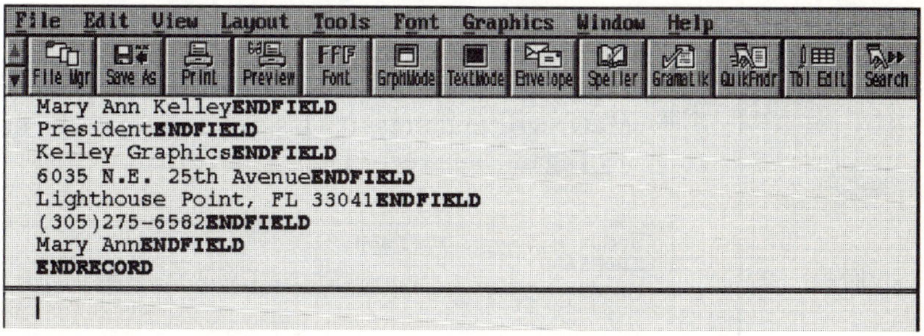

2. You can put multiple lines in a field. The same record that you typed can be entered with two lines in the address field instead of one. First,

type **Mary Ann Kelley** and press F9. Next, type **President** and press F9. Then, type **Kelley Graphics** and press F9.

You can use two lines for the address. Type **6035 N.E. 25th Avenue**, press Enter, type **Lighthouse Point, FL 33041**, and press F9 to end the field. The two lines look like this:

```
6035 N.E. 25th Avenue
Lighthouse Point, FL 33041ENDFIELD
```

To include the telephone number, type **(305)275-6582** and press F9. The last field in this record is the name to be used in the salutation. Type **Mary Ann** and press F9.

Finally, select **T**ools, M**e**rge, **D**efine or press Shift-F9. From the Merge Codes dialog box, select OK, since WordPerfect has correctly chosen the **D**ata [Text] option button for the type of file you are creating. Select **E**nd Record. This ends the record you have just entered and adds a page break to keep the records separate. The record now looks like this:

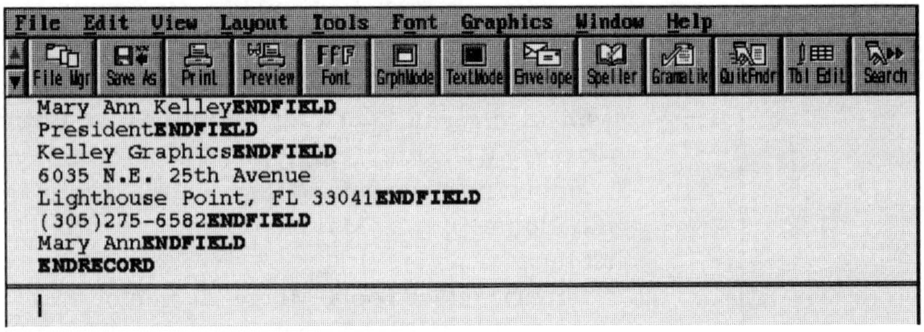

Keep this record on the screen to use in the next example.

3. You can create records that do not include information in all fields. However, you must tell WordPerfect which fields are empty so that it will continue to use the proper fields after it reaches a field you are skipping. Create a record without a title or company. First, type **Scott McGregor** and press F9. Next, since he does not have a title, press F9 again. The record looks like this:

```
Scott McGregorENDFIELD
ENDFIELD
```

The second ENDFIELD tells WordPerfect that the information to the left of it is for the second field. Since there is nothing to the left of it,

WordPerfect will recognize that the second field is blank. Since Scott McGregor does not have a company name, press F9 again.

Fill in the address field by typing **503 S.W. 6th Avenue**, pressing Enter, typing **Pompano, FL 33167**, and pressing F9. To complete the phone number field, type **(305)465-6734** and press F9. To include the first name for a salutation, type **Scott** and press F9.

Finally, since the salutation field is the last one, select **T**ools, M**e**rge, **D**efine or press Shift-F9. Select **E**nd Record to complete the record you have just entered. The completed record for Scott McGregor looks like this:

```
Scott McGregorENDFIELD
ENDFIELD
ENDFIELD
503 S.W. 6th Avenue
Pompano, FL 33167ENDFIELD
(305)465-6734ENDFIELD
ScottENDFIELD
ENDRECORD
```

The document now contains two records that are ready to be combined with a form file, which you will create in section 14.2. Save the document you just created as NAMES by selecting **F**ile, **E**xit or pressing F7. Then select **Y**es, type **names**, and press Enter. Select **N**o to stay in WordPerfect.

EXERCISES

1. Create a data file that contains the following four records:

B. J. Smith	231-46-4232
Carroll Lawrence	564-90-5327
Sara Graham	976-95-3194
Ellen Pelton	687-64-6546

2. Retrieve the NAMES file created in example 3. Using the same format, add the following record to the data file and save the revised file:

Paul Stevens
Vice President

Stevens & Stevens
635 Dover Street
Daytona Beach, FL 34240
(305)287-3863
Paul

3. Add another record to the NAMES data file, using your own information. Save the revised file.

14.2 CREATE A FORM FILE

A form file contains the text that is to appear in each form letter or other merge document. It also contains merge codes that instruct WordPerfect where to place the different fields when the form file merges with the data file. You do not have to use all of the available fields in the form file; you can use any of the fields you want, in any order you choose. You can also use a field more than once in the form file.

You might find it worthwhile to print a page of a data file format to help you correctly identify the field numbers when you create a form file. Each piece of data in a record that ends with an ENDFIELD is a field.

TO CREATE A FORM FILE

a. Type the text as you want it to appear in each merge document. Where the final documents will display individualized information, leave the form file blank.

b. Place the cursor where you want WordPerfect to substitute one of the fields from the data file.

c. Select **T**ools, Me**r**ge, **D**efine or press Shift-F9.

d. Select **F**ield.

e. Type the number of the field containing the information that you want inserted at that spot.

f. Press Enter.

g. Repeat steps b through f for each field in the data file that you want placed in the form file when WordPerfect merges the files.

h. Save the file.

The first time you perform step c, you must also select OK from the Merge Codes dialog box. This dialog box lets WordPerfect know that you are creating a form file rather than a data file. Once WordPerfect knows you are creating a data file, you will not see the dialog box again. In the form file document, WordPerfect displays FIELD(*n*), where *n* represents the field number. If you look at the codes for what you have just created, you will see [MRG:FIELD] before the field number and [mrg:field] after the field number.

EXAMPLES

1. You can create a form file that generates address labels. Since the address labels will include only text that is in the data file, the form file will consist of only field references. First, select **T**ools, M**e**rge, **D**efine or press Shift-F9. Select OK, since WordPerfect correctly selected the **F**orm option button. Select **F**ield. From the Parameter Entry dialog box, WordPerfect prompts you for a field number. Type **1** for the field containing the person's name in each record, and press Enter. Press Enter to move to the next line. The screen now looks like this:

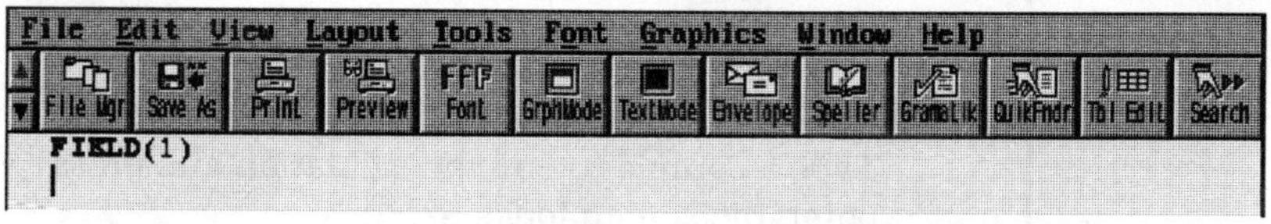

Add the merge code for the field containing the person's title by selecting **T**ools, M**e**rge, **D**efine or pressing Shift-F9. Select **F**ield, type **2**, and press Enter. Press Enter to move to the next line.

Add the merge code for the field containing the company name by selecting **T**ools, M**e**rge, **D**efine or pressing Shift-F9. Select **F**ield, type **3**, and press Enter. Press Enter to move to the next line.

Add the merge code for the field containing the company address by selecting **T**ools, M**e**rge, **D**efine or pressing Shift-F9. Select **F**ield, type **4**, and press Enter. Even though the address uses two lines in the data file, the form file requires only one, since WordPerfect will use the hard return in that field when it merges the files. The form file looks like this:

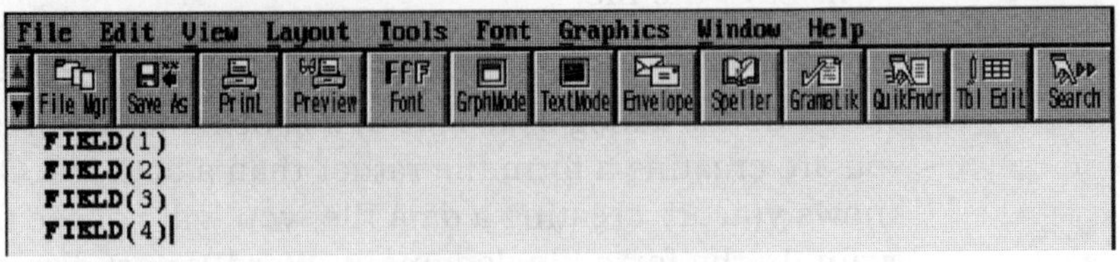

Finally, save this document as LABELS by selecting **F**ile, **E**xit or pressing F7. Then select **Y**es, type **labels**, press Enter, and select **N**o.

2. You can create a form letter that confirms reservations. The first part of a letter is the inside address. This address is the information contained in the data file that you created earlier. First, select **T**ools, M**e**rge, **D**efine or press Shift-F9. Select OK, since WordPerfect correctly selected the **F**orm option button. Select **F**ield. Type **1** in response to WordPerfect's prompt for a field number and press Enter. Press Enter to move to the next line.

   Add the field name for the title by selecting **T**ools, M**e**rge, **D**efine or pressing Shift-F9. Select **F**ield, type **2**, and press Enter. Press Enter to move to the next line.

   Add the merge code for the field containing the company name by selecting **T**ools, M**e**rge, **D**efine or pressing Shift-F9. Select **F**ield, type **3**, and press Enter. Press Enter to move to the next line.

   Add the merge code for the field containing the company address by selecting **T**ools, M**e**rge, **D**efine or pressing Shift-F9. Select **F**ield, type **4**, and press Enter. Since WordPerfect will use the hard return in field 4 in the data file when it merges the files, you need to use only one line for this field in the form file. Press Enter twice to place a blank line between the inside address and the salutation.

   To create the salutation, type **Dear**, press Spacebar, select **T**ools, M**e**rge, **D**efine or press Shift-F9. Select **F**ield, type **6**, and press Enter. Type a comma to end the salutation and press Enter twice. At this point, the screen looks like this:

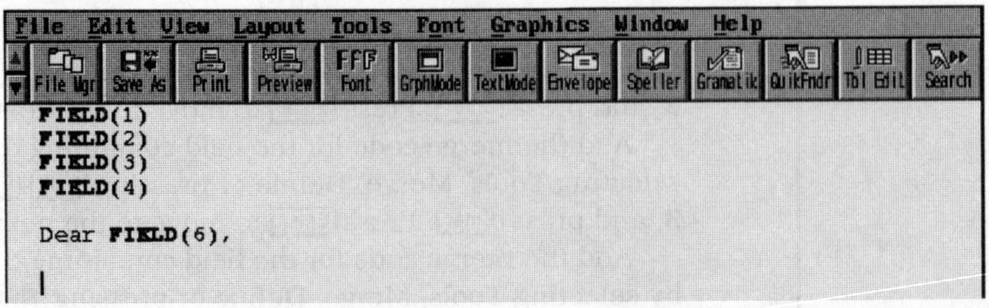

Type the body and closing of the letter as follows, using the 3.5-inch tab stop for the closing:

Enclosed are the registration materials for the upcoming forum, Taking Computer Graphics One Step Further. Please return the completed forms no later than the end of the month to insure that you are registered in time.

Sincerely,

Mark Scheimer
Chairman, Education and Development
Association of Computer Graphic Artists

Encl: (3)

This form file does not use field 5, which contains phone numbers. Save the file as REGIS. Select **F**ile, **E**xit or press F7. Then select **Y**es, type **regis**, press Enter, and select **N**o.

3. You can modify merge codes in a form file so that WordPerfect will not include blank data file fields. Select **T**ools, M**e**rge, **D**efine or press Shift-F9. Select OK, since WordPerfect correctly selected the **F**orm option button. Select **F**ield. Type **1** in response to WordPerfect's prompts for a field number and press Enter. Press Enter to move to the next line.

   Next, select **T**ools, M**e**rge, **D**efine or press Shift-F9. Select **F**ield, type **2?**, and press Enter.

   The ? after the field number tells WordPerfect to use this field in a merge only if the field contains information. If the field is blank, WordPerfect will not include it when it merges the record. Press Enter to move to the next line. The screen looks like this:

To include the third field, company name, select **T**ools, M**e**rge, **D**efine or press Shift-F9. Select **F**ield, type **3?**, and press Enter. Press Enter again to move to the next line.

For the address, select **T**ools, M**e**rge, **D**efine or press Shift-F9. Select **F**ield, type **4**, and press Enter. The address uses two lines, but the form file requires only one, since WordPerfect will incorporate the hard return in the data file when it merges the two. Press Enter twice to place a blank line between the address and the salutation.

To create the salutation, type **Dear**, press the Spacebar, and select **T**ools, M**e**rge, **D**efine or press Shift-F9. Select **F**ield, type **6**, and press

Enter. Type a comma and press Enter twice. The screen now looks like the following:

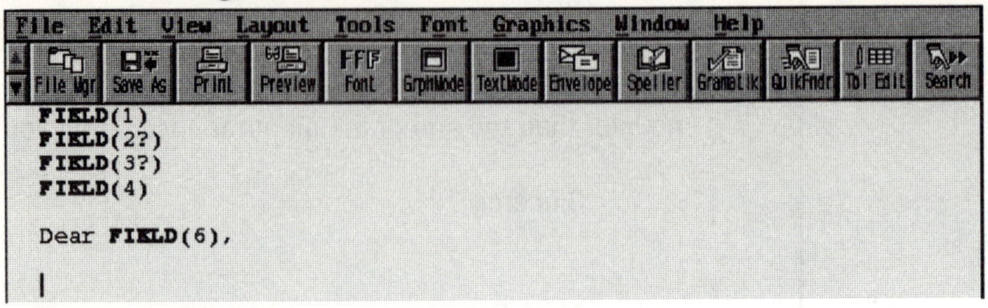

Type the body and closing of the letter as follows, using the 3.5-inch tab stop for the closing:

Enclosed are the registration materials for the upcoming forum, Taking Computer Graphics One Step Further. Please return the completed forms no later than the end of the month to insure that you are registered in time.

Sincerely,

Mark Scheimer
Chairman, Education and Development
Association of Computer Graphic Artists

Encl: (3)

If you did not use question marks, WordPerfect would print blank lines for Scott McGregor's title and company when it merged this form file with the data file containing his record.

Save this file by selecting **F**ile, **E**xit or pressing F7. Then press Enter (or select **Y**es), type **register**, and press Enter. Select **N**o to stay in WordPerfect.

EXERCISES

1. Create a form file for the following form letter, replacing the information in parentheses with merge codes for fields. Assume that the data file is in the format of the examples in section 14.1.

   The Association of Computer Graphic Artists wishes to thank (person's name) from (person's company) for assisting with the Taking Computer Graphics One Step Further forum.

Save this file as THANKS.

2. Create a form file for the following form letter, substituting the information in parentheses with merge codes for fields. Assume that the data file is in the format of example 2 in section 14.1. Use the 3.5-inch tab stop for the closing.

(full name)
(title)
(company)
(address)

Dear (first name),

To stimulate attendance at your display during the upcoming forum, we are providing cards for you to distribute. These cards are professionally printed on high-quality paper. The format of these cards is as follows:
(company name)
(address)
(phone number)

Contact: (person's name)
(title)

If you prefer a different format, call us at (501) 365-2352 by next Monday.

Sincerely,

Mark Scheimer
Chairman, Education and Development
Association of Computer Graphic Artists

Save the file as CARDS and clear the screen.

14.3 PRODUCE THE MERGE DOCUMENT

Once you have created the form and data files, you are ready to produce the merge document. When you merge the two files, you create another document that contains a copy of the form file for each record in the data file. The new copies have the information from each field substituted for the merge code for the field number in the form file. WordPerfect automatically inserts a page break after merging each data file record.

WordPerfect has many other merge features that are beyond the scope of this book. These features are covered in the WordPerfect manual, in *WordPerfect 6 Made Easy* by Mella Mincberg (Berkeley, CA: Osborne/McGraw-Hill, 1993), and in *The Best 1001 WordPerfect Tips Ever* by Mary Campbell (Berkeley, CA: Osborne/McGraw-Hill, 1993).

TO CREATE A MERGE DOCUMENT

a. Select **T**ools, M**e**rge, **R**un. You can also press Ctrl-F9 and select **M**erge.

b. Type the name of the form file and press Enter.

c. Type the name of the data file and press Enter.

d. Select the Merge button to create the merged document.

WordPerfect merges the files you specified. It automatically adjusts line spacing and word wrap to accommodate the substitution of the data file information for the merge codes for field numbers.

EXAMPLE

You can combine the form file created in the examples in section 14.2 with the data file created in the examples in section 14.1. Select **T**ools, M**e**rge, **R**un. You can also press Ctrl-F9 and select **M**erge. WordPerfect displays this dialog box:

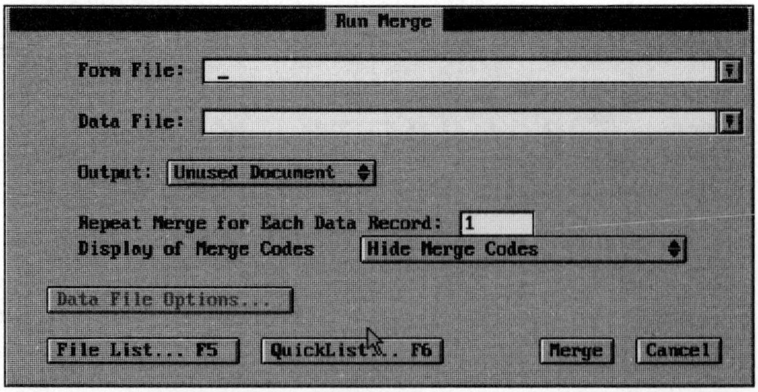

FIGURE 14-1
WordPerfect screen showing a merge document

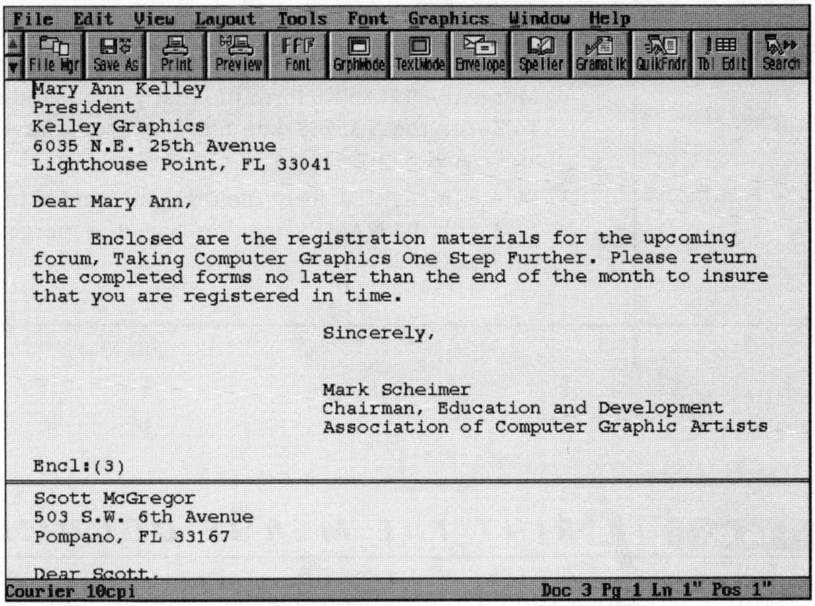

Type **register** as the name of the form file, and press Enter. Type **names** as the name of the data file and press Enter. Press Enter to merge the two documents.

The letter containing your name should appear on the screen. Press Home twice and ↑ once to view the first two letters. Figure 14-1 shows the beginning of two letters that result from WordPerfect's replacing the merge codes for field numbers in the form file with the contents of the fields in the data file.

Save the merge document by selecting **F**ile, **E**xit or pressing F7. Then press Enter, type **rgstr**, and press Enter. Select **N**o to remain in WordPerfect.

EXERCISES

1. Merge the THANKS form file that you created in exercise 1 in section 14.2 with the NAMES data file. You should save the merge document as THANKS.OUT.
2. Merge the CARDS form file that you created in exercise 2 in section 14.2 with the NAMES data file. Save the merge document as CARDS.OUT.

14.4 PRINT THE MERGE DOCUMENT

Once you have produced the merge document, you can print it. You can print a merge document from disk if you've saved it, or you can print it directly from memory. You can use the same print features that work with printing regular documents.

TO PRINT A MERGE DOCUMENT

a. Select **F**ile, **P**rint or press Shift-F7.
b. Select the **F**ull Document option button.
c. Select **P**rint to have WordPerfect print the merge document.

TO PRINT A MERGE DOCUMENT FROM DISK

a. Select **F**ile, **P**rint or press Shift-F7.
b. Select the **D**ocument on Disk option button.
c. Type the name of the merge document that you saved and press Enter.
d. Type the numbers of the pages that you want printed and select OK, or select OK to print the entire document.
e. Select P**r**int to cause WordPerfect to print the document.

EXAMPLE

You can print the merge document that you created in the example in section 14.3. Select **F**ile, **P**rint or press Shift-F7. Select **D**ocument on Disk, type **rgstr**, and press Enter twice. The printed pages look just like the ones you see on your screen in graphics display mode or when you preview the printed document.

EXERCISES

1. Print the merge document THANKS.OUT, which you created in exercise 1 in section 14.3.
2. Print the merge document CARDS.OUT, which you created in exercise 2 in section 14.3.

mastery skills check

1. Create a data file that contains records with the following information. Each line represents a separate field.

   Karen Simon
   34220 Euclid Avenue
   Cleveland, OH 44134

   Jim Darcy
   12353 Carnegie Avenue
   Lakewood, OH 44116

   Save the file as NAMES2. [14.1]

2. Create a form file that creates address labels when merged with the data file NAMES2. Save the form file as LBLS. Merge the form and data files and print the merge document. [14.2, 14.3, 14.4]
3. Retrieve the NAMES2 data file. Add a field below the first three fields for the first name, to be used as a salutation in form letters. Save the revised file as NAMES2. [14.1]
4. Create a form file containing a letter to be used with NAMES2. Use the following as the letter body:

   According to our records, we cannot finish processing the application until you send two ID-sized photos. Please send these photos so that your application to the Radio Controlled Planes Club may be processed.

   Sincerely,

   Tim Powers
   Membership Director

   Save the file as PHOTOS. Merge this file with the NAMES2 data file and print the merge document. [14.2, 14.3, 14.4]
5. Retrieve the PHOTOS form file and modify it so that the person's first name and a comma appear after "According to our records." Save the revised file. Merge the file with the NAMES2 data file and print the merge document. [14.2, 14.3, 14.4]

Teach Yourself: cumulative skills check

Do not clear the screen between exercises unless instructed to do so.

1. Create a data file that contains records with the following information:

Thomas Douglas
Dept. Manager, Accounting
X3963

Tanya Smith
Dept. Manager, Data Processing
X3959

Save the file as NAMES.TWO. Clear the screen. [2.4, 14.1]

2. Create a form file that contains the following memo. Replace the parenthetical information with a merge code, or fill in the information, as appropriate. Use the format of the data file created in exercise 1 for field numbers. [14.2]

Memo
To: (name)
(title)
(phone number)
Date: (today's date)
From: (your name)
Re: Smoking Areas

In compliance with local ordinances, the company must limit smoking to a designated area. The designated smoking area is the cafeteria's west end. Please inform the staff of your department. This is effective immediately.

3. Center the word "Memo." [4.3, 4.7]
4. Place a hyphenated line between "Memo" and "To." Save the file as SMOKERS and clear the screen. [1.2, 1.3, 2.4]
5. Merge the SMOKERS form file with the NAMES.TWO data file. [14.3]
6. Print two copies of the merge document. [12.1, 14.4]
7. Clear the screen. Retrieve the data file into document 1 and the form file into document 2. Resize and move the windows so you can see as much of the form document as possible, while seeing a complete record in the data document. [1.2, 2.5, 13.2]

15

Adding a Column of Numbers

chapter objectives

After completing this chapter, you should be able to

15.1 Obtain a total for a column of numbers

15.2 Use multilevel totals

WORDPERFECT'S math feature is not designed to do heavy-duty calculating like a spreadsheet program. It does, however, have basic math capabilities that can perform simple calculations. In this chapter, you will add a column of numbers to produce a subtotal. You will also add subtotals to produce a total and combine totals into a grand total.

You will want to master the basic math features presented in this chapter to guarantee that expense reports, invoices, and other such documents are accurate.

review skills check

1. Clear the default tab stops. Create tab settings at 1.5 inches, 2 inches, and 4 inches. Reset the tab stops to the default setting. [5.3]
2. Type the following paragraph, using bold and underline where indicated. [4.1, 4.2]

   We have written several times to inquire about the status of **order number 98754**. Please check the status of the back-ordered items. If you are unable to fill the remainder of the order within 10 days, please notify us so that we can contact other suppliers.

3. Type the following, using Ctrl-R to draw the line. [1.2, 5.3]

   150
    50
   100

   300

4. Type the following, using bold where indicated:

   You can use an 's to create the plural of letters, numbers, symbols, and words. For example, you could write that there are four s's and four i's in **Mississi**ppi.

   Print two copies of the paragraph. [3.1, 4.2]

5. Type the following:

   Errors, like straws, upon the surface flow;
   He who would search for pearls, must dive below.
   John Dryden

   Use the block feature to make two more copies of the quotation and author name. [8.3]

15.1 OBTAIN A TOTAL FOR A COLUMN OF NUMBERS

Many of the documents that you create may contain columns of figures. Rather than use a calculator to obtain the correct total at the bottom of a column, you can use WordPerfect's math features.

WordPerfect's math features require a bit of advanced planning and a little extra care on your part. You must follow a set procedure, placing the math entries in columns set with tab stops. The math features use a special symbol to tell WordPerfect that you wish to add the numbers in a column.

Once you have learned the process, abiding by the rules is not difficult. Your reward is column totals that are always accurate, whether you are preparing commission reports, purchase orders, or the company bowling team's scores.

TO CALCULATE A TOTAL FOR A COLUMN OF NUMBERS

a. Place the cursor where you wish to use the math features.
b. Set tab stops for the columns you plan to use.
c. Select **T**ools, Math, **O**n or press Alt-F7, select **M**ath, then select the Math **O**n check box, and click OK.
d. Type the labels and numbers as column entries.
e. Type a plus sign (+) where you want the total calculated.
f. Select **T**ools, Math, **C**alculate or press Alt-F7 and select **M**ath, **C**alculate to calculate the total.
g. Select **T**ools, Math, **C**alculate or press Alt-F7, select **M**ath, clear the Math **O**n check box, then select OK to turn math off.

The hidden codes [Math:On] and [Math:Off] mark the beginning and ending locations for math. These steps produce what WordPerfect refers to as a subtotal for the column. WordPerfect uses the hidden code [Do Subtot], entered when you type a plus sign, to mark where it computes the subtotal. In many documents, the subtotal is all you need.

EXAMPLES

1. You can use WordPerfect's math features to add amounts in an invoice. First, type the top of the invoice. Type the following three lines, pressing Shift-F6 at the beginning of each line to center it:

   ABC COMPANY
   Invoice Number 889-3452
   As of August 6, 1993

   Press Enter twice. The screen looks like this:

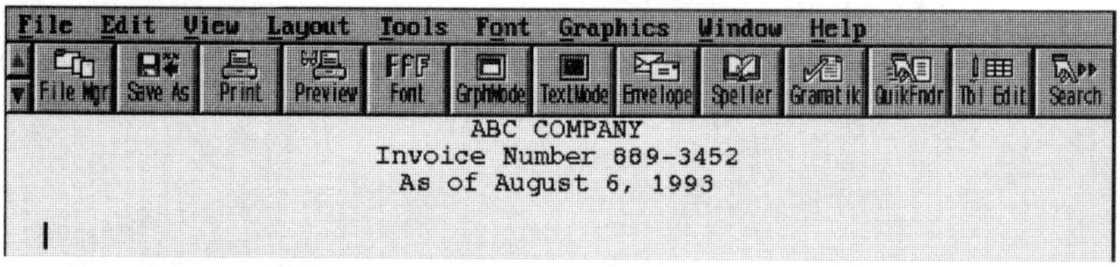

   You are now ready to set the tabs for the math columns. Since you can store the text descriptions at the left margin, you need only one tab stop for the numeric column. Select **L**ayout, **T**ab Set to open the Tab Set dialog box. Clear all the tabs by selecting the Clear **A**ll button. Move to the **S**et Tab text box, type **4.5**, and press Enter. Press D to change the tab to a decimal tab, which aligns numbers on their decimal points. Select OK to return to the document.

   Select **T**ools, Ma**t**h, **O**n or press Alt-F7, select **M**ath, then select the Math **O**n check box, and OK. WordPerfect can perform calculations only in an area of the document where the math feature is on.

   Type **Desk**, press Tab, and type **249.95**. WordPerfect places the decimal point at the tab stop. Press Enter, type **Chair (side)**, press Tab, and type **98.75**. Press Enter, type **Chair (desk)**, press Tab, and type **185.00**. For the last item, press Enter, type **Lamp**, press Tab, type **59.95**, and press Enter.

You can use a plus sign (+) to make WordPerfect add the numbers in the column. First, press the Tab key to position the cursor in the numeric column. Next, type a **+**. Nothing seems to happen, as the plus sign only marks the place where you want the calculation; it does not perform the calculation. If you have the Reveal Codes screen open, you can see that WordPerfect inserts the hidden code [Do Subtot] rather than a + at this place. The screen looks like Figure 15-1. Select **T**ools, Ma**t**h, **C**alculate or press Alt-F7 and select **M**ath, **C**alculate. The result on the screen should match Figure 15-2. When you print this document, the + sign will not appear on the printed copy.

You must now turn off the math feature. Press Enter, then select **T**ools, Ma**t**h, O**f**f or press Alt-F7, select **M**ath, and clear the Math **O**n check box. Select OK. WordPerfect inserts the [Math:Off] hidden code, and the math features are inactive at the current cursor position. A + sign typed outside of the document area where math is on cannot total a column of numbers.

Do not clear the screen, so you can use these entries in the next example.

2. You can revise mathematical calculations that have already been defined. Move the cursor to the 8 in 185.00. Notice that the **Math** indicator reappears on the status line. Press the Ins key to invoke typeover mode, type **7**, and press Ins again to turn typeover mode off. The new number appears in the column, but the subtotal is unchanged. You must recalculate the subtotal. Select **T**ools, Ma**t**h, **C**alculate or press Alt-F7 and select **M**ath, **C**alculate. The new subtotal, 593.65, appears at the bottom of the column.

   Do not clear the screen, so you can use these entries in the next example.

3. You can insert a new item in a column and include its value in the subtotal. First, move the cursor to the *L* in "Lamp." Press the Enter key

FIGURE 15-1

Plus sign used for subtotal

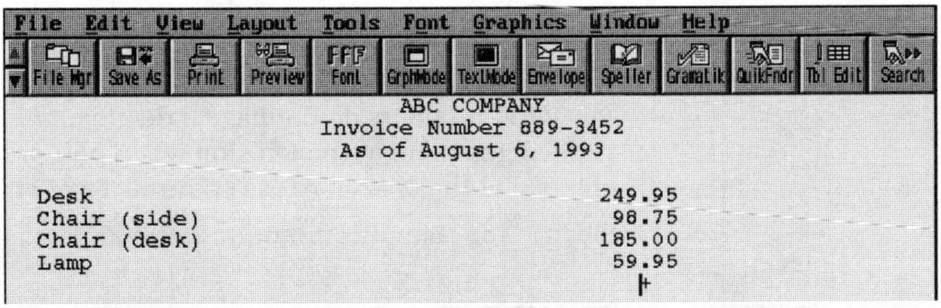

FIGURE 15-2 *Subtotal calculated*

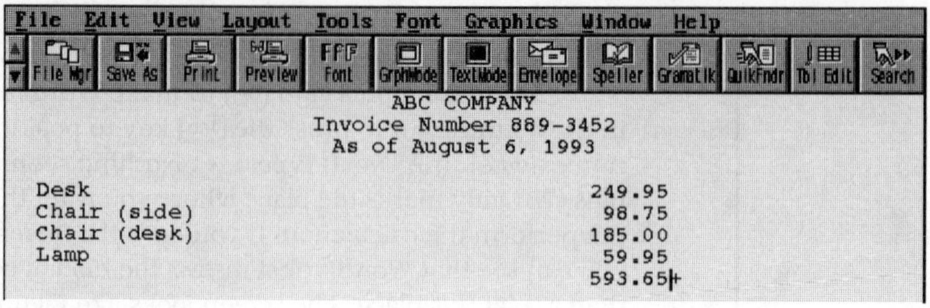

to add a new line and use the ↑ key to move the cursor to it. Type **Credenza** and press the Tab key. Type **205.75**. Again, the subtotal needs to be recalculated. Select **T**ools, Ma**t**h, **C**alculate or press Alt-F7 and select **M**ath, **C**alculate. The new subtotal, 799.40, appears at the bottom of the column.

Save the file by selecting **F**ile, **E**xit or pressing F7. Then select **Y**es, type **invoice**, and select OK. Select **N**o to remain in WordPerfect.

EXERCISES

As you perform the exercises, do not clear the screen unless you are told to do so.

1. Set a decimal tab stop at 3 inches and create math columns for the following entries:

Salaries	50,000
Benefits	8,500
Travel	18,000
Rent	120,000

   Since the numbers do not have a decimal point, WordPerfect right-aligns them at the tab stop when you press Enter. Calculate a subtotal at the bottom of the column. Turn off the math feature.

2. Change the "Benefits" amount to **8,900**. Recalculate the subtotal.

15.2 USE MULTILEVEL TOTALS

WordPerfect supports multiple levels of totals. You can calculate subtotals for columns of entries, add subtotals, and even create a grand total. Each level requires a different symbol to indicate which entries you want WordPerfect to add together.

You can place all of your totals in the same column, or you can use the columns to the right of your entries to show different levels of totals. If you elect to use extra columns, you must use another math feature to define the columns before making your entries.

TO CREATE MULTIPLE LEVELS OF TOTALS

a. Place the cursor where you wish to use the math features.

b. Set tab stops for the columns you plan to use.

c. Select **T**ools, Ma**t**h, **D**efine or press Alt-F7 and select **M**ath, **D**efine.

d. Change the settings as appropriate for each column you will use and select OK. If you used Alt-F7, select OK twice.

e. Select **T**ools, Ma**t**h, **O**n or press Alt-F7, select **M**ath, and the Math **O**n check box. Select OK to turn math on.

f. Type the labels and numbers as the column entries.

g. Press the Tab key to move the cursor to the appropriate column and type a plus sign (+) to calculate a subtotal, an equal sign (=) to calculate a total from subtotals, or an asterisk (*) to calculate a grand total.

h. Select **T**ools, Ma**t**h, **C**alculate or press Alt-F7 and select **M**ath, **C**alculate to calculate the total.

i. Select **T**ools, Ma**t**h, O**f**f or press Alt-F7, select **M**ath, and clear the Math **O**n check box. Select OK to turn math off.

The special code [Math Def] marks the math definition in the Reveal Codes screen; [Do Total] marks where WordPerfect will compute the total; and [Do Grand Tot] marks where WordPerfect will compute the grand total.

EXAMPLES

1. You can add subtotals together. You can place this total in the same column as the subtotals or in a separate column to the right. If you wish to use a separate column, you must be sure the column is defined appropriately.

   You can use this feature to find the total of the salaries paid to sales representatives on the East Coast. In addition to defining the columns for the numeric entries and totals, you can define other text columns to allow for the indentation of various levels of entries.

   The first step is to define the tab settings for all of the columns. Select **L**ayout, **T**ab Set. Select the Clear **A**ll button to clear the tab settings. Create left-aligned tab stops at 0.2 inches, 0.5 inches, and 0.7 inches by selecting **S**et Tab, typing these numbers and pressing Enter. Create decimal tab stops at 3.5 inches and 5.0 inches by selecting **S**et Tab, typing these numbers, pressing Enter, and selecting **D**ecimal. The tab settings look like this:

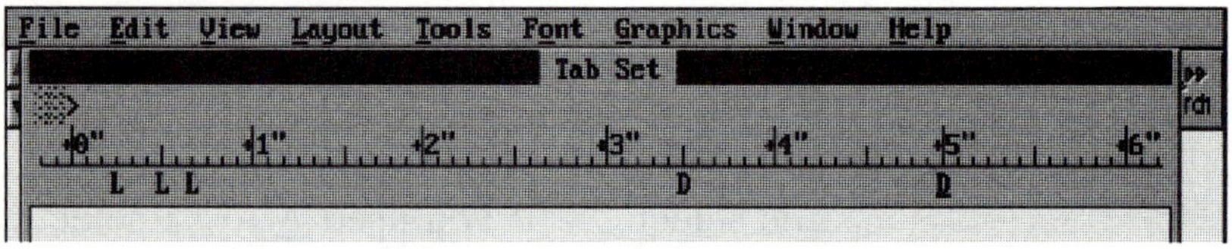

   Select OK to return to the document. Next, select **T**ools, Ma**t**h, **O**n, or press Alt-F7 and select **M**ath and the Math **O**n check box. Then select OK to return to the document.

   Now, select **T**ools, Ma**t**h, **D**efine or press Alt-F7 and select **M**ath, **D**efine to define the math columns. The Math dialog box looks like Figure 15-3. The letters at the top represent consecutive columns in the document, not including the column at the left margin. These columns match the tab stops in the document. You need to define only the columns you plan to use. The type of column is defined in the next line. As the information near the bottom of the screen explains, *X* indicates text columns, *N* is used for numeric columns, and *T* is used for columns containing calculated totals. If the setting for a column is incorrect, you will need to change the number under the column letter.

   The next row in the Math dialog box defines the appearance of negative numbers. For each column, you can choose a minus sign or parentheses. The entries in the next row indicate the number of digits to be placed after the decimal point in each calculation in each column.

FIGURE 15-3
Math dialog box

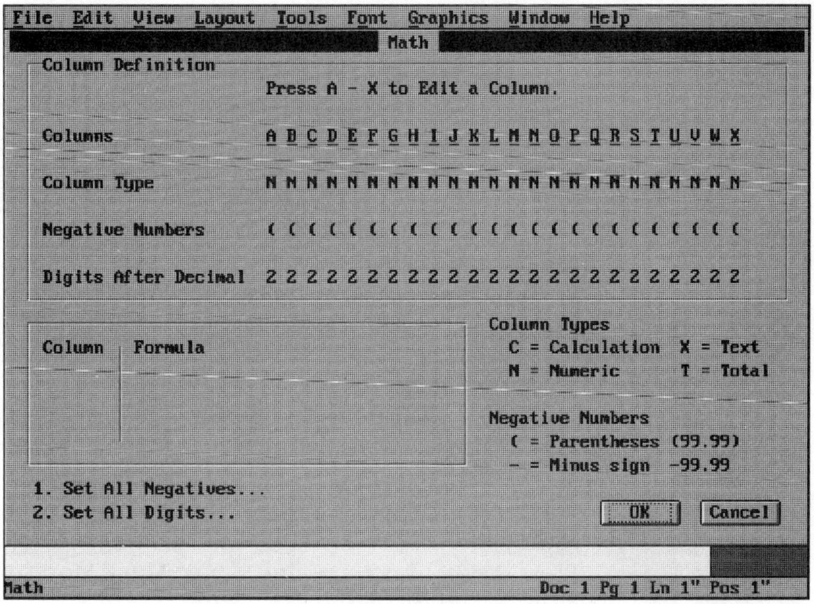

For the current example, the first three columns will be text columns. Press A for the letter of the first column, and the Define Math Column dialog box opens, as shown here:

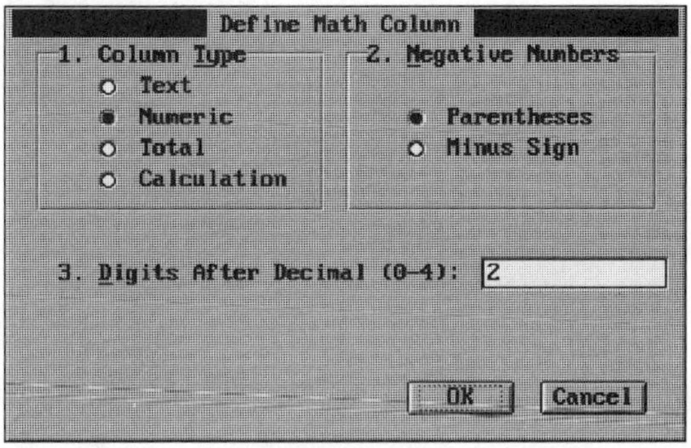

Select Column **T**ype, the Te**x**t option button, and OK. Repeat this for columns B and C.

The fourth column will be a numeric column, with no decimal places. From the Math dialog box, press D to select it, then Column **T**ype, and the **N**umeric option button. Select the **D**igits After Decimal text box and type **0**, then select OK. Press E to select the next column, select Column **T**ype, and the **T**otal option button to set it as a total column. Again, select the **D**igits After Decimal text box, type **0**, and select OK.

Figure 15-4 shows the top of the completed dialog box. Select OK to accept the math column definitions (twice if you used Alt-F7) and return to the document.

Next, type **Salary Report** and press Enter twice. Press the Tab key, type **East Coast**, and press Enter twice. Press the Tab key twice, type **New York**, and press Enter. Press the Tab key three times and type **Bob Jones**. Press the Tab key again, type **25,600**, and press Enter. Press the Tab key three times, type **Jane Doe**, press the Tab key again, type **26,850**, and press Enter.

Since these are the only two employees listed in the New York area, you can compute a subtotal for the salaries for New York. Press the Tab key four times and type a **+**. WordPerfect displays the + but does not perform the calculation automatically.

Press the Enter key twice, press the Tab key twice, type **Washington**, and press Enter. Press the Tab key three times, type **Nancy Smith**, press the Tab key again, type **32,500**, and press Enter. Press the Tab key three times, type **Mary Marvin**, press the Tab key again, and type **24,350**.

To include the subtotal for Washington, press Enter, press the Tab key four times, and type a **+**.

To make WordPerfect add the subtotals, press the Enter key, press the Tab key four times, and type an **=**. This symbol represents the total level. Select **T**ools, Ma**t**h, **C**alculate or press Alt-F7 and select **M**ath, **C**alculate. Then select OK. The results look like Figure 15-5.

Do not clear the screen, so you can use these entries in the next example.

2. You can add a grand total to a WordPerfect report. You can add data for the West Coast to the entries in example 1 and produce a grand total of the salaries in all locations.

FIGURE 15-4

Math dialog box after defining math columns for text, subtotal, total, and grand total

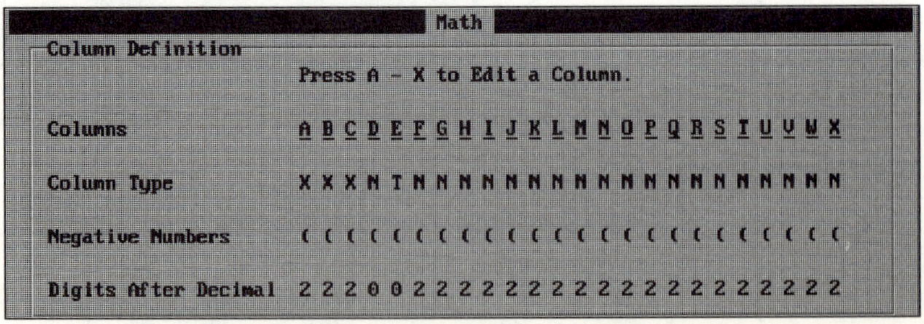

FIGURE 15-5

Using the equal sign to calculate a total

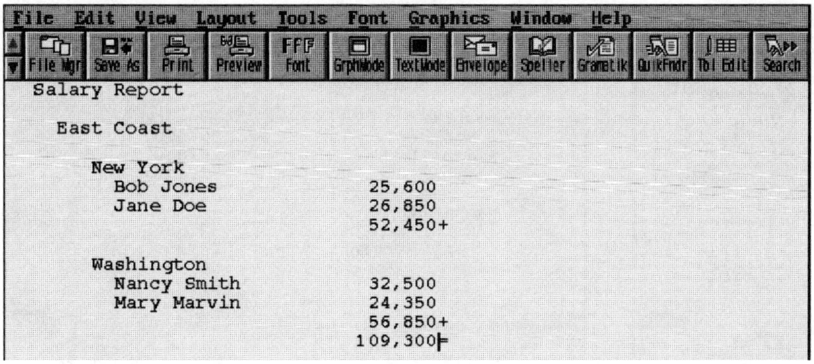

First, press the Enter key twice to begin entering the additional data. Next, press the Tab key, type **West Coast**, and press Enter twice. Press the Tab key twice, type **California**, and press Enter. Press the Tab key three times and type **Cindy Harper**. Press the Tab key again, type **42,870**, and press Enter. Press the Tab key three times, type **Jeff Parker**, press the Tab key again, type **39,700**, and press Enter.

Since these are the only two employees in the California area, you can have WordPerfect calculate a subtotal for the salaries. Press the Tab key four times, type a **+**, and press the Enter key twice.

Press the Tab key twice, type **Nevada**, and press Enter. Press the Tab key three times, type **Joan Carson**, press the Tab key again, type **18,750**, and press Enter. Press the Tab key three times, type **Frances Drake**, press the Tab key again, type **16,500**, and press Enter.

To tell WordPerfect where to place the subtotal for Nevada, press the Tab key four times and type a **+**.

To make WordPerfect calculate a total for the two subtotals, press Enter, press the Tab key four times, and type an **=**. Then, select **T**ools, Ma**t**h, **C**alculate or press Alt-F7 and select **M**ath, **C**alculate. WordPerfect calculates the subtotals for California and Nevada and a total for the West Coast.

You can have WordPerfect calculate a grand total for the East and West Coasts. Press Enter once and press the Tab key five times. Type an * to mark the location of the grand total. Then, select **T**ools, Ma**t**h, **C**alculate or press Alt-F7 and select **M**ath, **C**alculate. Press Enter and select **T**ools, Ma**t**h, O**f**f or press Alt-F7, select **M**ath, and clear the Math **O**n check box to turn math off.

Since WordPerfect shifted the screen display so that you can't see all the entries, Figure 15-6 displays the results of the grand total. You can make changes to the numbers that are in the math area, but you will need to recalculate to revise the totals.

FIGURE 15-6 *Using the asterisk to calculate a grand total*

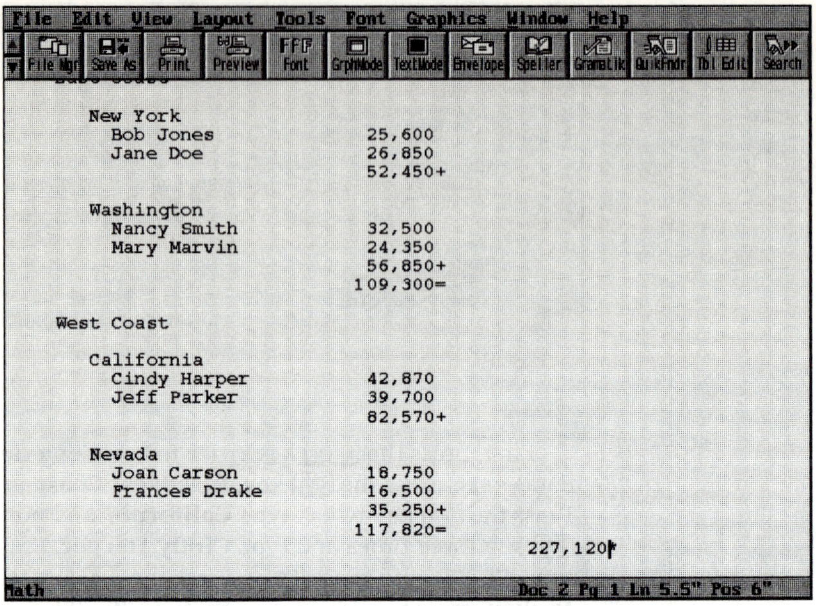

EXERCISES

1. Set a left-justified tab at 1.5 inches and a decimal tab at 5.0 inches. Use the math features to re-create the following information, with decimal places set to 0:

Machine repairs		
Model 5210		
Factory 1	10	
Factory 2	5	
Total Repairs 5210		+
Model 6511		
Factory 1	48	
Factory 2	9	
Total Repairs 6511		+
TOTAL ALL MODELS		=

Calculate the subtotals and the total.

2. Set left-justified tabs at 1.3 and 1.5 inches and decimal tabs at 5.5 and 6.5 inches. Re-create the following information with the math features:

EMPLOYEE BENEFIT PARTICIPATION			
Employees in Savings Plan			
Thrift	500		
S&L	250		
Bonds	250		
Total in Savings		+	
Employees in Stock Option Plan			
Plan A	100		
Plan B	100		
Total in Stocks		+	
Total Employees in Investment Plans			=
Employees in Medical Plan			
White Cross	500		
Cheap Docs	500		
Total Medical		+	
Employees in Life Insurance Plan			
Quick Save	100		
High Risk	100		
Total Life		+	
Total Employees in Insurance Plans			=
TOTAL NUMBERS IN BENEFIT PLANS			*

Have WordPerfect calculate the totals.

Teach Yourself

mastery skills check

1. Set the tabs and math features, type the following information, and calculate the subtotal. [15.1]

HEAD COUNT BY LOCATION	
Chicago	120
Dallas	38
Denver	105
New York	302
TOTAL	+

Do not clear the screen.

2. Edit "TOTAL" in exercise 1 to read "U.S. TOTAL." Add the following information to the list and calculate the subtotal. [15.1]

Paris	82
London	106
Lisbon	34
Frankfurt	192
FOREIGN TOTAL	+

3. Set a left-justified tab at 1.5 inches and a decimal tab at 4.0 inches. Use the math features to re-create the following information and calculate the subtotals and total, with decimal places set to 0. [15.2]

Product 1 Sales		
	Jim	12,500
	Fred	38,900
	Harry	23,500
Total Product 1		+
Product 2 Sales		
	Jim	23,450
	Fred	56,750
	Harry	78,900
Total Product 2		+
Total Products 1 & 2		=

4. Set tabs and the math features, re-create the following information, and calculate the totals. [15.2]

Office Supplies	
	10.00
	15.50
	25.60
Total Supplies	+
Office Furniture	
	345.00

	545.00		
Total Furniture		+	
Total Office Products			=
Coffee Supplies			
	25.00		
	15.80		
Total Coffee		+	
Paper Products			
	115.00		
Total Paper		+	
Total Miscellaneous			=
TOTAL PURCHASES			*

cumulative skills check

As you perform the Skills Check, do not clear the screen until you have completed the last exercise.

1. Type the following:

   Expenses for 1993 have risen dramatically. Please review the following figures with your managers.

   Add a header with "ABC Company" at the left and the date at the right. Add a footer with the page number in the middle preceded by the word "Page." [10.2]

2. Type the following information below the paragraph you typed in exercise 1, using the math features. Use 3- and 4.5-inch left-justified tabs for the column headers and 3.5- and 5-inch decimal tabs for the numbers.

	Last Year	This Year
Travel	52,900	86,900
Consultants	104,585	190,800
Entertainment	3,900	9,800
Supplies	1,200	15,900
Phone	25,000	49,000
TOTALS	+	+

Calculate the totals for the two columns. [4.1, 5.3, 15.1]

3. Turn off math, reset the tabs, and type the following paragraph. [5.1, 5.3]

   A meeting has been scheduled for June 20 to discuss emergency measures to cut costs. Please come prepared to offer your suggestions for both proven and innovative cost-cutting measures.

4. Print two copies of the document. [3.1, 12.1]

16

Drawing Lines and Boxes

chapter objectives

After completing this chapter, you should be able to

16.1 Draw a line

16.2 Create a box with lines

16.3 Erase a line

16.4 Move the cursor without drawing

16.5 Use a special character for the line

16.6 Add text to a box

WORDPERFECT'S line draw feature allows you to add borders, lines, boxes, and graphs to your documents. You can use lines to create your own custom forms or to add a dividing line beneath a letterhead. Organizational charts and flow diagrams are easy to create with the line draw feature.

You can use the line draw feature in a blank document, or you can type text and add lines around it. Ctrl-R allows you to control the length of a line. Special characters can be used to add variety to your drawings. You can erase existing lines or move the cursor without extending the current line.

These features provide a full set of options for jazzing up your documents with the addition of lines and boxes. You must use a monospaced font when you want to use the line draw feature. A *monospaced* font is a font that uses the same amount of space on the line for each character. A *proportionally spaced* font is a font that uses a different amount of space for different letters and symbols. For example, with a proportionally spaced font more space is allocated to *m* than to *l*.

When you draw lines and boxes, WordPerfect uses special codes to describe the symbols. When you reveal codes, these hidden codes appear different from the other codes you have used, but they operate like other keyboard characters.

review skills check

As you perform the Skills Check, do not clear the screen until you have completed the last exercise.

1. Create a directory called ACCOUNT on the same level as WPDOCS. [11.2]
2. Create a subdirectory of WPDOCS called LETTERS. [11.2]
3. Create a line of 55 asterisks with Ctrl-R. [1.3]
4. On the line below the asterisks, type the following text centered, boldfaced, and underlined. [4.1, 4.2, 4.3]

1993 Statement of Changes in Financial Position

5. Preview the printed document. [3.3]
6. Block the line of asterisks and reposition it below the centered text. [4.6, 8.2]

16.1 DRAW A LINE

You can draw single or double lines with a simple WordPerfect menu option. The graphics line draw feature lets you develop your own set of forms, to which you can add text. Depending on which direction you move the cursor, you can create lines vertically and horizontally. Usually you will want to move to where the line will begin before starting line draw. In a new document, you will have to start line draw first, then move to where you want the line to begin, as you will learn in section 16.4.

TO DRAW A LINE

a. Place the cursor where you want the line to start.
b. Select **G**raphics, Line **D**raw, or press Ctrl-F3 and select **L**ine Draw.
c. Select **1** to draw a single line or **2** to draw a double line.
d. Move the cursor to where you want the line to end.
e. Press F7 to finish the line drawing.

NOTE *You can use Ctrl-R to help you draw a line quickly. Instead of step d, you can press Ctrl-R, type the number of lines or spaces through which the line should move, then press one of the arrow keys to indicate the direction.*

As you move the cursor, WordPerfect draws the line. As you draw the line, WordPerfect inserts spaces and hard returns where appropriate to make the line fit the document format. The arrows that appear on the screen when you are in text mode will not be printed.

NOTE *You may want to use text mode rather than graphics mode with the line draw feature. Text mode is much faster than graphics mode when using this feature.*

EXAMPLES

1. You can use vertical lines to set off lines of text. First, type

   When you use the drill, remember to:

   Now press Enter to move to the next line. Select **G**raphics, Line **D**raw, **2**. Press ↓ three times, creating a double line. Press F7. The screen looks like this:

   ```
   When you use the drill, remember to:
   ║
   ║
   ║
   ```

   You can type text to be set off from the vertical line. Press ↑ twice and → once to place the cursor after the first double-line character. Press Spacebar and type

   Wear safety goggles and gloves.

   Since WordPerfect inserted a hard return for each line in which the double line was drawn, you do not need to press Enter. Instead, press ↓. Press the Spacebar and type

   Unplug the drill before changing bits.

   The screen now looks like this:

   ```
   When you use the drill, remember to:

   ║ Wear safety goggles and gloves.
   ║ Unplug the drill before changing bits.
   ```

   The actual characters that WordPerfect uses for the lines depend upon your printer.

2. You can use horizontal lines to set off text. First, type

   When you use the drill, remember to:

   Press Enter to move to the next line. Select **G**raphics, Line **D**raw, **1**. Press Ctrl-R, type **5**, and press → to draw a line four characters long. Exit from line draw by pressing F7. The screen looks like this:

   ```
   When you use the drill, remember to:
   ────
   ```

You can type the first line of text next to this line. Press the → key and type

Wear safety goggles and gloves.

Then, press Enter to move to the next line.

To draw the next line, select **G**raphics, Line **D**raw. Since WordPerfect retains the last line type selection, you do not have to select the type of line you want to draw. Press Ctrl-R, type **5**, and press →. To finish the line drawing, press F7. Press → and type

Unplug the drill before changing bits.

The screen appears as follows:

```
When you use the drill, remember to:
 ─────Wear safety goggles and gloves.
 ─────Unplug the drill before changing bits.|
```

EXERCISES

1. Type the first paragraph that follows. Draw a horizontal double line 40 characters long, then type the second paragraph.

   The new accounting system assigns each account a number. The numbers prevent confusion among accounts with similar names but different purposes.

   This change will improve internal control. It should prevent debits and credits to the miscellaneous account that belong in another account.

2. Draw a single line that extends three rows down. Then draw a double line six characters across. Draw another double line that extends five rows down. Preview how WordPerfect will print the lines at 100 and 200 percent.

16.2 CREATE A BOX WITH LINES

You can create a box with a series of four connecting lines. The secret to creating boxes with lines of the same length on opposite sides is to use Ctrl-R to draw the lines that make up the sides of the box. WordPerfect automatically adds corners to your boxes as you change directions. Text to the right of the cursor is pushed ahead to make room for the box. WordPerfect inserts spaces and hard returns to fill blank areas.

TO DRAW A BOX

a. Place the cursor where you want the upper-left corner of the box to appear.

NOTE *You will not be able to move the cursor beyond the end of the document, which limits your ability to move within an empty document. Later, in section 16.4, you will learn how to move without drawing a line in line draw.*

b. Select **G**raphics, Line **D**raw or press Ctrl-F3 and select **L**ine Draw.

c. Press Ctrl-R, type the number of rows through which the box will extend, and press the ↓ key.

d. Press Ctrl-R, type the number of spaces across which the box will extend, and press the → key.

e. Press Ctrl-R, type the number you typed in step c, and press the ↑ key.

f. Press Ctrl-R, type the number you typed in step d, and press the ← key.

g. Press F7 to exit line draw.

EXAMPLES

1. You can use boxes to show where information should be provided in a form. First, type

   Total amount remitted:

Next, select **G**raphics, Line **D**raw. Then, press Ctrl-R, type **3**, and press ↓. Create the bottom line of the box by pressing Ctrl-R, typing **10**, and pressing →. To create the right side of the box, press Ctrl-R, type **3**, and press ↑. Complete the box by pressing Ctrl-R, typing **10**, and pressing ←. Press F7 to exit line draw. The screen looks like this:

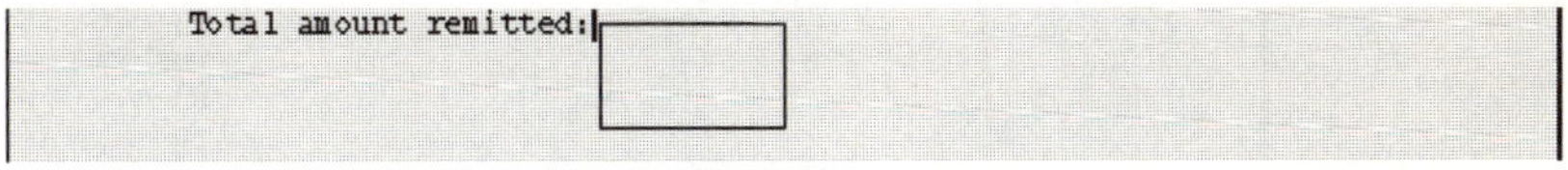

2. You can combine lines and boxes to create a blank organization chart. First, type

   Organization Chart

   Press Enter to move to the next line and press Tab four times.

   To begin drawing the first box, select **G**raphics, Line **D**raw, **2**. Press ↓ three times. To draw the bottom of the box, press Ctrl-R, type **15**, and press →. For the right side of the box, press ↑ three times. To complete the box, press Ctrl-R, type **15**, and press ←. Press F7 to exit.

   To create a second box, you can block and copy the first one. First, press ↓ three times, End once, and Enter twice to move below the box. Next, press ↑ five times and Ctrl-→ to move to the upper-left corner of the box. Press Alt-F4 or select **E**dit, **B**lock. Next, press ↓ three times and End once. Select **E**dit, **S**elect, **R**ectangle, and then select **C**opy and Paste.

   As the highlight shows, blocking a rectangle affects only the area between the cursor's first and last position. When you move, copy, or delete a rectangle, WordPerfect ignores the text or other material that is on the same line as any line of the block but not within the rectangle. Press ↓ five times and Enter once to place the copy of the box below and to the left of the original.

   To draw the third box, press End once and Tab five times to move to the location of the box. Select **E**dit, **P**aste. The screen looks like Figure 16-1.

FIGURE 16-1

Boxes for an organization chart

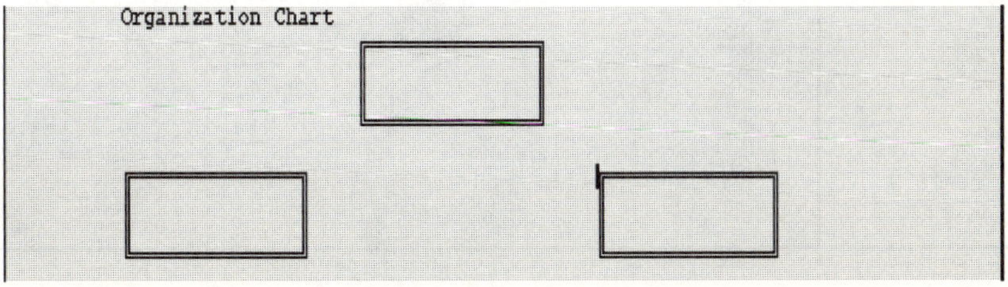

FIGURE 16-2

Lines connecting the organization chart boxes

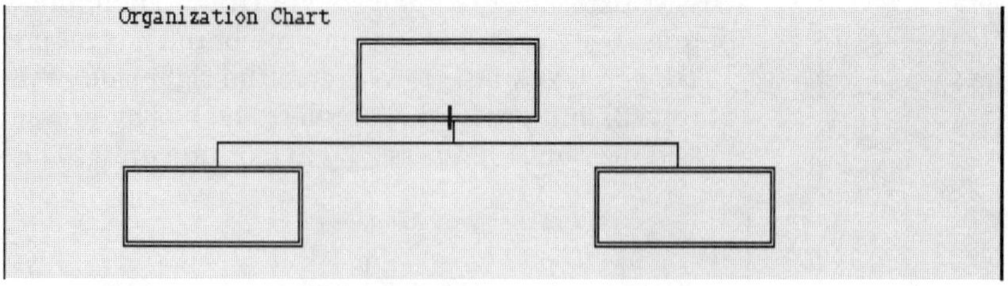

To draw the connecting lines, press Ctrl-R, type **7**, and press → to move to the middle of the box that you just drew. Next, select **G**raphics, Line **D**raw, **1**. Press ↑ once to draw a line leading up from the box on the right. Press Ctrl-R, type **39**, and press ← to draw a line to the box on the left. Press ↓ to connect the line to the box, then press F7 to complete the line drawing.

Next, press ↑, press Ctrl-R, type **20**, and press → to move to the middle of the line that you created. Then, select **G**raphics, Line **D**raw, press ↑ to connect all three boxes, and press F7. The organization chart looks like Figure 16-2.

EXERCISES

1. Create a form that asks for a person's first name and last name. For each place the form prompts for information, create a box to contain the information.
2. Using boxes 5 rows deep and 14 columns wide, draw boxes and lines for a flow chart that looks like this:

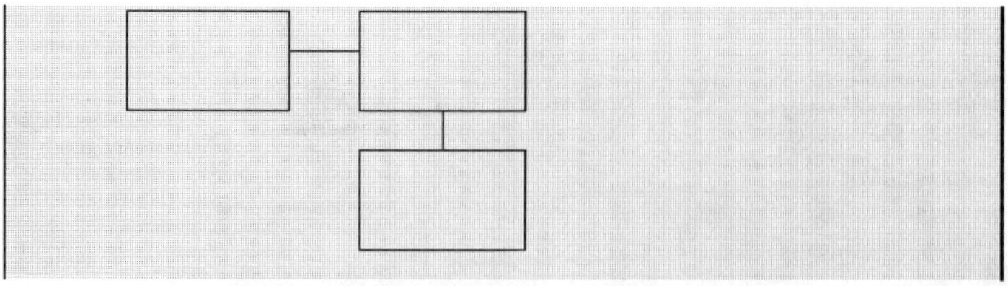

16.3 ERASE A LINE

WordPerfect's Erase option in the Line Draw menu lets you correct mistakes without starting over. As you move the cursor over a line, WordPerfect erases that part of the line. You can use this option to shorten or remove a line. WordPerfect adjusts spaces and hard returns to maintain the remaining portions of the line.

TO ERASE A LINE

a. Move the cursor to the end or beginning of the part of the line you want to erase.
b. Select **G**raphics, Line **D**raw.
c. Select **E**rase.
d. Move the cursor along the part of the line you want to erase.
e. Press F7 to end line draw.

Since WordPerfect erases every character over which you move the cursor when you erase lines, do not move the cursor over part of a line that you want to keep. If you want to move to another line to erase, press F7 to exit line draw first, so that you can move the cursor without changing the drawing. You can also erase lines and boxes by pressing Del or typing spaces in typeover mode.

EXAMPLES

1. You can use the Erase option when you have drawn a line incorrectly. First, select **G**raphics, Line **D**raw, **1**. Press Ctrl-R, type **20**, press →, and press F7 to exit line draw.

   To erase part of the end of the line, select **G**raphics, Line **D**raw, **E**rase, press ← twice, and press F7. You have shortened the line by two characters.
2. You can erase part of a line from the middle. First, select **G**raphics, Line **D**raw, **1** to select a single line. Next, press Ctrl-R, type **12**, press →, and press F7 to exit.

Now press the ← key six times to move the cursor to the middle of the line. Then, select **G**raphics, Line **D**raw, **E**rase. Press → three times and press F7. The line now looks like this:

3. You can use the line draw feature to create boxes representing an office layout and erase part of a box to represent a door. First, label the drawing by typing

   Office Layout

   Now press Enter to move to the next line and select **G**raphics, Line **D**raw, **1**. To draw the first room, press Ctrl-R, type **4**, and press ↓. Then, press Ctrl-R, type **20**, and press →. Press Ctrl-R, type **4**, and press ↑; then press Ctrl-R, type **20**, and press ←. Press F7 to exit line draw and relocate the cursor.

   For the second room, press Ctrl-R, type **4**, and press ↓. Then, select **G**raphics, Line **D**raw, **1**. Next, press Ctrl-R, type **8**, and press ↓; press Ctrl-R, type **10**, and press →; then press Ctrl-R, type **8**, and press ↑.

   For the third room, press Ctrl-R, type **8**, and press ↓; press Ctrl-R, type **10**, and press →; press Ctrl-R, type **8**, and press ↑. Then press F7. The screen looks like Figure 16-3.

   To move to the entrance, press ↑ four times, press Ctrl-R, type **11**, and press ←. To mark the door, select **G**raphics, Line **D**raw, **E**rase, and press → twice.

   To move to the next door without drawing or erasing, press F7, press ↓ four times, and press ← seven times. To indicate the door, select **G**raphics, Line **D**raw, and press → twice.

FIGURE 16-3 *Office layout with three rooms*

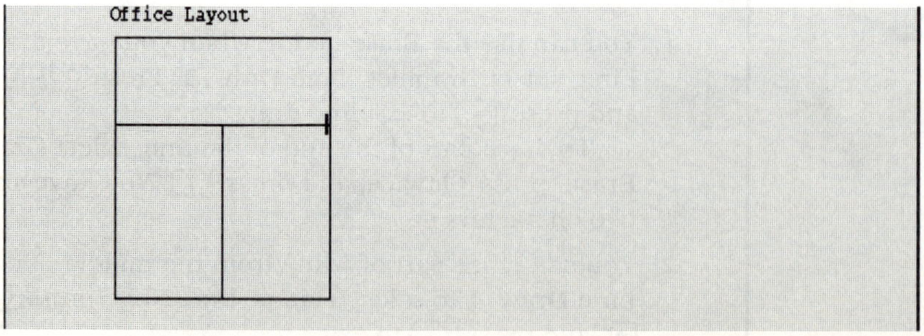

FIGURE 16-4

Using the Erase option to show doors in the office layout

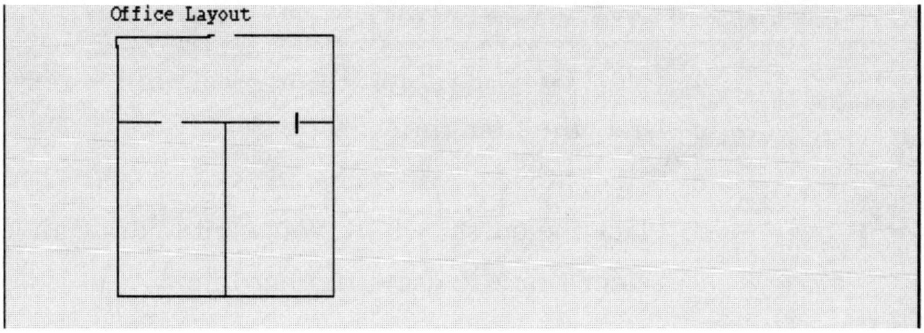

To erase the lines for the second door, type **1** so that WordPerfect draws a line where you move the cursor. Next, press Ctrl-R, type **9**, and press →. Then, select **E**rase and press → twice. Press F7. The screen looks like Figure 16-4.

EXERCISES

1. Draw a double line six characters across. Erase the line.
2. Create a single-line box that is five characters across and four rows deep. Erase the middle character in the top and the bottom of the box to split the box in half.

16.4 MOVE THE CURSOR WITHOUT DRAWING

Entering multiple unconnected lines on the screen requires a method for moving the cursor without extending the lines. WordPerfect's line draw feature provides an option for cursor movement without line creation.

TO MOVE THE CURSOR WITHOUT DRAWING (OR ERASING)

a. Select **G**raphics, Line **D**raw.

b. Draw the first line.

c. Select **M**ove.

d. Place the cursor where you want to draw another line.

e. Select **1** or **2** to draw another line.

WordPerfect adds the necessary spaces and hard returns to allow you to move in a straight direction.

EXAMPLES

1. You can move the cursor around in a document to reduce the steps you must perform when you want to draw multiple lines. To try this, type the following lines, pressing Enter once after "Name:" and "Phone:" and twice after "Address:". Type three spaces before "Name:" and two before "Phone:" to right-align the colons.

```
   Name:
Address:
  Phone:
```

To draw a line after each entry, press ↑ and End to move to the end of the "Phone:" line. Next, select **G**raphics, Line **D**raw, **1** to select the single line option. Press Ctrl-R, type **30**, and press →.

Instead of pressing F7 to move to the second "Address:" line, select **M**ove and press the ↑ key. WordPerfect automatically inserts spaces at the beginning of the second "Address:" line, so you can move up in a straight line. To draw the line for the second line of the address, select **1**, press Ctrl-R, type **30**, and press ←.

Move to the first "Address:" line by selecting **M**ove and pressing ↑. To draw the line for the first line of the address, select **1** for a single line, press Ctrl-R, type **30**, and press →.

Move to the "Name:" line by selecting **M**ove and pressing ↑. To draw the line for the name, select **1** for a single line, press Ctrl-R, type **30**, and press ←. Press F7 to end the drawing. The result looks like this:

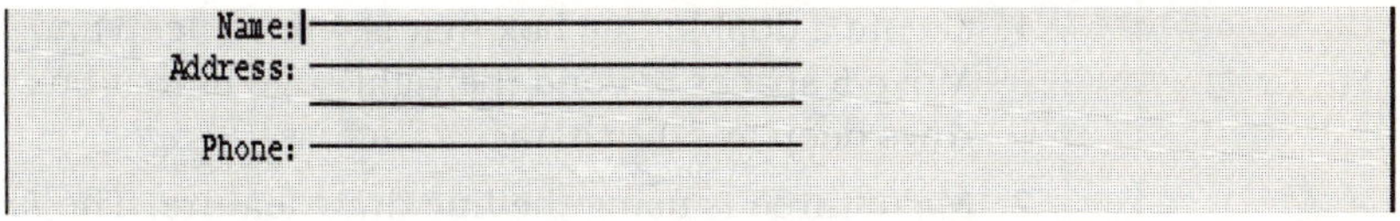

2. You can draw a competition list using WordPerfect. For this type of list, some of the lines connect and others do not. To draw the lines for the first set of competitors, select **G**raphics, Line **D**raw, **1**. Press Ctrl-R, type **20**, and press the → key. Press the ↓ key twice, press Ctrl-R, type **20**, and press the ← key. The screen looks like this:

To draw the lines for other competitors, select **M**ove and press the ↓ key twice. Press 1 to resume line drawing, press Ctrl-R, type **20**, and press the → key. Press the ↓ key twice, press Ctrl-R, type **20**, and press the ← key.

Next, draw lines for the finalists. First, Select **M**ove, press the ↑ key, press Ctrl-R, type **20**, and press the → key to move the cursor to the vertical line. Then, press 1 to resume line drawing, press Ctrl-R, type **20**, and press the → key. Next, press Ctrl-R, type a **4**, and press the ↑ key. Press Ctrl-R again, type **20**, and press the ← key.

To draw a line for the winner, first select **M**ove, press the ↓ key twice, and press the → key until the cursor is at the vertical line. Then, press 1 to resume line drawing, press Ctrl-R, type **20**, and press the → key. Press F7 to end the drawing. The drawing looks like Figure 16-5.

FIGURE 16-5

A competition list

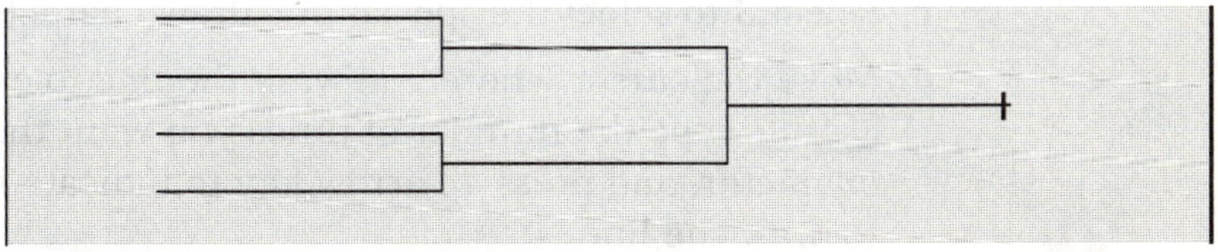

EXERCISES

1. Create a double-line box that is 4 rows deep and 15 characters across. Move 5 spaces beyond the right edge of that box and create a box 2 rows deep and 12 characters across.
2. Make three *I*s using the line draw feature. The *I*s should be 10 rows high, 10 characters wide, and 10 characters apart from each other.

16.5 USE A SPECIAL CHARACTER FOR THE LINE

You can draw lines with any character you choose. WordPerfect's default Line Draw menu offers the asterisk (*) as an option for drawing lines when you choose characters other than a single or double line. You can change the setting for this character and draw lines with any character of your choice.

TO USE THE SPECIAL CHARACTER TO DRAW A LINE

a. Place the cursor where you want the line to start.
b. Select **G**raphics, Line **D**raw.
c. Select **3** to select the special line draw character.
d. Move the cursor where you want the line to end, or press Ctrl-R, type the number of times you want the special character, and press an arrow key to indicate in which direction to draw the line.
e. Repeat step d for every line you want.
f. Press F7 to stop drawing.

TO CHANGE THE SPECIAL CHARACTER

a. Place the cursor where you want to start drawing with the special character.

b. Select **G**raphics, Line **D**raw.

c. Select **C**hange to change the special character.

d. Type the number representing the special character you want or **9** if the one you want is not displayed.

e. Type the character that you want to use if you typed **9** in step d.

f. Draw your lines with the special character.

EXAMPLES

1. You can create a box with asterisks. First, select **G**raphics, Line **D**raw, **3** to select the special line draw character, which is initially set to an asterisk (*). Next, press ↓ three times, → four times, ↑ three times, and ← three times. Finally, press F7 to exit line draw. The box looks like this:

2. You can change the special character to a shaded pattern. First, select **G**raphics, Line **D**raw, **C**hange. Then, select **1** to choose the character indicated by that number and press F7 to exit line draw.

3. You can use the special character you have just selected to create a gray box. First, select **G**raphics, Line **D**raw, **3**.

   Next, press ↓ twice, → seven times, ↑ twice, and ← six times. Finally, press F7. The box looks like this:

EXERCISES

1. Set the special character to the number sign (#). Create a box 10 lines deep and 20 characters wide.
2. Set the special character to the solid rectangle (█). Draw a line 30 characters long.

16.6 ADD TEXT TO A BOX

If you create organizational charts or flow diagrams, you will need to place text inside your boxes. You can create the text first and draw boxes around the text, or you can draw the box first and add the text. To add text to an existing box, you use the Ins key to set WordPerfect to typeover mode. (If you used insert mode, you would distort the box when you added the text.)

TO INSERT TEXT IN A BOX

a. Press the Ins key to go to typeover mode.
b. Place the cursor inside the box where you want the text.
c. Type the text.
d. Press the Ins key to return to insert mode.

EXAMPLES

1. You can put text in boxes to set off the text. First, start line draw by selecting **G**raphics, Line **D**raw, **2** to select a double line. Next, press Ctrl-R, type **3**, and press ↓. Press Ctrl-R, type **35**, and press →. Press Ctrl-R, type **3**, and press ↑. Press Ctrl-R, type **35**, and press ←. Then, press F7 to exit from line draw.

   Next, press the Ins key, press ↓, press → twice, and type

Bill must be paid by August 20th

For the next line of text, press the ↓ key, Ctrl-←, and the → key twice, and type

to prevent a late payment penalty

The final block looks like this:

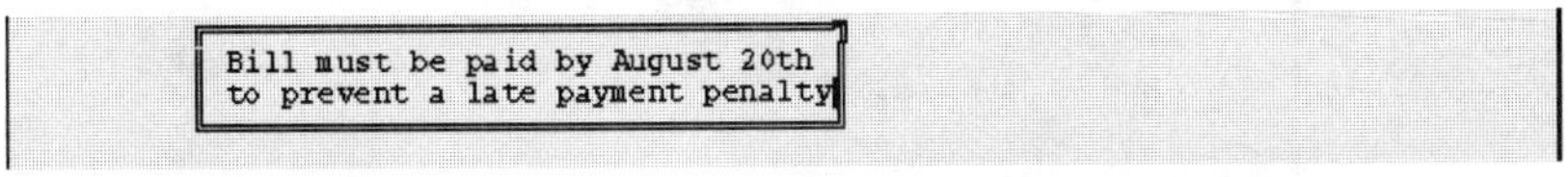

2. You can add the boxes after you type the text. You can use this feature to create, for example, a diagram of directories and subdirectories, such as a diagram of a root directory containing the WPDOCS and ACCOUNT directories. The WPDOCS directory has a subdirectory, called LETTERS. First, press Enter three times to create space to draw the boxes later. Then, press Tab four times and type **Root Directory**. Next, press Enter four times, press Tab, type **WPDOCS**, press Tab seven times, and type **ACCOUNT**. Then press Enter three times, press Tab, type **LETTERS**, and press Enter.

   To draw a box for the root directory, press Ctrl-R, type **9**, press ↑, and press Tab three times. Then, select **G**raphics, Line **D**raw, **2** to select a double line. Press ↓ twice, press Ctrl-R, type **23**, and press →. To complete the box, press ↑ twice, press Ctrl-R, type **23**, and press ←.

   To draw the box for the WPDOCS directory, select **M**ove and press ↓ four times. Select **2** for a double line, press Ctrl-R, type **15**, and press ←. Press ↓ twice, press Ctrl-R, type **15**, and press →. To complete the box, press ↑ twice.

   To draw the box for the ACCOUNT directory, select **M**ove, press Ctrl-R, type **26**, and press →. Then, select **2** for a double line, press ↓ twice, press Ctrl-R, type **15**, and press →. Press ↑ twice, press Ctrl-R, type **15**, and press ←.

   To draw the box for the LETTERS subdirectory, select **M**ove, and press ↓ three times. Press Ctrl-R, type **50**, and press ←. Select **2** for a double line and press ↓ twice. Press Ctrl-R, type **15**, and press →. Press ↑ twice. Press Ctrl-R, type **15**, and press ←. The screen looks like Figure 16-6.

   Once you have drawn the boxes, you can draw lines to connect them. First, select **M**ove, press Ctrl-R, type **8**, and press →. Select **1** for a single line and press ↑. Next, select **M**ove and press ↑ twice. Select **1** for a single line and press ↑. Press Ctrl-R, type **40**, and press →. Press ↓ to connect the WPDOCS and ACCOUNT directories. To connect the root directory to the other directories, press ↑, press

FIGURE 16-6

Boxes added around text

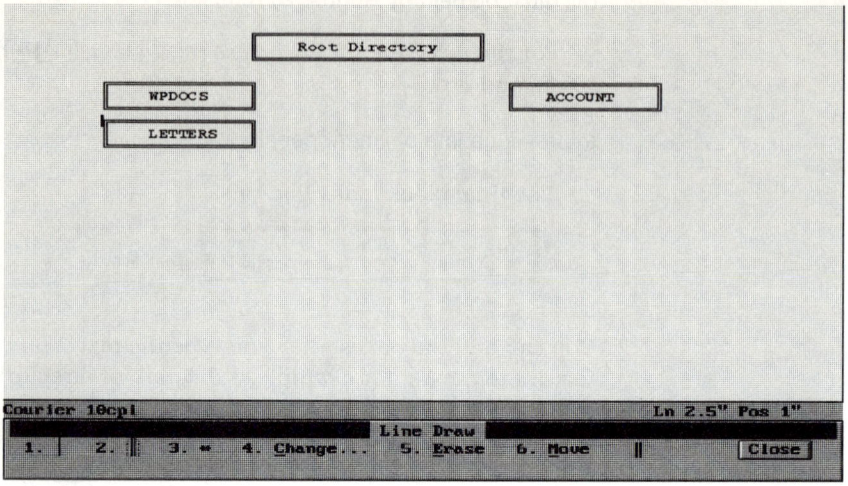

Ctrl-R, type **20**, press ←, and press ↑. Since this completes the diagram, press F7 to exit line draw. The screen looks like Figure 16-7.

FIGURE 16-7

Completed diagram of directories and subdirectories

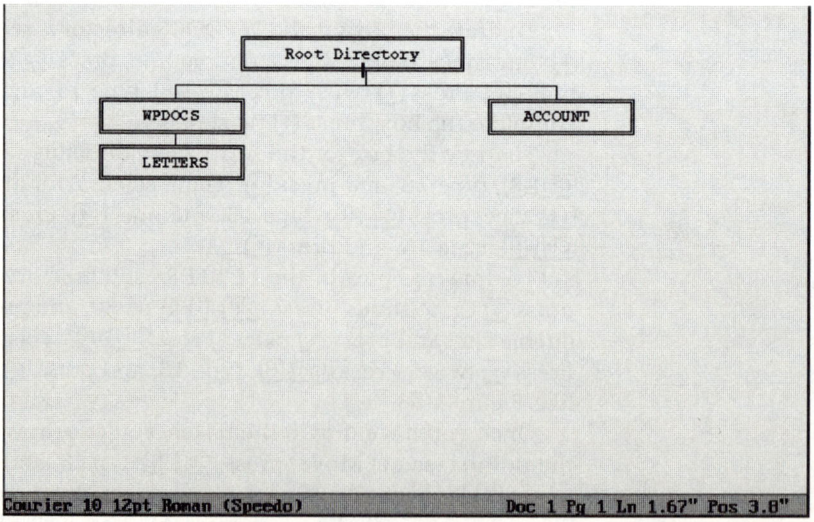

EXERCISES

1. Create a directory diagram with three directories under the root directory. Name them BUDGET, PRODUCT, and REPORTS.
2. Create a single-line box that is 50 characters across and 4 rows deep. Type the following text inside the box:

   All of the paintings displayed in this
   restaurant are for sale on a consignment
   basis. For more details, see the manager.

mastery skills check

As you complete the Skills Check, do not clear the screen between exercises unless instructed to do so.

1. Create a single line 40 characters across. Move 20 spaces to the left in the line and erase the 3 characters to the right. Clear the screen. [16.1, 16.3, 16.4]
2. Create this flow chart:

Clear the screen. [16.1, 16.2, 16.4]

3. Change the special character to colons. [16.5]
4. Create the following line diagram. Insert a blank line above the diagram and press Enter twice before typing each line of text. [16.1]

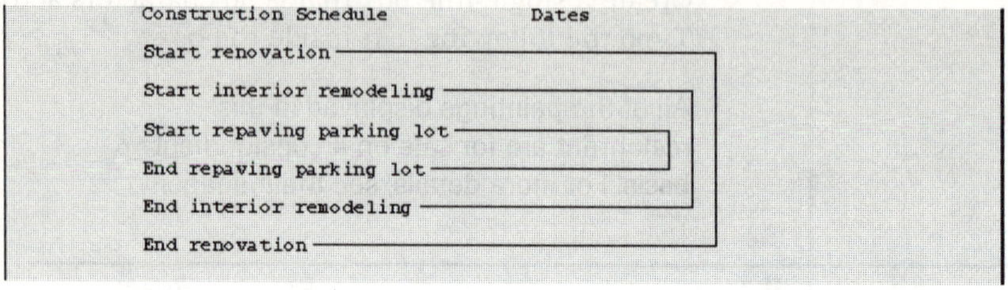

5. Delete the portion of the lines under the "Dates" heading. Then, insert the following dates. [16.3, 16.6]

Start renovation	5/1
Start interior remodeling	6/15
Start repaving parking lot	7/1
End repaving parking lot	7/31
End interior remodeling	8/30
End renovation	9/30

6. Draw a box of colon characters around the diagram. [16.2, 16.5]

cumulative skills check

1. Create a form for the entry of the following information. After each item, draw a box large enough to contain the information. [1.3, 16.2]

   Last name:
   First name:
   Department:
   Years with the company:

2. Type the following lines of text:

   Acme's Main Product Line
   Solder
   Silver necklaces
   Silver flatware

   Add lines that connect the items to the heading, "Acme's Main Product Line." [4.1, 16.1]

3. Remove the ACCOUNT directory that you created in the "Skills Check" at the beginning of the chapter. [16.3]

4. Remove the LETTERS subdirectory that you created in the "Skills Check" at the beginning of the chapter. [16.3]

5. Return the special character for line drawing to asterisks. Create a box 10 lines by 50 characters, and put the following text inside it. [4.2, 16.5]

   Clark Corporation Is Moving
   On Friday the 23rd, Clark Corporation is
   closing its Lakewood offices. Its new
   headquarters are in Barlow, Florida. It is
   moving there to be closer to its prospering
   land-development subsidiary.

6. Center the box and the text inside.

17

WordPerfect's Graphics Features

chapter objectives

After completing this chapter, you should be able to

17.1 Add graphics to a document

17.2 Place text in a graphics box

17.3 Edit and delete graphics boxes

17.4 Add a caption

17.5 Position and size a graphics box

17.6 Print documents that contain graphics

WORDPERFECT provides exciting features that allow you to combine text and graphics in a single document. You can use these features to create newsletters, letterheads, customized forms, and other special documents that convey your message by using both text and graphics.

You can incorporate graphics images that were created by using computer-aided design (CAD) systems, and you can use pictures that were created by using drawing software. If you would prefer not to create the images, third-party developers sell disks that contain a variety of graphics images. WordPerfect provides a number of sample graphics files that you can use to try out the techniques presented in this chapter.

WordPerfect also enables you to add graphics boxes to a document and to display text within the boxes. A list of objectives, a quotation, a sidebar, or other text can be set off from the main text by using this method.

WordPerfect also has an advanced equations editor that allows you to create complex equations. The equations editor graphics feature is not covered here, but it is a feature you might want to look at if you plan to produce documents that contain equations.

The full set of graphics features that WordPerfect offers requires some time to explore. In this chapter, you will be introduced to the basic options to get you started using these exciting features. Even these basic options require a little more time to master than some of the other topics in this book. You will find the time investment worthwhile if you want to create professional-looking documents that include text and graphics.

review skills check

Do not clear the screen until you have completed the last Skills Check exercise.

1. Type the following paragraph:

The objective of this chapter is to learn how to incorporate graphics boxes into your document. You will learn how to create these boxes, and you will use options to fill the boxes with images or text. WordPerfect also allows you to create captions for the boxes to provide labels and titles. Graphics boxes can be moved and deleted.

Underline "objective of this chapter." Save the document as GRAPHBOX. [4.7]

2. Switch to a second document window. Retrieve GRAPHBOX, and add the following paragraph to the end. [2.7]

   After your document is complete, you can print it. Most printers can print text and graphics simultaneously.

3. Create a header that reads "WordPerfect's Graphics Features." [10.2]
4. Boldface the words "captions," "labels," and "titles." [4.7]
5. Preview document 2. Preview document 1. [2.7, 3.3]

17.1 ADD GRAPHICS TO A DOCUMENT

WordPerfect can incorporate graphics images into a document. WordPerfect comes with many graphics images. You can add your own if you have graphics images in one of the formats that WordPerfect can use. Adding graphics to a document creates a graphics box.

Graphics boxes are like footnotes in that WordPerfect numbers them consecutively from the beginning of the document to the end and renumbers them as necessary when boxes are added, deleted, or moved. Graphics boxes can be placed anywhere in a document, including in headers and footers. WordPerfect has eight graphics box styles: figure box, table box, text box, user box, equation box, button box, watermark image box, and inline equation box. The box style that you select does not affect what can be stored in the box. The differences between the box styles are the default settings. In this book, you will focus on the figure box style. When you create a graphics box, WordPerfect wraps surrounding text around the graphics box. If WordPerfect cannot fit the entire graphics box on the current page, it moves the box to the next page.

NOTE *Working with a document that contains graphics is slower than working with a document that does not contain graphics. When you create a document that contains graphics, you might want to switch to text mode to make moving* *through the document faster. In text mode, graphics boxes appear as blank boxes that indicate where the graphics will appear. You can always select **F**ile, Print Pre**v**iew to see the graphics.*

When you are in text mode and you add a graphic to your document, you will see a box that indicates the location of the graphic. The graphic will appear when you print the document from text mode; you just can't see the graphic onscreen. When you first add the graphic to a document, the outline for the graphics box is added as you move down the document. Initially, only the top of the graphics box may be outlined.

TO ADD A GRAPHIC TO A DOCUMENT BY RETRIEVING AN IMAGE

a. Select **G**raphics or press Alt-F9, and then select **R**etrieve Image.
b. Type the filename of the file that contains the graphic you want to add to the document. Include the filename extension, if it is not .WPG.
c. Select OK to return to the document and bring the graphic into the document.

TO ADD A GRAPHIC TO A DOCUMENT BY CREATING A GRAPHICS BOX

a. Select **G**raphics or press Alt-F9, and then select Graphics **B**oxes, **C**reate.
b. Select **F**ilename.
c. Type the filename of the file that contains the graphic you want to add to the document. Include the filename extension, if it is not .WPG.
d. Select OK to enter the filename and return to the Create Graphics Box dialog box.
e. Select OK to return to the document and bring the graphic into the document.

The graphics box you create will have a code such as [Para Box:1; Figure Box] that you can see when you display the hidden codes. The size of the graphics box depends on the size of the image you put into it.

Using the Create Graphics dialog box to add a graphic also allows you to make other changes affecting such things as captions, size, and position, which you will learn about later in this chapter.

EXAMPLES

1. You can use WordPerfect's ready-made images, such as the hummingbird image in HUMBIRD.WPG, to enhance your documents. Select **G**raphics or press Alt-F9, and then select **R**etrieve Image. Type **humbird** as the name of the file that contains the graphic you want to add to the document. Press Enter to select OK. WordPerfect brings the graphic into the document. Your document looks like this:

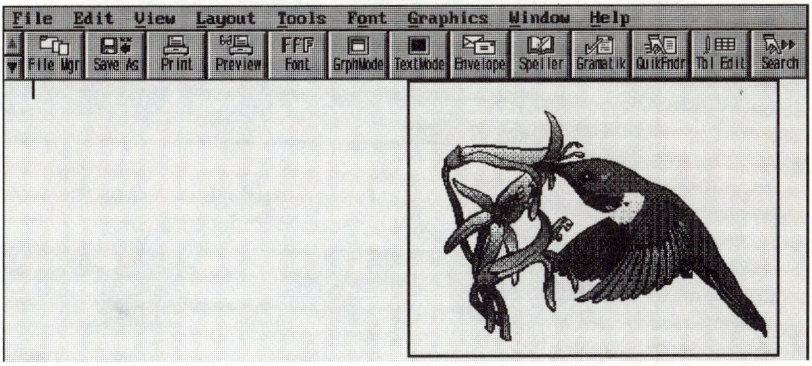

NOTE *If your graphics images are not in the WP60\GRAPHICS directory, you will need to type the full pathname of the images, instead of simply the image filenames, as you do the examples and exercises in this chapter. If you cannot find the named file, pick another one that is available.*

2. When you create a graphics box, WordPerfect wraps the document text around it unless you specify otherwise. Select **G**raphics or press Alt-F9, select Graphics **B**oxes, and select **C**reate. WordPerfect displays the Create Graphics Box dialog box, as shown in Figure 17-1. Select **F**ilename, type **hotrod**, and press Enter to add this image as a figure-box-style graphics box. Select OK to return to the document and add the picture of the car to the document.

   To see how WordPerfect wraps words around a graphics box, type

   WordPerfect allows you to add graphics boxes anywhere in your document. The options let you put graphics images or text into the boxes. You can also move or copy a box or change a box's size.

FIGURE 17-1

Create Graphics Box dialog box

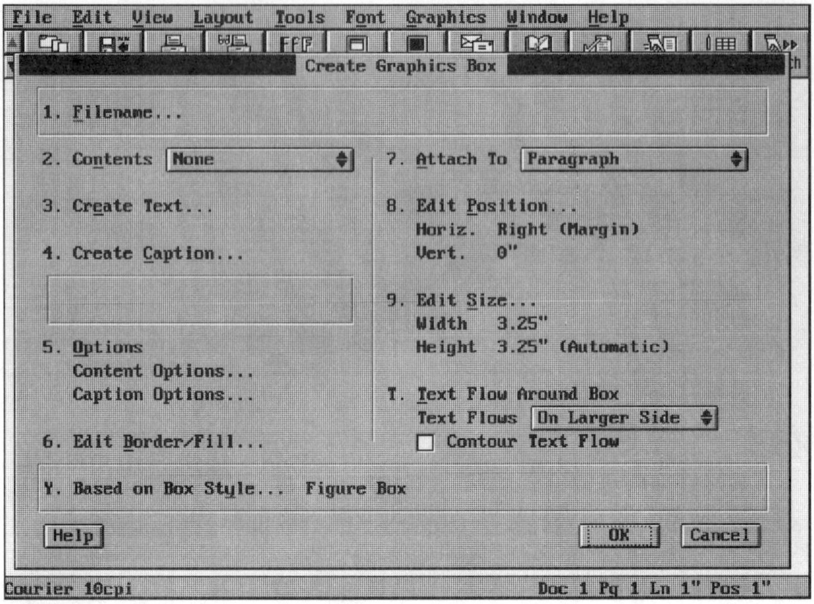

As you type the text, WordPerfect wraps the words around the graphics box. The screen looks like this:

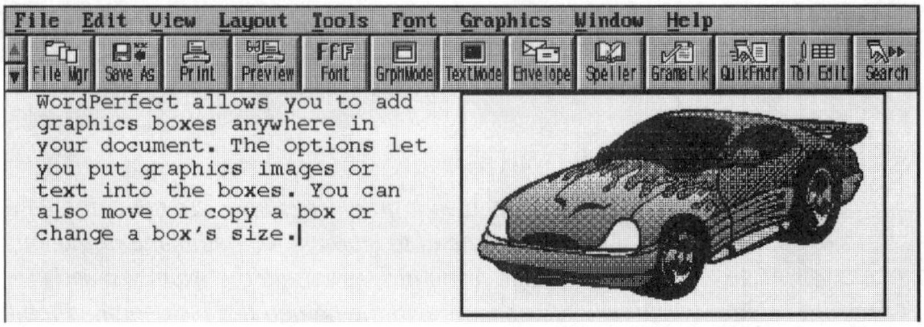

3. You can use graphics images in headers. First, select **L**ayout, **H**eader/Footer/Watermark, **H**eaders, Header **A**. With the **A**ll Pages option button selected, select the **C**reate button. Select **G**raphics or press Alt-F9, and then select **R**etrieve Image. Type **pheasant**, and press Enter to add this image as a figure-box-style graphics box. WordPerfect finds the file and loads the image into the header. Type **This is header text**. Press F7 to return to the dialog box, and select OK. Type **This is document text**. To view the document with the header, select **F**ile, Print Pre**v**iew, and then select **V**iew, **1**00%. The screen looks like Figure 17-2.
4. You can create multiple graphics boxes on the same page. As you add graphics boxes, WordPerfect tries to fit them next to one another. If

they will not fit next to one another, WordPerfect places them below one another. Select **G**raphics or press Alt-F9, and then select **R**etrieve Image. Type **hotair**, and press Enter to add this image. Select **G**raphics or press Alt-F9, and then select **R**etrieve Image again. Type **factory**, and press Enter to add this image to the document. WordPerfect adds the second graphic to the left of the first graphic. Select **G**raphics or press Alt-F9, and select **R**etrieve Image one more time. Type **windmill**, and press Enter to add this image to the document. WordPerfect adds the graphics image below the second graphic, as shown in Figure 17-3.

5. You can place graphics boxes below one another in a document. Select **G**raphics or press Alt-F9, and then select **R**etrieve Image. Type **skier1**, and press Enter to add this image to the document. Press Enter until the cursor is well below the graphics box that contains the skier—about 16 times. Select **G**raphics or press Alt-F9, and then select **R**etrieve Image. Type **wskier**, and press Enter to add this image to the document. This time, the second graphics box is added below the first box. If there is room, WordPerfect puts figure-style graphics boxes on the right side of the document. Because you have moved far enough down in the document so that there is room to have the graphic on the right side, that is where WordPerfect puts it.
6. WordPerfect can use graphics images from other software packages. This allows you to incorporate graphs and drawings that you have already made into your WordPerfect documents. This example requires a .PIC file from Lotus 1-2-3 and is included because many

FIGURE 17-2

Graphics box added to a header

FIGURE 17-3

Multiple graphics in a document

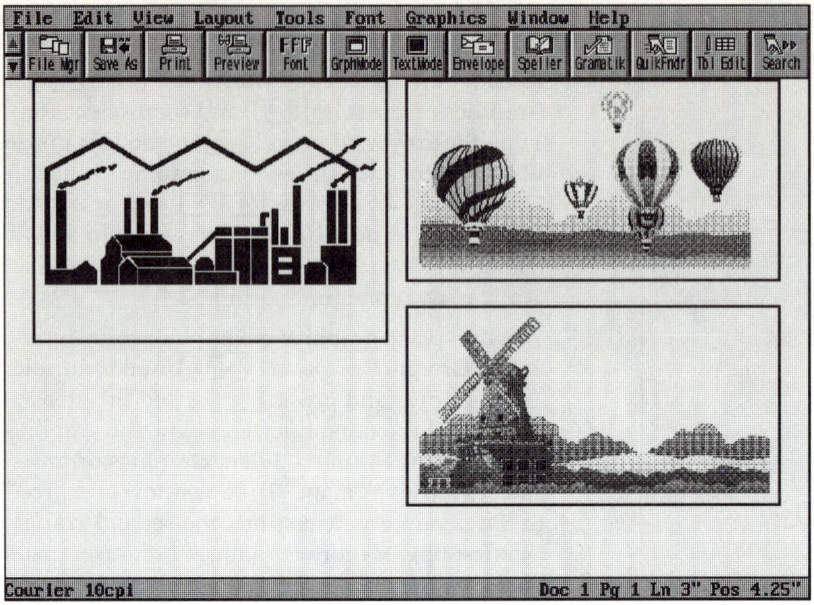

users wish to access this type of data. Although you might not have this particular graph or the spreadsheet program with which it was created, these steps demonstrate the process. If you do not have a Lotus 1-2-3 file, you can use a graphics image file from another program.

Select **G**raphics or press Alt-F9, and then select **R**etrieve Image. A Lotus 1-2-3 .PIC file named GRAPH is stored in the default directory for 1-2-3 Release 2.4. To add this image as a figure-box-style graphics box, type **c:\123r24\graph.pic** and press Enter. You must include the filename extension, .PIC, because the image does not have the default filename extension of .WPG. WordPerfect adds the graph stored in the .PIC file to your document, as shown here:

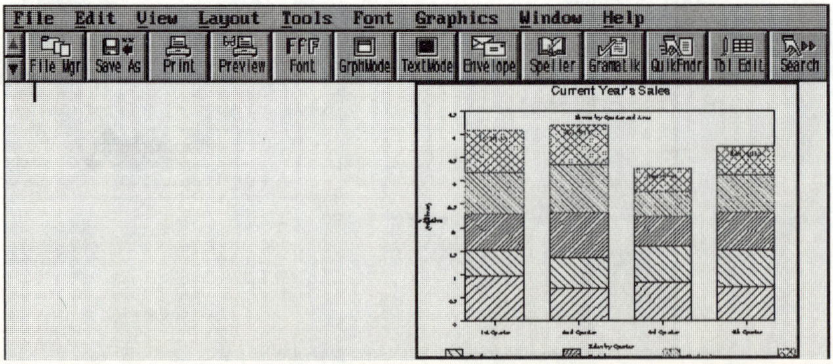

EXERCISES

1. Create a graphics box that displays the image PARROT.WPG.
2. Create a graphics box that displays the image TIGERHD.WPG.
3. Create a graphics box that displays the image PENPUSH.WPG. Type the following text, allowing WordPerfect to wrap the text as you type it.

   When you create a graphics box, WordPerfect wraps the document text around it. In text mode, if WordPerfect has not already drawn the box, it draws the box as you type the text. If you edit the text that you put next to the box, WordPerfect adjusts the text so that it is properly wrapped.

4. Add the image stored in GRIZZLY.WPG to a document. Then add the image stored in BORDER4.WPG to the same document.
5. Add the image stored in CONDUCT.WPG to a document. Press Enter until the cursor is below the graphics box. Add PLAN2.WPG to the same document.

17.2 PLACE TEXT IN A GRAPHICS BOX

You can put text in graphics boxes. You can display the contents of another document within a graphics box, and you can also type the text for a graphics box when you create the graphics box. Placing text in a graphics box can be an effective way to highlight project objectives or to set off quotations or other important text in a document. You can edit or create the text for a graphics box in a screen that is accessible through the graphics box menu selections.

When you use another document as the text for a graphics box, WordPerfect copies the text from the document on disk into the graphics box in the current document. Because the graphics box reflects the contents of the document on disk at the moment you copy it, the text in the graphics box is not updated to include any changes you subsequently make to the original document. Likewise, any changes you make to the copy of the document in the graphics box do not affect the original file. When you place text in a graphics box, the size of the graphics box changes to accommodate the text.

TO USE TEXT FROM A DOCUMENT STORED ON DISK IN A GRAPHICS BOX

a. Select **G**raphics or press Alt-F9, and then select Graphics **B**oxes, **C**reate.

b. Select **F**ilename.

c. Type the filename of the file containing the text that you want to appear in the graphics box.

d. Select OK to enter the filename and return to the Create Graphics Box dialog box.

e. Select OK to return to the document and add the graphics box to the document.

TO ENTER TEXT IN A GRAPHICS BOX OR EDIT A GRAPHICS BOX THAT CONTAINS TEXT

a. Select **G**raphics or press Alt-F9, and then select Graphics **B**oxes, **C**reate.

b. Select **E**dit Text or Cr**e**ate Text.

c. Type the text that you want to appear in the graphics box, or edit the existing text.

d. Press F7 to return to the dialog box.

e. Press Enter to select OK. You are returned to the document. If you created a graphics box, it is added to the document.

When you place text in a graphics box, WordPerfect sets the size of the graphics box to the size needed for the text. When you edit the text in a graphics box, you can use all of WordPerfect's formatting features, such as bold and underline. If you are using another document in the graphics box, the text contains all of the codes from the document on disk; if this text contains margin codes, you should remove them.

EXAMPLES

1. You can place text in a graphics box to have the text treated as a unit. Select **G**raphics or press Alt-F9, and then select Graphics **B**oxes,

Create. Select Create Text. The document area on the screen becomes smaller to indicate the smaller width where the text will appear. Type

Graphics boxes allow you to treat text as a unit. You can move graphics boxes without affecting the text in them.

Do not press Enter at the end of the paragraph. Press F7. WordPerfect sets the size of the graphics box to 3.25 inches by .86 inch. (The size of your graphics box might be different, depending on the default font you have selected.) Select OK to return to the document, and type

Text in a document that contains graphics boxes is moved to accommodate the graphics boxes. When you insert or move graphics boxes, or when you change the text in them, causing the boxes to change size, WordPerfect adjusts the way the remaining text wraps around the boxes. The text in the graphics boxes is unaffected by the other text.

The screen looks like this:

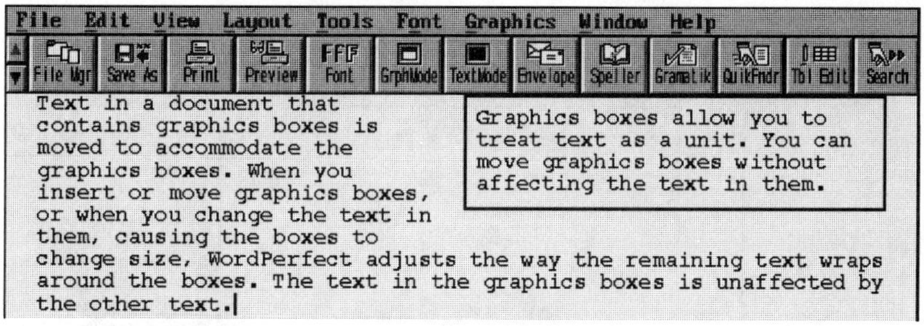

2. You can display text from another document in a graphics box. First, type

On August 17, 1993, the board of directors approved the company's long-term goals as presented by the Development Committee. The approved goals include:
Increase the return on investment from 8 to 10 percent.
Renovate the Hamburg facilities and develop a community-responsible attitude in that area.
Focus research and development on the electrochemical market.

Select **F**ile, **E**xit or press F7, press Y, type **goals**, press Enter, and press N to clear the screen. Next, select **G**raphics or press Alt-F9, select Graphics **B**oxes, and select **C**reate. Select **F**ilename, type **goals**, and press Enter. WordPerfect retrieves the GOALS file and sets the

Contents setting in the dialog box to Text. Select OK to return to the document.

Do not clear the screen; you will use this document in the next example.

3. You can edit the text in a graphics box. If the text came from another document, your edits will not change the original document. You might want to take this approach to use WordPerfect's formatting features on text in a graphics box. Select **G**raphics or press Alt-F9, and then select Graphics **B**oxes, **E**dit. Press Enter to select **E**dit Box. WordPerfect displays the Edit Graphics Box dialog box. This dialog box shows the settings for the graphics box you created in the prior example. This time, the dialog box displays the option Edit Text rather than Create Text. Select **E**dit Text. Press Ctrl-F4, select Pa**r**agraph, and select **D**elete. Then press F8 to turn on the underline feature, and type

   The long-term goals are:

   Press F8 and press Enter. Then press F7 and select OK. The document looks like this:

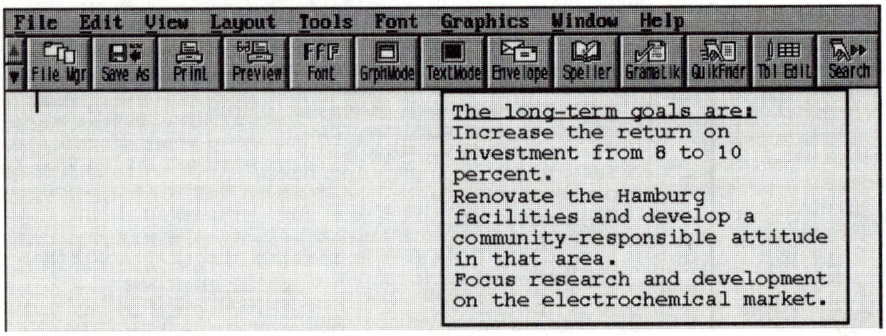

EXERCISES

1. Create a graphics box that contains the following text:

Project	Date
Systems analysis	5/1
Order equipment	6/15
Design software	7/1
Test software	7/31

Implement software	8/30
Evaluation	9/30

2. Type the following paragraph:

   You can put text in graphics boxes. In the previous section, you learned how to create a graphics box that contained an image. You do not need to create the image first, because WordPerfect provides several ready-made images.

   Save the document as PICTURE, and clear the screen. Create a graphics box that contains the text from the PICTURE file.

3. Create a graphics box that contains the following text:

   Steps for Creating a Graphics Box with Text in It:
   1. Select the Graphics menu.
   2. Press G to select Graphics Boxes.
   3. Press C to select Create.
   4. Press E to select Create Text.
   5. Type the text to appear in the graphics box.
   6. Press F7 to end the edit.
   7. Press Enter to select OK and return to the document.

17.3 EDIT AND DELETE GRAPHICS BOXES

When you edit a graphics box, you can change any of the settings for the box. Supplying the same filename or a new filename can update or change the contents of a graphics box. In the subsequent sections, you will learn how to make some other changes.

You can remove the contents of a graphics box by using the Edit option; however, to eliminate a box, you must delete the hidden code for the box. You can accomplish this easily in the Reveal Codes screen. You can also delete and restore the hidden code for a box to move the box from one location to another.

TO EDIT A GRAPHICS BOX

a. Select **G**raphics or press Alt-F9, and then select Graphics **B**oxes, **E**dit.

b. Type the number of the box you want to edit, and press Enter to select **E**dit Box.

c. Change any options that you want changed.

d. Press Enter to select OK. You are returned to the document. Any changes you made to the graphics box appear in the document.

You can also edit a graphics box by double-clicking it with the mouse. *Double-clicking* means pointing to an item and then pressing the left mouse button twice quickly.

TO DELETE A GRAPHICS BOX

a. Select **V**iew, Reveal **C**odes, press Alt-F3, or press F11.

b. Move the cursor to the code that represents the graphics box.

c. Press Del.

d. Select **V**iew, Reveal **C**odes, press Alt-F3, or press F11 again to return to the normal display.

You can also delete a graphics box by clicking it with the mouse and then pressing Del. When you delete a graphics box, WordPerfect renumbers all of the remaining graphics boxes.

TO MOVE A GRAPHICS BOX

a. Select **V**iew, Reveal **C**odes, press Alt-F3, or press F11.

b. Move the cursor to the code that represents the graphics box.

c. Press Del.

d. Place the cursor where you want the graphics box to be moved to.

e. Press Esc or select **E**dit, U**n**delete.

f. Select **R**estore to restore the graphics box.

g. Select **V**iew, Reveal **C**odes, press Alt-F3, or press F11 again to return to the normal display.

You can use Backspace instead of Del if the cursor is to the right of the hidden code for the graphics box.

EXAMPLES

1. When you specify a filename for a graphics box, WordPerfect places a copy of a document or image from disk into the current document. The copy of the image or text in the graphics box will not include any changes made to the original document at a later time. If you resupply the filename, you can update the graphics box contents. First, type the following:

   At the next board of directors meeting, they will discuss:
   The upcoming stockholders' meeting
   The company's reaction to the negative press involving the Indiana plant closing

   Select **F**ile, **E**xit or press F7, press Y, type **bodmeet**, press Enter, and press N to save the document and clear the screen. Next, select **G**raphics or press Alt-F9, and select Graphics **B**oxes, **C**reate. Select **F**ilename, type **bodmeet**, and press Enter. Select OK to return to the document. The document looks like this:

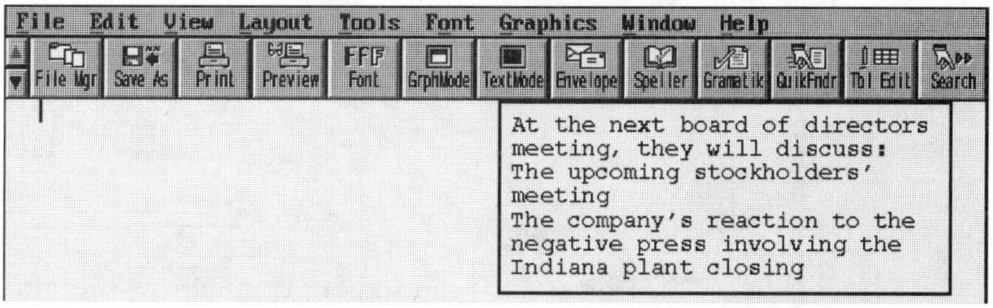

   Now select **W**indow, **S**witch or press Shift-F3, select **F**ile, **R**etrieve, type **bodmeet**, and press Enter. Press Pg Dn to move to the bottom of the document, press Enter, and type

   Suggestions for new board members to replace Ima L. Shark

   Select **F**ile, **E**xit or press F7, and select **Y**es twice to save the document and return to the first document. When you return to the first document, the screen does not show the new text that you entered in the BODMEET file. To update the graphics box, select **G**raphics or press Alt-F9, and then select Graphics **B**oxes, **E**dit. WordPerfect displays the following dialog box:

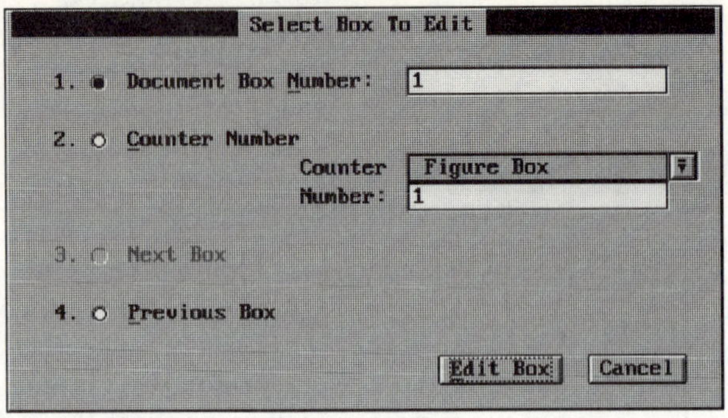

The number after "Document Box Number" is the number of the graphics box you want to edit. Because the 1 is correct, press Enter to select **E**dit Box. Select **F**ilename. Because WordPerfect displays the correct filename, press Enter. When WordPerfect prompts you for a confirmation to delete the current contents of the box, select **Y**es. Now the graphics box uses the updated copy of the BODMEET file. Select OK to return to the document. The graphics box looks like this:

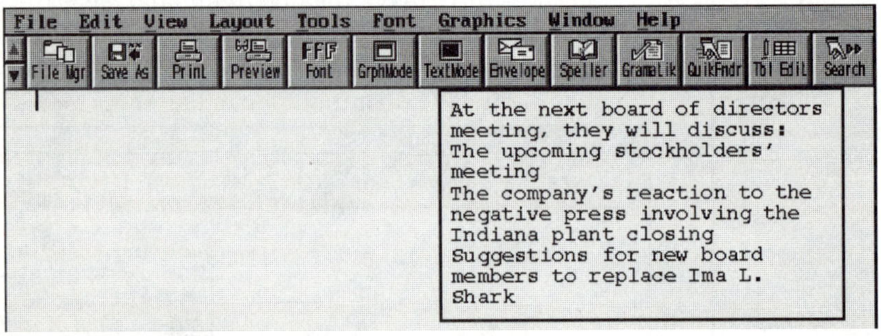

Do not clear the screen; you will use this graphics box in the next example.

2. You can remove the filename setting for a graphics box. To remove the filename setting for the graphics box that contains BODMEET, select **G**raphics or press Alt-F9, and then select Graphics **B**oxes, **E**dit. Press Enter to select **E**dit Box. Select **F**ilename. WordPerfect displays the current filename setting. Press Del and Enter. When WordPerfect prompts you for a confirmation to clear the contents, select **Y**es. Select OK to return to the document. Because you have removed its contents, the box is empty.

   Do not clear the screen; you will use this graphics box in the next example.

3. You can remove a graphics box from a document. To remove the empty graphics box, select **V**iew, Reveal **C**odes or press Alt+F3. In the bottom of the screen, you can see the following codes:

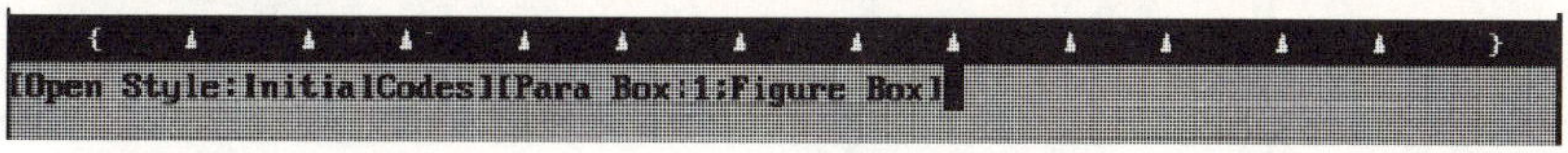

[Para Box:1;Figure Box] is the code for the graphics box. Press Backspace to remove the graphics box. Select **V**iew, Reveal **C**odes or press Alt+F3 to hide the codes.

4. You can move a graphics box by using its hidden code. Select **G**raphics or press Alt+F9, and then select Graphics **B**oxes, **C**reate. Select **F**ilename, type **bodmeet**, and press Enter. Select OK to return to the document. Press Enter until the cursor is several lines below the bottom of the graphics box. Next, select **G**raphics or press Alt+F9, and select **R**etrieve Image. Type **humbird**, and press Enter. Press Enter until the cursor is several lines below the bottom of the second graphics box. To move the graphics box that contains the text below the graphics box that contains the picture, select **V**iew, Reveal **C**odes or press Alt+F3. Press Home twice and ↑ once to move the cursor to the right of the hidden code for the first graphics box. Then press Backspace to delete the code.

   To insert the graphics box at its new location, press Home twice and ↓ once. Then select **E**dit, U**n**delete or press Esc. WordPerfect displays the code for the graphics box. Select **R**estore to restore the graphics box. Notice how the graphics box that contains the text is now the second graphics box. You can tell this by its code, which contains ":2." Select **V**iew, Reveal **C**odes or press Alt+F3 to hide the codes again.

5. If you have a mouse, you can use some shortcuts to manipulate graphics boxes. Select **G**raphics or press Alt+F9, and then select **R**etrieve Image. Type **dragon**, and press Enter. Click the graphics box so that its outline looks like this:

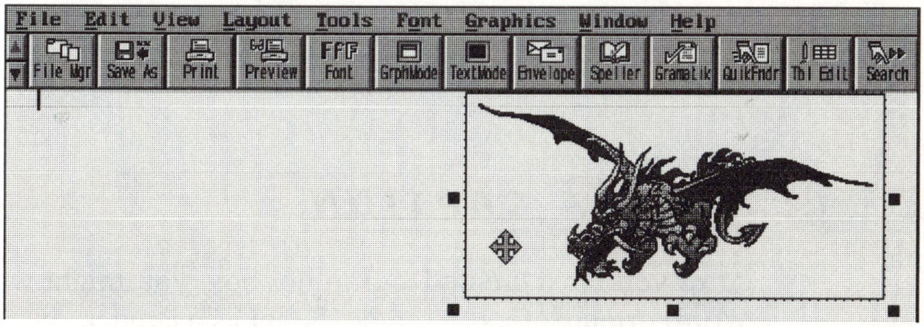

Double-click the graphics box by pressing the left mouse button twice quickly. The Edit Graphics Box dialog box appears. Click the Cancel button. Click the graphics box again. Press Del to delete the graphics box. WordPerfect prompts you to confirm that you want to delete the selected graphics box. Click the **Y**es button. You can use these two mouse shortcuts anytime you want to edit or delete a graphics box.

EXERCISES

1. Create a graphics box that contains the image named JEEP.WPG. Change the image to HOTROD.WPG.
2. Create a graphics box that contains the image BORDER4.WPG. Remove the filename setting.
3. Create a graphics box with nothing in it. Delete the graphics box.
4. Create a graphics box that contains the image named SKIER1.WPG. Press Enter until the cursor is several lines below the bottom of the graphics box. Create a graphics box that contains the image named WSKIER.WPG. Press Enter until the cursor is several lines below the bottom of the graphics box. Move the graphics box with the SKIER1.WPG image below the graphics box with the WSKIER.WPG image. Move to the beginning of the document, and delete the hard returns until the graphics box that contains the WSKIER.WPG image is at the first line.

17.4 ADD A CAPTION

After you have created a graphics box, you might want to label it. WordPerfect refers to the box label as a *caption.* WordPerfect will add a default caption, such as "Figure" followed by the figure number, if you want. You can provide additional information in the caption; for example, you can use the caption to provide a title for the graphics box. When you have multiple graphics boxes, the numbers and labels in the captions distinguish the various box entries.

TO ADD A CAPTION TO A GRAPHICS BOX

a. Select **G**raphics or press Alt-F9, and then select Graphics **B**oxes, **E**dit.

b. Type the number of the box you want to edit, and select **E**dit Box.

c. Select the Create **C**aption option.

d. Type the text that you want to appear in the caption.

e. Press F7 to return to the Edit Graphics Box dialog box.

f. Select OK to return to the document. Any changes you made appear in the document.

When you add a caption, you can use all of WordPerfect's formatting features, such as underline and bold. You can change or remove the initial caption that WordPerfect provides by editing the caption text. To move the default caption from the beginning of the caption area to another location within the caption area, first delete the caption by using the Backspace key. Then reinsert the caption by pressing Alt-F9, selecting **C**aption Number Style, and selecting **I**nsert. WordPerfect wraps the text in the caption to fit the width of the graphics box.

EXAMPLES

1. You can use captions to identify graphics images that are referenced in your text. When you use captions, a reader who is browsing through your document can quickly identify the information that each graphics box presents. Select **G**raphics or press Alt-F9, and then select Graphics **B**oxes, **C**reate. Select **F**ilename, type **tigerhd**, and press Enter. Select Create **C**aption. Press Spacebar, type **Make your products roar**, and press F7. Select OK to close the dialog box. The graphics box looks like this:

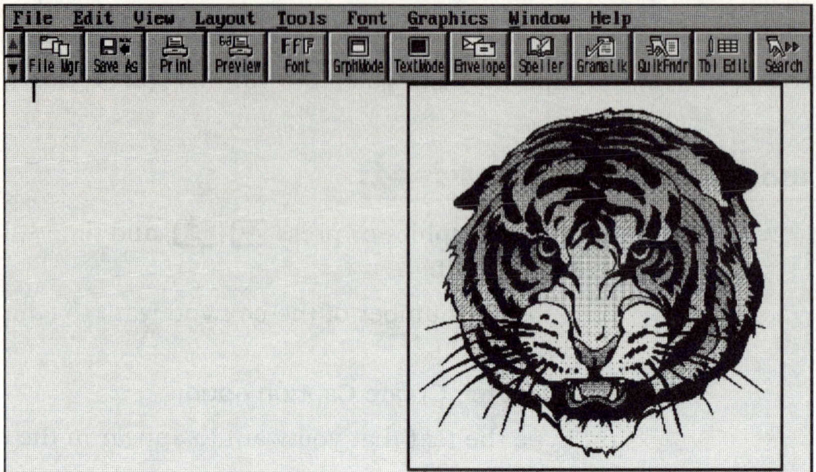

Figure 1 Make your products roar

Do not clear the screen; you will use this graphics box in the next example.

2. You can use WordPerfect formatting features on captions. Select **G**raphics or press Alt-F9, and then select Graphics **B**oxes, **E**dit. The 1 after "Document Box Number" is correct, so press Enter to select **E**dit Box. Select Edit **C**aption. Select **E**dit, **B**lock or press Alt-F4, and then press → to highlight "Figure 1." Press F8 to underline this text. Press F7 and select OK to finish editing the caption and the graphics box. The caption now has "Figure 1" underlined.

EXERCISES

1. Create an empty graphics box that has the caption "To be filled in later."
2. Create a graphics box that contains the text "insert Ms. Mitchell's picture here" and a caption that reads "Susan Mitchell, President."
3. Create a graphics box that contains the image named CONDUCT.WPG and has the caption "We are always on time for you."
4. Create a graphics box that contains the image named DRAGON.WPG and has the caption "We put fantasy to flight."

17.5 POSITION AND SIZE A GRAPHICS BOX

You can control the size of a graphics box and its placement on the page. The placement options allow you to specify vertical and horizontal positions. The options available for both position settings depend on how the graphics box is attached to the surrounding text. The default is attaching the graphics box to a paragraph, so you will use the position options for this attachment type. Graphics boxes attached to paragraphs remain with the text that is wrapped around them. For paragraph boxes, the vertical setting is the number of inches that the graphics box is placed from the top of the paragraph. The horizontal settings are left, right, center, and both left and right.

You can accept WordPerfect's calculations for a box size, or you can change the size of a box by altering its height or its width. You can also choose to alter both the height and the width. If you set only one dimension of the box, WordPerfect calculates the other dimension.

TO SET THE HORIZONTAL AND VERTICAL POSITIONS OF A GRAPHICS BOX

a. Select **G**raphics or press Alt-F9, and then select Graphics **B**oxes, **E**dit.

b. Type the number of the box to edit, and select **E**dit Box.

c. Select Edit **P**osition.

d. Select **D**istance from Top of Paragraph to specify the box's vertical position.

e. Type the number of inches between the top of the paragraph and the box, and press Enter.

f. Select **H**orizontal Position.

g. Select **L**eft to align the box with the paragraph's left margin, **R**ight to align the box with the paragraph's right margin, **C**entered to center the box between the paragraph margins, or **F**ull to stretch the box between the left and right margins.

h. Select OK to return to the Edit Graphics Box dialog box.

i. Select OK to return the document. Any changes you made appear in the document.

WordPerfect ignores the vertical setting if it prevents the image from fitting on the page.

TO SET THE SIZE OF A GRAPHICS BOX

a. Select **G**raphics or press Alt-F9, and then select Graphics **B**oxes, **E**dit.

b. Type the number of the box to edit, and select **E**dit Box.

c. Select Edit **S**ize to specify the size of the graphics box.

d. Select the Set **W**idth option button. Then type the number of inches for the box's width or select the **A**utomatic Width, Based on Box Content Width option button to let WordPerfect determine the width.

e. Select the Set **H**eight option button. Then type the number of inches for the box's height or select the A**u**tomatic Height, Based on Box Content Height option button to let WordPerfect determine the height.

f. Select OK to return to the Edit Graphics Box dialog box.

g. Select OK to return to the document. Any changes you made appear in the document.

When you set the size of a graphics box that contains a graphics image, WordPerfect changes the size of the image to fill as much of the box as possible. After the image is as large as possible, remaining space is left blank. When you set the size of a graphics box that contains text, WordPerfect fits as much of the text as possible into the box. If WordPerfect cannot display all of the text in the box, it displays as much as possible and keeps the rest in memory. If the box has more room than the text requires, WordPerfect leaves the remaining space blank.

EXAMPLES

1. You can set the vertical position of a graphics box when you want one or more lines of a paragraph that is wrapped around the graphics box to appear unwrapped above the box. First, type

   Dragons do not really exist, but they make great villains in epic tales. Their abilities to breathe fire and fly make them the fiercest of villains, and only the true of heart can conquer them. Most cultures have tales involving dragons that give their heros a target for a battle. For example, Beowulf had to kill three dragons, each worse than the previous. This is a dragon. He does not like fire extinguishers.

Select **G**raphics or press Alt-F9, and then select Graphics **B**oxes, **C**reate. Select **F**ilename, type **dragon**, and press Enter. WordPerfect finds the file and loads the image. Select Edit **P**osition, **D**istance from Top of Paragraph. Type **.5**, and press Enter three times to close the two dialog boxes and return to the document. WordPerfect adjusts the graphics box to fit below the first two lines of text in the paragraph. The text and graphics box look like Figure 17-4.

Do not clear the screen; you will use this text and graphics box in the next example.

2. You can set the horizontal position of a graphics box when you want to change how the box aligns with the left or right margin. Select **G**raphics or press Alt-F9, and then select Graphics **B**oxes, **E**dit. The 1 after "Document Box Number" is correct, so press Enter to select **E**dit Box. Select Edit **P**osition, **H**orizontal Position. To stretch the graphics box from the left margin to the right margin, select **F**ull. Press Enter twice to return to the document. The document looks like Figure 17-5. WordPerfect shifts the graphics box to start after the first two lines of the paragraph.

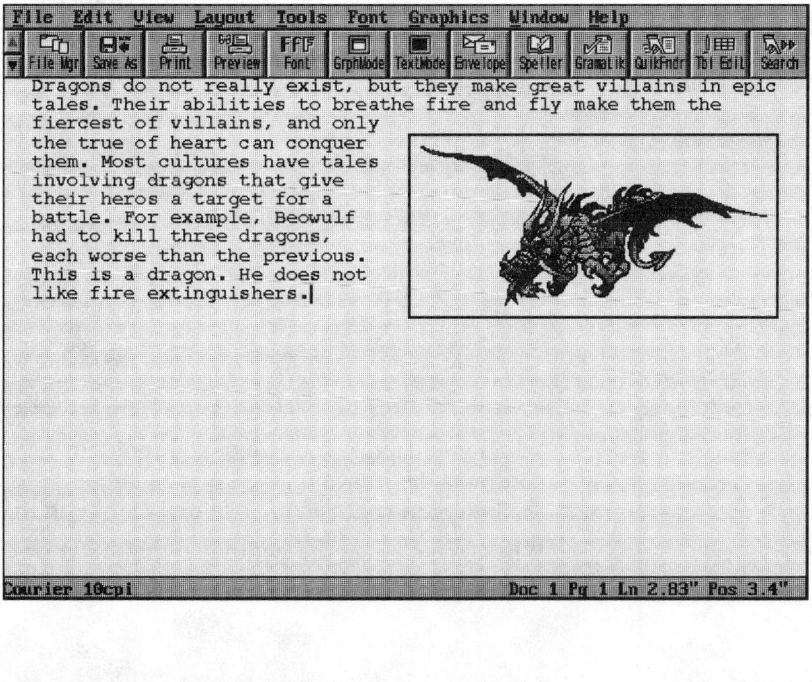

FIGURE 17-4
Graphics box with a vertical-position setting

FIGURE 17-5

Graphics box with a horizontal setting that stretches the box between the left and right margins

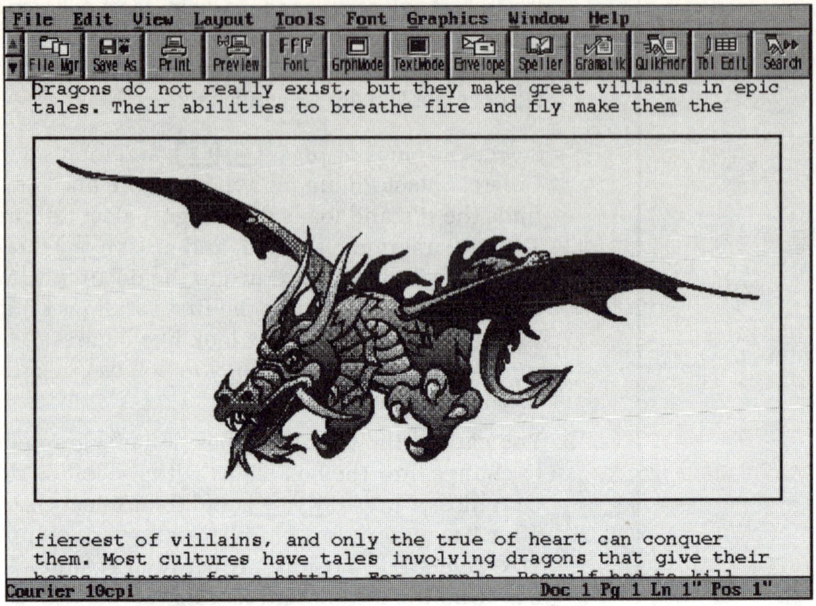

3. For most graphics boxes, you will not need to change the height and width settings that WordPerfect calculates. If you want to, however, you can change them at any time. Select **G**raphics or press Alt-F9, and then select Graphics **B**oxes, **C**reate. Select **F**ilename, type **hotair**, and press Enter. WordPerfect loads the image into the document, using a predetermined size. To change the size, select Edit **S**ize. For the width, select Set **W**idth, type **3**, and press Enter. For the height, select Set **H**eight, type **1.5**, and press Enter. To return to the document, press Enter twice. The document looks like this:

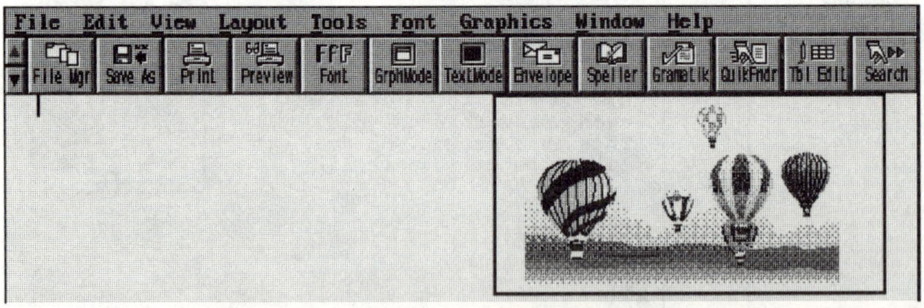

When you change the size of a graphics box, WordPerfect expands or contracts the image to display it as large as possible without changing the height-to-width ratio. The extra space in the box remains empty.

4. When you change the width of a graphics box that contains text, WordPerfect rewraps the text in the box to fit. Select **G**raphics or press

Alt-F9, and then select Graphics **B**oxes, **C**reate. Select Cr**e**ate Text. Then type

Four score and seven years ago, our fathers brought forth upon this continent, a new nation, conceived in liberty, and dedicated to the proposition that all men are created equal.

Press F7. Notice that WordPerfect changed the size of the graphics box to 3.25 inches by 1.36 inches. (The size of your graphics box might vary, depending on the default font you have selected.) Select OK. The graphics box looks like this:

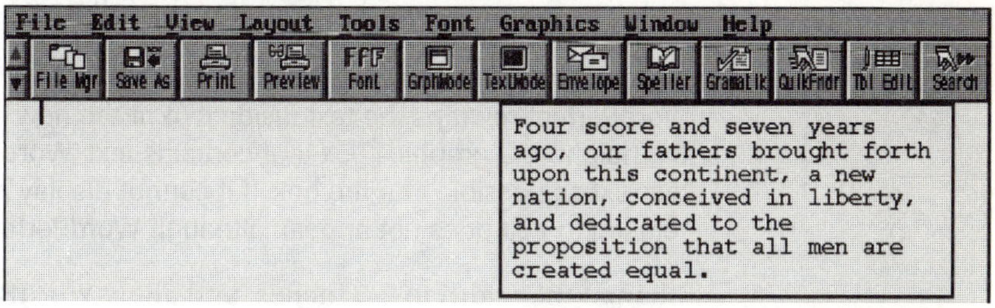

To change the size of the box, select **G**raphics or press Alt-F9, and then select Graphics **B**oxes, **E**dit. Because 1 is the appropriate graphics box number, press Enter to select **E**dit Box. Select Edit **S**ize, Set **W**idth. Type **5**, and press Enter for the new width. WordPerfect adjusts the height of the box to accommodate the text. Finally, select OK twice to return to the document. The graphics box looks like this:

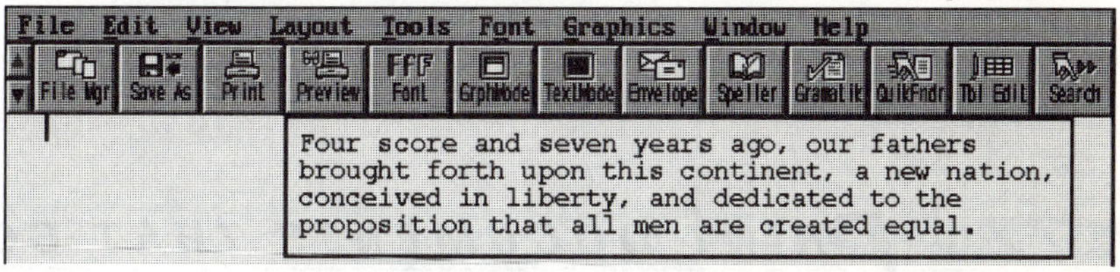

EXERCISES

1. Create a blank graphics box, and set its vertical position to .5 inch. Then return to the document, and type the following paragraph:

When you create a graphics box, WordPerfect wraps the document text around it. In text mode, if the box does not fully appear on the screen, WordPerfect completes the box as you type the text. If you edit the text that you put next to the box, WordPerfect adjusts the text so that it is properly wrapped.

2. Create an empty graphics box at the left margin.
3. Create a graphics box that contains the image named MEDICAL1.WPG. Set the height to 5 inches, and let WordPerfect determine the appropriate width.
4. Create a graphics box that contains the following paragraph:

   When you change the width of a graphics box that contains text, WordPerfect rewraps the text inside it to fit the new width. When you set the height of a graphics box that contains text, WordPerfect fits as much of the text as possible into the box. If it cannot display all of the text, the remaining text does not appear, although WordPerfect remembers it.

   Change the width to 2.5 inches, and allow WordPerfect to set the height. Change the width to 3 inches and the height to 2 inches.
5. Create a graphics box that contains the image HOTROD.WPG. Set the height to 4 inches, and allow WordPerfect to set the width. Set the horizontal position so that the box is centered.

17.6 PRINT DOCUMENTS THAT CONTAIN GRAPHICS

Most printers can print your graphics boxes as they print your document. A few printers can print graphics and text, but they cannot print both at one time. If you try to print a document that contains text and graphics and one or the other does not print correctly, your printer will not support the combined printing of text and graphics.

Depending on your printer, you might be able to set the quality of the printing. As you improve the print quality of text or graphics in a document, especially the latter, you increase the time your printer takes to print the document.

TO PRINT A DOCUMENT THAT CONTAINS TEXT AND GRAPHICS ON A PRINTER THAT CAN PRINT BOTH AT ONE TIME

a. Select **File**, **Print** or press Shift+F7.

b. Select **G**raphics Quality.

c. Select **D**raft, **M**edium, or **H**igh.

d. Select **T**ext Quality.

e. Select **D**raft, **M**edium, or **H**igh.

f. Select the P**r**int button to start printing the document.

TO PRINT A DOCUMENT THAT CONTAINS TEXT AND GRAPHICS ON A PRINTER THAT CANNOT PRINT BOTH AT ONE TIME

a. Select **File**, **Print** or press Shift+F7.

b. Select **G**raphics Quality.

c. Select Do **N**ot Print.

d. Select **T**ext Quality.

e. Select **D**raft, **M**edium, or **H**igh.

f. Select the P**r**int button to start printing the document.

g. When the text is printed, insert the printed pages into the printer so that the printer will start printing at the beginning of the first page.

h. Select **File**, **Print** or press Shift+F7.

i. Select **T**ext Quality.

j. Select Do **N**ot Print.

k. Select **G**raphics Quality.

l. Select **D**raft, **M**edium, or **H**igh.

m. Select the P**r**int button to start printing the document.

EXAMPLES

If your printer can print graphics and text at the same time, do example 1. If your printer cannot print graphics and text at the same time, do example 2.

1. Printing documents that contain text and graphics is a simple process with most printers. To create a document that contains text and

graphics, select **G**raphics or press Alt-F9, and then select Graphics **B**oxes, **C**reate. Select **F**ilename, type **penpush**, and press Enter. Select Edit **S**ize, Set **W**idth. Type **2**, and press Enter twice to change the size of the graphics box. Align this image with the left margin by selecting Edit **P**osition, **H**orizontal Position, **L**eft. Select OK twice to return to the document, and type

At next Tuesday's meeting, several important points will be discussed. It is imperative that you be there.

To print this document, select **F**ile, **P**rint or press Shift-F7. Select **G**raphics Quality, **H**igh. The default for the Text Quality option is High, so you do not need to change that option. Press Enter to select the P**r**int button. The printed document looks like this:

At next Tuesday's meeting, several important points will be discussed. It is imperative that you be there.

2. If you have a printer that cannot print graphics and text at the same time, you must use a different set of steps. Select **G**raphics or press Alt-F9, and then select Graphics **B**oxes, **C**reate. Select **F**ilename, type **penpush**, and press Enter. Select Edit **S**ize, Set **W**idth. Type **2** and press Enter twice to change the size of the graphics box. Align this image with the left margin of the paragraph by selecting Edit **P**osition, **H**orizontal Position, **L**eft. Select OK twice to return to the document, and type

   At next Tuesday's meeting, several important points will be discussed. It is imperative that you be there.

   To print this document, select **F**ile, **P**rint or press Shift-F7. Select **G**raphics Quality, and select Do **N**ot Print to suppress the printing of the graphics. Unless Text Quality is not set to High, you do not need to change it. Press Enter to select the P**r**int button.

   To print the graphics, reinsert the paper into the paper tray, if your printer uses one, or move the paper back in the traction feeders so that WordPerfect will start printing the graphics at the beginning of the document. Select **F**ile, **P**rint or press Shift-F7. Select **T**ext Quality, Do **N**ot Print to keep WordPerfect from printing the text.

Then select **G**raphics Quality, **H**igh to set the graphics quality to high. Press Enter to select the P**r**int button. WordPerfect will skip over where it printed the text and print the graphic in its appropriate place. The result looks like the illustration from the previous example.

Because printing graphics and text separately can be a cumbersome process, you might want to perform these steps for one page at a time if only a few pages in your document have graphics.

EXERCISES

1. Create a graphics box that contains the image named PLAN2.WPG. Print the document, using draft quality for the graphics.
2. Create a graphics box that contains the image named CONDUCT.WPG. Return to the document, and type the following paragraph:

   To check out a key for the computer room, you must register your name with the department secretary, Karen Martin. Then you must sign up for a night on the calendar outside Martin's office. On the day that you have signed up, you must pick up the key by 5:00 p.m.

   Print the document with medium graphics quality and high text quality.
3. Create a graphics box that contains the image WIZARD.WPG. Then return to the document, and type the following paragraph:

   Calligraphy is the art of writing beautifully. Although some calligraphers use quill pens, you can learn calligraphy by using special pens that are available in most art stores. To learn calligraphy, you need a pen, ink, paper, and patience.

   Print the document with the graphics quality set to High.

mastery skills check

As you complete these Mastery Skills Check exercises, do not clear the screen between exercises unless instructed to do so.

1. Create a graphics box that contains the image in BORDER4.WPG. [17.1]
2. Create a blank graphics box that is aligned at the left margin. [17.5]
3. Edit the second graphics box to contain the following text. [17.2]

   Points to remember:
   A bird is known by its note, and a man by his talk.
   Proverb
   The secret of success is constancy to purpose.
   Benjamin Disraeli
   Thrift is too late at the bottom of the purse.
   Seneca

4. Change the image used in the first graphics box to the image named PLAN2.WPG. [17.3]
5. Add a caption to the second graphics box that reads "A few thoughts to ponder." [17.4]
6. Change the width of the first graphics box to 1 inch. [17.5]
7. Change the height of the second graphics box to 4.5 inches. [17.5]
8. Insert blank lines between the sayings in the second graphics box. [17.2]
9. Print the document with text quality set to Medium and graphics quality set to High. [17.6]

cumulative skills check

Do not clear the screen between exercises.

1. Type the following paragraph:

   The images that you use for a graphics box can come from a variety of sources. WordPerfect provides several images, all of which have the .WPG extension. You can also use pictures generated by other software. For example, you can use .PIC files that you generate by using Lotus 1-2-3. You can learn more about graphics boxes from WordPerfect 6 Made Easy, by Mella Mincberg.

   Open a second document, and create an empty graphics box. Switch back to the first document, block the paragraph, and copy the paragraph to the Clipboard. Then paste the Clipboard's contents into the graphics box in the second document. Press Enter until the cursor is several lines below the bottom of the graphics box. [13.3, 17.2]

2. Create a graphics box that displays the image PHEASANT.WPG. Create a caption that says "A bird in the hand is worth two in the bush." Set both the height and the width of the graphics box to 4 inches. [17.1, 17.4, 17.5]

3. Set the font of the graphics box that contains text to Swiss 721 Roman. [12.6]

4. Edit the graphics box that contains text to underline "WordPerfect 6 Made Easy." [4.7, 17.3]

5. Set graphics and text quality to Draft. Print two copies of the document. [12.1, 17.6]

6. Split the document window so that you can see the document that contains just text and the document that contains the two graphics boxes. [13.2]

7. Save the document that contains the text as IMAGES. Save the document that contains the graphics boxes as GRAPHICS. Copy these two files to a floppy disk. [11.2]

8. Create a footer for the GRAPHICS document that contains a graphics box that displays the image named DRAGON.WPG. Set the horizontal position to stretch the box from the left to the right margin. [10.2, 17.5]

9. Add the following text below the text in the IMAGES document:

   Some of the images include:
   DRAGON A picture of a dragon
   HUMBIRD A picture of a hummingbird

   Put two extra lines between this text and the text above it. Put three spaces at the beginning of the three lines of text you have just added. Draw a double line around the three lines of text. [16.2, 16.5]

10. Set the graphics quality to High, and print the GRAPHICS document. Print the IMAGES document, and then cancel this print job. [12.3, 17.6]

18

Creating an Outline

chapter objectives

After completing this chapter, you should be able to

18.1 Create an outline

18.2 Change an outline

18.3 Change the outline numbering style

18.4 Collapse and expand an outline

YOU can use WordPerfect to create outlines. Your outline entries can be complete sentences or just topic words or phrases. You can use these outlines as the basis for a more detailed document with additional, descriptive text. You can also use them to show meeting agendas, project tasks, personnel assignments, and other materials.

If you use WordPerfect's outline feature to create your outline, WordPerfect numbers the outline entries for you. As you add, delete, and move entries in the outline, WordPerfect renumbers them.

WordPerfect supports up to eight levels of outlining, and it uses a different numbering style for each level. Arabic numbers, uppercase letters, lowercase letters, and Roman numerals are combined with periods and parentheses to make each level unique. You can use the default settings for each level, use other predefined style options, or define your own outline levels.

review skills check

1. Type the following text, indenting it from the left margin. [5.1]

   WordPerfect has many features that are missing from other word processing packages. After you master the basics, you will feel comfortable exploring some of the advanced features that WordPerfect offers.

2. Retype the paragraph in exercise 1, indenting it from both margins. [5.1]
3. Change the tab setting to one tab stop at 4 inches, and type the following list. [5.3]

Joe Jones	Accounting
Paul Balber	Finance
Norlin Rugers	Management
Mary Rogers	Accounting

4. Change the left and right margin settings to 2 inches, and type the following paragraph.

WordPerfect's outline feature makes entering and updating an outline an easy process. Each outline entry requires several steps, but after the outline is entered, WordPerfect updates the numbers.

Print two copies of the document. [6.2, 12.1]

18.1 CREATE AN OUTLINE

An outline can help you organize and focus your thoughts when you write lengthy documents. An outline can also serve as a useful end product when you need to share a set of summary data with others.

WordPerfect makes it easy to create outlines. When you turn on the outline feature, WordPerfect treats each new paragraph as another entry in your outline. You press Tab to change to the next lower outline level. You press Shift-Tab (back tab) to change to the preceding outline level. WordPerfect maintains perfect order for each level in your outline.

TO CREATE AN OUTLINE IN WORDPERFECT

a. Position the cursor where you want to begin the outline.

b. Select **T**ools, **O**utline or press Ctrl-F5, and then select **B**egin New Outline.

c. Highlight the outline style you want to use, and press Enter.

d. Press Tab or Shift-Tab (back tab) one or more times to change the outline level of the current entry.

e. Type the text of the entry.

f. Press Enter to create the next outline entry.

g. Repeat steps d, e, and f as necessary to complete the outline.

h. Select **T**ools, **O**utline or press Ctrl-F5, and then select **E**nd Outline.

The default numbering style, called Paragraph, which WordPerfect uses for levels in an outline, uses numbers and letters to mark the level of the paragraphs. You can also choose from many other styles.

If you want to indent the text of an outline entry, press Spacebar after pressing Tab in step d to change the outline level. An [Outline:*style*] code is inserted when you turn on the outline feature. *Style* is replaced by a code that indicates which style of numbering you selected. Another [Outline:*style*] code is inserted when you turn off the outline feature. Pressing Enter within an outline to create a new entry generates another hidden code: [Para Style:Level #;;].

EXAMPLES

1. You can use WordPerfect's outline feature to create a topic outline. You might use such an outline to record the various points that you want to discuss at an upcoming management meeting. First, type the following title for the outline:

   August 20 Meeting Agenda

   Press Enter to position the cursor at the beginning of the line. Select **T**ools, **O**utline or press Ctrl-F5, and then select **B**egin Outline. The Outline Style List dialog box opens, as shown in Figure 18-1. Highlight the outline style called Outline, and press Enter to have WordPerfect generate the number I for the first entry. Type the following lines, pressing Enter after each line except the last.

FIGURE 18-1

The Outline Style List dialog box

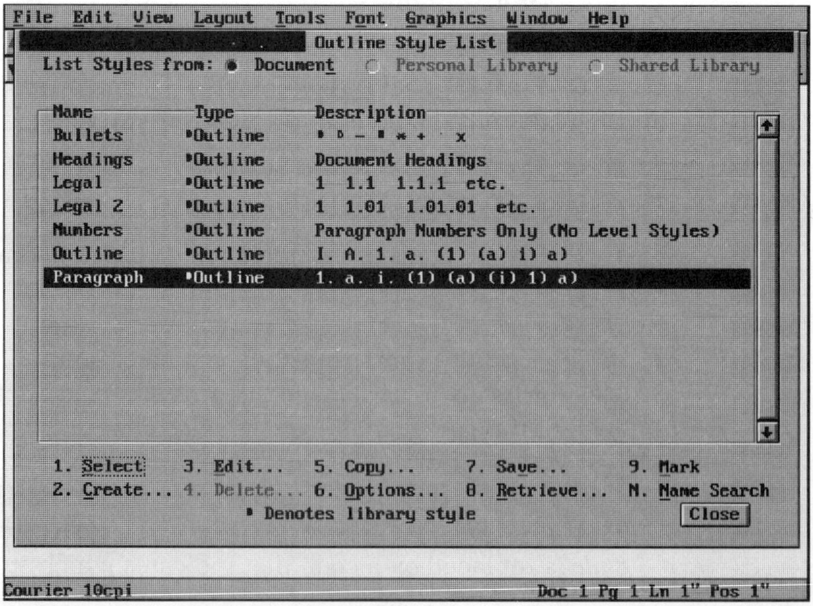

Sales bonus program
Insurance coverage options
Construction proposals
Meeting with security personnel
Position announcements before publication

The completed outline should look like this:

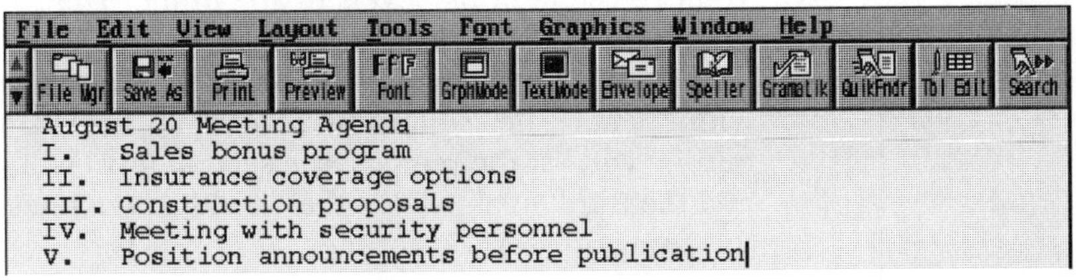

To turn off the outline feature, select **T**ools, **O**utline or press Ctrl-F5, and select **E**nd Outline.

Save the document by pressing F7, selecting **Y**es, typing **agenda**, and selecting OK. Select **N**o to clear the screen and remain in WordPerfect.

2. You can use WordPerfect's outline feature to create a sentence outline. You can outline tasks for a project in the order in which they will be completed. First, turn on the outline feature by selecting **T**ools, **O**utline or press Ctrl-F5, and select **B**egin Outline. Highlight the style called Outline, and press Enter. Type the following entries, pressing Enter after each line except the last to generate the next outline number.

   Meet with architect to discuss building plans and zoning requirements.
   Complete excavation and other site preparation tasks. Complete roadbed preparation.
   Review architect's drawings, make suggested changes, and discuss construction schedule.
   Begin construction on main building, drive pilings for pier, and begin paving parking lots.

   The outline looks like this:

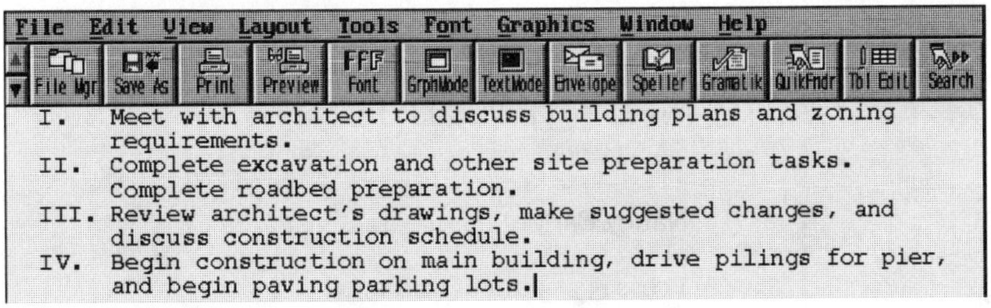

Select **T**ools, **O**utline or press Ctrl-F5, and select **E**nd Outline to turn off the outline feature. After you turn off the outline feature, you can add text below the outline without WordPerfect adding outline numbers to the text. Press F7, select **Y**es, type **constrt** as the filename for the document, select OK, and then select **N**o to clear the screen without leaving WordPerfect.

3. You can use multiple levels in an outline. You use Tab and Shift-Tab (back tab) to indicate to WordPerfect which level you want to use for each entry. You can create an outline structure that shows the winners in a sales contest by region and branch. The first level of the outline will list the regions, the second level will list the branches, and the third level will list the employees' names. First, type the following title for the outline:

   Better Boat Brigade Contest

   Press Enter. Then select **T**ools, **O**utline or press Ctrl-F5, and select **B**egin Outline to turn on the outline feature. Highlight the style called Outline, and press Enter. Type

   Eastern Region

   Press Enter, and then press Tab to generate a number one level down. Type

   Boston Branch

   Press Enter, and press Tab to generate a number one more level down. Type

   John Jones

   Press Enter, and type

   Mary Smith

   To begin another branch entry, press Enter and press Shift-Tab (back tab) once. Then type

   New York Branch

   Press Enter. To add the names for New York, press the Tab key, and type

   Nancy Carter

   Press Enter once, and type

Jeff Greenhoff

The screen looks like this:

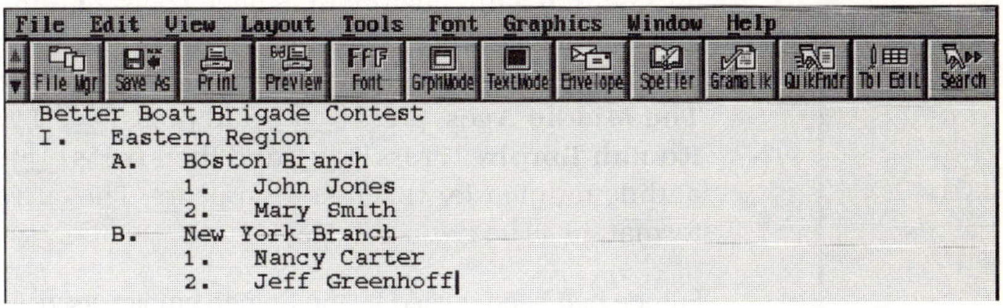

Complete the entries for the western region by using the same approach. Press Enter twice, and then press Shift-Tab (back tab) twice. Pressing Enter twice generates a blank line between the entries. Type

Western Region

Press Enter, press Tab, and type

Las Vegas Branch

Press Enter, press Tab once, and type

Jill Cravens

Press Enter. For the last entry, type

George Moore

The screen looks like this:

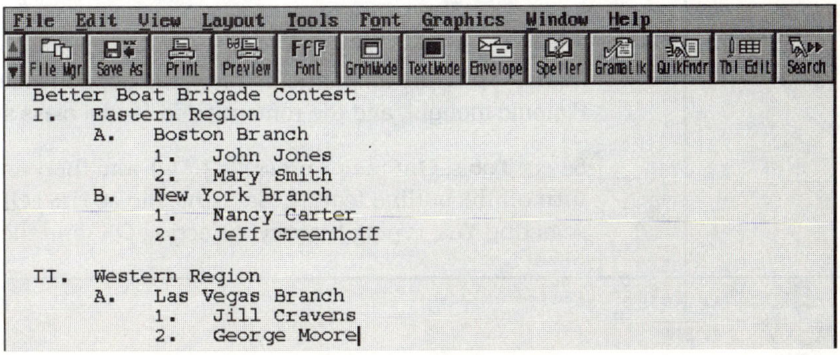

Select **T**ools, **O**utline or press Ctrl-F5, and then select **E**nd Outline to turn off the outline feature. Save the file and clear the screen by

pressing F7, selecting **Y**es, typing **prizes**, selecting OK, and then selecting **N**o.

4. You can add paragraphs of body text to an outline to expand an outline into a full document. Select **T**ools, **O**utline or press Ctrl-F5, and then select **B**egin Outline. Highlight the style called Outline, and press Enter to enter the first outline number in the document. Type **The Middle Ages**, press Enter, and press Tab. Type **The Fall of the Roman Empire**. Press Enter, and then press Ctrl-T. Notice that the outline number for this line disappears. The current paragraph is now formatted as body text. Type

   Europe had been unified by the Roman empire, its well-maintained roads, and regular trade. With the fall of the Roman empire, travel became less common and more risky, as the empire was fragmented by locally powerful leaders.

   Press Enter, press Ctrl-T, and type **The Dark Ages**. Notice that this line has the appropriate outline number. Press Enter, and press Ctrl-T to remove the outline number. Type

   Europe fell into the hands of numerous tribal leaders and enterprising warriors. As trade became less safe, there was less of it. Small communities had to be effectively self-providing.

   Press Enter and Ctrl-T, and then type **The High Middle Ages**. Press Enter, and press Ctrl-T to remove the outline number. Type

   The more stable political environment made long distance trade less risky, and trade and merchants flourished, providing the economic base for the cultural developments of the period.

   Press Enter and Ctrl-T, and type **The Renaissance**. Press Enter, and press Ctrl-T to remove the outline number. Type

   The Renaissance is marked by a break with the traditions of the High Middle Ages: the emphasis on piety, the dependence on the Bible and Platonic thought, and the romanticized feudal class structure.

   Select **T**ools, **O**utline or press Ctrl-F5, and then select **E**nd Outline to turn off the outline feature. Save this file as HISTORY by pressing F7, selecting **Y**es, typing **history**, selecting OK, and then selecting **N**o.

EXERCISES

1. Create the following outline:

   HIGH SCHOOL SPORTS
   I. BASEBALL
   II. FOOTBALL
   III. SWIMMING
   IV. HOCKEY

   Save the file as SPORTS.

2. Create the following outline:

   BREEDS OF DOGS
   I. Hounds
      A. Greyhound
      B. Whippet
   II. Sporting Dogs
      A. Labrador Retriever
      B. Irish Setter
   III. Terriers
      A. Airedale
      B. Welsh Terrier
   IV. Working Dogs
      A. Collie
      B. Siberian Husky

   Save the file as DOGS.

18.2 CHANGE AN OUTLINE

WordPerfect not only creates the numbering for an outline, it also maintains it as you change the outline. When you add items at any level, WordPerfect assigns the appropriate numbers to those items and renumbers entries affected by the addition. Likewise, if you remove an entry, WordPerfect adjusts the numbering of the remaining entries in that level. Moving entries by changing their levels or by moving them to new locations also causes WordPerfect to adjust the outline numbering. You can insert body text documents into your outline to expand the outline into a full document.

TO DELETE AN ITEM FROM AN OUTLINE

a. Position the cursor on the outline item you want to remove.

b. Select **T**ools, **O**utline, or press Ctrl-F5 and select **M**ove/Copy.

c. Select **C**ut Family.

When you delete an item from an outline, you delete that item and any items subordinate to it. For example, if you delete an outline item labeled III, and item III has items labeled A and B subordinate to it, the items labeled A and B are also deleted. If you want the items below the item you will delete to remain in the outline, you should move them to a higher level by moving to them and pressing Shift-Tab. Then you can delete the intended item without deleting the items below it.

TO ADD AN ITEM TO AN OUTLINE

a. Position the cursor on the outline item above where you want to add the item.

b. Press Enter.

c. Press Tab or Shift-Tab to change the level of the outline item you will add.

d. Type the text for the new outline item.

When you add an item to an outline, WordPerfect renumbers the remaining items in the outline.

TO MOVE AN ITEM IN AN OUTLINE

a. Position the cursor on the outline item that you want to move.

b. Select **T**ools, **O**utline, or press Ctrl-F5 and select **M**ove/Copy.

c. Select **M**ove Family.

d. Move to where you want the outline item placed.

e. Press Enter.

When you move an outline item, you move that item and any items subordinate to it. For example, if you move an outline item labeled II, and this item has items labeled A and B subordinate to it, the A and B outline items are also moved. Just like when you add an item to an outline, WordPerfect handles renumbering the outline items.

EXAMPLES

1. You can delete entries in an outline and have WordPerfect maintain the correct numbers for the outline entries. Open the file named AGENDA by selecting **F**ile, **O**pen or pressing Shift-F10, typing **agenda**, and selecting OK. The outline you created in example 1 of section 18.1 appears. You can delete the fourth item in the outline. Move to any position in the line containing "IV. Meeting with security personnel." Then select **T**ools, **O**utline, or press Ctrl-F5 and select **M**ove/Copy. Select **C**ut Family. The revised outline looks like this:

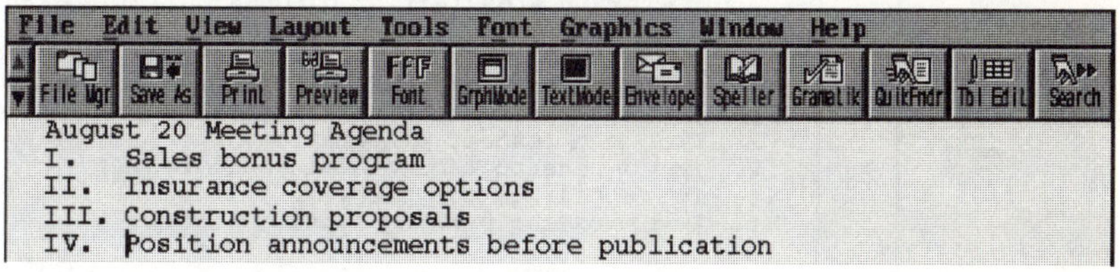

Save this revised outline by pressing F7 once, selecting **Y**es, and then selecting **N**o to clear the screen and remain in WordPerfect.

2. You can add items to an existing outline by typing new entries or by splitting existing entries. Open the file CONSTRT created in example 2 of section 18.1 by selecting **F**ile, **O**pen, or by pressing Shift-F10, typing **constrt**, and selecting OK.

   Move to the last outline entry, placing the cursor on the comma that follows "building." Press Del three times to eliminate the comma, the space, and the *d*. Type a period, press Enter, and type **D**. Since you are making the changes between the point where you turned on the outline feature and where you turned it off, the outline is updated.

   Move to the comma following "pier," press Del seven times, type a period, press Enter, and type **B**. WordPerfect assigns the two new outline entries the appropriate numbers, creating a revised outline that looks like this:

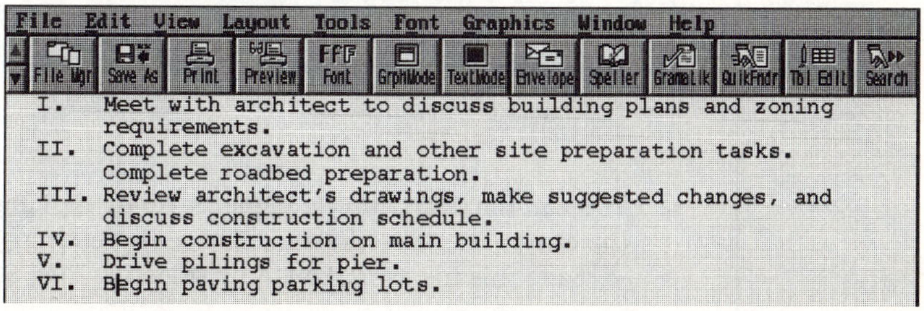

Do not clear the screen; you will use this outline in the next example.

3. WordPerfect adjusts the item numbers when you relocate outline entries. The revised outline from example 2 indicates that excavation will start before the architect's plans are approved. To delay this step until after approval, you can rearrange the outline.

   Move to the second outline entry. Select **T**ools, **O**utline, or press Ctrl-F5 and select **M**ove/Copy. Select **M**ove Family. Press ↓ to move to the third outline item. Press Enter. The item numbers are adjusted as shown here:

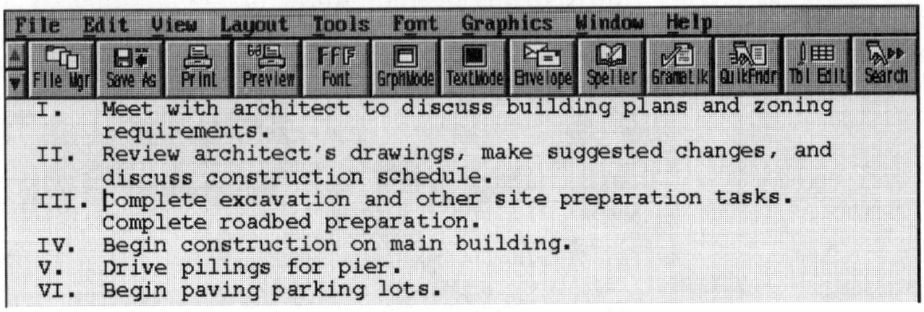

   Save this revised file as CONSTRT by selecting **F**ile, **S**ave.

4. When you change the level of an outline item, WordPerfect updates the rest of the outline accordingly. Open the file named AGENDA by selecting **F**ile, **O**pen or pressing Shift-F10, typing **agenda**, and selecting OK.

   Move to the end of the first outline entry. Press Enter, type **Branch managers**, press Enter, and type **Sales personnel**. Numbers II and III have been assigned to these two entries. To change the level of the "Branch managers" entry, move to the *B* in "Branch," and press Tab. To change the level of the "Sales personnel" entry, move to the *S* in "Sales," and press Tab. WordPerfect adjusts all of the levels properly, as shown here:

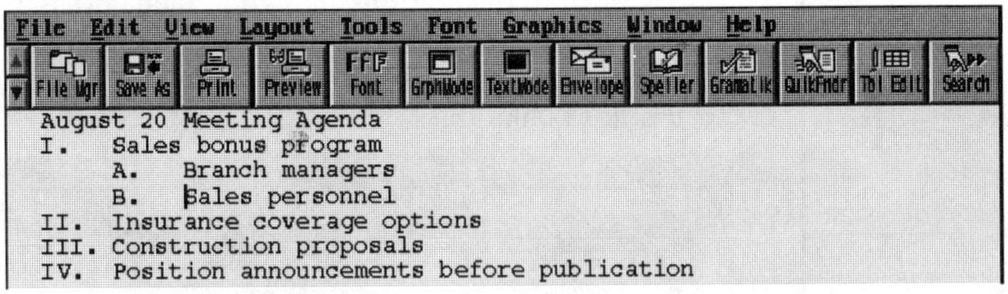

   You can make an entry a higher level by moving to the beginning of the entry, after the hidden codes, and pressing Shift-Tab.

   Save this file as AGENDA by selecting **F**ile, **S**ave.

EXERCISES

1. Retrieve the SPORTS file that you created in exercise 1 of section 18.1. Add the entries "BASKETBALL" and "TRACK." Add another level under each sport, and list the names of the team captains. Use your friends' names for the team captains' names. Save the revised outline.
2. Retrieve the DOGS file that you created in exercise 2 of section 18.1. Move the entries for "Sporting Dogs" to the end of the outline. Save the revised outline.

18.3 CHANGE THE OUTLINE NUMBERING STYLE

The default outline numbering style is adequate for many tasks. If you must conform to a set of established standards, however, you can select from a number of other predefined styles or create your own. This section explores the predefined bullet, legal, and heading styles.

TO CHANGE THE OUTLINE NUMBERING STYLE

a. Position the cursor in the outline whose style you want to change.
b. Select **T**ools, **O**utline or press Ctrl-F5, and then select **O**utline Style. The Outline Style List dialog box opens.
c. Highlight the numbering style you want to use.
d. Select **S**elect. If you used Ctrl-F5, select OK to close the Outline dialog box.

EXAMPLES

1. The bullets style offers an attractive solution for an outline of ideas or other entries that do not require numbers or letters. To create an outline in this style, select **T**ools, **O**utline, or press Ctrl-F5 and then select **B**egin Outline. The Outline Style List dialog box opens.

Select the bullets style by highlighting it and pressing Enter. WordPerfect closes the dialog box and creates the first bullet marker. Type **Complete filing**, and press Enter. Type **Create form letter**. Your two entries should be marked with bullet indicators, like this:

Turn off the outline feature by selecting **T**ools, **O**utline, or pressing Ctrl-F5 and then selecting **E**nd Outline.

2. The legal style allows you to create outline entries in which each item number displays the complete level of the entry in the context of the outline. For example, if your entry is the third item in the first section, it will be labeled 1.3. The second item one level below this entry would be labeled 1.3.2.

   To use the legal style, position the cursor where you want to create the outline, select **T**ools, **O**utline, or press Ctrl-F5 and then select **B**egin Outline. Highlight the legal style, and press Enter. Type **Easements to Title**. Press Enter and Tab to generate a number at the second level, and type **Water Rights**. Press Enter, and type **Building Rights**. Press Enter and Tab once to generate a number at the third level, type **Special deed rights**, and press Enter. Type **Lateral support**. Press Enter, press Shift-Tab, and type **Right of Way**. Press Enter, and type **Way of Necessity**. The completed outline looks like this:

   Turn off the outline feature by selecting **T**ools, **O**utline, or pressing Ctrl-F5 and then selecting **E**nd Outline.

3. The headings style makes creating a document from an outline quite simple. Select **F**ile, **O**pen or press Shift-F10, type **history**, and select OK to open the HISTORY file you created in the example 4 of section 18.1.

   With your cursor in the first line, select **T**ools, **O**utline, or press Ctrl-F5 and then select **O**utline Style. Highlight the headings style, and press Enter. Your document looks like Figure 18-2. Save the modified version by selecting **F**ile, **E**xit or pressing F7. Select **Y**es and then select **N**o to save the document and clear the screen.

FIGURE 18-2

Using the Headings style

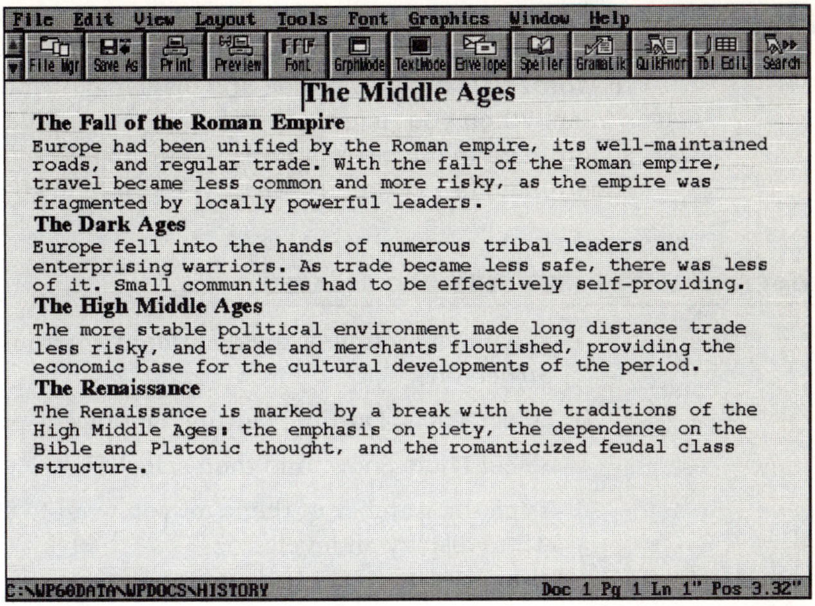

EXERCISES

1. Change the outline style to legal, and create the following outline:

    1 Estate Planning
    1.1 Trust
    1.2 Will

2. Change to the bullet outline style, and create the following entries with the level-four bullet indicators:

    The following employees are being honored for 25 years of service:

    ◇ Jane Parker
    ◇ Bill Black

18.4 COLLAPSE AND EXPAND AN OUTLINE

In WordPerfect, you can hide and display parts of your outline on the screen. When you hide an *outline family,* you hide all of the entries subordinate to the current entry. You can also hide all outline levels subordinate to a certain level, or you can hide body text.

TO SET THE LEVEL OF THE OUTLINE DISPLAYED

a. Move to a section of the document where the outline feature is turned on.

b. Select **T**ools, **O**utline, Outl**i**ne Options or press Ctrl-F5.

c. Select **H**ide/Show, and then select **S**how Levels.

d. Type the number of the level you want to show, or press A for **A**ll to display all levels.

TO HIDE OR DISPLAY THE BODY TEXT OF AN OUTLINE

a. Move to a section of the document where the outline feature is turned on.

b. Select **T**ools, **O**utline.

c. Select Hide Body **T**ext or Show Body **T**ext to hide or display the body text.

EXAMPLES

1. You can display only certain levels of your outline. Open the PRIZES file by selecting **F**ile, **O**pen or pressing Shift-F10, typing **prizes**, and selecting OK. Move to the *E* in "Eastern" so that you are in the section of the document where the outline feature is turned on. Select **T**ools, **O**utline, Outl**i**ne Options or press Ctrl-F5 to open the Outline dialog box. Select **H**ide/Show, and then select **S**how Levels. Select the number that corresponds to the lowest level you want to show—in this case, select **1**. The lower levels are hidden, and your screen looks like this:

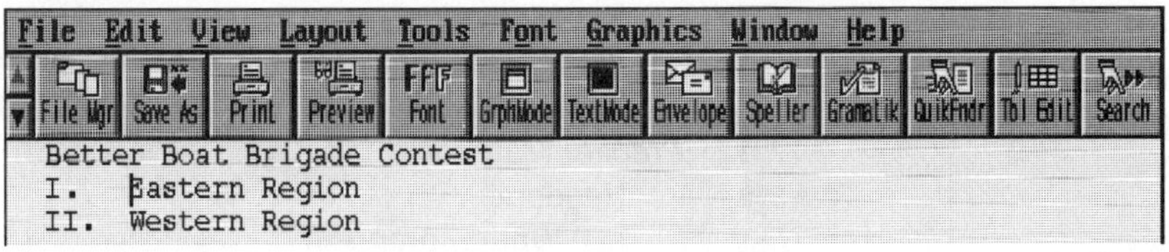

If you reveal the hidden codes, you will see that where the lower-level entries used to appear, WordPerfect has inserted the code [Hidden Text]. If you print this document now, only the displayed levels of the outline will appear. To restore the display to normal, first select **T**ools, **O**utline, Out**l**ine Options or press Ctrl-F5. Select **H**ide/Show, and then select **S**how Levels. Select **A**ll. WordPerfect expands the outline to show all of the outline text.

2. You can change the display of body text as well as the display of outline entries. Select **F**ile, **O**pen or press Shift-F10, type **history**, and select OK to open the HISTORY file you modified in example 2 of section 18.3. Select **T**ools, **O**utline, Hide Body **T**ext. All of the body text paragraphs disappear, although the outline entries do not. Your document looks like this:

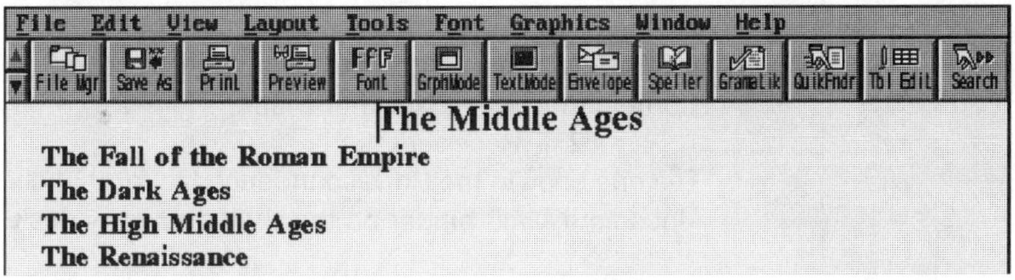

You could now print these outline entries to create an accurate and timely outline for the document. To restore the document's body text, select **T**ools, **O**utline, Show Body **T**ext. The body text paragraphs reappear, and you can use the document normally.

EXERCISES

1. Create the following outline:

I. Preparing for the Presentation
   A. Write Speech
      1. Research Issues

        a. Marketing surveys
        b. Product analyses
    2. Prepare Outline
B. Prepare Materials
    1. Handouts
        a. Written proposal
        b. Company brochure
        c. Chart of potential sales
    2. Display Slides
        a. Photograph site
        b. Have Cindy organize

Display only the first two levels. Display three levels. Display all levels, and save the outline as PRESENT.

2. Create the following outline. The levels without outline numbers are body text.

I Filing
    A. Letters
        1. Sent
File one copy in the binder marked "Outgoing Letters" on the shelf above my desk, in order by the date sent, and a second copy in the Correspondence file for that client.
        2. Received
File one copy in the Correspondence file for that client, and a second in the "Incoming Mail" binder on the shelf above my desk.

Hide the body text. Display the outline levels through the second level.

mastery skills check

As you work through these Mastery Skills Check exercises, do not clear the screen between exercises unless instructed to do so.

1. Create the following outline by using WordPerfect's automatic level-numbering feature. [18.1]

PORTFOLIO HOLDINGS
I. Zero coupon bonds
II. Treasury bills
III. Blue chip stocks
IV. Mutual fund shares

2. Revise the outline so that "Treasury bills" is the last entry. [18.2]
3. Add the following entry to the outline:

   V. Stock options

   Save the file as INVEST, and clear the screen. [18.2]
4. Create the following outline. [18.1, 18.4]

   I. New Construction
      A. Mayfield Village
      B. Highland Heights
         1. 1114 Miner Road
         2. 4811 Highland Avenue
   II. Remodeling Projects
      A. Gates Mills
         1. 112 Sherman Road
         2. 230 Saddleback Lane
      B. Chagrin Falls

   Display only two levels, and print a copy.
5. Add an entry for a remodeling project in Solon. Add an entry for a new construction project at 5311 Wilson Mills Road in Highland Heights. Save the file as JOBS. [18.2]

Teach Yourself cumulative skills check

1. Create the following memo, using the outline feature for the bulleted entries:

   From: John Smith
   To: George Carson
   Subject: Expense Reports

A recent audit of expense reports indicated that several of your employees have exceeded the per diem allowed for travel expenses on several occasions. A list of the employees who violated this policy is enclosed.

◇ Jim Miller
◇ Mary Parker
◇ Paul Drake

Insert a hard page break above the outline entries, and print a copy of the document. [1.3, 3.1, 18.1, 18.3]

2. Create a form letter to address to the three employees mentioned in the previous exercise. The form letter uses the following variable information stored in a data file named TRIPS1:

Jim Miller
Jim
Las Vegas; Atlantic City

Mary Parker
Mary
Washington, D.C.; Pittsburgh

Paul Drake
Paul
Miami; Orlando; New York City

The form letter looks like the following, with the information in parentheses replaced by the variable information.

From: George Carson
To: (employee's name)

Dear (employee's first name),

It has come to my attention that the expense reports from several of your last trips exceed the per diem amount the company allows for travel. The trips that have had this problem include:
(trip locations)
Please contact me so that we can discuss how to prevent this problem on future trips.

Add an extra line at the top, and draw a double-line box around the From and To information. Print two copies each of the three form letters. [12.1, 14.1, 14.2, 14.3, 14.4, 16.2]

3. Create the following outline:

   1 WordPerfect's Math Features
   1.1 Add numbers
   1.1.1 Produce a subtotal for a column of numbers
   1.1.2 Add subtotals to create totals
   1.1.3 Add totals to produce a grand total
   1.2 Perform formula calculations across columns

   Save the outline as MATH. Display only the first two levels. [2.4, 18.1, 18.3, 18.4]

4. Retrieve MATH, and add a graphics box that starts on the same line as the WordPerfect's Math Features outline item and displays the image PENPUSH.WPG. Add a caption to the graphics box that says "WordPerfect's Math Features Make Calculations Easy." [17.1, 17.4]

5. Create the following outline, using the underline feature for the titles:

   I. WordPerfect Books
      A. WordPerfect 6 Made Easy
   II. 1-2-3 Books
      A. 1-2-3 Made Easy
      B. 1-2-3: The Complete Reference

   Add **Teach Yourself WordPerfect 6** as item B in the first section. Print two copies of the outline. [12.1, 18.1, 18.2]

6. Create the following outline:

   I. Vacation days
   II. Sick leave
   III. Holidays
      A. Christmas
      B. Thanksgiving
      C. Memorial Day
      D. Halloween
      E. Independence Day
      F. Labor Day

   Move the third section, with all of its second-level entries, to the top of the outline. Delete the entry for Halloween. [18.2]

7. Open HISTORY. Change to the style called Outline, and hide the body text. Print the outline. Change back to the headings style, and redisplay the body text. Print the document. [2.6, 3.1, 18.1, 18.3, 18.4]

19

Changing Setup Parameters

chapter objectives

After completing this chapter, you should be able to

19.1 Change backup options

19.2 Change display options

19.3 Change other options

MANY people use WordPerfect for years without changing the settings that control the software. Although you can use WordPerfect with the default settings, customizing the settings personalizes your copy of the software to better meet your needs. In addition, some of the changes that you find yourself making to every document that you create can be made once and will then apply to every new document that you create.

The options in the File, Setup menu allow you to customize the display and other features that affect your use of the software. WordPerfect's display options allow you to customize the way in which various text styles, sizes, and features are displayed on the screen. If you have a color monitor, you can select from an entire palette of colors for each feature.

WordPerfect offers other options that are not located in the File, Setup menu. You can change the format used for a date inserted in a document, you can customize how the beep is used to respond to errors, and you can change the codes that are placed at the beginning of new documents.

In this chapter, you will explore only a few of the many customizing changes that you can make to WordPerfect. Because the process you learn here can be used to update other settings, you can explore additional options on your own.

review
skills check

Do not clear the screen until you have completed the last Skills Check exercise.

1. Type the following lines, using the bold and underline features where indicated. [4.1, 4.2]

   WordPerfect allows you to change several settings. You can set WordPerfect to back up files automatically. You can also change the screen's appearance by selecting the colors WordPerfect uses. These are just a few of the selections available.

2. Save the document as DEFAULT. [2.4]
3. Rename the DEFAULT file as SETTINGS. [11.5]
4. Reveal codes to see WordPerfect's code for a soft return. [4.4]

19.1 CHANGE BACKUP OPTIONS

WordPerfect creates a backup of your current document every ten minutes. You will notice a slight delay as you type when WordPerfect writes your document to disk. If you are working with multiple documents, it creates files named WP{WPC}.BK1, WP{WPC}.BK2, and so on. These backup files are useful because if your system goes down without warning, you can rename the backup files when you start another WordPerfect session and use them to replace the files that were lost. You can change the number of minutes between backups, or you can set WordPerfect to not make backups.

TO CHANGE THE TIMING OF WORDPERFECT'S BACKUPS OF YOUR WORK

a. Select **F**ile, **S**etup or press Shift-F1.
b. Select **E**nvironment.
c. Select **B**ackup Options. If the check box is filled with an *X*, selecting the check box removes the *X*, which causes WordPerfect to not make backups.
d. Select **M**inutes Between Backups, and type the desired number of minutes between saves.
e. Select OK twice.
   If you used Shift-F1 instead of the menu selections in step a, you need to select Close to close the Setup dialog box.

EXAMPLES

1. Timed backups offer protection against power failures or other accidents that can remove a document from your computer's memory. To have WordPerfect back up your documents every half

hour, first select **F**ile, Se**t**up or press Shift-F1. Next, choose **E**nvironment, select **B**ackup Options, select **M**inutes Between Backups, type **30**, and press Enter. Select OK twice.

2. If you lose a document, you can rename the backup copy of the document when you start WordPerfect again. Select **F**ile, Se**t**up or press Shift-F1, and then choose **E**nvironment. Select **B**ackup Options, select **M**inutes Between Backups, and type **1**. Press OK twice. To have something to back up, type

WordPerfect has an automatic timed backup feature.

To have WordPerfect back up the document, wait a minute. WordPerfect briefly displays a message box indicating that a timed backup is being made.

To see how you can use this timed backup, reboot your computer without exiting WordPerfect. First, open the door on drive A, if you have a disk in drive A, to force your computer to boot from drive C. Next, press Ctrl-Alt-Del. After the computer has loaded DOS, load WordPerfect. When you load WordPerfect, it displays this dialog box:

You can rename the file by selecting **R**ename and typing the new name in the Backup Filename text box. You can also delete the file or open the file to look at it.

Select **R**ename, and type **newfile** as a name. Press Enter to display WordPerfect's document screen.

EXERCISES

1. Set the timed backup interval to 2 hours (120 minutes).
2. Set the timed backup interval to 15 minutes.

19.2 CHANGE DISPLAY OPTIONS

WordPerfect allows a significant amount of screen customization. If you have a color monitor, you can change the screen colors to make various WordPerfect features and screen attributes look different onscreen. In graphics mode you can change the appearance of screen elements such as the menu bar, and in text mode you can change the colors used to distinguish bold or redlined text from normal text. Before attempting to change colors for either mode, activate the mode you want to change. Otherwise, your changes will not be reflected onscreen.

You can alter the special character used to display hard returns on your screen. You can also choose whether to display the filename of the current document on the screen.

TO CHANGE THE SCREEN COLORS

a. Select **F**ile, Se**t**up or press Shift-F1, and then select **D**isplay.

b. Select either **G**raphics Mode Screen Type/Colors or **T**ext Mode Screen Type/Colors, depending on which settings you want to change.

c. Select **C**olor Schemes.

d. Select **C**reate, type a name and select OK, or highlight one of the color schemes you have created and select **E**dit. You cannot change the default color schemes.

e. Select **A**ttributes if you are changing the text mode options, or select **S**creen Elements if you are changing the graphics mode options.

f. Highlight the desired text attribute or screen element, and press Enter to select **C**olors.

The colors that are available depend on the equipment you are using.

g. Use the arrow keys to frame the desired option.

If you change your mind while selecting colors, press Esc to return to your document.

h. Select OK twice and Close twice to return to your document with the new option in effect.

You can also use the F7 key in place of OK and Close.

TO CHANGE THE CHARACTER THAT REPRESENTS A HARD RETURN

a. Select **V**iew, Scree**n** Setup.

b. Select **D**isplay Characters.

c. Select **H**ard Return Character.

d. Type the character you want to represent a hard return.

e. Select OK.

Each time you press Enter, the character you set to indicate a hard return appears in the document window. The hard return code [HRt] appears as usual when you select **V**iew, Reveal **C**odes or press Alt-F3.

TO CHANGE THE DISPLAY OF THE FILENAME IN THE STATUS LINE

a. Select **V**iew, Scree**n** Setup.

b. Select **W**indow Options.

c. Select **S**tatus Line.

d. Select **N**othing to remove the filename from the display, F**o**nt to display the current font at all times, or **F**ilename to display the current filename.

e. Select OK.

EXAMPLES

1. You can change the colors WordPerfect uses to indicate blocked text. First, select **V**iew, **T**ext Mode. Next, select **F**ile, Se**t**up, **D**isplay. Select **T**ext Mode Screen Type/Colors, **C**olor Schemes, and **C**reate. Type **junk**, press Enter, and select OK to open the Edit Text Screen Colors dialog box.

   Select **A**ttributes, highlight the attribute for which you want to alter the color, select **B**locked, and press Enter to display a palette of colors. Move the box to the top row where the foreground letters are black, and move to the left to highlight the green background. Depending on your monitor, your screen might look something like Figure 19-1.

   Keep pressing F7 until you select OK twice, and then select Close twice to return to your document. Select **V**iew, **G**raphics Mode to return to graphics display mode.

The available options and the effects they have on your screen depend on your computer equipment.

2. You can change the character that represents a hard return. WordPerfect's default setting displays a hard return as a blank space. You can have WordPerfect display a different character for a hard return when you are unsure of the locations of hard returns and want them to be more obvious. First, type

   Hard Return Character

   Emphasizing the hard return characters allows you to discover where you have pressed ENTER and where WordPerfect has wrapped the text for you.

   Press (Enter), select **V**iew, Scree**n** Setup, and then select **D**isplay Characters. Select the **H**ard Return Character text box. To display the hard return character as a plus sign, type +. Then select OK. The text looks like this:

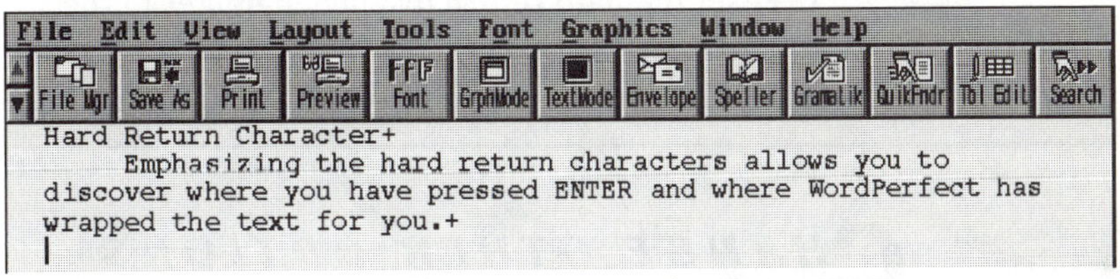

3. You can suppress the display of the current filename in the status line. Select **V**iew, Scree**n** Setup. Select **W**indow Options and then

FIGURE 19-1

Palette of color options for changing the appearance of text

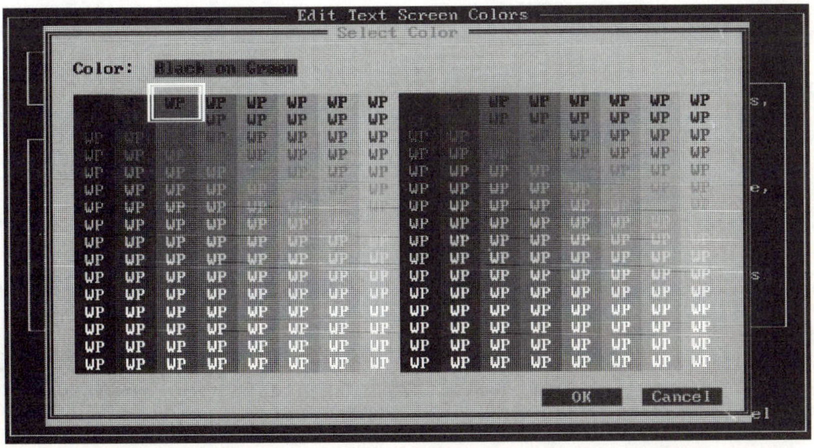

Status Line. Select **N**othing, and then select the OK button. The filename no longer appears in the status line after you open a document or save a new document without exiting from it.

EXERCISES

1. Change the foreground color of bold text for the junk color scheme to black.
2. Set the colors of italic text for the junk color scheme to the same colors used for normal text.
3. Change the hard return display character to the less-than symbol (<).
4. Reset the hard return display character to the space.
5. Set WordPerfect to display the filename in the status line.

19.3 CHANGE OTHER OPTIONS

There are many more customizing changes that you can make to WordPerfect. You can change the display of the date, and you can specify when the computer beeps a warning. Also, you can set which WordPerfect codes appear at the beginning of all new documents. In WordPerfect 6, not all customizing changes are made by using the File, Setup menu.

TO CHANGE THE OCCURRENCE OF THE BEEP

a. Select **F**ile, Se**t**up, **E**nvironment.

b. Select B**e**ep Options.

c. Select the Beep on **E**rror, Beep on **H**yphenation, or Beep on **S**earch Failure check boxes to set when the beep sounds.

   WordPerfect's second beep option, Beep on Hyphenation, determines whether WordPerfect beeps when it prompts you to select a location for a hyphen in a word that won't fit on a line.

d. Select OK twice to return to your document.

TO CHANGE THE DATE DISPLAY

a. Select **T**ools, **D**ate, **F**ormat.

b. Select a predefined numbered format, or select **E**dit.

c. If you select **E**dit in step b, alter the Edit text box entry, or delete it by using Ctrl-End. You can press F5 to select date code entries or Shift-F5 to select time code entries. Select OK when you are finished editing the date format.

d. Select OK.

TO ENTER FORMAT CODES THAT WILL BE PLACED AT THE BEGINNING OF EACH NEW DOCUMENT

a. Select **L**ayout, **D**ocument, Initial Codes Se**t**up.
The Initial Codes Setup dialog box appears. It will display the codes for any formatting you select.

b. Use the menus or the function keys to select formats for lines, margins, pages, or the initial font.

c. Press F7 to finish entering the initial format codes.
All new documents will use the format settings you defined in the Initial Codes Setup dialog box.

d. Select OK to return to the document.

EXAMPLES

1. You can direct WordPerfect to beep when it cannot find the text for which it is searching. This alerts you when WordPerfect cannot find a search string or when it finishes a replace operation. Select **F**ile, Se**t**up, **E**nvironment. Select B**e**ep Options, and then select the Beep on **S**earch Failure check box so that it is filled with an *X*. This sets WordPerfect to beep when a search fails. Finally, select OK twice. When you search the document for text or codes, WordPerfect beeps when it cannot find the search string.

2. WordPerfect can insert the current date into a document. You can change the date format for WordPerfect's date feature. Select **T**ools,

Date, **F**ormat. A dialog box opens that provides many options to format dates and times. Select **E**dit.

To set the date in the format of MM/DD/YY, press Ctrl-End to delete the existing format. Next, press F5, highlight Month#, press Enter, and type /. Press F5, highlight Day#, press Enter, and type /. Press F5, highlight Year(2), and press Enter. The dialog box now looks like Figure 19-2. Press Enter twice. To have WordPerfect insert the date in a document, select **T**ools, **D**ate, **T**ext. WordPerfect inserts the date at the cursor location, using the format that you specified.

3. You can use the date feature to insert the current time in your document. First, select **T**ools, **D**ate, **F**ormat. Select **E**dit. Press Ctrl-End to delete the old setting. To set the time in the format of the hours, a colon, and the minutes, press Shift-F5. Next, select Hour(00), and type **:**. Press Shift-F5, and select Minute#, leading zero. The dialog box now looks like Figure 19-3. Press Enter twice. To have WordPerfect insert the time in a document, select **T**ools, **D**ate, **T**ext. WordPerfect inserts the time at the cursor's location, using the format that you specified.
4. WordPerfect's default justification is set to left justification. If you prefer full justification, which was the default in WordPerfect 5.1, you might want to make a change to the default initial codes. Select **L**ayout, **D**ocument, Initial Codes Se**t**up. Then select **L**ayout, **J**ustification, **F**ull. Select OK. Press F7 to end the initial code entries. Select OK to return to the document. When you create new

FIGURE 19-2

Changing the date format

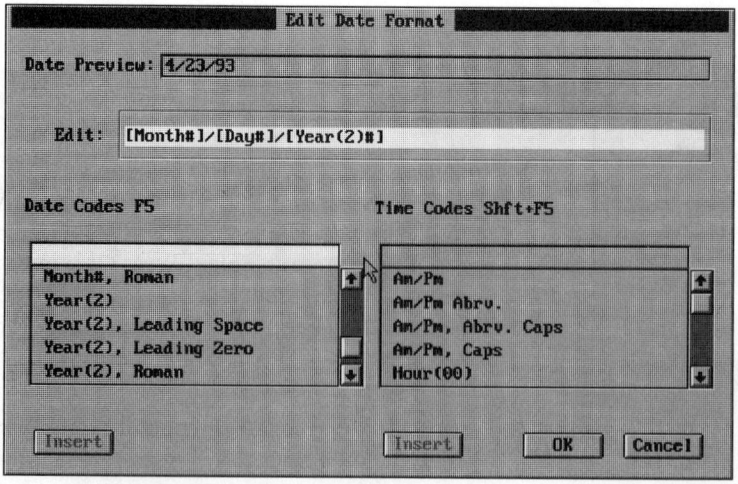

FIGURE 19-3

Using time codes for the date format

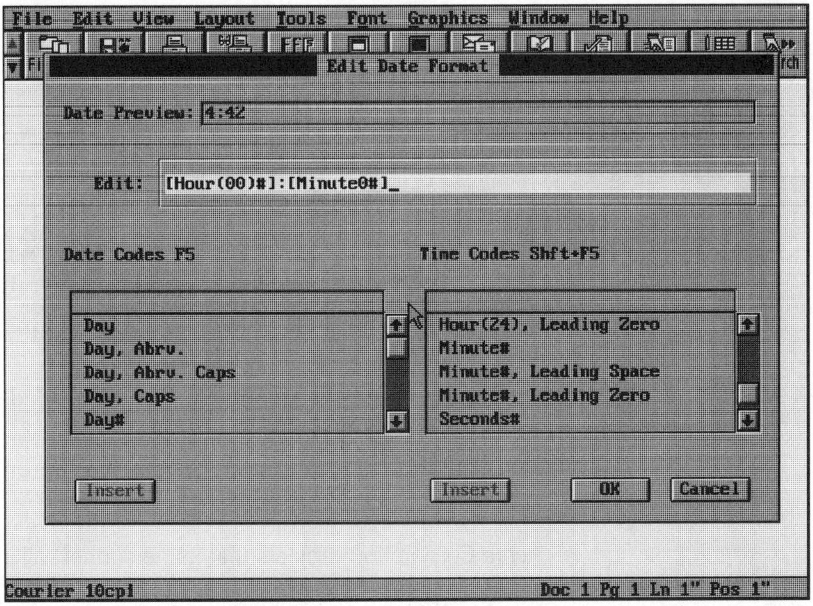

WordPerfect documents, they will have full justification as the default. You can override a document's default settings by making format changes in the document.

EXERCISES

1. Set WordPerfect not to beep when an error occurs.
2. Set WordPerfect to use the date format of the day of the week, a comma, a space, the month, another space, and the day of the month.
3. Type the following sentence. Where the sentence has four *X*s, use the date feature to insert the current date.

   On XXXX, the Okra Vegetable Company begins marketing its new product line, the Seeing Green frozen foods.

mastery skills check

1. Set the automatic timed backup to every 20 minutes. [19.1]
2. Set the background for normal text for the junk text mode color scheme in text mode to black. [19.2]
3. Set the date format to insert the month spelled out, a space, and four digits for the year. [19.3]
4. Type the following sentence. Where the sentence has four *X*s, use the date feature to insert the current date. [19.3]

   Acme Corporation projects that its personnel will increase 5% during XXXX.

5. Set WordPerfect not to beep when it cannot find the text that you want during a search. [19.2]

cumulative skills check

As you complete these exercises, do not clear the screen between exercises unless instructed to do so.

1. Set the automatic timed backup to back up your files every minute. Type **Testing Backups**. Wait until WordPerfect backs up your document. Reboot your system without exiting WordPerfect, and then rename the backup file WP{WPC}.BK1 as BCKUPTST. [19.1]
2. Set the automatic timed backup so that it does not back up your files. [19.1]
3. Set the date format to the month spelled out, a space, the day of the month, a comma, a space, and four digits for the year. [19.3]
4. Type the following paragraphs. Use the date feature to replace the four *X*s with the current date. [19.3]

The company picnic is on XXXX.

Each person should bring one dish. Please review the schedule, which breaks down the type of dish based on the person's last name.

5. Make the first sentence bold. Underline the words "one dish." [4.1, 4.2]
6. Set the hard return display character to an asterisk. [19.2]
7. If you have a color monitor, set the underlined text background to red and the bold text background to light blue in text mode. [19.1]
8. Save the document as DISH, and exit WordPerfect. Load WordPerfect. Set the automatic timed backup to back up your files every 30 minutes. [1.1, 2.4, 19.1]
9. Set WordPerfect to not put any codes as part of the initial codes setup. [19.2]

20

Using Styles

chapter objectives

After completing this chapter, you should be able to

20.1 Create a character or paragraph style

20.2 Use character and paragraph styles

20.3 Create an open style

20.4 Use an open style

20.5 Modify a style

20.6 Create a style library

20.7 Use styles from a style library

WORDPERFECT'S style feature is a useful tool for formatting documents or parts of documents. A *style* is a stored group of codes or text that you create, which can be retrieved into a document to control its formatting. Most of the formatting you are likely to use in a document can be incorporated into a style. Styles also offer you some expanded capabilities compared to normal formatting.

Styles simplify the process of formatting documents (or sections of documents). If, for example, you always change the justification, tabs, and margins for letters, you could create a style to do the same thing for you.

Styles can be used to standardize the appearance of documents. Creating sets of styles for each type of document you produce can make formatting easier and quicker, and it also produces a uniform appearance among similar types of documents.

With styles, you can also change the formatting of documents or parts of documents easily. To change the formatting of text produced with a style you need only change the codes associated with that style. Within the document, all text that is associated with the edited style is automatically modified.

Styles become a part of the document in which they are used. They can also be saved as a *style library* and later retrieved and used in other documents.

The capabilities of WordPerfect's style feature form a powerful tool for formatting documents. This chapter presents the basic features of styles. Once mastered, you can use them to create professionally formatted documents quickly and easily.

review skills check

As you perform the Skills Check, do not clear the screen between exercises unless instructed to do so.

1. Type the following paragraphs:

Styles

Styles are an exciting feature of WordPerfect. Many people use them to simplify document production. One advantage of styles is that they can help you create all types of documents, long or short. Mary Smith of the Accounting Department says:

"I was afraid that using styles would be too complicated and would take too much time. However, I'm glad I tried them. I'm constantly finding new and better uses for styles."

As you and your co-workers will discover, styles can be used to simplify document formatting and to create document standards throughout your department.

2. Preview the document. [3.3]
3. Bold and center the heading. [4.2, 4.3, 4.7]
4. Change the line spacing to double spacing for the first and third paragraphs, but the second paragraph should be single spaced. [5.5]
5. Delete the quotation marks from the quote and indent the quote from both sides. [5.1]
6. Underline Mary Smith. [4.1, 4.7]
7. Preview the document. [3.3]
8. Save the document as STYL.DOC and clear the screen. [1.2, 2.4]

20.1 CREATE A CHARACTER OR PARAGRAPH STYLE

Before you can use styles in your documents, you must first create (or define) the styles. Character and paragraph styles have beginnings and ends. You can place formatting codes at the beginning of the style to affect the entered text. Most codes that are placed at the beginning of the style are automatically turned off by WordPerfect at the end of the style. Sometimes, you will also want codes to occur after the text, because you have other features you will want to invoke.

The difference between character styles and paragraph styles is the kind of formatting you can use them for. A character style can be used to change the character formatting features; for example, those for a single letter, a word in a sentence, or parts of several sentences. A paragraph style sets formatting for entire paragraphs, and can only be applied to complete paragraphs. Despite these differences, creating character and paragraph styles is essentially the same.

NOTE *If you are a previous user of WordPerfect 5.0 or 5.1 styles, you will notice that paired styles are not discussed here. WordPerfect 6 does not use paired styles because character and paragraph styles are refinements of paired styles. Where you previously used a paired style, you now use either a character or a paragraph style.*

TO CREATE A CHARACTER OR PARAGRAPH STYLE

a. Select **L**ayout, **S**tyles or press Alt-F8.

b. Select **C**reate to create a style.

c. Type a name for the style (1 to 12 characters long).

d. Select Style **T**ype, then **C**haracter Style or **P**aragraph Style.

e. Select OK.

f. Select **D**escription and type a description of the style and its purpose.

g. Select the Show Style **O**ff Codes check box if you want the style to turn on WordPerfect features when you turn the style off.

h. Select Style **C**ontents to enter the formatting codes and text that the style uses. Type the text and enter the codes, using the same steps you would use to apply formats in a document.

i. Press F7 when finished entering the codes and text.

j. Select **E**nter Key Action to select an option button that will determine what happens when you press Enter. Select **I**nsert a Hard Return to have the Enter key work normally; select Turn Style O**f**f to turn the style off; select Turn Style Off and Back **O**n to turn the style off, then back on for the next paragraph; or select **T**urn Style Off and Link To to turn the style off, then turn on the style you specify.

k. Select OK twice and Close once to return to the document.

If you select the Show Style **O**ff Codes check box in step g, the Style **C**ontents box is split in two by a boxed comment when you select it. Your entries are made either above or below this comment. The cursor starts in the top half of the box, above the boxed comment. You can think of the comment as a placeholder for the text that will be affected by this style. The area above the comment is the Style On area, and the area below is the Style Off area. Place formatting codes that you want to affect the text the style is applied to before the comment (in the Style On area), and place any codes or text to go into effect after the comment (in the Style Off area). Many codes that you turn on in the Style On area are automatically turned off for you by the character or paragraph style.

Step j determines how pressing Enter within the style affects the style. With character styles, you can have WordPerfect insert a hard return code [HRt] without affecting the style when you press Enter. Or you can have WordPerfect turn the style off when you press Enter, turn the style off and then back on again when you press Enter, or turn the style off and then turn on another style. In paragraph styles, pressing Enter always inserts a hard return. You can choose to have WordPerfect turn the style off when you press Enter, as well as enter a hard return. Or you can have WordPerfect turn the style off and then on again for the next paragraph, or turn the style off and turn on a new style for the next paragraph.

If you choose to have the Enter key turn off the style, you eliminate having to turn off the style yourself. This technique is often used for headings within documents. Headings are usually short phrases that fit on one line. This is also very useful with character styles.

Having the Enter key turn the style off and then on again can be used for styles in lists, where each item in the list is no more than a paragraph long. You'll understand better how this kind of style works when you get to section 20.2.

EXAMPLES

As you complete the following examples, do not clear the screen until you are told to do so.

1. You are going to create a style for a main heading. This heading is to be centered from left to right on the page and boldfaced. Because this style will be applied to paragraphs, and not to words or sentences within a paragraph, you will use a paragraph style.

   First, select **L**ayout, **S**tyles or press Alt-F8. The Style List dialog box appears on the screen, as shown in Figure 20-1.

FIGURE 20-1

Style List dialog box

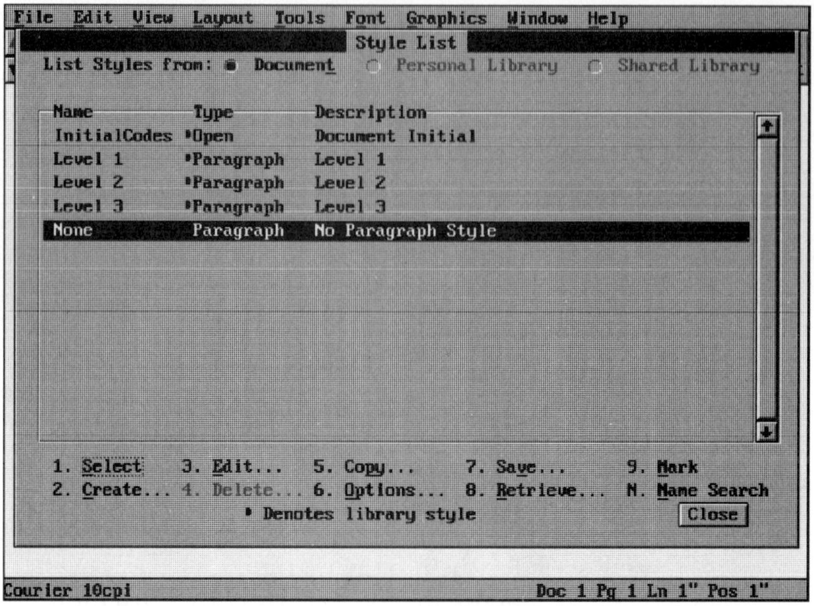

Second, select **C**reate to create the style. The Create Style dialog box appears, shown here:

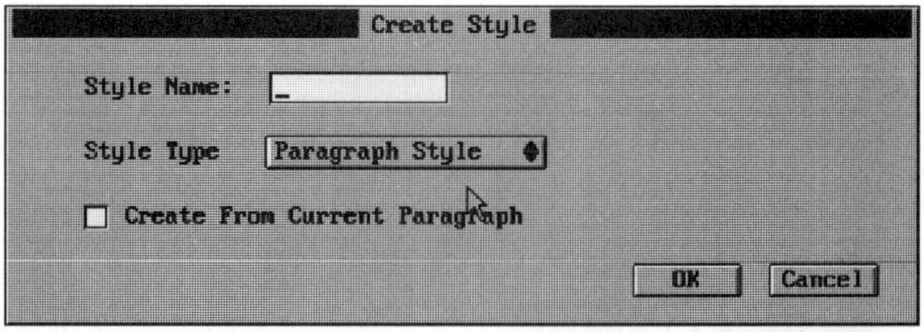

To give this style a name, type **Main Heading** and press (Enter). (If you did not give the style a name, WordPerfect would assign the style a number.) The **P**aragraph Style is already selected for Style **T**ype, so you do not need to select it. Now, select OK. The Edit Style dialog box, shown here, opens:

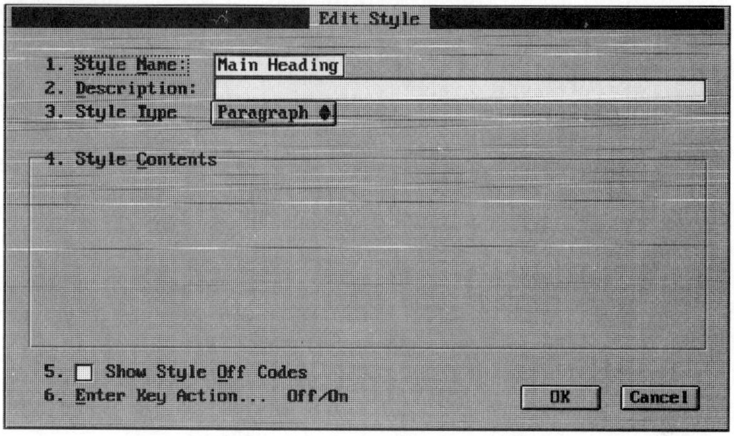

Next, select **D**escription to describe fully the purpose of this style, then type **First level of headings for document**, and press Enter. This step is not required, but it makes it easier to identify the style you wish to use.

Select Style **C**ontents to define what the style actually does. Any codes you enter now will affect text formatted with the style. Press Shift-F6 to center the heading. Press F6 to boldface it. Notice that the [Bold On] code appears but there is no [Bold Off] code. Don't worry, the Style Off section of this style automatically turns off the boldfacing for you.

Press F7 to exit the Style **C**ontents box.

For this example, you want to change the normal function of the Enter key. Select **E**nter Key Action, opening the Enter Key Action dialog box shown here:

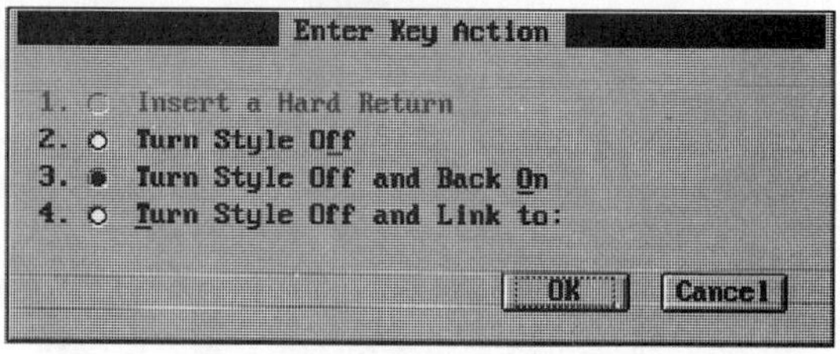

Select the Turn Style O**f**f option button and then select OK. To end the definition of this style, select OK, then press F7 to return to the document.

Do *not* clear the screen. Even though there is no text in your document, the style you created is part of the document. You will want all the styles created in these examples available to you when you do section 20.2.

2. Creating bulleted lists is another instance where paragraph styles are useful. Many times, the tab settings within a document may change. You cannot count on the tabs always being set properly for specific types of text, such as bulleted lists.

   To create a bulleted list style, first select **L**ayout, **S**tyles or press Alt-F8. The Style List dialog box appears again. The Main Heading style should be listed.

   Second, select **C**reate to create the style, type **Bullet List**, and press Enter. Since the type of style chosen is already a paragraph style, you can skip the second item. Select OK, and the Edit Style dialog box appears on the screen.

   Next, select **D**escription to describe more fully the purpose of this style. Type **Indented bulleted lists style** and press Enter. Select the Show Style **O**ff Codes check box.

   Then select Style **C**ontents to define what the style actually does. The first thing you want to do is make sure the tabs have been set for bullets. Select **L**ayout, **T**ab Set, which opens the Tab Set dialog box. Select Clear **A**ll to delete the current tab settings. Set the tabs by positioning the cursor at the correct location and pressing Spacebar. Use this method to set left-aligned tabs at 0.5 and 0.8 inch. Select OK to return to the Style **C**ontents box. Press Tab, type an asterisk (*) for the bullet, and press F4 for indenting.

   Press ↓ to move below the comment separating the Style On and Style Off areas. Press Enter to place a line between bulleted items and press ↑. The dialog box should look like this:

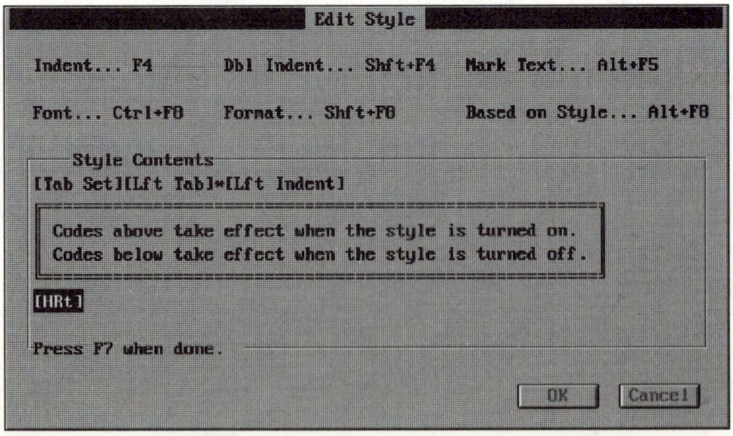

Press F7 to exit the Style **C**ontents box.

For this example, you will not change what Enter does, which is to turn the style off and on again for the next paragraph when you press Enter. To end the definition of this style, select OK, then press F7 to return to the document window.

3. Character styles are used less frequently than paragraph styles because they are used to affect a character, word, sentence, or block of text, rather than a complete paragraph.

   Begin creating a character style by selecting **L**ayout, **S**tyles, **C**reate. Type **Temp** as the style's name and press Enter. Select Style **T**ype and **C**haracter Style. Now, select OK to open the Edit Style dialog box.

   Select **D**escription, type **Style for words that might change**, and press Enter. This style is applied to words in your document that might have to change because they are incorrect or incomplete. You will want to underline and boldface these names so that they do not look like any other text in your document.

   Select Style **C**ontents to set the style's codes. The dialog box now looks like this:

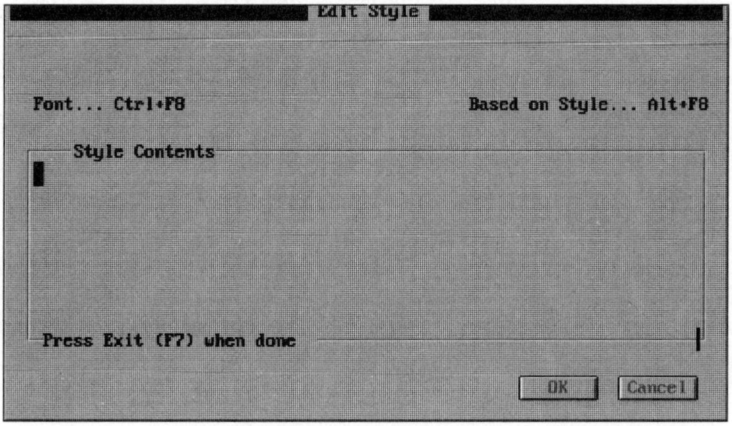

   You will notice that this dialog box is a little different than the one you used to set paragraph style codes, because you use these styles for different purposes.

   Now press F8 for underlining and F6 for bold. The [Und On] and [Bold On] codes appear in the Style **C**ontents box. Press F7 to leave this box.

   Change the function of Enter by selecting the **E**nter Key Action and the Turn Style O**f**f option button. Select OK.

Then select OK and press F7 to return to the document. Once you have returned to the blank document screen, save the document by pressing F7, selecting **Yes**, typing **style1.doc**, and then selecting OK and **N**o.

EXERCISES

Do not clear the screen until you have completed the last exercise and are told to do so.

1. Create a paragraph style called Header Lvl 1. This style boldfaces and centers the heading and puts a centered line of 45 asterisks on the next line when the style is turned off. As a word of caution, you will want the first code after the comment to be a hard return.
2. Create a character style called Names. This style applies the Small Caps character format to text it is applied to. You can find the Small Caps font option on the F**o**nt menu.
3. Create a paragraph style called Header Lvl 2. The style turns itself off when you press the Enter key. The formatting for the style includes underlining and one hard return when the style is turned off.
4. Create a paragraph style called Long Quotes. Define this style to set line spacing to single spacing and to indent the paragraph from both sides. Define Enter within the style to make it turn the style off when it is pressed.
5. Save the document as STYLE2.DOC and clear the screen.

20.2 USE CHARACTER AND PARAGRAPH STYLES

Using a paragraph or character style is easy once it has been created. Paragraph and character styles can be turned on to affect text as you type it in, or they can be applied to text that is already part of the document. In fact, paragraph and character styles work much the way that paragraph and character formats, such as tab settings or underlining, do.

TO USE A STYLE ON TEXT AS YOU TYPE IT IN

a. Select **L**ayout, **S**tyles or press Alt-F8.

b. Using ↑ and ↓, highlight the style you want to use.

c. Select **S**elect to turn the style on.

d. Type the text that is to be part of the style.

e. Turn off the style. This step depends on the action you assigned to Enter. If Enter works normally, press → to move beyond the code turning the style off. If Enter turns the style off, press Enter. If Enter turns the style off and then on again, you can type the next paragraph of text using that style. You can return to the default of no style by selecting **L**ayout, **S**tyles or pressing Alt-F8; then choose **S**elect and select None.

TO USE A STYLE ON EXISTING TEXT

a. Block the text to be affected by the style.

b. Select **L**ayout, **S**tyles or press Alt-F8.

c. Highlight the style and select **S**elect to turn it on.

If you are adding a paragraph style to only one paragraph, you can add the style by placing the cursor anywhere in that paragraph. You do not have to select the whole paragraph to apply the paragraph style.

EXAMPLES

Do not clear the screen until you have completed the last example and are told to do so.

1. You can use the styles created in section 20.1 to format a document that already exists. Open STYLE1.DOC by selecting **F**ile, **O**pen, typing **style1.doc**, and selecting OK.

   Type the following:

   My Summer Vacation
   I did some very interesting and fun things this summer. Some of the things I did included working for the City Park Commission, taking a vacation in Yellowstone National Park, and meeting some new people.

   "My Summer Vacation" is the main heading for this document. To use the Main Heading style created for this document, you must indicate the text to be included within the style. Move the cursor to the *M* in "My." (Since Main Heading is a paragraph style, you do not have to select the whole paragraph.)

Select **L**ayout, **S**tyles or press Alt-F8. Using ↑, highlight the Main Heading style. Select **S**elect to turn on the style. You are returned to the document, and "My Summer Vacation" is now centered and boldfaced at the top of the screen.

Select **V**iew, Reveal **C**odes or press Alt-F3. Then press End to highlight the [HRt] code at the end of the line. When highlighted, the code changes, as shown here:

```
[Open Style:InitialCodes][Para Style:Main Heading;]My Summer Vacation[Para Style
 End::[HRt]
[Bold Off]]I did some very interesting and fun things this summer. Some of[SRt]
the things I did included working for the City Park Commission,[SRt]
taking a vacation in Yellowstone National Park, and meeting some[SRt]
C:\WPDOCS\SUMMER.JOB                                  Doc 1 Pg 1 Ln 1" Pos 5.15"
```

When you created the Main Heading style, you did not put in the [Bold Off] code. The paragraph style automatically created it for you. Now press Home, ← to position the cursor adjacent to the code that turns the style on. The code is [Para Style:Main Heading;]. Press ← one more time so that the cursor is now highlighting the code. The code looks like this:

```
[Open Style:InitialCodes][Para Style:Main Heading;[Cntr on Mar][Bold On:Courier
Bold; 12pt]]My Summer Vacation[HRt]
I did some very interesting and fun things this summer. Some of[SRt]
the things I did included working for the City Park Commission,[SRt]
taking a vacation in Yellowstone National Park, and meeting some[SRt]
C:\WPDOCS\SUMMER.JOB                                  Doc 1 Pg 1 Ln 1" Pos 1"
```

2. Now you will use a style as you type in the text. This time you will use the Temp character style. This style turns the style off when you press the Enter key.

   First, make sure that the Reveal Codes screen is displayed. Then press Home, Home, ↓ to move to the end of the document. Make sure that there are two [HRt]s after the existing text, then type

   Working for the

   Press Spacebar, then select **L**ayout, **S**tyles or press Alt-F8. Highlight the Temp style and select **S**elect, then type

   City Park Commission

   Notice that both a [Char Style On:Temp] and a [Char Style Off:Temp] code were inserted when you selected the character style. Now press

Enter twice. As you press Enter the first time, the cursor moves to the right of the Char Style Off code. When you press Enter the second time an [HRt] code is inserted, as usual, and you move down one line.

3. Continue typing the document with the following paragraph:

   I learned a lot this summer working for the City Park Commission. I performed a variety of jobs because my main job was to act as a fill-in for regular employees on vacation. Some of my more interesting duties included:

   Press Enter twice to get ready to type in some bulleted items. The Bullet List style you created was a paragraph style, where the Enter key turns the style off and then on again.

   Select **L**ayout, **S**tyles or press Alt-F8. Highlight the Bullet List style and select **S**elect to turn this style on. Type the following, pressing Enter at the end of each item:

   Washing the elephants
   Selling balloons
   Cleaning out animal stalls
   Acting as a guide in the monkey pavilion

   As you type in the list, the bullets are created for you, as shown in Figure 20-2. If you are not in Reveal Codes, select **V**iew, Reveal **C**odes or press Alt-F3.

FIGURE 20-2

Bulleted list created with styles

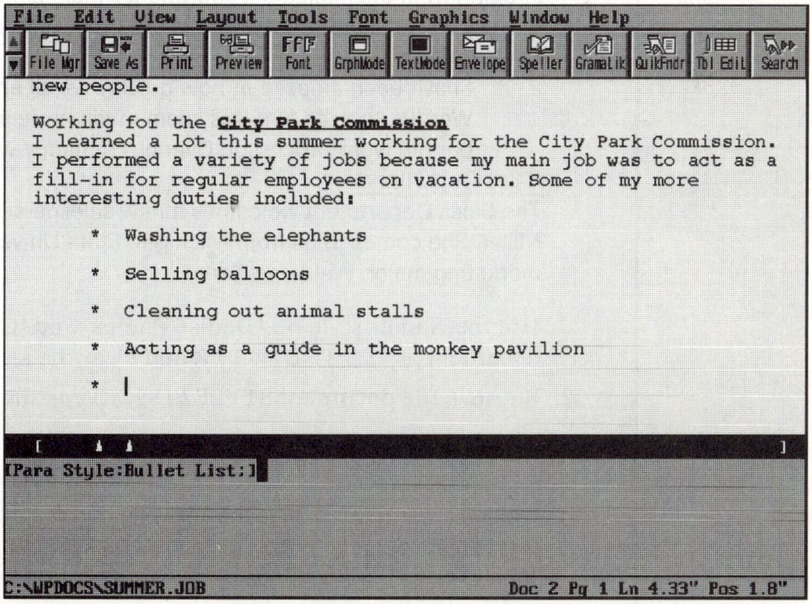

Notice that your cursor is currently located after a [Para Style] code. This is because you pressed Enter after "pavilion," and WordPerfect automatically generated a new style code. To stop the style at this point, press Backspace. This deletes the extra style code.

Select **F**ile, Save **A**s, type **summer.job**, and select OK. Then press F7 and select **N**o twice to clear the screen. Hide the codes by selecting **V**iew, Reveal **C**odes or pressing Alt-F3.

EXERCISES

1. Retrieve the file named STYLE2.DOC. No text will appear in the document screen, but the previously defined styles are there. Change the line spacing to double spacing. Type in the following text using the Header Lvl 1 style for the main heading, the Header Lvl 2 style for the department headings, and the Long Quotes style for the quote.

   Department Comments and Concerns
   ****

   Accounting Department
   Judging from the mail, the Department's main concern has to do with the current conversion from ACME's Word Processor to WordPerfect 6. Denise Phelps writes:

   > I have been amazed at how quickly we all are learning WordPerfect. Its features seem much more intuitive than our old word processor. Overall, I'm happy with the change.

   Sales Department
   The Sales Department welcomes a new salesperson. Her name is Carla Miller. She comes to us from Michigan State University where she was a marketing major. Welcome Carla!

   Use the Names style on "Denise Phelps" and "Carla Miller." Save this document as DEPTNEWS.LTR and clear the screen.

2. Retrieve the document STYLE2.DOC. Type the following text:

   Welcome!

   We give a warm welcome to the following transferees to our main headquarters.
   John Smith
   John joins us from our Tucson office, where he was the top salesman for

the past three quarters. Congratulations, John!
Jane Brown
Jane comes to us from the New York office, where she managed the MIS department. She joins us here as Chris Robertson's second-in-command in our own MIS department. Welcome!

Use the Header Lvl 1 style on "Welcome!" Use the Header Lvl 2 style on "John Smith" and "Jane Brown." Save the document as WELCOME and clear the screen.

20.3 CREATE AN OPEN STYLE

Open styles, unlike paragraph and character styles, have only a beginning. The formatting codes you put in an open style stay on for the whole document, or at least until the formatting is either changed within the document or by another style. Open styles are useful for formatting that affects the entire document. That is why they are often used at the beginning of documents.

TO CREATE AN OPEN STYLE

a. Select **L**ayout, **S**tyles or press Alt-F8.
b. Select **C**reate to create a style.
c. Type a name for the style (1 to 12 characters long) and press Enter.
d. Select Style **T**ype and **O**pen Style.
e. Select OK.
f. Select **D**escription, type a description of the style, and press Enter.
g. Select Style **C**ontents. Using the same formatting steps you would use in a document, enter the formatting codes. Press F7 when finished.
h. Select OK to exit the Edit Style dialog box.
i. Press F7 to exit the Style List dialog box.

There are two main differences between creating a paragraph or character style and an open style. The first difference appears in step d, which requires that you tell WordPerfect that the style is to be an open one. The second difference is that there is no selection for changing the function of the Enter key. Because there is no ending to an open style, there is no need to define what the Enter key means to the creation of the style.

EXAMPLES

1. One advantage of using styles is that they save time. You are now going to create an open style that can be used to start all correspondence from John Smith. Open the document named STYLE1.DOC by selecting **F**ile, **O**pen or pressing Shift-F10. Then type **style1.doc** and select OK. The screen is blank.

   Select **L**ayout, **S**tyles or press Alt-F8. Then select **C**reate to create a style. To give this style a name, type **Letter** and press Enter. Select Style **T**ype and **O**pen Style. Now select OK. Select **D**escription, type **Opening of Letter from John Smith**, and press Enter.

   Now you are ready to insert the codes. Select Style **C**ontents. For this letter, you are going to change the tabs, change to full justification, turn on Widow/Orphan protection, and insert the return address for the letter.

   To set the tabs, select **L**ayout, **T**ab Set. Select Clear **A**ll to delete all the tabs. Place the cursor at 1 inch on the ruler and press Spacebar. Repeat this at 1.4 inches and 5 inches. Select OK.

   To change to full justification, select **L**ayout, **J**ustification, **F**ull. To turn Widow/Orphan protection on, select **L**ayout, **O**ther, then select the **W**idow/Orphan Protect check box, so that it is filled with an *X*, and select OK.

   For the return address, enter the following address, pressing Tab twice before each line:

   John Smith
   123 Washington Boulevard
   Adrian, Michigan 49221

   Press Enter twice after the last line. Press the Tab key twice. After pressing F7, the box should look like this:

```
4. Style Contents
[Tab Set][Just][Wid/Orph][Lft Tab][Lft Tab]John Smith[HRt]
[Lft Tab][Lft Tab]123 Washington Boulevard[HRt]
[Lft Tab][Lft Tab]Adrian, Michigan 49221[HRt]
[HRt]
[Lft Tab][Lft Tab]
```

Select OK and press F7 to return to the document window. To save the document (which currently is blank but in which styles have been defined) and clear the screen, select **F**ile, Save **A**s, type **letter**, and select OK. Then select **F**ile, **E**xit or press F7, and select **N**o twice.

2. Styles are also handy when you know ahead of time that you will eventually want to change the formatting of a document. With this in mind, this example creates an open style designed for the initial drafts of a research paper. Later on in this chapter, you will modify this style for the final version of the research paper.

   The draft of a research paper should be double spaced with a large right margin so there is plenty of room to pencil in corrections and changes. Also, the header of each page should indicate that the document is a draft and include a page number.

   Retrieve the document named STYLE1.DOC by selecting **F**ile, **R**etrieve, typing **style1.doc**, and selecting OK. The screen is blank.

   To produce this style, select **L**ayout, **S**tyles or press Alt-F8, then select **C**reate. Type **Research Ppr** for the style's name and press Enter. Select Style **T**ype and **O**pen Style, then select OK. Select **D**escription, type **Main Document Formatting for Research Paper**, and press Enter. Select Style **C**ontents to enter the codes for this open style.

   To set the double line spacing, select **L**ayout, **L**ine. Then select the Line **S**pacing text box, type **2**, and select OK. To increase the right margin, select **L**ayout, **M**argins, **R**ight Margin, type **2**, press Enter, and select OK.

   Select **L**ayout, **H**eader/Footer/Watermark, then **H**eaders, and Header **A**. With the **A**ll Pages option button selected, select the **C**reate button. Type **DRAFT**. Press Alt-F6 to have text right-aligned, then type **Page**, press Spacebar, and Ctrl-P. Press F7, select OK, and press F7 again.

   The Style **C**ontents box should now look like this:

```
4. Style Contents
[Rgt Mar][Ln Spacing][Header A]
```

   Select OK, then press F7 to return to the document window. To save the document (which currently is blank but in which styles have been defined), select **F**ile, Save **A**s, type **research.ppr**, and select OK. Select **F**ile, **E**xit or press F7. Then select **N**o twice to clear the screen.

EXERCISES

1. Open the document called STYLE2.DOC. No text will appear in the document screen, but the previously defined styles are there.

   Create an open style called "Letters" that will be used frequently for correspondence. Describe it as "General Correspondence." The left margin should be 1.5 inches, with a tab set at 2 inches. Include within the style your name and address for the return address, centered from left to right. Skip a line and use the date code feature to insert the current date, centered. Skip four lines. Save the document as LETTER2.DOC and clear the screen.
2. Open the document called STYLE2.DOC. No text will appear in the document screen.

   Create an open style for Acme Corporation's company newsletter named "Newsletter." This is a draft format and, therefore, should be double spaced. The newsletter heading should be centered and say "Acme Corporation Newsletter." Save the document as NEWS.LTR and clear the screen.

20.4 USE AN OPEN STYLE

Using an open style is easy once it has been created. Open styles work much the same way as adding any formatting code to a document.

TO USE AN OPEN STYLE IN A DOCUMENT

a. Move the cursor to the location where you want the style to begin.
b. Select **L**ayout, **S**tyles or press Alt-F8.
c. Using ↑ and ↓, highlight the style you wish to use.
d. Select **S**elect to turn the style on.
e. Continue creating the rest of your document.

In step a, make sure the cursor is located where you want the style to begin. In the case of a style that is intended to format the entire document, you need to make sure that you are at the beginning of the document. This, of course, is usually easy to do because you will turn on the style before you begin typing the contents of the document.

EXAMPLES

1. You can create a letter from John Smith using the open style created in the previous section. First, you need to retrieve the document LETTER, which contains the style. Select **F**ile, **O**pen or press Shift-F10. Then type **letter** and select OK. The screen will be blank, but it includes the Letter style.

   To start the letter, select **L**ayout, **S**tyles. Using ↑, highlight Letter and select **S**elect to turn the style on.

   Type the following text, pressing Enter four times after you type in the date. Because of the way you defined the style, the date should line up with the return address of the letter. Press the Tab key twice before typing each section of the letter's closing.

   April 15, 1994

   James T. Brown, President
   Consolidated Corporation
   1234 Mason Drive
   Lansing, Michigan 48913

   Dear J.T.:

   This letter is to inform you that I will no longer be your service representative because I've been transferred to our company's main headquarters. I've turned your account over to the capable hands of Jane Albrecht. She is already familiar with your company and will be contacting you soon.

   Sincerely,

   John Smith

   Your document should look like Figure 20-3. Select **F**ile, Save **A**s, type **Consol**, and select OK. Then select **F**ile, **E**xit or press F7. Select **N**o twice to clear the screen.

2. You are now ready to start a research paper using the open style you created in section 20.3. Retrieve the document called RESEARCH.PPR by selecting **F**ile, **O**pen, typing **research.ppr**, and selecting OK. The screen will be blank, but it includes the Research Ppr style.

   To start the research paper, select **L**ayout, **S**tyles. Using ↓, highlight Research Ppr and select **S**elect to turn the style on.

FIGURE 20-3

Using open styles to create a letter

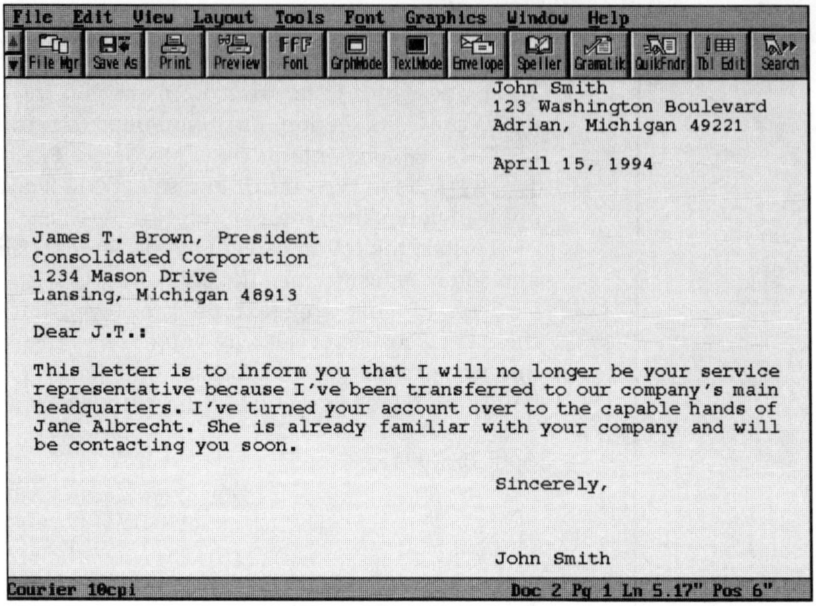

Type the following text:

Rocks
There are many different kinds of rocks found on the earth. In fact, the earth is composed primarily of rock. These rocks differ in the minerals they are made of, how they were formed, and their age.

Select **F**ile, Print Pre**v**iew, then select **V**iew, **1**00%. Notice the line spacing, the header, and the margins. Press Esc to leave the print preview screen. Save the document and clear the screen by selecting **F**ile, **E**xit or pressing F7. Then select **Y**es, then **N**o.

EXERCISES

1. Retrieve the file LETTER2.DOC. Using the open style named Letters, type the following letter. Save the document as TRAVEL.LTR.

Worldwide Travel Agency
12340 Center Parkway
New York, NY 10011

Sir or Madam:

We are planning a trip to London, England, in September. Please send me any travel information on hotel accommodations, air fare, and points of interest for sightseeing.
After we have looked the information over, we will arrange an appointment to finalize our plans.

Sincerely,

{type your name}

2. Retrieve the file NEWS.LTR. Using the style Newsletter, create the formatting for the following document. Use the style named Header Lvl 2 to format the heading. Type the following:

   NEW EQUIPMENT FOR SALES DEPARTMENT
   A new microcomputer network will be installed in the Sales Department next month. It will consist of five workstations and a file server with a 150MB drive. The configuration also includes two laser printers. The system will run WordPerfect 6 and other popular software.

   Save the document as NEWSVOL1.DOC.

20.5 MODIFY A STYLE

So far in this chapter, you have seen how styles can save time in formatting documents. You have also seen how styles can be useful in creating consistent formatting for documents and parts of documents. This section will show you what may be the most valuable feature of styles: the ability to modify styles and have the modifications immediately go into effect for your document.

TO EDIT FORMATTING CODES IN A STYLE

a. Select **L**ayout, **S**tyles or press Alt-F8.
b. Using ↑ and ↓, highlight the style you want to edit.

c. Select **E**dit.

d. Select Style **C**ontents to edit the formatting codes. Modify the formatting codes as required.

e. Press F7 when finished editing the formatting codes.

f. Select OK, then press F7 to return to the document.

EXAMPLES

In this set of examples, do not clear the screen until you have completed the last example.

1. To explore this feature of styles, you need to work with a document that already has some styles applied to text. You will use the document, RESEARCH.PPR. To open the document, select **F**ile, **O**pen or press Shift-F10. Then type **research.ppr** and select OK. The start of the research paper called "Rocks" will appear in your document screen.

   Use the Main Heading style to format the title of the paper. To do this, put the cursor on the *R* in "Rocks" and select **L**ayout, **S**tyles or press Alt-F8. Then highlight the Main Heading style and select **S**elect. "Rocks" is now centered and in bold.

   Press Home, Home, ↓, Enter, and type the following paragraph:

   Rocks that were formed from dust, sand, seashells, and other materials settling long ago at the bottom of lakes and seas are called sedimentary rocks. Examples of sedimentary rock are:

   Press the Enter key twice. At this point, you are ready to type a bulleted list. To do this, you will use the style you created called Bullet List. This style turns the style off and back on whenever you press the Enter key.

   To turn on the Bullet List style, select **L**ayout, **S**tyles or press Alt-F8. Then highlight the Bullet List style and select **S**elect. Now, turn on the Temp character style by selecting **L**ayout, **St**yles, highlighting Temp, and selecting **S**elect. Type **limestone** and press Enter, which turns off the Temp character style. Next, press the Spacebar, type **(made from shells)**, and press Enter. Pressing Enter this time turns off the Bullet List style, then turns it back on for the next paragraph. Type the next two lines, applying the Temp style to the rocks' names. Don't forget to press Enter at the end of each line.

sandstone (made from sand)
shale (made from clay and mud)

To turn the Bullet Style off completely, select **L**ayout, **S**tyles or press Alt-F8. Then highlight None and choose **S**elect. Type the metamorphic rocks section, using the same techniques you used for sedimentary rocks. Use the Bullet List style and apply the Temp style to the rock names.

Rocks that have been changed from one kind of rock to another by heat and pressure are called metamorphic rocks. Metamorphic rocks are usually stronger and harder than the rocks they were changed from. Examples of metamorphic rock are:

slate (which comes from shale)
marble (which comes from limestone)

Your document should now look like Figure 20-4. Save the document by selecting **F**ile, **S**ave.

2. Now that you have a document to work with, you are going to see how changing styles can affect the appearance of a document. The Research Ppr style was set up for creating drafts. Let's assume that

FIGURE 20-4

A draft paper created with styles

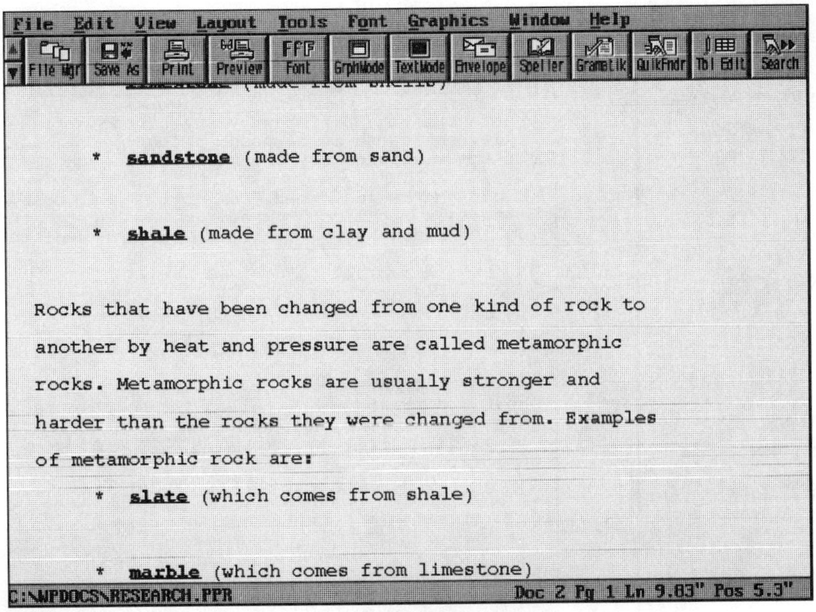

you have finished modifying the paper and are now ready to put it in final form. To do this, you will need to edit the Research Ppr style.

Select **L**ayout, **S**tyles or press Alt-F8. Then highlight the Research Ppr style and select **E**dit. Select Style **C**ontents in the Edit Style dialog box.

Press the Del key three times to delete the line spacing, margins, and header codes. Add a page numbering code by selecting **L**ayout, **P**age, then Page **N**umbering, and Page Number **P**osition. Select the Bottom **C**enter option button and OK. Select Page Number **F**ormat, type **Page**, press the Spacebar, type a hyphen, press the Spacebar, and press Enter to finish the page number's appearance. Select OK twice to return to the Edit Style dialog box.

Press F7, select OK, and press F7 again to return to the document. Press Home, Home, ↑ to move to the beginning of the document. Your document should look like Figure 20-5. Notice the line spacing and margins. Do not clear the screen.

3. You will now change the appearance of the words formatted with the Temp style. You want these words italicized and in small caps, indicating that they are special words.

   Select **L**ayout, **S**tyles or press Alt-F8. Then highlight the Temp style and select **E**dit. Select Style **C**ontents to change the font formatting applied with this style.

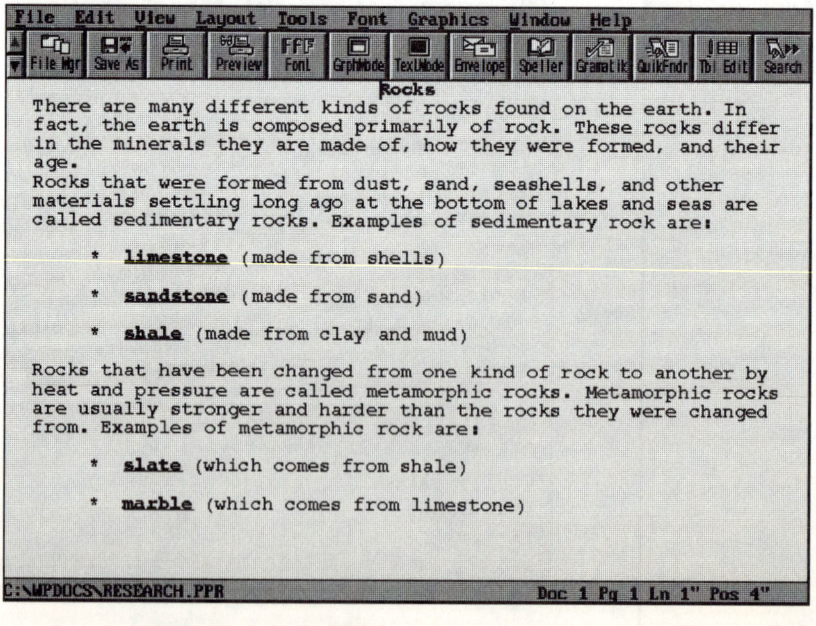

FIGURE 20-5

Modifying styles to create a final version

FIGURE 20-6

Exchanging styles to reformat a paper

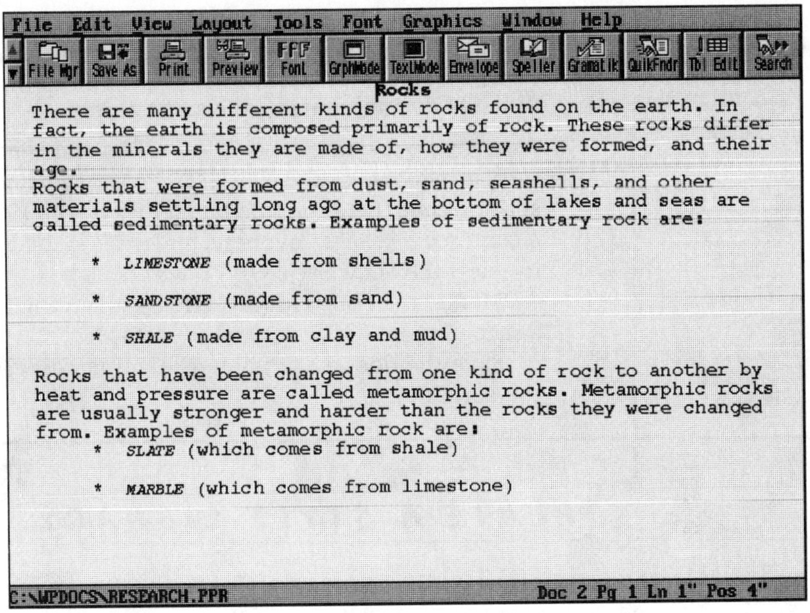

Press [Del] twice to delete the [Bold On] and [Und On] codes. Select F**o**nt, Small **C**aps, then F**o**nt, **I**talics. Press [F7] to return to the Edit Style dialog box.

Select OK, then press [F7] to return to the document window. Your document should now look like Figure 20-6. Save the document by selecting **F**ile, Save **A**s, typing **rockdone.ppr**, and selecting OK.

EXERCISES

As you perform these exercises, do not clear the screen until you are instructed to do so.

1. Retrieve the document named NEWSVOL1.DOC. Add the following text to the end of the document, using the Long Quotes style to format the quote:

   Ron Adams, the MIS coordinator, states that:
   "All systems are go. All equipment and cabling has been received,

assembled, and tested. We anticipate no problems."
Training sessions are planned for the next three Fridays at 1:00 p.m.

Save the document using the same name.

2. Assume the document has been edited and is now ready for final formatting. Modify the Newsletter style by deleting the double spacing code. Bold the title by modifying the Header Lvl 2 style. Add a centered line of 27 hyphens underneath the heading. (You will need to select the Show Style **O**ff Codes check box.)

   Modify the Long Quotes style by indenting the text from both sides a second time.

   Save the document using the name NEWSVOL1.FIN and clear the screen.

20.6 CREATE A STYLE LIBRARY

Another powerful feature of styles is that you can save styles in style libraries, to be used by any or all of your documents. All you need to do is give the set of styles a filename.

TO CREATE A STYLE LIBRARY FROM STYLES IN A DOCUMENT

a. Open the document that contains the styles you want saved in a style library.
b. Select **L**ayout, **S**tyles or press Alt-F8.
c. Select Sa**v**e to save the styles.
d. Type the filename for the style library.
e. Select the Save **U**ser Create Styles check box to save the styles that you created in this style library, or clear it if you do not want to save these styles in this library.
f. Select the Save WP **S**ystem Styles check box to save the styles that came with WordPerfect in the style library, or clear it if you do not want to save these styles in this library.
g. Select OK, then press F7 to return to the document window.

EXAMPLES

1. You are going to create a style library from the document named RESEARCH.PPR. First, open the document by selecting **F**ile, **O**pen or pressing Shift-F10. Then type **research.ppr** and select OK.

   Select **L**ayout, **St**yles or press Alt-F8. Select Sa**v**e and type **research.sty** as the filename. By default, the Save **U**ser Created Styles check box is selected, and the Save WP **S**ystem Styles is not, which is the way that you want it. Select OK, then press F7 to return to the document window.

2. You are going to create a style library from the document named ROCKDONE.PPR. First, open the document by selecting **F**ile, **O**pen or pressing Shift-F10. Then type **rockdone.ppr** and select OK.

   Select **L**ayout, **St**yles or press Alt-F8. Select Sa**v**e to save the styles, type **donepapr.sty** as the filename, and select OK. Press F7 to return to the document window.

EXERCISES

1. Create a style library called NEWSLTR.DFT using the styles found in the NEWSVOL1.DOC document.
2. Create a style library called NEWSLTR.FIN using the styles found in the NEWSVOL1.FIN document.

20.7 USE STYLES FROM A STYLE LIBRARY

Once you have created a style library, you can use it to create other documents. You can retrieve a style library into either a new or existing document. More than one style library can be incorporated into a single document. Thus you can combine libraries to create additional, larger libraries.

TO RETRIEVE A STYLE LIBRARY INTO YOUR DOCUMENT

a. Select **L**ayout, **S**tyles or press Alt-F8.
b. Select **R**etrieve to retrieve the style library.
c. Type the filename for the style library.
d. Select or clear the Retrieve **U**ser Created Styles and Retrieve WP **S**ystem Styles check boxes to choose which styles you want to retrieve from the style library.
e. Select OK.
f. Press F7 to return to the document window.

EXAMPLES

1. Clear the screen by pressing F7 and selecting **N**o twice. To retrieve the style library you created called RESEARCH.STY, select **L**ayout, **S**tyles, or press Alt-F8. Select **R**etrieve, type **research.sty**, and select OK, and then **Y**es. This extra prompt tells WordPerfect what to do when an incoming style has the same name as a style already in the document. Selecting **Y**es replaces the style in the document with the style in the incoming style. Selecting **N**o keeps the style in the current document and ignores the style from the incoming document with the same name.

   To use the styles you have brought into the current document, use ↓ to highlight Temp and choose **S**elect. Type the following sentence:

   This document uses the same styles as the document used to create the saved styles.

   You can see how the text is already bold and underlined because of the Temp style. Clear the document without saving by selecting **F**ile, **E**xit or pressing F7. Then select **N**o twice.
2. When you retrieve a style library into a document that already contains styles, WordPerfect first checks to see if there are any new styles with the same name. If there are styles with names in common, WordPerfect asks if you want to replace the current styles with the

new ones. Select **Y**es if you do, or **N**o if you do not want your current styles to be replaced by the new ones.

Sometimes, it is to your advantage to create two or more style libraries that have style names in common. The research paper about rocks is an example of this.

Open the document named RESEARCH.PPR by selecting **F**ile, **O**pen or pressing Shift-F10. Then type **research.ppr** and select OK. This is the draft version of your research paper.

Assume that you have finished editing the paper and are now ready to put it in final form. To incorporate the styles for a finished paper, retrieve the style library called DONEPAPR.STY. Select **L**ayout, **S**tyles or press Alt-F8. Select **R**etrieve, type **donepapr.sty**, and select OK.

WordPerfect asks for confirmation that you want the current styles replaced by the new ones. Select **Y**es. Press F7 to return to the document. Notice that the formatting is now for a finished research paper.

EXERCISES

Do not clear the screen until you have completed the exercises and are told to do so.

1. Make sure you have a clear screen. Retrieve the style library called NEWSLTR.DFT. Use the Newsletter style to format a newsletter. Type the following:

   An office party to celebrate the coming new year is scheduled for Monday, December 29, at 4:30 p.m. All employees are welcome to join in the festivities.

   Print the document.

2. Assume that the newsletter has been edited and is ready to be put in its final form. Retrieve the NEWSLTR.FIN style library into the newsletter, allowing the styles to be overwritten.

   Print the document and clear the screen.

mastery skills check

Do not clear the screen between exercises unless instructed to do so.

1. Create a paragraph style named "Title" that consists of a centered line of 54 asterisks (*), an [HRt], a centered message, an [HRt], another centered line of 54 asterisks (*), and an [HRt]. [20.1]
2. Create a character style named "Emphasize" that consists of the font features, 16-point Roman-WP Bold. [20.1]
3. Create an open style named "Announcement" that sets all four margins at 1.5 inches. [20.3]
4. Create a document using the Announcement style to set the document formatting. Using the Title style, start the document with the message:

   New Medical Reimbursement Procedures

   Type the following paragraph:

   The application for medical reimbursement has been streamlined. Contact the personnel department for copies of the new forms.

   Print and save the document as ANNOUNCE.DOC but do not clear the screen. [20.2, 20.4]
5. Create a style library called STYLE.ANN. Clear the screen. [20.6]
6. Type the following document:

   New Safety Rules Regarding Eye Protection
   Anyone caught not wearing goggles in Labs C and D as required will be warned once. Any further infractions will result in the employee being suspended for one day without pay. Any employee breaking this rule four or more times within a one-year period will be fired.

   Retrieve the style library called STYLE.ANN. Use the Announcement style to format the document. Use the Title style to format the heading. Use the Emphasize character style to format the word "fired" in the last sentence. [20.3, 20.4, 20.6]

7. Modify the Title style by eliminating the first row of asterisks (*) and boldfacing the rest of the style. Print the document and then clear the screen. [20.5]

cumulative skills check

In the following exercises, do not clear the screen unless instructed to do so.

1. Type the following document. [2.1]

   Amalgamated Electronics is pleased to announce the release of its latest computer. The Data-Blaster is the latest and fastest in our series of high-speed electronic data crunchers. "No other computer in its price range can compare with the Data-Blaster's performance," says Amalgamated's president, Joshua Miller.

2. Create an open style called Press Rel that formats a document with double spacing. The style should also include a footer with the following message centered at the bottom. [4.3, 5.5, 10.3, 20.3]

   PRESS RELEASE – PRESS RELEASE – PRESS RELEASE

3. Create a paragraph style that turns itself off when you press Enter. Call the style "Main Heading." It should consist of boldfaced, centered text that is followed by one [HRt]. [4.2, 4.3, 20.1]
4. Create a character style that turns itself off when you press Enter, and consists of small caps and italics. These formats can be selected from the F**o**nt menu. Call this style "Logo." [20.1]
5. Use the Press Rel style created in exercise 2 to format the document currently on your document screen. [20.4]
6. Use the Main Heading style to add a heading at the beginning of the document titled "Data-Blaster Blasts the Competition." [20.2]
7. Use the Logo style to format every occurrence of the company name in the press release. [20.2]
8. Print the press release. [3.1]
9. Modify the Press Rel style to include a header that contains the same text as the footer. [10.2, 20.5]
10. Print the press release. Clear the screen. [1.2, 3.1]

21

Working with Text Columns

chapter objectives

After completing this chapter, you should be able to

21.1 Create newspaper columns

21.2 Create parallel columns

21.3 Modify column entries

OCCASIONALLY, information contained in a document either looks better or is more understandable if it is printed in columns. Sometimes you can create these columns by setting tabs and using Tab to move from one column to the next. This is especially true if the columns consist primarily of numbers or if the column entries are very short. However, there are times when you'll want text to appear in column format. WordPerfect's column feature is designed to do just that.

You can use the column feature to create two types of text columns: newspaper columns and parallel columns. *Newspaper columns* are commonly seen in newspapers and magazines. The text of an article, for example, continues down a column until it reaches the end of the page, and then it continues in the next column. Some people refer to newspaper columns as snaking columns because the text snakes from top to bottom through each of the columns. WordPerfect 6 offers a variation of the newspaper column that is called the balanced newspaper column. With this selection, the first column isn't filled before the text snakes to the second column. Instead, the column lengths are kept equal. For example, if you have two columns and you type two lines of text, one line appears in each column.

Parallel columns are used when text entries that relate to each other must remain side by side. They are ideal when at least one of the columns contains text that is more than one line long. WordPerfect wraps the text within the columns in the same way it normally wraps text from one page to the next. WordPerfect 6 supports a type of parallel column called parallel with block protect. With this option, corresponding entries in columns are not split between pages. If the entry in any column is long enough to require lines on the next page, all corresponding entries are moved to the next page. This prevents situations such as a name appearing on one page and the last two lines of the associated address appearing at the top of the next page.

You can use both newspaper and parallel columns in a single document, but only one type of column can be used at a time. You can also use columns at one place in your document, change to normal page formatting, and then change back to column formatting. WordPerfect provides you with a great deal of flexibility.

Both parallel and newspaper columns can be very helpful when you are preparing specialized documents. With WordPerfect, they are also easy to create. Throughout this chapter you might find that your screen does not exactly match the examples because different printer selections cause different default font sizes and might cause column text to break in different locations.

review
skills check

Do not clear the screen until you have completed the last Skills Check exercise.

1. Set the top margin to 2 inches and the bottom margin to 3 inches. [6.2]
2. Change the justification to full justification, and then set it back to left justification. [5.6]
3. Center the following line, and press Enter once. [4.3]

   Memory Upgrades Available

4. Center 35 hyphens, and press Enter twice. [1.3, 4.3]
5. Type the following paragraph, underlining the word "finally." [4.1]

   The memory chips we ordered three months ago have finally arrived. Those of you who have been waiting to upgrade your system should schedule a time with MIS for swapping memory chips at your earliest convenience

6. Use WordPerfect's spell feature to check for spelling errors. [9.1]
7. Save the document as MEMORY, and clear the screen. [2.4]

21.1 CREATE NEWSPAPER COLUMNS

WordPerfect 6 has simplified the creation of columns to a one-step process. As soon as you define the columns you want, you can begin to enter data in them. When you are finished with the column format, you simply turn it off. If you want to use the same column definition again later in the document, you copy the column definition code that appears on the Reveal Codes screen.

When defining columns, you must first specify which type of columns you want to use. You can then specify how many columns are going to appear on a page (24 is the maximum) and how much space you want between the columns. WordPerfect uses these settings to create columns of equal size, although you can customize the column sizes. WordPerfect provides default column settings that you can choose to accept or change at any time.

TO DEFINE NEWSPAPER COLUMNS

a. Select **L**ayout, **C**olumns, or press Alt-F7 and select **C**olumns.

b. Select **N**umber of Columns, and type the number of columns you want.

c. If you want to set the distance between columns, select **D**istance Between Columns. Type the distance, and press Enter.

d. Select OK, and enter text in the columns you just defined.

e. When you are finished using the columns and want to return to the full page width, select **L**ayout, **C**olumns, and then select O**f**f.

Because the default setting is for newspaper columns, you do not need to make any selections after step b if you want equal-size columns with 1/2 inch between them.

After newspaper columns are turned on, WordPerfect treats each column as if it were a separate page. It wraps lines of text to the next line, and it moves text to the next column when one column is full.

EXAMPLES

To minimize the amount of typing required to learn about newspaper columns, you will reduce the size of the page by increasing the bottom margin in each of the following examples. The other option would be to use balanced newspaper columns so that you would see the snaking effect as soon as you entered the second line of text.

1. To change the bottom margin to 8 inches, select **L**ayout, **M**argins, **B**ottom Margin, type **8**, and press Enter. Select OK. This will shorten the page so that you will be able to see how WordPerfect places text in the next column when it reaches the end of the first column.

   Start a newsletter by typing a heading. Press Shift-F6 or select **L**ayout, **A**lignment, **C**enter to turn on the centering feature, and type

Acme Corporation Newsletter

Press Enter. To add a centered dividing line between the heading and the area where the columns will be, press Shift-F6, press Ctrl-R to set the repeat number, type **35**, and press =. Press Enter twice.

Now you are ready to create two newspaper columns. Select **L**ayout, **C**olumns. The Text Columns dialog box appears, as shown in Figure 21-1. Because newspaper columns are the default column type, you are going to accept all of the default choices in this dialog box except the number of columns. Select **N**umber of Columns, type **2**, press Enter, and select OK.

NOTE *If you want to see the widths that WordPerfect has established for your columns, select Custom Widths before leaving the dialog box. After looking at the entries for each column, select OK twice to return to your document.*

Select **V**iew, Reveal **C**odes or press Alt-F3 to display the [Col Def] code. Use ← to highlight the code. It reads [Col Def:Newspaper;2]. This code indicates a column definition for two newspaper-style columns. Press → to move off the code. To clear the Reveal Codes display, select **V**iew, Reveal **C**odes or press Alt-F3 again.

FIGURE 21-1

Text Columns dialog box

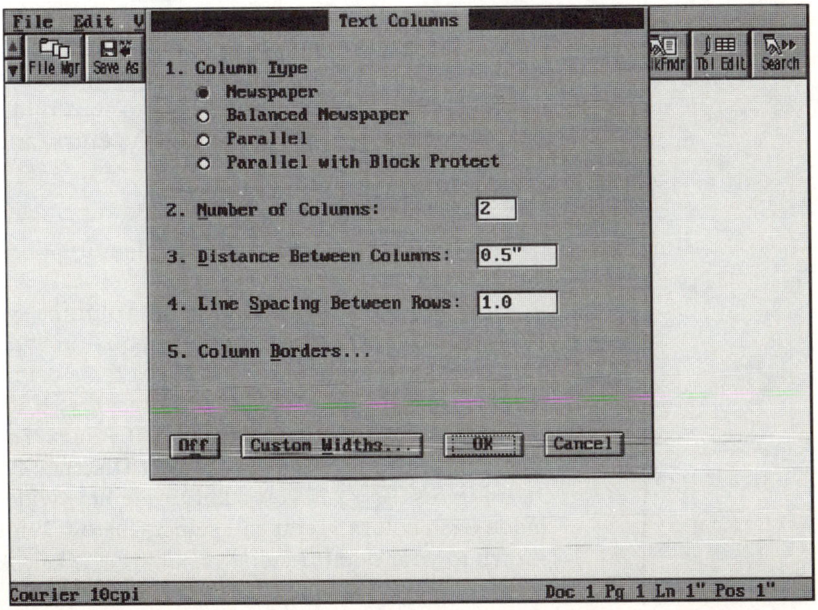

Now you are ready to enter the column text. The title for the paragraph is "New Benefits." You can underline and center the title at the beginning of the first column by using the same technique you would use on a regular page. Select **L**ayout, **A**lignment, **C**enter or press Shift-F6. Press F8 to start underlining, and type

New Benefits

Press F8 to turn off the underline feature, and press Enter twice. Type the following text as you normally would, allowing WordPerfect to wrap text as usual. As you approach the sentence, "A sign-up card will also be included," note how the text scrolls up to the next column.

Starting May 1, all employees will have a choice in their health plans. Three different plans will be offered. Information will be sent to all departments by May 1. A sign-up card will also be included. These cards must be filled out and returned to Personnel no later than May 25. The health benefits will begin on June 1. Insurance cards will be mailed the same week. If you have any questions, please call the Personnel office.

When you are finished, the screen should look like Figure 21-2, although different printers will cause WordPerfect to use different fonts, which might affect column breaks.

To turn off the columns, select **L**ayout, **C**olumns, O**f**f. Save the document and clear the screen by selecting **F**ile **E**xit, pressing Y, typing **acmecorp.ltr**, and pressing Enter twice.

2. For this example, you will define three newspaper columns. First, change the bottom margin to 8 inches by selecting **L**ayout, **M**argins, **B**ottom Margin, typing **8**, pressing Enter, and selecting OK. For the heading of this example, press F8 to start underlining, press Caps Lock, press Shift-F6 to center the entry, and type

   PC SOFTWARE TRAINERS CLUB

   Press F8 to turn off the underline feature, press Caps Lock, and press Enter twice.

   Now you are ready to define the columns. Select **L**ayout, **C**olumns. The three columns are going to be equal in width; however, you will tell WordPerfect that you want them to be 0.4 inch apart. Select **N**umber of Columns, type **3**, and press Enter. The default distance between columns is approximately 0.5 inch. To change the distance between columns to 0.4 inch, select **D**istance Between Columns, type **.4**, and press Enter. If you want to see how wide WordPerfect has made each column, you can select Custom **W**idths. You select OK to return to your document.

FIGURE 21-2

Entries in two newspaper columns

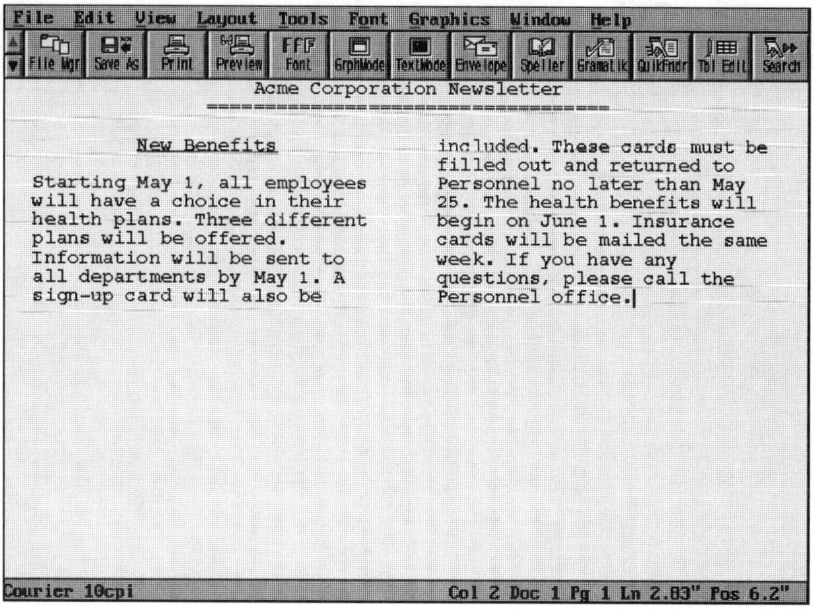

The title for the paragraph is "Featured Speaker." You can underline the title at the beginning of the first column in the same way you would underline on a regular page. Press F8 to start underlining, and type

Featured Speaker

Press F8, and press Enter twice. Type the following text as you normally would, allowing WordPerfect to wrap text as usual:

We are proud to welcome Jan Smithers from WordPerfect Corporation for our May 15th, 12:00 pm meeting. She will be demonstrating some of the new features of WordPerfect 6. Come and see for yourself what all the hoopla has been about these last few months. Send in your reservation card as soon as possible to be guaranteed a good seat. Lunch will be served promptly at 12:15 pm. For members, the fee is $7.00. For non-members, it is $10.00. Bring a friend.

Turn off the columns by selecting **L**ayout, **C**olumns, O**f**f. When you are finished, the screen should look similar to the screen in Figure 21-3, although the columns might break differently.

Save the document and clear the screen by selecting **F**ile, **E**xit, pressing Y, typing **pcclub.ltr**, and pressing Enter twice.

FIGURE 21-3

Entries in three newspaper columns

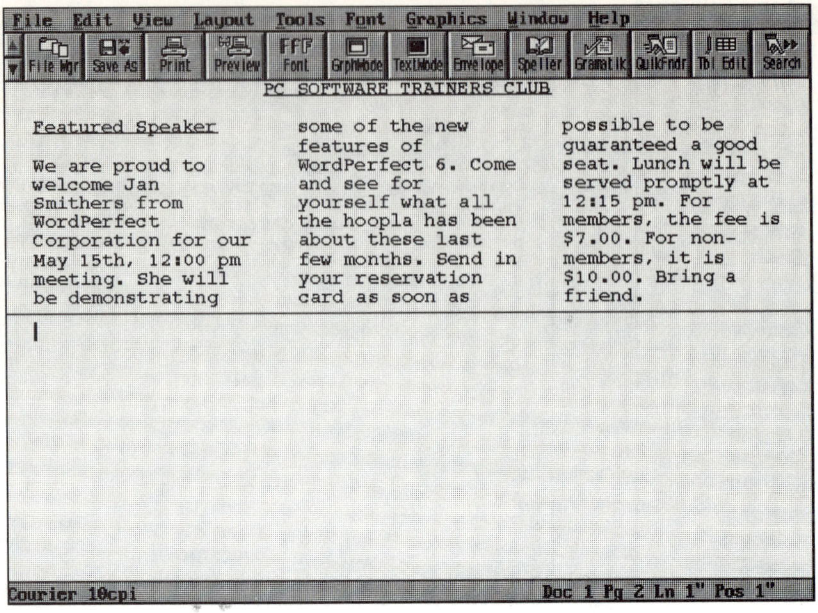

3. Later in this chapter you will learn keystroke combinations that make editing columns easier. For now, it is sufficient to say that editing text in the normal page format is easier than editing text in newspaper columns. You can create text for newspaper columns in the normal page format and then turn the text into columns. For an example of how this is done, type the following text, pressing Enter twice after the headings and between the paragraphs.

   EMPLOYEE OF THE MONTH

   The employee of the month award at Acme Corporation was awarded to Jessica Lancaster for her outstanding sales performance last month. She sold more than $125,000 in office furniture and supplies, setting a new company record. The old record, set in 1991 by Terry Smith, was $120,000. Jessica also increased her customer base by 15%. Congratulations, Jessica!

   SOFTWARE FAIR

   Last month's PC Software Trainers Club meeting featured a mini-fair. Several vendors set up booths and provided demonstrations of various software packages. These ranged from spreadsheet and database programs to word processing programs. Sales literature from the participating vendors is available upon request from the club's secretary, Brian Robertson.

Press Home, Home, ↑ to move to the beginning of the document. Now you are ready to define the columns. Select **L**ayout, **C**olumns. Select **N**umber of Columns, type **2**, press Enter, and select OK. The document will reformat itself.

The page is long enough to contain both paragraphs in column 1. If you move to the last line, the screen looks like Figure 21-4.

To force the second paragraph to the beginning of the next column, you can press Ctrl-Enter (the same way you force a new page). Move the cursor to the *S* in SOFTWARE and press Ctrl-Enter. The document should now look like Figure 21-5.

Press Home, Home, ↓ to move to the end of the document. Turn off the columns by selecting **L**ayout, **C**olumns, O**f**f. Press Enter twice, and type

NORTH COAST GETS POOL
The North Coast Community recreation department is happy to announce the opening of their new swimming pool. The pool is olympic size and features an L extension that is three feet deep. Pool hours and classes will be posted soon.

Because this paragraph occurs after the [Col Def:Off] code, it is formatted to fit the full width of the page. The screen should look similar to this:

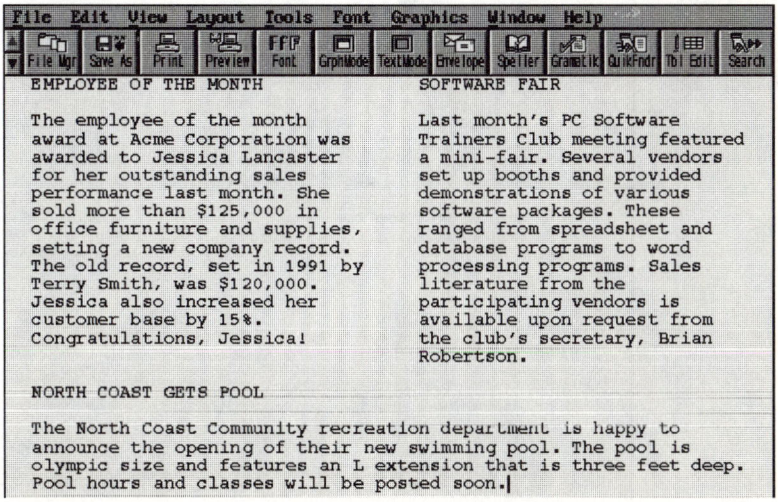

FIGURE 21-4

Text entries in column 1

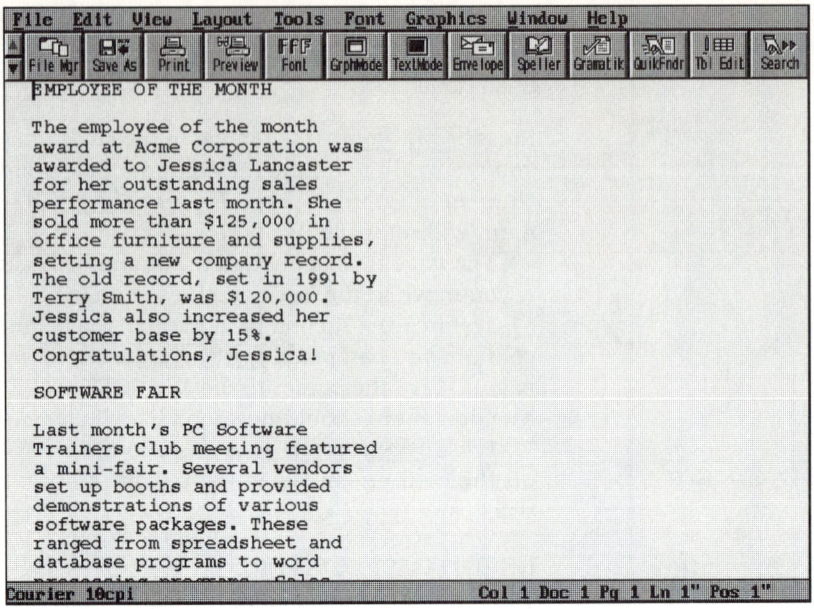

Save the document by selecting **F**ile, **E**xit, pressing (Y), typing **pr.doc**, and pressing (Enter) twice.

FIGURE 21-5

Text entries in two columns

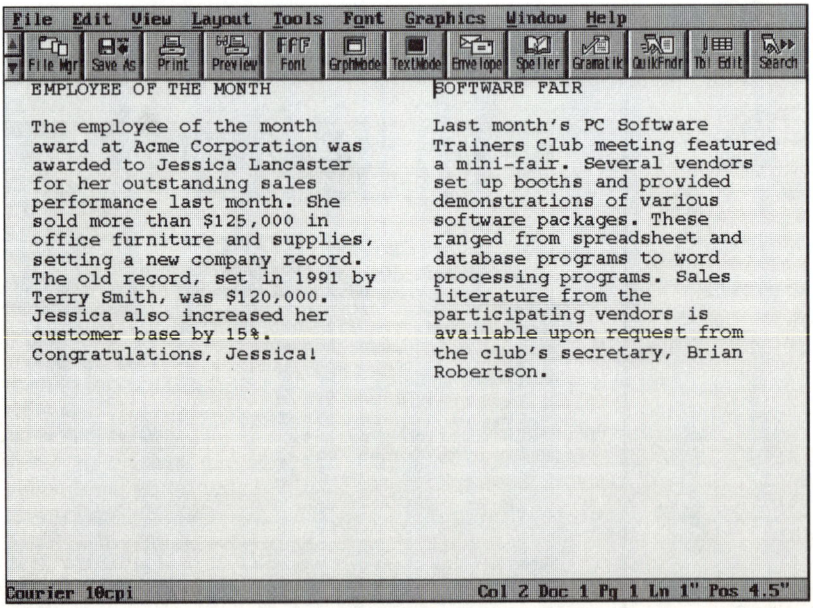

EXERCISES

1. On a page that has an 8-inch bottom margin, start a document by centering this heading:

   ACME CORPORATION

   Underneath the heading, insert 65 centered equal signs (=), and press Enter twice. Define two newspaper columns that use WordPerfect's default settings. Type the following column text, centering and underlining the heading and pressing Enter twice after the heading and after the first paragraph.

   SAFETY SEMINAR

   On May 5th, the Acme Corporation will host a seminar on industrial safety for Acme employees. Frances Wilkens, a well-known speaker from Ohio's American Red Cross, will be our key speaker. She offers a wealth of information regarding safety on the job. Those who attend the seminar will have hands-on training in the first aid skills required in common emergency situations.

   The seminar begins at 9:00 am and ends at 4:00 pm.

   Save the document as NEWSLTR.DOC, and clear the screen.

2. On a page that has an 8-inch bottom margin, center and boldface the following heading:

   NORTH COAST COMMUNITY NEWS

   Center 26 equal signs (=) underneath the heading, and press Enter twice. Define three newspaper columns spaced 0.3 inch apart. Type the following text, centering the heading and pressing Enter twice after the heading and after each of the first two paragraphs.

   KIDDIE CALENDAR

   Summer is almost here and our children have much to look forward to.

   With the opening of the new swimming pool, open swimming hours and swimming classes for the summer will soon be scheduled. The new schedule will be included in the next newsletter and posted at the pool.

   Games and activities are scheduled in the rec hall every weekday afternoon between 12:00 pm and 4:00 pm for children ages three to seven.

Save the document as COMMNEWS, and clear the screen.

3. Define two newspaper columns. Type the following paragraph in column 1.

   Paragraph 1
   This is the first paragraph of this exercise.

   Force a new column. Type the following paragraph in the second column.

   Paragraph 2
   This is the second paragraph of this exercise. It appears in column 2.

   Turn off the columns, and type the following paragraph.

   Paragraph 3
   This is the third paragraph of this exercise. It should appear below the first two paragraphs.

   Save the document as COLUMNS, and clear the screen.

21.2 CREATE PARALLEL COLUMNS

Parallel columns are used to create tables, charts, or other documents in which the text appears in columnar form but must be read from left to right. When related material that appears in separate columns must remain side by side, the parallel columns feature is a good choice. When the side-by-side entries need to remain on the same page, you can select the Parallel with Block option to keep them together.

The procedure used to define parallel columns is similar to that used to define newspaper columns. It is more common to vary the width of columns when using the parallel columns feature, however. Often the amount of text that appears in a parallel column varies depending on the column's purpose. Usually you will make columns that contain a lot of text wider than columns that contain less text.

You can also use the tables feature to produce documents that have parallel columns. See Chapter 22, "Using Tables in a Document," for more information about tables.

TO DEFINE PARALLEL COLUMNS

a. Select **L**ayout, **C**olumns.

b. Select Column **T**ype, and then select **P**arallel or Parallel with **B**lock Protect.

c. Select **N**umber of Columns, type a number, and press Enter.

d. If you want to set the distance between columns, select **D**istance between Columns, type the distance, and press Enter.

e. If you want to adjust the column widths, select Custom **W**idths, highlight the column or space you want to change, select **E**dit, select **W**idth, type the new width, press Enter, and select OK.

f. Select OK, and enter your column text.

In step b, you can select one of two variations of parallel columns. The basic parallel columns format (without block protection) is used for text where one or more columns can run on to the next page. Although the columns must always remain side by side, parts of the text can be pushed to the beginning of the next page. Parallel columns with block protection are used when all related text must remain side by side on the *same* page.

TO ENTER TEXT IN PARALLEL COLUMNS

a. Type the first entry for the first column.

b. Press Ctrl-Enter or select **L**ayout, **A**lignment, Hard **P**age. This jumps you to the next column.

c. Type the related entry for the second column.

d. Press Ctrl-Enter. This jumps you to the next column (or back to the first column, when there are only two columns defined).

e. Continue in this manner until you have made all the entries.

f. When you are finished making column entries, select **L**ayout, **C**olumns, O**f**f.

EXAMPLES

1. Change the bottom margin of a document to 8.5 inches by selecting **L**ayout, **M**argins, **B**ottom Margin, typing **8.5**, and selecting OK. This will shorten the page so that you will be able to see how parallel columns work with a minimum of typing.

   Press Shift-F6 to turn on the centering feature, and then type

   Flower Glossary

   Press Enter twice.

   You are going to define two parallel columns to be used to create a glossary of terms. The first column will contain terms and the second column will contain definitions, so the first column can be narrower than the second.

   Select **L**ayout, **C**olumns. The Text Columns dialog box appears, as shown in Figure 21-1. Select Column **T**ype, **P**arallel. Select **N**umber of Columns, type **2**, and press Enter. Select Custom **W**idths. The highlight in the upper-right corner is on column 1, for the first column. Select **E**dit, **W**idth, type **1.5** for the new width, press Enter and select OK.

   Because you narrowed the first column, there is room to enlarge the second column. Press ↓ twice to move to the setting column 2. Select **E**dit, **W**idth, type **4.5**, and press Enter. The dialog box now looks like Figure 21-6. Select OK twice.

   Start your column entries by typing the column headers. Press Caps Lock, type **TERM**, press Ctrl-Enter, type **DEFINITION**, press Ctrl-Enter, and press Caps Lock again. The headers are now in place.

   Type the following text, pressing Ctrl-Enter after each section of text. For example, type **Azalea**, press Ctrl-Enter, type the definition of an azalea, press Ctrl-Enter, type **Crocus**, press Ctrl-Enter, and so on.

Azalea	A shrub with flower blooms of various colors that belongs to the heath family. It thrives in dry, acid soil.
Crocus	A spring-blooming plant of the iris family with grass-like leaves and a yellow, purple, or white flower.
Tulip	A bulb plant with a large cup-shaped flower. Some of the best varieties are imported from the Netherlands.

When completed, your document screen should look something like Figure 21-7. If your screen splits sooner due to a different printer font, you can add an extra line to the definition of the crocus.

FIGURE 21-6

Customizing the column widths

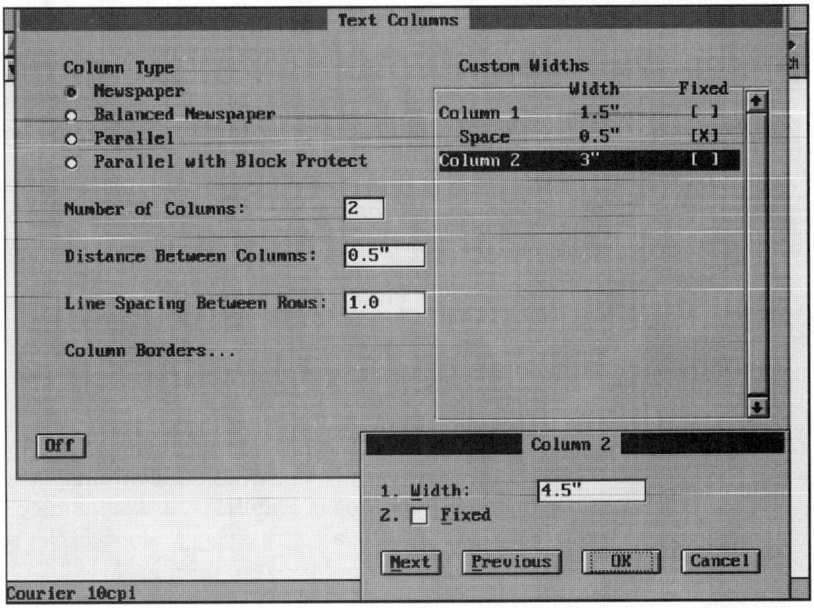

FIGURE 21-7

Glossary entries in parallel columns

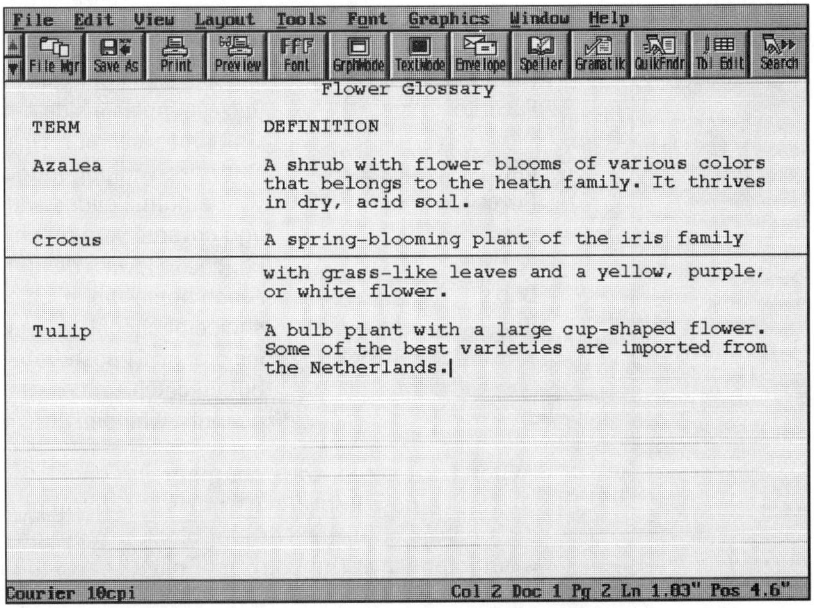

Notice how the definition of the crocus is split between pages. This happens because the parallel columns were defined without block protection.

Save the document and clear the screen by selecting **F**ile, **E**xit, selecting **Y**es, typing **flowers**, and selecting OK and **N**o.

2. For this example, you will define three parallel columns that have block protection turned on. First, change the bottom margin to 7.5 inches by selecting **L**ayout, **M**argins, **B**ottom Margin, typing **7.5**, pressing Enter, and selecting OK. For the heading of this example, press F8 to turn on the underline feature, press Shift-F6 to turn on the centering feature, and type

   Dessert Menu

   Press F8 to turn off the underline feature, and press Enter twice. Now you are ready to define the columns. Select **L**ayout, **C**olumns, Column **T**ype. Select Parallel with **B**lock Protect. Select **N**umber of Columns, type **3**, and press Enter. WordPerfect adjusts the column widths to allow for three equal-size columns. Select **D**istance Between Columns, type **.4** and press Enter. Select **W**idth, type **1.8**, press Enter, and select OK. Press ↓ twice to move to the row for column 2. Select **E**dit, **W**idth, type **.5** for the width of column 2, press Enter, and select OK. Press ↓ twice to move to the row for column 2. Select **E**dit, **W**idth, type **3** for the width of column 3, and press Enter. Select OK twice.

   Type the following text, pressing Ctrl-Enter after each section of text. Don't worry if you make a typographic error and can't get back to fix it; this will be discussed in section 21.3.

Grandpa's Favorite	$3.50	A deep-dish apple pie made from the juiciest apples inside a flaky pie crust. Grandma's secret recipe.
Patti's Prize	$2.75	Our prize-winning fudge brownies that melt in your mouth. Loaded with toasted walnuts and covered with rich chocolate icing. A chocolate lover's delight.
Bob's Boast	$2.50	A rich home-made ice cream sundae with your choice of chocolate, vanilla, or butter pecan ice cream. Choose from hot fudge, caramel, or butterscotch sauces. Don't forget the fresh peanuts, whipped cream, and cherry on top.

   When completed, the document screen should look like Figure 21-8.

   Notice how Bob's Boast starts at the top of a new page. If you had defined the columns without block protection, part of Bob's Boast would appear at the bottom of page 1, and the rest of column 3 would

FIGURE 21-8

Menu entries in parallel columns with block protection

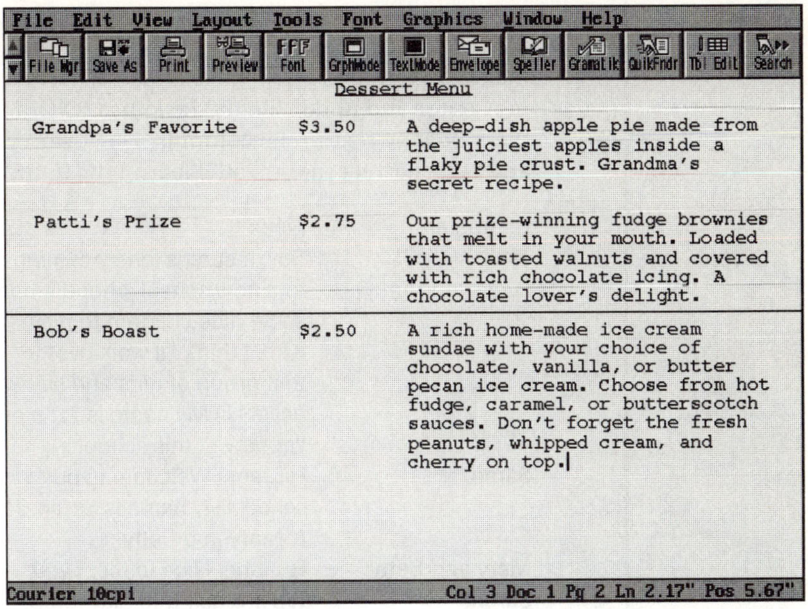

appear at the top of page 2. Instead, the entire entry pertaining to Bob's Boast is moved to page 2.

Save the document and clear the screen by selecting **F**ile, **E**xit, pressing Y, typing **dessert**, and pressing Enter twice.

EXERCISES

1. Create a play script by using two parallel columns without block protection. First, center the following headings, pressing Enter twice after "Friends", "By:", and "Class."

   MEETING NEW FRIENDS

   A Play Presented By:

   Ms. Walker's First Grade Class

Set up the columns with these specifications: the first column's width should be 1.5 inches, the second column's width should be 4.5 inches, and there should be a .5-inch space between them.

Center and underline the headings "Character" and "Lines." Type the following text in the columns. Don't worry if you make mistakes and can't correct them; you'll learn how in the next section.

Character	Lines
Jane:	Boy, it sure is lonely coming to a new school. I hope I meet some nice children to play with. I think I'll walk over to that group of girls and say hello. Hi! My name is Jane and I'm new at this school.
Sarah:	Hi, Jane! Welcome to our school. My name is Sarah. This is Mary and Betty.
Mary and Betty:	Hi, Jane! Nice to meet you.
Sarah:	We are going to play jump rope. Would you like to join us?
Jane:	I'd love to. Thanks for being so nice to me.

Save the document as PLAY.DOC, and clear the screen.

2. Set the bottom margin of a document to 8 inches. Center and boldface the following heading, and then press Enter twice.

Name & Address Listing

Define three parallel columns that have block protection on. Set the first column's width to 1.5 inches. Set the second column's width to 3 inches. Set the third column's width to 1 inch, and set a .5-inch space between columns.

Enter the following text into the three columns. Press Ctrl-Enter after the second line of the second column. Don't worry if you make mistakes and can't correct them; you'll learn how in the next section.

Sandy Clark	121 S. Main St Cleveland, OH 44114	287-1120
Joe Kent	2780 Bluebird Lane North Oak, OH 44013	452-7655
Sally Jones	5891 Sunny Vale Little Creek, OH 44410	552-1732

Save the document as N&A.LST.

3. Set the bottom margin of a document to 8.5 inches. Define an inventory list for the Acme Corporation. Center the following headings at the top of the page, and press Enter twice.

ACME CORPORATION
Equipment Inventory

Define three parallel columns that have block protection on. The three column widths should be set so that column 1 has a width of .8 inches, column 2 has a width of 1.8 inches, and column 3 has a width of 3.1 inches. There should be a .4-inch space between columns.

Enter the following text in the three columns. Don't worry if you make mistakes and can't correct them; you'll learn how in the next section.

PART NO.	PRODUCT NAME	DESCRIPTION
100459	Personal Computer	1MB RAM, monochrome monitor, 40MB hard drive, one 5 1/4" floppy disk drive
122989	Laser Printer	8 pages per minute, 250-page paper tray, envelope feeder
223348	Dot Matrix Printer	300 cps - draft mode, 150 cps - letter quality mode

Turn off the column feature, and save the document as INVTY.DOC.

21.3 MODIFY COLUMN ENTRIES

Editing text within columns is a little different than editing normal text. WordPerfect treats the text within a column similarly to the way it treats text on a page. Jumping from one column to the next thus requires a special keystroke combination.

TO MOVE FROM ONE COLUMN OF TEXT TO ANOTHER

a. To move one column to the right, press Ctrl-Home or select **E**dit, **G**o To, and then press →.

b. To move one column to the left, press Ctrl-Home or select Edit, **G**o To, and then press ←.

If you are using a mouse, you can click on the column you want.

After you are within the column you want to edit, use the cursor movement keys as you would within a normal page.

Changing the width of columns is a common modification. If you have already entered text into columns, you probably want to avoid having to reenter the text. You can position the cursor on the column definition in the Reveal Codes screen or anywhere in the column text and redefine the column widths. Because the default setting of WordPerfect 6 is auto-code placement, WordPerfect 6 will replace the old definition with the new one.

TO CHANGE THE WIDTH OF PREVIOUSLY CREATED TEXT COLUMNS

a. Move the cursor to a section of the document that contains the columns you want to change.

b. Select **L**ayout, **C**olumns.

c. Select Custom **W**idths, and then adjust the column widths by highlighting information in the desired column, selecting **E**dit, **W**idth, typing a new width, pressing Enter, and selecting OK.

d. Select OK to return to the document.

EXAMPLES

1. To experiment with editing columns, retrieve the document ACMECORP.LTR by selecting **F**ile, **R**etrieve, typing **acmecorp.ltr**, and pressing Enter. Press ↓ three times so that the cursor is at the beginning of the line where the heading "New Benefits" appears. This puts your cursor at the beginning of the first column.

You are going to change the due date for submitting the insurance cards from May 25 to May 26. This date appears in the second column. To move quickly to the second column, press Ctrl-Home, and then press →. This moves the cursor to the beginning of the second column.

Place the cursor on the period after 25. Press Backspace to delete the 5, and type **6**.

For more practice, change the second sentence to read "Four different health plans will be offered." Move to the left column by pressing Ctrl-Home and then pressing ←. This moves you to the left side of the first column. Move to the word "Three." Press Ctrl-Backspace to delete the word "Three," type **Four**, and press Spacebar. Press Ctrl-→ to move to the beginning of the word "plans," type **health**, and press Spacebar. You are now done editing this document.

Save the document and clear the screen by selecting **F**ile, **E**xit, and pressing Enter twice.

2. To practice editing a three-column document, retrieve the document named DESSERT by selecting **F**ile, **R**etrieve, typing **dessert**, and pressing Enter.

   This example has three parallel columns that have block protection on. First, you will eliminate the word "toasted" from the description of Patti's Prize. Press ↓ twice. This moves the cursor to the *G* in "Grandpa's." Move the cursor to the third column by pressing Ctrl-Home, → twice.

   Press ↓ to move to the line where "toasted" appears. Move to the word "toasted," and delete it by pressing Ctrl-Backspace.

   Change the price of Bob's Boast to $2.75. Press ↓ three times. Press Ctrl-Home, ← to move to column 2. Press → three times, press Del twice, and type **75**. The corrections have been made.

   Save the document and clear the screen by selecting **F**ile, E**x**it, and pressing Enter twice.

3. Occasionally you will want to change the widths of columns after you have entered the text. To practice editing column widths, retrieve the document named FLOWERS by selecting **F**ile, **R**etrieve, typing **flowers**, and pressing Enter.

   Press ↓ twice to move to the *T* in TERM. This moves the cursor to part of the document where the column definition is in effect. Select **L**ayout, **C**olumns. Column 1 has a width of 1.5 inches, and column 2 has a width of 4.5 inches. Adjust the column widths by selecting Custom **W**idths and then selecting **E**dit with the highlight on column 1. Select **W**idth, type **1**, and press Enter twice. Press ↓ twice to move to the column width setting for column 2. Select **E**dit, **W**idth, type **5**, and press Enter twice to change column 2's width. Select OK to return to the document. The right column adjusts to the new width setting.

EXERCISES

1. Retrieve the document named COMMNEWS. Change the starting time in the last paragraph to 2:00. Change the title "KIDDIE CALENDAR" to "KIDDIE NOTES."
   Save the document by using the same filename, and clear the screen.
2. Retrieve the document named N&A.LST. Change the second phone number to 555-5555. Change "Sally Jones" to "Sally Smith."
   Save the document by using the same filename, and clear the screen.
3. Retrieve the document named PLAY.DOC. Change the width of column 1 to 1 inch and the width of column 2 to 5.1 inches.
   Save the document by using the same filename, and clear the screen.

mastery skills check

Do not clear the screen until you have completed the last Mastery Skills Check exercise.

1. Define a page that has 4-inch top and bottom margins. Center the title "The Greenville Library." On the next line, center the title "Eager Reader Club." Skip a line, and define newspaper columns by using WordPerfect's default settings. Enter the following text. [21.1]

   Story Hour

   Eager readers can take part in story hour every Monday from 10:00 am. to 11:00 am. Every week, we will feature a new story read by everyone's favorite, Mr. Rabbit. After the reading, the children are encouraged to participate in a lively discussion about the story. Mr. Rabbit tries to teach a valuable lesson from every story he reads to our Eager Readers.

Mr. Rabbit is looking forward to seeing you next week.

2. Turn off newspaper columns, and add a hard page break. [21.1]
3. Center the title "The Top Four Favorites," and then skip a line. Define three parallel columns. The first column should have a width of 2 inches. The second column should have a width of 2.5 inches. The third column should have a width of 1 inch. Center the headings "Title," "Author," and "Rating." Enter the following text. [21.2]

A B C, 1 2 3	Jeffries, Kenneth B.	****
Seven Little Fish	Weston, Meryl Ann	***
The Dancing Flowers	Philips, Jocelyn M.	***
Big Eddie, Little Sam, and Susie	Duley, Katherine Louise	**

4. Turn off parallel columns, enter a blank line, and then enter the following text, indented one tab stop from the left margin. [21.2]

Book Sale

On May 5th, the Greenville Teen Readers will be sponsoring a book sale of books donated by various members of the community. All are welcome to browse and pick up a few favorites at very low prices. If you have books you would like to donate, please bring them to the library on May 4th during business hours.

5. Preview the document, change the ratings for some of the titles, and clear the screen. [21.3]

Teach Yourself — cumulative skills check

Do not clear the screen until you have completed the last exercise.

1. Make the following formatting changes to a document: change justification to full justification, and set the left, right, top, and bottom margins to 1.5 inches. [5.6]

2. Define two newspaper columns, with the distance between columns set to 0.4 inch. [21.1]
3. Center and boldface the following heading on the page:

   Looking for the Perfect Candy Bar?

   Skip two lines. [4.2, 4.3, 10.2]
4. Type the following text. At the end of the first sentence, force the following sentence to the top of the next column. [21.1]

   Capital Foods announces the release of their first no-calorie, no-cholesterol candy bar, called Perfect-Bar.

   The product received rave reviews during its test marketing. Now you can eat a delicious candy bar guilt free!
5. Turn off the columns. Skip two lines. [21.1]
6. Center and boldface the following heading on the page:

   Perfect-Bar Taste Testers Survey

   Skip two lines. [4.2, 4.3, 10.2]
7. Type the following paragraph as normal text, skipping two lines at the end of the paragraph. [21.1]

   Capital Foods test marketed Perfect-Bar in three areas of the country. The customer comments were generally favorable. Some of the comments are reproduced here:
8. Define two parallel columns; the first column should be 1 inch wide, and the second column should be 4.1 inches wide. Specify a .4-inch space between the columns. Type the following text. [21.2]

Area A	Tasty nougat center. The chocolate coating is rich and creamy.
Area B	Where did you put the calories? This tastes just like the stuff I'm not supposed to have.
Area C	Anything that tastes this good has to have something wrong with it.

22

Using Tables in a Document

chapter objectives

After completing this chapter, you should be able to

22.1 Create a table

22.2 Enter text into a table

22.3 Change the width of a column

22.4 Add or delete a row or column

22.5 Join cells

22.6 Change cell attributes

22.7 Incorporate simple math features into a table

WORDPERFECT'S table feature lets you add a grid to a document and fill it with text. The table feature can be used to create a variety of documents, including forms, scripts, and documents similar to spreadsheets. You can use the table feature to create any document that requires a column-and-row format. Tables can perform simple arithmetic calculations, similar to the calculations a spreadsheet program can perform. Any attributes that can be used within a document (for instance, bold text, right justification, or different fonts) can be assigned to the entire table, to a column, or to a cell (the intersection of a row and a column). These capabilities and others make the table feature very powerful.

Using tables is a two-step process. First, you create the table by defining the number of columns and rows that make up the table. After you have created the table, you are presented with a table edit screen that allows you to change the way the table looks.

The second step is adding the text and numbers to the table. This editing is done while you are in the regular document window. After you have created a table, exited the table edit screen, and entered text, you can return to the table edit screen to change the table's formatting. Text that already exists within the table immediately conforms to the new format settings. This capability is one of the reasons the table feature is so powerful.

Before you begin working with tables, you must learn the basic vocabulary associated with them. Tables are made up of *rows,* which run horizontally across the page, and *columns,* which run vertically down the page. Rows are assigned numbers (starting with number 1 and going down the page), and columns are assigned letters of the alphabet (starting with *A*).

The location where a row and column intersect is called a *cell.* Cells are assigned names based on their relative positions within the table. The cell located at the intersection of the first column and the first row is called A1 because it is in column A and row 1. The cell located at the intersection of the third column and fifth row is called C5 because it is located in column C and row 5. See Figure 22-1 for an example of a table. The row heading "Game 1" is located in cell A2. The score "201" is located in cell C3.

This chapter does not cover the full set of features offered by tables. It does cover basic features that will allow you to produce a large variety of documents. After you have mastered the concepts covered

FIGURE 22-1

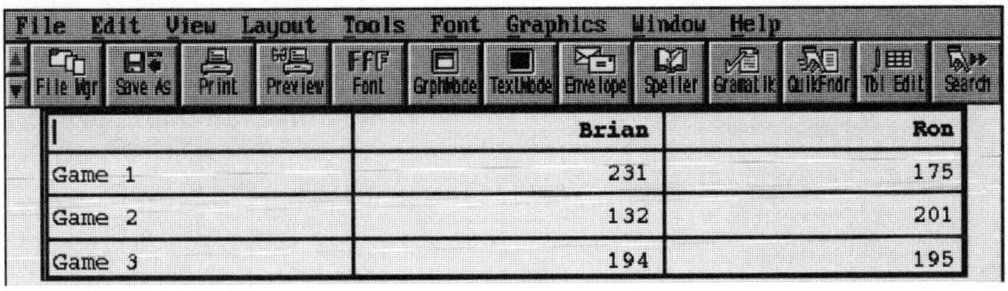

Completed table

in this chapter, you will easily be able to master the more advanced and specialized features of tables.

Because different printer and font selections affect the number of characters that WordPerfect will display on one line, you might not obtain exactly the same word-wrap breaks shown in this chapter. The examples in this chapter were all developed for use on a Hewlett-Packard LaserJet Series III printer using the default Courier font.

review skills check

Do not clear the screen until you have completed the last Skills Check exercise.

1. Delete all tab stops. Set left-justified tab stops at 0 inches and 0.5 inch. Set decimal tabs at 5 inches and 6 inches. [5.3]
2. Create a centered heading for the document that includes the following information:

   Acme Corporation
   Statement

On the third line of the heading, enter the current date by using WordPerfect's date feature. [4.3, 5.4, 10.2]

3. Use Tab to create the following statement. [4.1, 5.3]

Previous Balance		$1,234.56
Expenses		
Rent	400.00	
Utilities	119.90	
Total Expenses		(519.90)
Income		
Client 012	150.00	
Client 110	1,210.00	
Total Income		1,360.00
Current Balance		$2,074.66

4. Exit the document, and clear the screen. [2.4]

22.1 CREATE A TABLE

As previously noted, a minimum of two steps is required to work with the table feature. First you must define the table. Afterwards, you can enter the text (data) into the table from the normal document window. This section shows you how to do the first step, creating a table.

TO CREATE A TABLE

a. Select **L**ayout, Ta**b**les, **C**reate. You can also press Alt-F7 and then select **T**ables, **C**reate.

b. Type the number of columns to be created for the table, and press Enter.

c. Type the number of rows to be created for the table, and press Enter.

d. Select OK to create the table.

e. When you are finished editing the formatting for the table, press F7 to return to the document window.

EXAMPLES

1. Creating a table is easy. You will start by creating a table that has three columns and four rows. First, select **L**ayout, Ta**b**les, **C**reate, or press Alt-F7 and then select **T**ables, **C**reate. WordPerfect displays this dialog box:

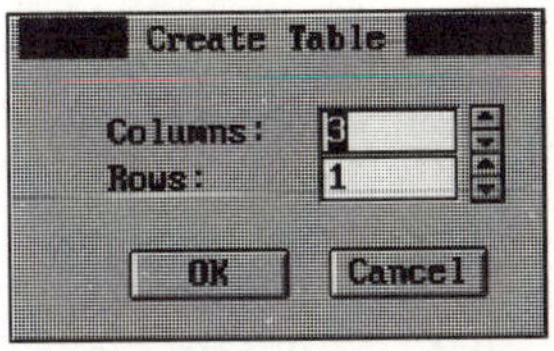

Type **3** for the number of columns, and press Enter. Type **4** for the number of rows, and press Enter. Select OK. The table edit screen appears, displaying the table, as shown in Figure 22-2.

The cursor is located in the top-left cell of the table. In the status line below the table, next to the document number, is an additional entry indicating that your cursor is located in cell A1. Later in this chapter, you will learn about the table editing features that appear at the bottom of the screen.

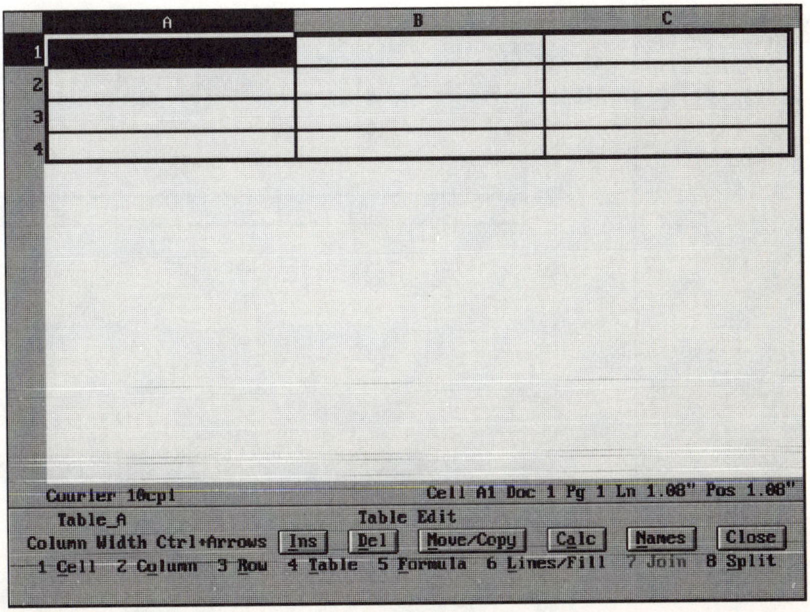

FIGURE 22-2 *Table edit screen*

Press F7 to exit the table edit screen. You are now in the normal document window, and your cursor is in cell A1. Select **V**iew, Reveal **C**odes or press Alt-F3 to display the codes inserted for this table, as shown in Figure 22-3. The [Tbl Def] code appears where the table has been defined. Anything between this code and the [Tbl Off] code is part of the table. When you move to the [Tbl Def] code, you will see a code like [Tbl Def:Table_A;2.17";2.17";2.17"] to indicate that the table has three columns that are 2.17 inches wide. "Table_A" identifies this table as the first table you defined. Tables you define after table A will have letters after *A*.

The four [Row] codes represent the four rows of the table. The [Cell] codes separate the contents of each cell. If your cursor is located in cell A1, you'll find it at the first [Cell] code that is after the first [Row] code in the Reveal Codes screen.

Turn off the Reveal Codes screen by selecting **V**iew, Reveal **C**odes or pressing Alt-F3. Move to the end of the document by pressing Pg Dn. Your cursor will move to just below the table. Press Enter, and type

The above table lists the scores from last week's series of games for Brian and Ron. The following table lists this week's scores, showing the improvement both players made in one week.

Press Enter twice, and create a second table similar to the first. Select **L**ayout, Ta**b**les, **C**reate, or press Alt-F7 and select **T**ables, **C**reate.

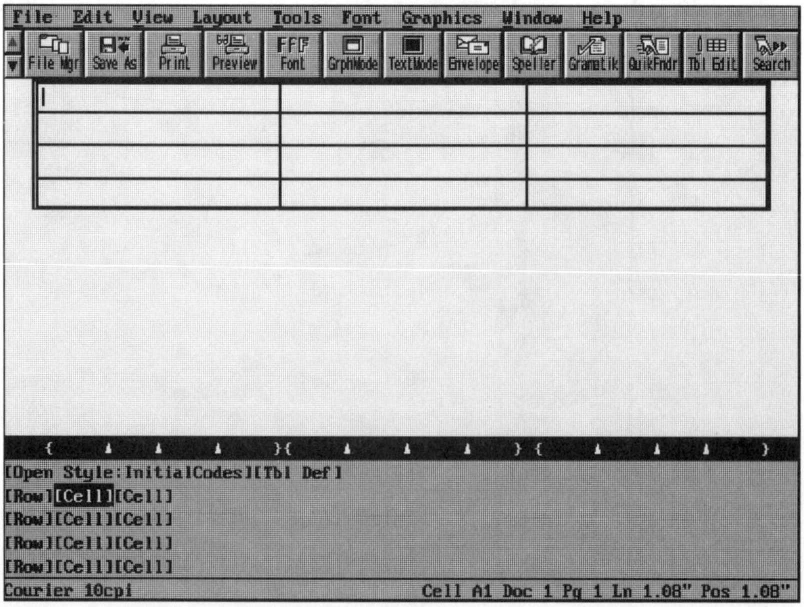

FIGURE 22-3

Codes displayed that show table structure

Select OK to create a table that has three columns and four rows. Press F7 to exit the table edit screen and return to the normal document window.

Save the document by pressing F7, selecting **Y**es, typing **games**, and selecting OK. Select **N**o to clear the screen and remain in WordPerfect.

2. To create a table that contains three columns and five rows, first press Enter to leave an empty line at the top of the document. Select **L**ayout, Ta**b**les, **C**reate, or press Alt-F7 and select **T**ables, **C**reate. Type **3** for the number of columns in the table, and press Enter. Type **5** for the number of rows, and press Enter. Select OK to create the table. When the table edit screen appears, press F7 to return to the document screen.

   Save the document by pressing F7, selecting **Y**es, typing **3by5**, and selecting OK. Select **N**o to clear the screen and remain in WordPerfect.

3. Press F6, and type the following title:

   1993 MACRS Deductions

   Press F6 again to turn off the bold feature, and press Enter twice. Create a two-column by four-row table by selecting **L**ayout, Ta**b**les, **C**reate, or by pressing Alt-F7 and selecting **T**ables, **C**reate.

   Type **2** and press Enter for the number of columns in the table. Type **4** and press Enter for the number of rows. Select OK to display the table edit screen with the created table. Press F7 to return to the document screen.

   Save the document by pressing F7, selecting **Y**es, typing **macrs**, and selecting OK. Select **N**o to clear the screen and remain in WordPerfect.

4. You can use tables to create a form such as an employment application. Center a heading for this document by selecting **L**ayout, **A**lignment, **C**enter or pressing Shift-F6. Press F6 to turn on the bold feature, and type

   Acme Corporation Employment Application

   Press F6 once, and press Enter twice. Create a three-column by four-row table by selecting **L**ayout, Ta**b**les, **C**reate, or by pressing Alt-F7 and selecting **T**ables, **C**reate.

   Type **3** and press Enter for the number of columns in the table. Type **4** and press Enter for the number of rows. Select OK to create the table and display the table edit screen. Press F7 to return to the document screen.

Save the document by pressing F7, selecting **Y**es, typing **employee.tbl**, and selecting OK. Select **N**o to clear the screen and remain in WordPerfect.

EXERCISES

1. Type the following bold heading:

   Office Supplies Inventory - Top Shelf

   Insert a blank line. Create a table that has three columns and four rows. Insert a blank line. Type the following bold heading:

   Office Supplies Inventory - Bottom Shelf

   Insert a blank line. Create a table that has three columns and five rows. Save the document as SUPPLIES, and clear the screen.
2. Center and boldface this heading:

   Faculty Evaluation Form

   Insert a blank line. Type the following paragraph:

   Place an X under the Agree category if you believe the statement regarding the instructor is true. Place an X under the Neutral category if you have no opinion or do not know whether the statement applies to the instructor. Place an X under the Disagree category if you believe the statement regarding the instructor is not correct.

   Insert a blank line. Create a table that contains four columns and five rows. Insert a blank line underneath the table. Type this sentence:

   Return this form to the department's faculty secretary.

   Save the document as FACULTY.TBL, and clear the screen.
3. Type the following:

   Attachment C:

   Insert a blank line. Create a table that has two columns and four rows. Insert a blank line underneath the table. Type

See page 14-7 for more details.

Save the document as ATTACH.C, and clear the screen.

4. Create a table that is two columns wide by four rows long. Save the document as BILL.SHT, and clear the screen.

22.2 ENTER TEXT INTO A TABLE

Entering text into a table is similar to entering text into a normal document. While you are within a cell, you type the text for the cell in much the same way you would type text in a normally formatted document. One exception to this is the use of Tab. Within tables, Tab moves from cell to cell.

TO ENTER TABLE DATA

a. Move the cursor to the cell in which the data is to be entered.
b. Type the text into the cell. Press Enter to end short lines, but do not press Enter at the end of the data.
c. Press Tab to move to the next cell.

Pressing Tab or pressing Ctrl-Home, → moves the cursor forward from cell to cell. Pressing Shift-Tab (back tab) or pressing Ctrl-Home, ← moves the cursor backward from cell to cell. If you need to use the tab function within a cell, press Home and then Tab. Pressing any of the arrow keys moves the cursor in the direction of the arrow. If your cursor is located at the outer edge of the text in a cell, pressing the arrow key that points in that direction moves the cursor to the next cell. If you press Tab when the cursor is in the last cell of a table, WordPerfect adds a new row to your table.

EXAMPLES

1. You will now enter text into a previously created table. Retrieve the document GAMES by selecting **F**ile, **R**etrieve, typing **games**, and selecting OK. With the cursor in cell A1, press Tab once to move to

cell B1. Type **Brian**, press Tab to move to cell C1, and type **Ron**. Press Tab again, which moves the cursor to cell A2.

Type **Game 1**, press Tab, type **231**, press Tab, and type **175**. Press Tab, type **Game 2**, press Tab, type **132**, press Tab, and type **201**. Finally, press Tab, type **Game 3**, press Tab, type **194**, press Tab, and type **195**. The first table should like this:

	Brian	Ron
Game 1	231	175
Game 2	132	201
Game 3	194	195

Using ↓ and ←, move the cursor to cell B1 in the second table. Make sure that the status line says "Cell B1" before continuing with this example. You will now enter text into the second table. This time, however, you will use → to move from one cell to the next.

Type **Brian**, press →, and type **Ron**. Press → to move to cell A2. Type **Game 1**, press →, type **220**, press →, type **196**, and press →. Type **Game 2**, press →, type **195**, press →, type **212**, and press →. Finally, type **Game 3**, press →, type **180**, press →, and type **194**. The second table should look like this:

	Brian	Ron
Game 1	220	196
Game 2	195	212
Game 3	180	194

At this point, assume you have discovered a typographic error. You realize that in the second table, Brian's first game score should have been 230. Press ↑ twice to move up to cell C2, and press Shift-Tab (backtab) once to move to cell B2. Press →, press Del, and type **3** to change the number to 230.

Save this revised document by pressing F7 once, selecting **Y**es, and selecting **N**o.

2. You can try entering data in another table by using the 3BY5 document. Retrieve the document 3BY5 by selecting **F**ile, **R**etrieve, typing **3by5**, and selecting OK. In a later section of this chapter, you will create a table heading within the first row of this table. For now, leave this row blank. Press ↓ twice to move to cell A2.

   Press Caps Lock, type **TEAM**, press Tab to move to cell B2, type **WINS**, press Tab to move to cell C2, type **LOSSES**, and press Tab. Your cursor should be located in cell A3. Press Caps Lock again.

   Type **Redmen**, press Tab, type **10**, press Tab, type **0**, and press Tab. Your cursor should be located in cell A4. Type **Patriots**, press Tab, type **9**, press Tab, type **1**, and press Tab. Your cursor should be located in cell A5. Type **Bruins**, press Tab, type **8**, press Tab, and type **2**.

Now add some text before the table. To do this, press Home, Home, ↑. This moves the cursor to the beginning of the document. Type the following:

This year's high school basketball conference has been very exciting for our readership. The following table lists the current standings of our local teams.

Press Enter to produce a blank line between the paragraph and the table that follows it. Save this revised document with a new filename by selecting **F**ile, Save **A**s or pressing F10, typing **baskball** as the new filename, and selecting OK. Clear the screen as usual.

3. You can use document formatting features to change the appearance of text within a cell in much the same way you use these features in a normal document. If you attempt to use a formatting feature that conflicts with the table formatting defined for the cell, WordPerfect ignores your attempt. Because you have not yet added formatting to any tables, you need not worry about conflicting formats at this time.

   Retrieve the document named MACRS by selecting **F**ile, **R**etrieve, typing **macrs**, and selecting OK. The 1993 MACRS Deductions table should appear on your screen.

   Move to cell A1 by pressing ↓ twice. The first row will contain the headings "Property" and "1993 Deduction." Boldface and center the headings as you type them. Press F6 and Shift-F6, and then type **Property**. Press Tab, F6, and Shift-F6, and type **1993 Deduction**.

   You needed to press F6 for the second column heading because formatting codes do not transfer from one cell to another. For the same reason, you do not need to turn off the bold feature after typing the second heading.

   Press Tab to move to cell A2. You are now ready to enter the text. In this example, the text does not fit into one line of the cell. Just type normally, and let WordPerfect wrap the line as needed.

   Type **3-year property (fully depreciated)**, press Tab, and type **0.00**. The word "depreciated" scrolls to the second line of the cell, which lengthens to accommodate the entry. The table should now look like this:

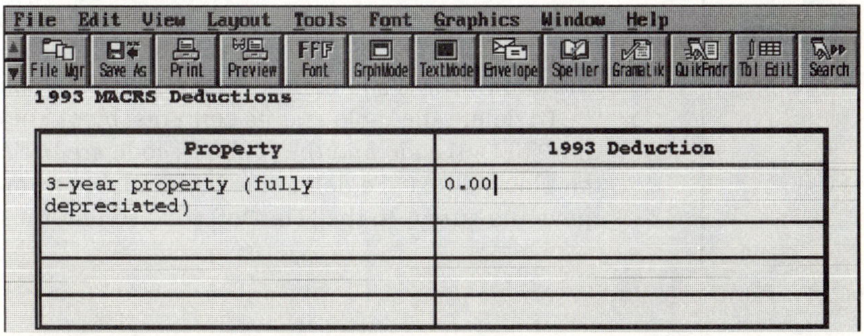

Press Tab so that the cursor is located in cell A3. Type the following four entries, pressing Tab after each one except the last:

5-year property (21% each year)
9,450.00
10-year property (10% each year)
5,000.00

Save this revised document by selecting **F**ile, **E**xit or pressing F7, selecting **Y**es, and selecting **N**o.

4. To delete a table, you must delete its codes. You are now going to experiment with deleting a table structure and deleting an entire table. Retrieve the document GAMES by selecting **F**ile, **R**etrieve, typing **games**, and selecting OK. Select **V**iew, Reveal **C**odes or press Alt-F3 to display the codes for this table. The cursor is located at the first [Cell] code in the Reveal Codes screen.

   Press Del. The [Cell] code is not deleted, but the cursor moves one cell to the right. The cursor is at the *B* in "Brian." If you press Del now, you will delete the *B* in "Brian." Press → until the next [Row] code is highlighted. Press Del again. Again, nothing is deleted, but the cursor now moves to the *G* in "Game." You cannot delete the [Cell] and [Row] codes.

   To delete the table *structure,* press ↑ and ← to move to the [Tbl Def] code. The only way you can delete a table is to delete the [Tbl Def] code. Deleting a table deletes the structure of the table but leaves the contents of the table intact. Any text that was in the table remains. Press Del to delete the [Tbl Def] code. The [Cell] codes are replaced by [Lft Tab] codes, and the [Row] codes are replaced by [HRt] codes. Because WordPerfect's default tabs are set at every half inch, the headings do not line up with the game scores. If you want to delete a table structure but retain the text within the table, it is normally a good idea to adjust the tab stops after you delete the [Tbl Def] code.

   To change the tab stops, select **L**ayout, **T**ab Set, and then select the Clear **A**ll button. Set a tab by selecting **S**et Tab, typing **3**, and pressing Enter. Set a second tab by selecting **S**et Tab, typing **5**, and pressing Enter. Press F7 to select OK and return to the document. The game scores should now line up with the column headings.

   To delete the table and its contents, block the table, making sure the [Tbl Def] code and the [Tbl Off] code are both contained within the blocked text. To delete the bottom table from this document, move the cursor to the [Tbl Def] code so that the code is highlighted.

Select **E**dit, **B**lock or press Alt-F4. Press ↓ until the cursor is to the right of the [Tbl Off] code. Press Del to delete the table. The entire table disappears from the document.

Turn off the Reveal Codes screen by selecting **V**iew, Reveal **C**odes or pressing Alt-F3. Exit without saving the document by selecting **F**ile, **E**xit or pressing F7, and then selecting **N**o twice.

5. Sometimes the tables you create will not require that text be placed in all of the cells. You can leave some cells empty, to be filled in at a later time; or the document can be used as a form in which someone will enter information by hand. A sign-up sheet is a good example of this type of table. This example shows a useful table in which some of the cells remain empty.

   Retrieve EMPLOYEE.TBL by selecting **F**ile, **R**etrieve, typing **employee.tbl**, and selecting OK. The first column of this table will contain a question. The remaining two columns will be used to indicate a yes or no response.

   If the answer is yes, the applicant will place a check mark in column B. If the answer is no, the applicant will place a check mark in column C. Normally you would want column A to be as wide as possible to accommodate the space required for the questions. Columns B and C would normally be narrow. You'll learn to change column widths in the next section of this chapter. For now, the table will look strange because so much of the text of the questions will have to be wrapped within a relatively narrow cell.

   Press ↓ until the cursor is located in cell A1. Press Caps Lock, and type the following, without pressing Enter:

   ANSWER THE FOLLOWING. PLACE A CHECK MARK IN THE YES COLUMN IF THE ANSWER TO THE QUESTION IS YES. PLACE A CHECK MARK IN THE NO COLUMN IF THE ANSWER TO THE QUESTION IS NO.

   Press Tab, type **YES**, press Tab, type **NO**, and press Tab. The cursor should be located in cell A2. Press Caps Lock.

   Type the following three questions, pressing Tab three times after each of the first two questions. (Do not press Enter.)

   Have you ever applied for a position with Acme Corporation before?
   Have you ever been convicted of a felony?
   Are you a citizen of the United States?

   Save this revised document by selecting **F**ile, **E**xit or pressing F7, selecting **Y**es, and selecting **N**o.

EXERCISES

1. Retrieve the document named SUPPLIES. Enter the following data into the first table, using bold text where indicated.

ITEM	**TOTAL**	**UNITS**
Pencils	10	Boxes
Pens	8	Boxes
Note Pads	15	Dozen

Enter the following data into the second table.

ITEM	**TOTAL**	**UNITS**
Letterhead	3	Boxes
Second Sheet Paper	4	Boxes
Bond Paper	15	Reams
Laser Labels	2	Packages

Save the revised document by using the same filename.

2. Retrieve the document named FACULTY.TBL. Enter the following headings into the four cells of the first row (one heading per cell).

STATEMENT AGREE NEUTRAL DISAGREE

Enter each of the following statements into a separate cell in column A. Leave the remaining cells in columns B, C, and D empty.

1. He/she comes prepared to class.
2. He/she has command of the subject matter.
3. He/she seems genuinely concerned with whether students learn the course material.
4. The course's contents were taught in a manner that promoted learning of the course material.

Save the revised document by using the same filename.

3. Retrieve the document named ATTACH.C. Leave the first row of cells blank. You will be adding a table header later. Enter the following information in the indicated cells (leaving cell B4 empty).

Cell A2: 1993 MACRS deduction: $12,000 x .20 =
Cell B2: 2,400.00
Cell A3: 1994 MACRS deduction: $12,000 x .32 x
1/2 year =
Cell B3: 1,920.00
Cell A4: Total MACRS deduction:

Save the document by using the same filename.

4. Retrieve the document named SUPPLIES. Delete the structure of the second table. Adjust the tab stops to 3 inches and 5 inches. Save the document as TOPSHELF.
5. Retrieve the document named BILL.SHT. Enter into cell A4 the following:

   Total Charges:

   Save the document by using the same filename, and clear the screen.
6. Create a table that contains 12 columns and 15 rows. Delete the entire table.

22.3 CHANGE THE WIDTH OF A COLUMN

WordPerfect provides two methods for changing the width of a column. You perform both methods from the table edit screen. One method allows you gradually to increase or decrease the width of a specified column and immediately see the results. The other method allows you to specify in inches the new width of a column. With the second method, the reformatting occurs after you set the column's width.

TO CHANGE THE WIDTH OF A COLUMN USING THE Ctrl METHOD

a. Move the cursor to a location inside the table.
b. Select **L**ayout, Ta**b**les, **E**dit. You can also press Alt-F7 and then select **T**ables, **E**dit.
c. Move the cursor to any cell in the column whose width is to be changed.
d. Press Ctrl-← to narrow the column or Ctrl-→ to widen the column. Continue until the column's width is acceptable.
e. Press F7 to exit the table edit screen.

In step d, WordPerfect will not let you make the rightmost column larger if the table is already the full width of the page. With other columns, WordPerfect will decrease the size of columns to the right to accommodate making a column larger when the table is already the full width of the page.

TO CHANGE THE WIDTH OF A COLUMN USING THE MENU METHOD

a. Move the cursor to a location inside the table.

b. Select **L**ayout, Ta**b**les, **E**dit. You can also press Alt-F7 and then select **T**ables, **E**dit.

c. Move the cursor to any cell in the column whose width is to be changed.

d. Select C**o**lumn.

e. Select the **W**idth text box.

f. Type the width for the column in inches, and press Enter.

g. Select OK to close the Column Format dialog box.

h. Press F7 to exit the table edit screen.

If you have a mouse, you can edit the table's structure by clicking the Tbl Edit button in the Button Bar in place of step b.

EXAMPLES

1. You can change the widths of columns in a table. Retrieve the document GAMES by selecting **F**ile, **R**etrieve, typing **games**, and selecting OK. Because you are currently within the table, activate the table edit screen by selecting **L**ayout, Ta**b**les, **E**dit, or by pressing Alt-F7 and selecting **T**ables, **E**dit. If you have a mouse, you can activate the table edit screen by clicking the Tbl Edit button in the Button Bar. The Tbl Edit button looks like this:

Because your cursor is in cell A1, first decrease the width of column A by pressing Ctrl-← ten times. As you do this, the table readjusts itself to reflect each decrease in the size of the column.

Press → and ↓. Your cursor should be in cell B2. WordPerfect does not care which row you are in when you change a column's width. To decrease column B's width by eight characters, press Ctrl-← eight times. Press → once so that your cursor is in cell C2. Decrease column C's width to be the same as column B's by pressing Ctrl-← eight times. Press F7 to exit the table edit screen.

Move the cursor to any cell within column A of the second table. Activate the table edit screen for this table by selecting **L**ayout, Ta**b**les, **E**dit, or by pressing Alt-F7 and selecting **T**ables, **E**dit. Select C**o**lumn, **W**idth. Type **1.17** and press Enter twice to change the width of column A to 1.17 inches. Press → to move to column B. To change the width of column B, select C**o**lumn, **W**idth. Type **1.37** and press Enter twice to change the width of column B to 1.37 inches. Press → to move to column C. To change the width of column C, select C**o**lumn, **W**idth. Type **1.37** and press Enter twice to change the width of column C to 1.37 inches. The widths of the columns in the second table should be the same as the widths of the columns in the first table in this document. Press F7 to exit the table edit screen. At this point, your table looks like Figure 22-4.

Save this revised document by pressing F7 once, selecting **Y**es, and selecting **N**o.

2. You can change the size of a column in which text is wrapped, and the text will adjust to the new column size. Retrieve the document

FIGURE 22-4

Tables containing data

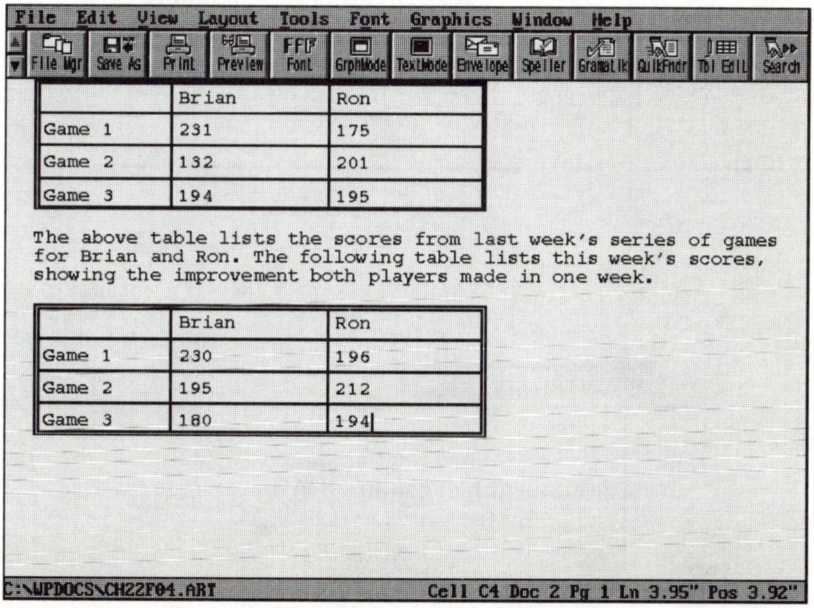

	Brian	Ron
Game 1	231	175
Game 2	132	201
Game 3	194	195

The above table lists the scores from last week's series of games for Brian and Ron. The following table lists this week's scores, showing the improvement both players made in one week.

	Brian	Ron
Game 1	230	196
Game 2	195	212
Game 3	180	194

MACRS by selecting **F**ile, **R**etrieve, typing **macrs**, and selecting OK. Press ↓ until the cursor is in cell A1 of the table.

Activate the table edit screen by selecting **L**ayout, Ta**b**les, **E**dit, or by pressing Alt-F7 and selecting **T**ables, **E**dit. Because your cursor is in cell A1, first increase the width of column A by pressing Ctrl-→ ten times. As you do this, the table readjusts itself to reflect each increase in the size of column A. Column B's width decreases to make room for the increased size of column A. Press F7.

Save this revised document by pressing F7 once, selecting **Y**es, and selecting **N**o.

3. Changing column widths by using the Column Format dialog box changes text wrapping in a column just like using the Ctrl and arrow-key combinations does. Retrieve the document EMPLOYEE.TBL by selecting **F**ile, **R**etrieve, typing **employee.tbl**, and selecting OK. Press ↓ until the cursor is in cell A1 of the table.

   Activate the table edit screen by selecting **L**ayout, Ta**b**les, **E**dit, or by pressing Alt-F7 and selecting **T**ables, **E**dit. Press → once to move the cursor into the YES column (column B). Decrease the width of this column by selecting C**o**lumn, **W**idth. Type **.5** and press Enter twice to change the width of column B to .5 inch. Press → to move to the NO column (column C).

   Make column C's width the same as column B's. Select C**o**lumn, **W**idth. Type **.5** and press Enter twice to change the width of column C to .5 inch.

   Now that columns B and C have been decreased in width, it is time to increase the width of column A. Press ← twice to move the cursor to column A. Select C**o**lumn, **W**idth. Type **5.5** and press Enter twice to change the width of column A to 5.5 inches. Press F7.

   Save this revised document by pressing F7 once, selecting **Y**es, and selecting **N**o.

EXERCISES

1. Retrieve the file named SUPPLIES. In the first table, decrease the width of column B by ten characters. Decrease the width of column C by five characters.

In the second table, use the menu method to change the width of column B to 1.17 inches and the width of column C to 1.67 inches. Save the revised document.

2. Retrieve the document named FACULTY.TBL. Use the menu method to change the widths of the four columns. Change the width of column D to 1.1 inches, column C to .9 inch, column B to .7 inch, and column A to 3.8 inches. Save the revised document.
3. Retrieve the document named ATTACH.C. Increase the width of column A by 15 characters. Save the revised document.
4. Retrieve the document named BILL.SHT. Increase the width of column A by 15 characters. Save the revised document.

22.4 ADD OR DELETE A ROW OR COLUMN

Sometimes you will find it necessary to add a row or column to a previously created table. You will also need to remove a row or column from a previously created table. You can add or remove columns or rows from the table edit screen. The new column or row that you add takes on the attributes (formatting) of the column or row where the cursor is located. WordPerfect also has a shortcut for adding rows to the bottom of a table.

TO ADD A COLUMN OR ROW TO A TABLE

a. Move the cursor to a location inside the table.
b. Select **L**ayout, Ta**b**les, **E**dit. You can also press Alt-F7 and select **T**ables, **E**dit.
c. Move to the cell closest to where you want to add the column or row.
d. Select **I**ns, or press Ins.
e. Select **C**olumns or **R**ows.
f. Select **H**ow Many?, type the number of rows or columns to add, and press Enter.
g. Select the **B**efore Cursor Position option button to insert columns to the left of the cursor position or to insert rows above

the cursor position, or select the **A**fter Cursor Position option button to insert columns to the right of the cursor position or to insert rows below the cursor position.

h. Select OK to insert the rows or columns.

i. Press F7 to exit the table edit screen.

TO ADD ROWS TO THE END OF A TABLE

a. While in the normal document window, move the cursor to the lower-right cell of the table.

b. Press Tab to add a row.

c. Make entries in the row, and then repeat steps a and b for each of the new rows you want to add.

TO REMOVE COLUMNS OR ROWS FROM A TABLE

a. Move the cursor to a location inside the table.

b. Select **L**ayout, Ta**b**les, **E**dit. You can also press Alt-F7 and select **T**ables, **E**dit.

c. Move to a cell in the first column or row you want to delete.

d. Select **D**el, or press Del.

e. Select **R**ows or C**o**lumns.

f. Select **H**ow Many?, type the number of rows or columns to remove, and press Enter.

g. Select OK to delete the rows or columns.

h. Press F7 to exit the table edit screen.

EXAMPLES

1. Adding rows and columns to a table is fairly easy. In this example, you will add a row to the bottom of a table and a column to the right edge of a table. Retrieve the document GAMES by selecting **F**ile,

Retrieve, typing **games**, and selecting OK. With the cursor in cell A1 of the first table, activate the table edit screen by selecting **L**ayout, Ta**b**les, **E**dit, or by pressing Alt-F7 and selecting **T**ables, **E**dit. To add a row at the bottom of the table, press ↓ three times and → twice to move to cell C4. Select **I**ns to display this dialog box:

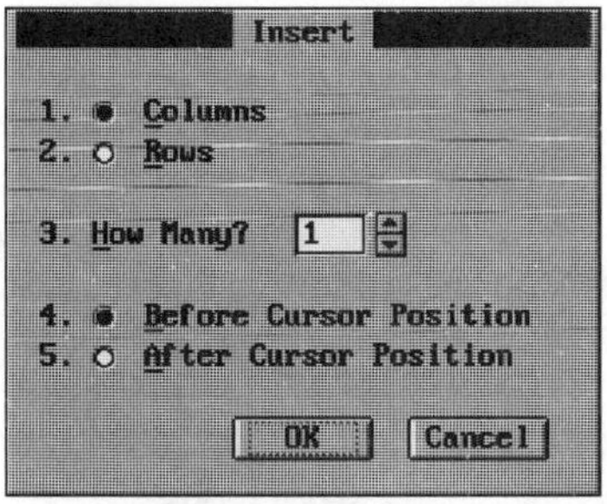

Select **R**ows and select **A**fter Cursor Position to insert one row below the cursor's position. Because you want to insert only one row, the number in the How Many? text box is correct. Select OK to insert the row.

To add a column to the right side of the table, select **I**ns. Select **C**olumns and select **A**fter Cursor Position to insert one column to the right of the cursor's position. Because you want to insert only one column, the number in the How Many? text box is correct. Select OK to insert the column. Press ↑ four times to move to cell D1, which is where you will start making entries.

Exit the table edit screen by pressing F7. Add text to these cells by typing **John**, pressing ↓, typing **140**, pressing ↓, typing **151**, pressing ↓, typing **170**, and pressing Tab. Type **Total** in cell A5. You will have WordPerfect generate the totals in a later section of this chapter. At this point, your new table looks like this:

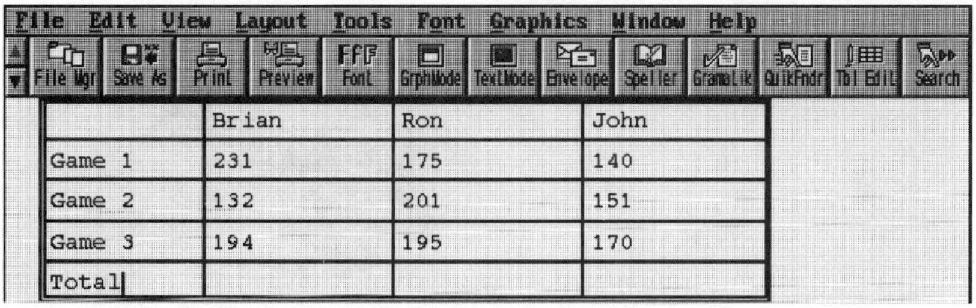

	Brian	Ron	John
Game 1	231	175	140
Game 2	132	201	151
Game 3	194	195	170
Total			

Edit the paragraph that separates the two tables. Move the cursor to the *B* in "Brian." Press Ctrl-Backspace three times to delete "Brian and Ron." Type **the Boomers.**, and press Spacebar. Move the cursor to the *b* in "both." Press Ctrl-Backspace twice, type **the Boomers**, and press Spacebar.

Make similar changes to the second table by pressing ↓ twice to move the cursor to cell A1. Select **L**ayout, Ta**b**les, **E**dit, or press

Alt-F7 and select **T**ables, **E**dit. To add a row at the bottom of the table, press ↓ three times and → twice to move to cell C4. Select **I**ns, select **R**ows, select **A**fter Cursor Position, and select OK to insert one row below the cursor's position.

To add a column to the right side of the table, select **I**ns again. Select **C**olumns, select **A**fter Cursor Position, and select OK to insert one column to the right of the cursor's position. Press ↑ four times to move to cell D1, which is where you will start making entries. Exit the table edit screen by pressing F7.

Add text to these cells by typing **John**, pressing ↓, typing **153**, pressing ↓, typing **161**, pressing ↓, typing **190**, and pressing Tab. Type **Total** in cell A5.

Save this revised document by selecting **F**ile, **E**xit or pressing F7, and then selecting **Y**es and **N**o.

2. You can practice adding and removing rows and columns. Retrieve the document BASKBALL by selecting **F**ile, **R**etrieve, typing **baskball**, and selecting OK. Press ↓ until you are in cell A1 of the table. Activate the table edit screen by selecting **L**ayout, Ta**b**les, **E**dit, or by pressing Alt-F7 and selecting **T**ables, **E**dit.

   First, add two rows between "Redmen" and "Patriots" to allow room for a new basketball team. Press ↓ three times to move the cursor to cell A4. Press Ins, select **R**ows, **H**ow Many?, type **2**, press Enter, and select OK to indicate that you want to add two rows.

   Now add two columns to the table. These columns will be located between the TEAM and WINS columns and will list the names of the schools. Press Ins, select **C**olumns, **A**fter Column Position, **H**ow Many?, type **2**, press Enter, and select OK to add two new columns.

   At this point, your table has an extra column and row that you can use to practice deleting columns and rows. With the cursor in cell B4, press Del to display this dialog box:

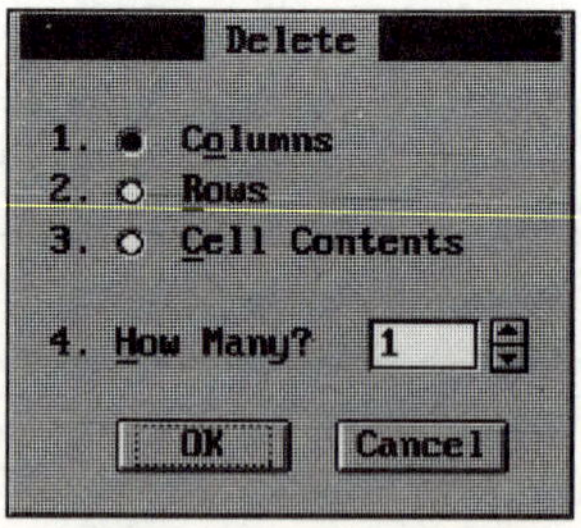

The default settings are correct, so select OK. Now you have only one empty new column. Delete the extra row by pressing Del, selecting **R**ows, and selecting OK.

Press Ctrl-→ 11 times to make the new column larger. Exit the table edit screen by pressing F7. Move the cursor to cell B2 by pressing ↑ twice. Type **SCHOOL**, press ↓, type **Maple City**, press ↓, type **Rochester**, press ↓, type **Broadview Heights**, press ↓, and type **Cranbrook**. Press ↑ three times to move to cell B4, and press Shift-Tab once. Type **Warriors**, press Tab twice, type **9**, press Tab, and type **1**.

Save this revised document by selecting **F**ile, **E**xit or pressing F7, and then selecting **Y**es and **N**o.

3. You can easily add a row to the bottom of a table by using Tab. Retrieve the document MACRS by selecting **F**ile, **R**etrieve, typing **macrs**, and selecting OK. Press ↓ until the cursor is in cell A4 of the table. Press Tab twice. The first time, the cursor moves to the last cell in the table. The second time, you insert a row in the table and move the cursor to the first cell in the new row. Type **Total Deduction:** in cell A5. Leave cell B5 empty. You will make WordPerfect generate a total in a later section of this chapter.

   Save this revised document by selecting **F**ile, **E**xit or pressing F7, and then selecting **Y**es and **N**o.

4. You can add a row to the top of a table and use the row as a heading for the table. Retrieve the document EMPLOYEE.TBL by selecting **F**ile, **R**etrieve, typing **employee.tbl**, and selecting OK. Press ↓ until the cursor is in cell A1 of the table. Select **L**ayout, Ta**b**les, **E**dit, or press Alt-F7 and select **T**ables, **E**dit.

   You will add a row at the top of this table. This row will be used in a later section of this chapter to add a table heading. Because the cursor is in the top row of the table and the row to be added is above this point, press Ins. Select **R**ows and select OK to add one row. Exit the table edit screen by pressing F7.

   You will also add a row at the bottom of this table, but you will want to do this from the normal document window. To do so, press ↓ until the cursor is at the *A* in "Are." Press Tab three times. A row is immediately added to the bottom of the table. Type

   Have you ever served in a branch of the armed services?

   Save this revised document by selecting **F**ile, **E**xit or pressing F7, and then selecting **Y**es and **N**o.

EXERCISES

1. Retrieve the document named SUPPLIES. Add a column named "ORDER NO." before the TOTAL columns of both tables. Add a row called "Envelopes" between "Second Sheet Paper" and "Bond Paper" in the second table. Add the following column entries in the first table:

   ORDER NO.
   PX-3
   ST-2
   RX-5

   Add the following column entries in the second table:

   ORDER NO.
   345
   23
   X35
   RX-34
   RX-1

   Add the following row entries in the second table:

   Envelopes X35 4 Boxes

   Save the revised document by using the same filename.

2. Retrieve the document named FACULTY.TBL. Add a row to the bottom of the table. Type the following statement in column A of the new row:

   5. As a student, you were interested in learning the course material.

   Save the revised document by using the same filename.

3. Retrieve the document TOPSHELF. Add a column named REORDER to the far right of the table. Except for the heading REORDER, leave the other cells blank.

   Save the revised document by using the same filename.

4. Retrieve the document BILL.SHT. Add three columns before the two columns in the table. Remove the columns you have just added. Clear the screen without saving the document.

22.5 JOIN CELLS

You can join two or more cells in a table. Sometimes joining cells to make one cell is very useful. This is especially true for table headings that are used to describe more than one column. WordPerfect provides a simple means for joining cells.

TO JOIN TWO OR MORE CELLS

a. Move the cursor to a location inside the table.

b. Select **L**ayout, Ta**b**les, **E**dit. You can also press Alt-F7 and select **T**ables, **E**dit.

c. Move the cursor to the first cell to be joined.

d. Press Alt-F4 to turn on the block feature.

e. Use the cursor movement keys to move to the last cell to be joined. All the cells to be joined should be blocked.

f. Select **J**oin to join the cells, and select **Y**es to confirm that the cells are to be joined.

g. Press F7 to exit the table edit screen.

Cells can be joined horizontally, vertically, or both ways. The following examples, however, will join cells only horizontally because creating table headings is the most common reason for joining cells.

EXAMPLES

1. You can join cells when you want to create a heading for a table. Retrieve the document BASKBALL by selecting **F**ile, **R**etrieve, typing **baskball**, and selecting OK. Press ↓ until the cursor is in cell A1 of the table. Activate the table edit screen by selecting **L**ayout, Ta**b**les, **E**dit, or by pressing Alt-F7 and selecting **T**ables, **E**dit.

   Now you will join the cells in the first row. Because the cursor is in cell A1, you are ready to block the row of cells. To do this, press Alt-F4 once and then press → three times. Select **J**oin to join the cells, and select **Y**es to confirm that the cells are to be joined. Press F7 to exit the table edit screen. Type the following title:

   Local High School Basketball Standings

   The table looks like this:

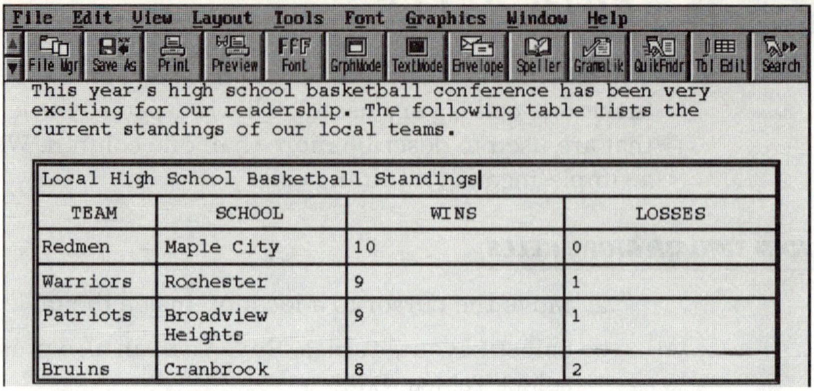

This year's high school basketball conference has been very exciting for our readership. The following table lists the current standings of our local teams.

Local High School Basketball Standings			
TEAM	SCHOOL	WINS	LOSSES
Redmen	Maple City	10	0
Warriors	Rochester	9	1
Patriots	Broadview Heights	9	1
Bruins	Cranbrook	8	2

Save this revised document by selecting **F**ile, **E**xit or pressing F7, and then selecting **Y**es and **N**o.

2. For more practice, retrieve the document EMPLOYEE.TBL by selecting **F**ile, **R**etrieve, typing **employee.tbl**, and selecting OK. Press ↓ until the cursor is in cell A1 of the table. Activate the table edit screen by selecting **L**ayout, Ta**b**les, **E**dit, or by pressing Alt-F7 and selecting **T**ables, **E**dit.

   Now you will join the cells in the first row. Because the cursor is in cell A1, you are ready to block the row of cells. To do this, press Alt-F4 once and then press → twice. Select **J**oin and select **Y**es to join the three cells into one. Press F7 to leave the table edit screen.

   Type the following title:

   SECTION 5: Background Information

   Save this revised document by selecting **F**ile, **E**xit or pressing F7, and then selecting **Y**es and **N**o.

EXERCISES

1. Retrieve the document named ATTACH.C. Join the cells in the top row. Type the following title, pressing Enter after the first two lines. Save the revised document.

   Acme Corporation of North America
   MACRS deduction calculation for XYZ Gizmo
   April 1, 1994

2. Retrieve the document named BILL.SHT. Join the cells in the top row. Type the following title, pressing Enter after the first line. Save the revised document.

   Service Bill
   Please pay upon receipt.

22.6 CHANGE CELL ATTRIBUTES

You can easily make several formatting changes to tables. You can specify the type style, justification, vertical alignment, underlining, boldfacing, and other attributes. These attributes can affect individual cells, individual columns, or the entire table. After you make formatting selections, any text that you enter in a cell uses the attributes you have added to the table, column, or cell. Attributes can be set before or after text has been added to a table. You can directly apply formats to text by using the WordPerfect menus or shortcut keys but not override formatting selected for the cell, column, or table. Using the table formatting features lets you quickly apply formats to entire columns or tables.

TO CHANGE A CELL'S APPEARANCE OR SIZE

a. Move the cursor to a location inside the table.

b. Select **L**ayout, Ta**b**les, **E**dit. You can also press Alt-F7 and select **T**ables, **E**dit.

c. Move the cursor to the cell where you want to change the attribute.

d. Select **C**ell to change the format of the cell's entry, C**o**lumn to change the format of the column's entries, or **T**able to change the format of all the entries in the table.

e. Select **A**ppearance or **S**ize.

f. Select the check box of the size you want to use, or of the appearance attributes you want to use.

g. Select OK to apply the change to the text in the cell, column, or table.

h. Press F7 to exit the table edit screen.

The size and appearance selections are the same ones you can select by using the WordPerfect menus.

TO CHANGE A CELL'S JUSTIFICATION

a. Move the cursor to a location inside the table.
b. Select **L**ayout, Ta**b**les, **E**dit. You can also press Alt-F7 and select **T**ables, **E**dit.
c. Move the cursor to the cell or column where you want to change the justification.
d. Select **C**ell to change the alignment of the cell's entry, C**o**lumn to change the alignment of the column's entries, or **T**able to change the alignment of all the entries in the table.
e. Select **J**ustification.
f. Select the radio button of the justification method you want to use.
g. Select OK to apply the change to the text in the cell, column, or table.
h. Press F7 to exit the table edit screen.

Whenever a block of cells is to have the same formatting, you can save yourself some work. Modify step c in either of the previous two sets of instructions by placing the cursor on the first cell to be formatted, pressing Alt-F4, and using the arrow keys to block the cells to be formatted. Then continue with the rest of the instructions as written.

EXAMPLES

1. You can try the justification options by using the GAMES document. Select **F**ile, **R**etrieve, type **games**, and select OK. With the cursor in cell A1 of the first table, activate the table edit screen by selecting **L**ayout, Ta**b**les, **E**dit, or by pressing Alt-F7 and selecting **T**ables, **E**dit.

   You are going to right-align most of this table. Select **T**able to display the Table Format dialog box, as shown in Figure 22-5. The Appearance, Size, and Justification options are the same when you select **C**ell, C**o**lumn, or **T**able. Select **J**ustification, **R**ight, OK. The text for all of the cells is right-aligned.

Although right justification works best for most of the columns, you will want to left-align the entries in column A. With the cursor in cell A1, select C**o**lumn, **J**ustification, **L**eft, OK. The entries in the first column are left aligned, and the rest of the entries remain right- aligned.

Next you will change the three column headings to bold text. Move the cursor to cell B1 by pressing ←. Press Alt-F4. Press → twice. The three headings should now be blocked. Select **C**ell, **A**ppearance, **B**old, OK. Bold the "Total" header by pressing ← three times and ↓ four times. Select **C**ell, **A**ppearance, **B**old, OK. Press F7 to exit the table edit screen. At this point, the table looks like this:

	Brian	**Ron**	**John**
Game 1	231	175	140
Game 2	132	201	151
Game 3	194	195	170
Total			

Move the cursor to the *J* in "John." Press Ctrl-Backspace to delete "John." Type **Jack**. Notice that "Jack" is boldfaced and right-aligned as you type the text. If you had used F8 and Alt-F6 or their menu equivalents to boldface and right-align "John," when you deleted "John," you would have also deleted the codes for bold text and right-

FIGURE 22-5

Table Format dialog box

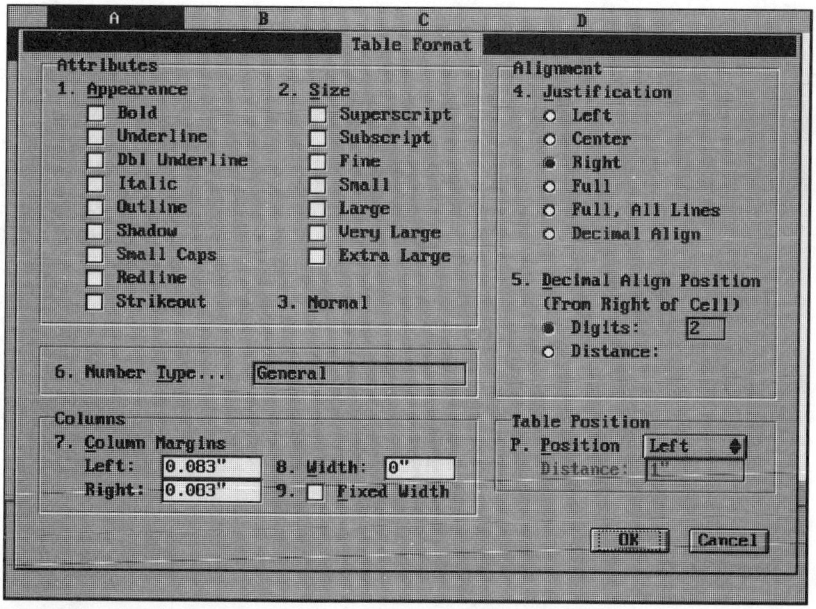

alignment. Because you added right alignment and bold text by editing the table's format, the attributes remain with the cell.

Now you will make the same changes to the second table. Press ↓ until the cursor is in the line above the second table, and then press → to move to cell A1 of the second table. Select **L**ayout, Ta**b**les, **E**dit, or press Alt-F7 and select **T**ables, **E**dit to display the table edit screen. Select **T**able, **J**ustification, **R**ight, OK to right-align all the cells in the table. With the cursor in cell A1, Select C**o**lumn, **J**ustification, **L**eft, OK.

To add the bold text, press → and Alt-F4, and then press → twice. Select **C**ell, **A**ppearance, **B**old, OK. Press ← three times and ↓ four times to move to the cell containing "Total." Select **C**ell, **A**ppearance, **B**old, OK. Press F7 to exit the table edit screen. Now both tables use the same formatting.

Move the cursor to the *J* in "John." Press Ctrl-Backspace to delete "John," and then type **Jack**. Save this revised document by selecting **F**ile, **E**xit or pressing F7, selecting **Y**es, and selecting **N**o.

2. When you format joined cells, the formatting applies to the entire entry. Retrieve the document BASKBALL by selecting **F**ile, **R**etrieve, typing **baskball**, and selecting OK. Press ↓ until the cursor is in cell A1 of the table. Select **L**ayout, Ta**b**les, **E**dit, or press Alt-F7 and select **T**ables, **E**dit.

   You are going to center the column headings. Press Alt-F4 and ↓. The first two rows of cells should be highlighted. Select **C**ell, **J**ustification, **C**enter, OK to center the entries in these two rows.

   Boldface the top row heading by first pressing ↑. Select **C**ell, **A**ppearance, **B**old, OK. Exit the table edit screen by pressing F7. Save this revised document by selecting **F**ile, **E**xit or pressing F7, selecting **Y**es, and selecting **N**o.

3. Retrieve the document EMPLOYEE.TBL by selecting **F**ile, **R**etrieve, typing **employee.tbl**, and selecting OK. Press ↓ until you move to cell A1 of the table. Activate the table edit screen by selecting **L**ayout, Ta**b**les, **E**dit, or pressing Alt-F7 and selecting **T**ables, **E**dit.

   Boldface the top row heading by selecting **C**ell, **A**ppearance, **B**old, OK. Exit the table edit screen by pressing F7. Save this revised document by selecting **F**ile, **E**xit or pressing F7, selecting **Y**es, and selecting **N**o.

4. Retrieve the document MACRS by selecting **F**ile, **R**etrieve, typing **macrs**, and selecting OK. Press ↓ until the cursor is in cell A1 of the table. Activate the table edit screen by selecting **L**ayout, Ta**b**les, **E**dit, or by pressing Alt-F7 and selecting **T**ables, **E**dit.

   You will now decimal-justify the dollar amounts under the heading for 1993 deductions. Press → to move to column B. Select C**o**lumn,

Justification, **D**ecimal Align, OK. The dollar amounts will immediately move to the right and line up by their decimal points.

Exit the table edit screen by pressing F7. Save this revised document by selecting **F**ile, **E**xit or pressing F7, selecting **Y**es, and selecting **N**o.

EXERCISES

1. Retrieve the document named SUPPLIES.
   For both the first and second tables, do the following:
   - Center the three column headings named "ORDER NO.," "TOTAL," and "UNITS."
   - Boldface all four column headings.
   - Decimal-align the numbers within the TOTAL column.
   - Change the total number of boxes of letterhead from 3 to 10. Save the revised document.
2. Retrieve the document named FACULTY.TBL. Bold the four column headings. Save the revised document.
3. Retrieve the document named ATTACH.C. Center and boldface the top row. Decimal-align the three cells in the right column that contain dollar amounts. Save the revised document.
4. Retrieve the document named BILL.SHT. Center and boldface the top row of the table. Decimal-align the three cells B2, B3, and B4.
   Type the following text and numbers in rows 2 and 3:

4.3 hours of typing services	55.90
1 disk	2.50

Save the revised document.

22.7 INCORPORATE SIMPLE MATH FEATURES INTO A TABLE

The table feature can do simple arithmetic. The arithmetic that can be performed in tables is divided into two categories. The first category, adding columns of numbers, is similar to the math feature used with tabular columns. (See Chapter 15, "Adding a Column of Numbers," for more information.) The second category, formulas, allows you to do calculations that use addition, subtraction, multiplication, and division, based on the contents of other cells.

After you have incorporated a math feature into a table, you need to be conscious that the calculations are not done automatically. Whenever a cell's contents that affect a calculation are changed, you need to tell WordPerfect to recalculate everything in the table.

Another concern when using the math feature in tables is that tables assume all cell entries are numeric. If you have a cell that falls within the range of cells to be added together but is not part of the calculation, you must tell WordPerfect that the cell is to be ignored for calculating purposes.

This section walks you through the creation of simple math functions. Because you learned about WordPerfect's math feature in Chapter 15, you have a head start in learning to use math in tables.

TO CREATE A SUBTOTAL FOR A COLUMN OF NUMBERS

a. Move the cursor to a location inside the table.
b. Select **L**ayout, Ta**b**les, **E**dit. You can also press Alt-F7 and select **T**ables, **E**dit.
c. Move the cursor to the cell where you want the subtotal.
d. Select **F**ormula.
e. Type **+** for a subtotal, and press Enter. (You type = for a total and * for a grand total.)
f. Select OK to close the dialog box.
g. Press F7 to exit the table edit screen.

TO CREATE A FORMULA

a. Move the cursor to a location inside the table.
b. Select **L**ayout, Ta**b**les, **E**dit. You can also press Alt-F7 and select **T**ables, **E**dit.
c. Move the cursor to the cell where you want the result of the formula to be displayed.

d. Press 5 or F to select **F**ormula.

e. Type the formula, and press Enter. The operators that can be included within the formula are + for addition, - for subtraction, * for multiplication, and / for division.

f. Select OK to close the dialog box.

g. Press F7 to exit the table edit screen.

TO RECALCULATE ALL ARITHMETIC FROM THE TABLE EDIT SCREEN

Select C**a**lc.

TO RECALCULATE ALL ARITHMETIC FROM THE NORMAL DOCUMENT WINDOW

Select **L**ayout, Ta**b**les, C**a**lculate. You can also press Alt-F7 and select **T**ables, C**a**lculate All.

TO OMIT A CELL IN A COLUMN FROM CALCULATIONS

a. Move the cursor to a location inside the table.

b. Select **L**ayout, Ta**b**les, **E**dit. You can also press Alt-F7 and select **T**ables, **E**dit.

c. Move the cursor to the cell that you want to omit from calculations.

d. Select **C**ell.

e. Select **I**gnore When Calculating.

f. Select OK to close the dialog box.

g. Press F7 to exit the table edit screen.

EXAMPLES

1. You can use math features to calculate totals in a table column. Retrieve the document MACRS by selecting **F**ile, **R**etrieve, typing **macrs**, and selecting OK. Press ↓ until the cursor is in cell A1 of the table. Activate the table edit screen by selecting **L**ayout, Ta**b**les, **E**dit, or by pressing Alt-F7 and selecting **T**ables, **E**dit.

Press ↓ four times and → once to move to cell B5. In this cell, you want to total the deductions.

Select **F**ormula. WordPerfect prompts you for a formula. Type + and press Enter twice to enter the formula and select OK. WordPerfect calculates the total for the column and displays 16443. Give this cell the double underline attribute by selecting **C**ell, **A**ppearance, **D**bl Underline, OK.

Notice that the total 16443 is not the total of the three preceding numbers. Instead, 16443 is the total of 1993 (from the column heading) and the three numbers. To avoid the inclusion of the heading as part of the calculation, you need to tell WordPerfect not to include 1993 in the calculation. Press ↑ four times to move the cursor to cell B1. Select **C**ell, **I**gnore When Calculating, OK. The result of the calculation remains 16443. This is because WordPerfect does not automatically produce recalculations. To update the calculation, select C**a**lc. The total now displays as 14450, which is correct. Press F7 to exit the table edit screen. At this point, the table looks like this:

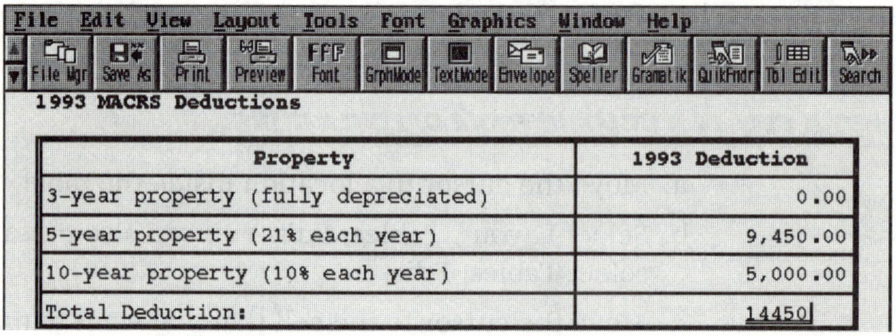

Save this revised document by selecting **F**ile, **E**xit or pressing F7, selecting **Y**es, and selecting **N**o.

2. You can try entering simple formulas to calculate average bowling scores. Select **F**ile, **R**etrieve, type **games**, and select OK. You need to add another row to this table, so press ↓ until the cursor is at the *T* in "Total" and then press Tab four times to add a row. Select **L**ayout, Ta**b**les, **E**dit, or press Alt-F7 and select **T**ables, **E**dit to display the table edit screen.

   Next, add some formulas that total the bowling scores. Press ↑ and → to move to cell B5. To create a subtotal for Brian, select **F**ormula, type +, and press Enter twice. Press → to move to Ron's column. Select **F**ormula, type +, and press Enter twice. Press → to move to Jack's column. Select **F**ormula, type +, and press Enter twice.

   Press ↓ once. This cell is where the average score for Jack is to appear. Select **F**ormula, type **D5/3**, and press Enter twice. D5/3 is a formula that takes the value located in cell D5 (Jack's total) and divides it by 3, producing the average. Press ← once to move to Ron's column. Select **F**ormula, type **C5/3**, and press Enter twice. Press ← once more to move to Brian's column. Select **F**ormula, type **B5/3**, and press Enter twice. Press F7 to exit the table edit screen. Move to cell A6. Type **Average**.

Move to Brian's third game score by pressing ↑ twice and Tab once. Press Del to delete the 1 in 194, and type **2** to make the score 294.

Because the numbers have changed, the total and average for Brian are no longer accurate. To recalculate, select **L**ayout, Ta**b**les, C**a**lculate All, or press Alt-F7 and select Tables, C**a**lculate All. The total and average change to reflect the changes made in Brian's score. The table looks like this:

	Brian	Ron	Jack
Game 1	231	175	140
Game 2	132	201	151
Game 3	294	195	170
Total	657	571	461
Average	219	190.33333333 3	153.66666667

Save this revised document by selecting **F**ile, **E**xit or pressing F7, selecting **Y**es, and selecting **N**o.

EXERCISES

1. Retrieve the document named ATTACH.C. Create a subtotal at the bottom of column B of the table. Omit the table header cell from the computations. Recalculate the subtotal. Save the revised document.
2. Retrieve the document named BILL.SHT. Add two rows to the bottom of the table.

   Make cell B4 a subtotal of the two previous cells.

   Make cell B5 a sales tax calculation cell by creating a formula that multiplies the contents of cell B4 by the sales tax rate of .07. Use an asterisk to indicate multiplication.

   Make cell B6 a total cell by creating a formula that adds the contents of cells B4 and B5.

   Exit the table edit screen. In cell A6, type

Sales Tax:

In cell A5, type

Total Amount Due:

Save the revised document.

mastery skills check

As you work through these Mastery Skills Check exercises, do not clear the screen until you have completed the last exercise.

1. Create a table that has two columns and eight rows. [22.1]
2. Join the two cells of the first row to form one cell. Set the joined cell to center its contents and to be ignored in calculations. [22.5, 22.6, 22.7]
3. Set cells A2 and B2 to center their contents. Set cell B2 to also be ignored in calculations. [22.6, 22.7]
4. Decimal-align cells B3 through B8. [22.6]
5. Create a math formula in cell B8 that adds cells B6 and B7, and double underline the answer. [22.6, 22.7]
6. Create a math formula in cell B7 that multiplies cell B6 by .07, and underline the answer. [22.6, 22.7]
7. Create a math formula in cell B6 that is the sum of cells B3, B4, and B5. Exit the table edit screen. [22.7]
8. Enter the following information in the table. [22.2]

JOE'S HARDWARE

Item	Amount
Nails	9
Hammer	5
Screwdriver	7
Subtotal	
Tax @ 7%	
Total	

9. Update the calculations in the table. The subtotal should be 21, the tax should be 1.47, and the total should be 22.47. [22.7]
10. Change the widths of the columns so that the first column is 3 inches wide and the second column is 1 inch wide. [22.3]

Teach Yourself cumulative skills check

Do not clear the screen until you have completed the last exercise.

1. Create a table that has three columns and six rows. [22.1]
2. In the first row, join all three cells. Center the cell, and have WordPerfect ignore the cell's contents for calculations. [22.5, 22.6, 22.7]
3. In row 2, center all three cells and have cells B2 and C2 ignored by calculations. [22.6, 22.7]
4. Right-align cells B3 through B6 and C3 through C6. [22.6]
5. Sum cells C3, C4, and C5 in cell C6. [22.7]
6. Sum cells B3, B4, and B5 in cell B6. [22.7]
7. Underline cells B5 and C5. Exit the table edit screen. [22.6]

8. Enter the following information in the table.

SALES BY DEPARTMENT		
DEPT	JAN	FEB
Clothing	25000	20000
Shoes	15000	12000
Housewares	40000	42000
Total		

   Calculate the totals. They should be 80000 and 74000. [22.2, 22.7]

9. Add a column at the right edge of the table. Add a formula to cell D6 that totals the values in the new column. Insert the following figures:

MAR
23000
14000
37000

   Recalculate the totals. The March total should be 74000. [22.2, 22.4, 22.7]

part IV

Appendixes

A

Installing WordPerfect and Selecting a Printer

IF you do not have WordPerfect installed on your computer, you will need to install the program before you can use it. The process is not difficult and can be completed in a short time if you follow the instructions provided. Part of the installation process involves selecting one or more printers to use with WordPerfect. If your system is already installed, you may need to update the WordPerfect system files to incorporate any new printer you might add to your system. This appendix has the steps for installing WordPerfect or the Runtime help program on your system, instructions for adding a printer, instructions for updating your WordPerfect system files, and instructions for adding WordPerfect to Windows.

- *Installing WordPerfect on your system* Use these instructions if you wish to install WordPerfect on your hard disk.
- *Installing Runtime* Use these instructions to install Runtime, which provides help on how to use WordPerfect.
- *Adding printer files* Use these instructions if you need to install a new printer file after WordPerfect has been installed.
- *Updating WordPerfect's system files* Use these instructions if you need to install updated WordPerfect system files after WordPerfect has been installed.
- *Installing WordPerfect in Windows* Use these instructions if you have Windows installed on your system and you want to be able to run WordPerfect 6 while you run Windows.

The instructions use drive A as the floppy disk drive, but you may need to substitute drive B depending on the configuration of your disk drives and the size of your WordPerfect disks. Drive C is the normal default for a hard disk, although some computers may have hard disks that use other labels.

A.1 INSTALLING WORDPERFECT ON YOUR SYSTEM

Before you can use WordPerfect, it must be installed. Installing WordPerfect transfers the files from the WordPerfect diskettes to your hard drive. You *must* use the installation program to install WordPerfect. The program files have been compressed on the installation disks and must be expanded using the installation program. Besides installing WordPerfect on your hard disk through WordPerfect's installation program, you can also install the Runtime help information and set up WordPerfect as a program item if you are using Windows.

To install WordPerfect, follow these steps:

1. Turn on your computer. The computer loads DOS from the hard disk into your computer's memory. You may also need to respond to prompts for the date and time, pressing Enter after each entry.
2. Insert the WordPerfect installation disk labeled "Install 1" into drive A.
3. Type **a:install** and press Enter. WordPerfect displays a screen welcoming you to the WordPerfect installation program and asks you whether you see three colored boxes at the bottom of the screen. Select **Y**es to tell WordPerfect to use color installation screens or select **N**o to tell WordPerfect to use black-and-white screens.
4. The WordPerfect Installation menu appears. Because you are doing a standard system installation of WordPerfect, press **1** or **S** for **S**tandard Installation.
5. WordPerfect prompts for the location that you are installing WordPerfect from, and where you are installing WordPerfect to. Select **N**o to install WordPerfect in the default directory, C:\WP60. If you select **Y**es, you can type a new directory and press Enter in response to the two prompts for directories. Then select **N**o at the prompt about changing the directories.
6. Press Y to continue with the installation when prompted. You may need to respond to a prompt for adding WordPerfect to your path statement. If you want to start WordPerfect from any directory, select **Y**es; otherwise, select **N**o.
7. WordPerfect prompts you to indicate when it should replace a file on your hard disk with a WordPerfect file of the same name. Select **A**lways prompt before replacing if you always want to choose whether or not to replace the file, **N**ever prompt before replacing to let WordPerfect replace any file, or **S**mart prompting to have WordPerfect prompt you only when the file on your disk is newer than the WordPerfect file. This prompt is most important if you are reinstalling or updating WordPerfect on your system.

8. WordPerfect automatically installs the display drivers for EGA and VGA screens. If this matches your system, you can select **N**o at the prompt for installing additional graphics drivers. If you want to install other display drivers, select **Y**es at the prompt, highlight the video display your system will accept, press Enter, and select **Y**es to confirm selecting the video display. Then select **Y**es to add another video driver or **N**o to continue with installation.
9. When prompted for installing printer drivers, select **Y**es to add the files you will need to select your printer.
10. Press ↑, ↓, Pg Up, and Pg Dn to scroll through the list of printers and locate the name of your printer. Once located on the screen, press Enter and then select **Y**es. You may be prompted to insert a different installation disk and press Enter. You can then select **Y**es to install another printer and repeat this step for each printer you plan to use with your system. When you have installed the printers you want, select **N**o when prompted about installing another printer.
11. Follow the directions on the screen for inserting disks. After replacing the disk in the drive with the one prompted for onscreen, press Enter.
12. When prompted about installing sound drivers, if your system has a sound board, select **Y**es; otherwise select **N**o.
13. Next, WordPerfect is loaded and you are prompted for the serial number of your product. Type this number and press Enter. Now you are in WordPerfect, but you will not do anything for a moment because WordPerfect is running a macro that sets your printer up to be used in WordPerfect.
14. If you are prompted for a default font for the printer you selected, press ↑, ↓, Pg Up, and Pg Dn to scroll through the list of fonts and select the font that you want to use for most of your work. When the font you want is highlighted, press Enter. The examples in this book use Courier 10cpi or 12 points. If you select a different font, your examples may look different.
15. After setting up the printer, the installation program exits WordPerfect. You are now back in DOS and ready to start learning WordPerfect. Store the original WordPerfect disks in a safe place.

16. If you directed the installation program to modify the AUTOEXEC.BAT file, open the door for drive A; then press the Ctrl, Alt, and Del keys simultaneously to reboot the system with the newly revised system files.

A.2 INSTALLING RUNTIME

Runtime provides help for WordPerfect features. It is installed separately from WordPerfect.

1. Turn on your computer as described in step 1 of the previous procedure if it is not already on.
2. Insert the first WordPerfect Documentation disk into drive A.
3. Type **cd\wp60** and press Enter to switch to the directory containing the WordPerfect files. If you installed WordPerfect in another directory, replace WP60 with the directory where WordPerfect is installed.
4. Type **copy a:*.*** and press Enter. DOS copies the files from the disk to your WordPerfect directory. Repeat this for all the Documentation disks. At this point, you can start Runtime by typing **runtime** and pressing Enter.

A.3 ADDING PRINTER FILES

If you add a new printer to your system, you will want to check to see if the printer driver is already available on your system. Load WordPerfect onto your computer. If you do not know how to do this, see Chapter 1.

1. If it is not already on, turn on your computer as described in step 1 of the procedure to install WordPerfect.
2. Type **cd\wp60** and press Enter to switch to the directory containing the WordPerfect files. If you installed WordPerfect in another directory, replace WP60 with the directory where WordPerfect is installed.
3. Type **wp** and press Enter to start WordPerfect.
4. Press Alt-= to activate the menus, then select **F**ile, **P**rint, **S**elect.

5. Make the necessary selections to choose the printer you want. You will perform one of three steps:
   a. If you see the printer you want to use and it has an asterisk next to it, press Esc twice since WordPerfect is set to use the printer you want.
   b. If you see the printer you want to use and it does not have an asterisk next to it, press ↑ or ↓ to highlight it, choose **S**elect, then press Enter to leave the menu system.
   c. If you want to use a printer that is not listed, select **A**dd Printer. Find the printer you want in the list of printers, press Enter twice, press F7, press Enter, and choose **S**elect. Then press Enter to leave the menu system. If the printer you want is not in the list, you will need to run the installation program to install the printer, so you need to press F7 three times to leave the menu system.
6. At this point, your printer is installed, unless you need to use the installation program to add the printer. Press F7, then N and Y to exit to DOS. If your printer is selected, you can skip the remaining steps.
7. Place the first Install disk in drive A (or B), then type **a:install** and press Enter. WordPerfect displays a screen welcoming you to the WordPerfect installation program and asks you whether you see three colors at the bottom of the screen. Select **Y**es to tell WordPerfect to use color installation screens or select **N**o to tell WordPerfect to use black-and-white screens.
8. Select **D**evice (Printer, Sound, Graphics) Files. WordPerfect prompts for the location of your WordPerfect diskettes and where you installed WordPerfect. The defaults are the drive you started the install program from and C:\WP60, respectively, but you can type other directory locations before you press Enter at the two prompts.
9. Select **P**rinter Files.
10. Press ↑, ↓, Pg Up, and Pg Dn to scroll through the list of printers and locate the name of your printer. Once located on the screen, press Enter and select **Y**es. You may be prompted to insert a different installation disk and to press Enter. You can then select **Y**es to install another printer and repeat this step for each printer you plan to use with your system. When you have

installed the printers you want, select **N**o when prompted about installing another printer.

11. Next, WordPerfect is loaded and a macro handles running WordPerfect to add the printer you selected in the installation program.
12. When WordPerfect prompts you for the port the printer is connected to, select OK to accept LPT1 or select another port before selecting OK.
13. If you are prompted for a default font for the printer you selected, press ↑, ↓, Pg Up, and Pg Dn to scroll through the list of fonts and select the font that you want to use for most of your work. When the font you want is highlighted, press Enter.
14. At this point, the printer you installed is added and selected, so you are ready to create documents that use this printer. Press F7, N, and Y to exit to DOS.

A.4 UPDATING WORDPERFECT'S SYSTEM FILES

You may need to update the system files after WordPerfect has been installed. This happens occasionally when WordPerfect comes out with a new release of the same program. The new release may fix problems with the original program or it may enhance the program. To take advantage of the new release, you need to use WordPerfect's installation program to update your system files.

1. If it is not already on, turn on your computer as described in step 1 of the procedure for installing WordPerfect.
2. Insert the first Install disk in drive A (or B).
3. Type **a:install** and press Enter. WordPerfect displays a screen welcoming you to the WordPerfect installation program and asks you whether you see three colors at the bottom of the screen. Select **Y**es to tell WordPerfect to use color installation screens or **N**o to tell WordPerfect to use black-and-white screens.
4. Press U to indicate you are updating the system files. WordPerfect prompts for the location of your WordPerfect diskettes and where you installed WordPerfect. The defaults are the drive

you started the Install program from and C:\WP60, respectively, but you can type other directory locations before you press Enter at the two prompts.

5. Press S for **S**mart prompting when prompted for how WordPerfect's Installation program should handle updating a file that already exists among your WordPerfect files. Smart prompting lets WordPerfect decide whether a file should be replaced, so you only see prompts when WordPerfect can't make a decision. You can also press A for **A**lways prompt before replacing if you want to confirm each replacement, or press N for **N**ever prompt before replacing.
6. Select **I**nstall and Program to update your WordPerfect files on the Install and Program disks, or select **O**ther to update your WordPerfect files with some other disks. Put the disk the program prompts for in the drive and press Enter. WordPerfect compares the file dates to check whether the file dates are newer and only copies files from the diskettes that have later dates than the ones on your hard disk. After the files are copied, you are either prompted for another disk or you return to the Install: Update menu.
7. Select **E**xit to return to the WordPerfect Installation menu. Then select **E**xit and **Y**es to return to DOS.

A.5 INSTALLING WORDPERFECT IN WINDOWS

If you are using WordPerfect 6 with Windows, you will want to have Windows create a program item for WordPerfect 6. You can do this by following these steps:

1. Type **win** and press Enter to start Windows.
2. Press Alt-F to display the File menu at the top of the Program Manager window. Press N to select **N**ew and Enter to add a program item.
3. Type **WordPerfect 6** in the text box after **D**escription and press Tab.
4. Type **c:\wp60\wp.pif** in the text box after **C**ommand Line.

5. Press Enter to select OK and add an icon with WordPerfect 6 below it that you can use to run WordPerfect 6 to the currect window.

At this point, you have an icon for WordPerfect 6. To start WordPerfect while using Windows, you want to switch to the window in the Program Manager that contains this icon. Then use the arrow keys to highlight this icon and press Enter. With a mouse, you can point to the icon and double-click it. When you leave WordPerfect, you will return to Windows rather than the DOS prompt.

A.6 SETTING UP A DIRECTORY FOR YOUR WORDPERFECT DOCUMENTS

Every individual and company structures their hard disk a little different. To help you keep your WordPerfect documents separate from your other files and access them quicker, you can create a directory specifically for your WordPerfect documents. WordPerfect is set up to use the directory WPDOCS for your WordPerfect documents if the directory is available. You can create this directory if it does not exist by following these steps:

1. Switch to your hard disk where you want to create this directory. Usually, this means typing **C:** and pressing Enter.
2. Type **MD \WPDOCS** and press Enter.

If you see the message "Invalid switch," you have typed a slash (/) rather than a backslash (\). If you see the message "Too many parameters," you have typed a space between the \ and WPDOCS. If you see the message "Directory already exists," your drive already has a WPDOCS directory.

B

WordPerfect Screen Elements

IF you have used other programs you are probably already familiar with using menus and dialog boxes. This appendix is provided in case you have never used menus and dialog boxes and are unfamiliar with what they are. You will also learn how to use the mouse and keyboard to activate different objects and select them.

B.1 PULL-DOWN MENUS

WordPerfect 6 automatically displays a menu bar of options at the top of your screen. Although it is possible to customize the package to eliminate the menu bar, it is assumed that you used the default installation procedure and have not customized the appearance of the screen.

Each option on the menu bar can be activated to display a pull-down menu of choices. You can activate the menu bar by typing Alt-=, then type the underlined or boldfaced letter in the choice you want to make. If you prefer to use the mouse, you can select an option by moving the mouse pointer to it and clicking it. A *click* is a single quick press and release of the left mouse button. When the menu bar option is selected, a pull-down menu appears on the screen listing the various selections that are possible.

The pull-down menus display the names of options at the left side. If a function key sequence such as Shift-F10 provides an alternative to using the menus, it will be shown to the right of the menu option. If a shortcut key sequence such as Ctrl-R offers an alternative to the menu, it will also be shown to the right of the menu option. Menu options with an ellipsis (...) following them indicate that a dialog box must be completed. A menu choice with a right arrowhead at the far right indicates that selecting it displays another menu of choices. Figure B-1 shows the pull-down Layout menu with the Tables menu also displayed.

To make a selection from the pull-down menu or a subsequent menu, you can click it with the mouse. If you prefer to use the keyboard, type the underlined letter to make the selection. Selections which are dimmed are not available at the current time.

FIGURE B-1

Pull-down menu

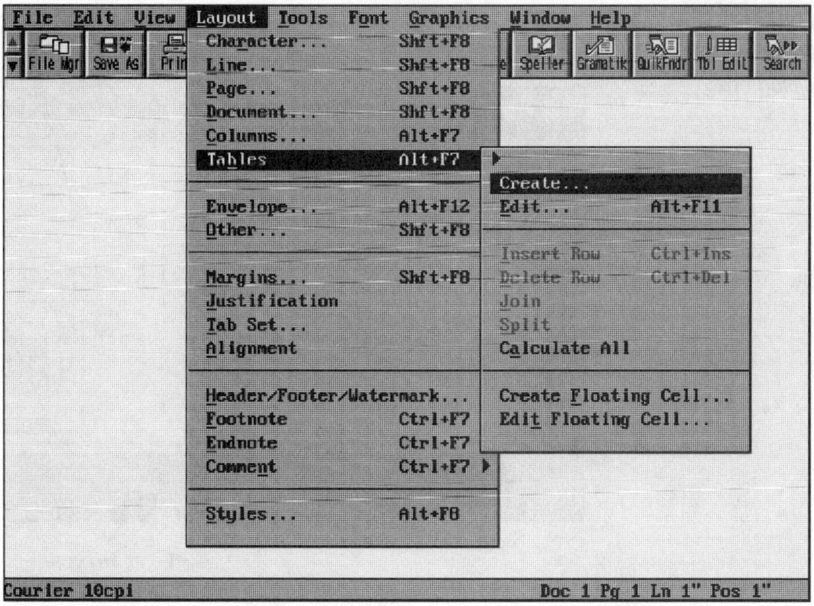

B.2 DIALOG BOXES

You use dialog boxes to refine the selections you have made with menus, function key combinations, or shortcut keys. If a menu command has a key equivalent, it does not matter which method you use to activate the command, the dialog box looks the same in most cases.

Dialog boxes have more elements than menus since there are different types of information that they expect you to specify. Dialog box elements have a different appearance depending on whether you have text or graphics mode selected. You can make this selection through the View menu. Figure B-2 shows a text mode dialog box. The same dialog box in graphics mode is shown in Figure B-3. As you look at a dialog box, only the selections that have numbers or letters next to them can be selected with the keyboard at the current time. Mouse selections can be made for any dialog box element.

The Tab Set option in the dialog box in Figures B-2 and B-3 has an ellipsis after it, which indicates that selecting it will display another dialog box. If you choose to use the keyboard to select it, you would press T or 1 for the underlined or highlighted letter in the name of the option or the number next to it. The entry in the selection box that

FIGURE B-2

Text mode dialog box

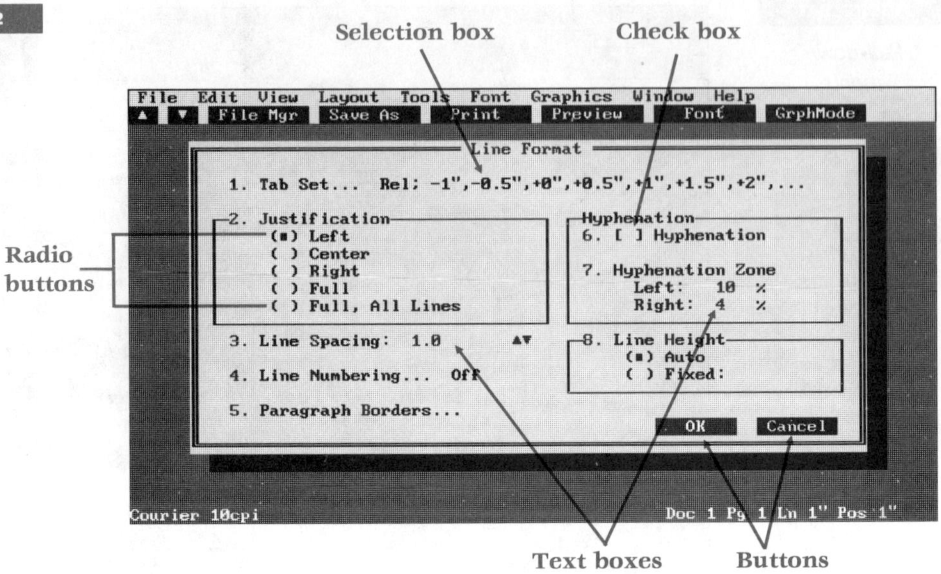

FIGURE B-3

Graphics mode dialog box

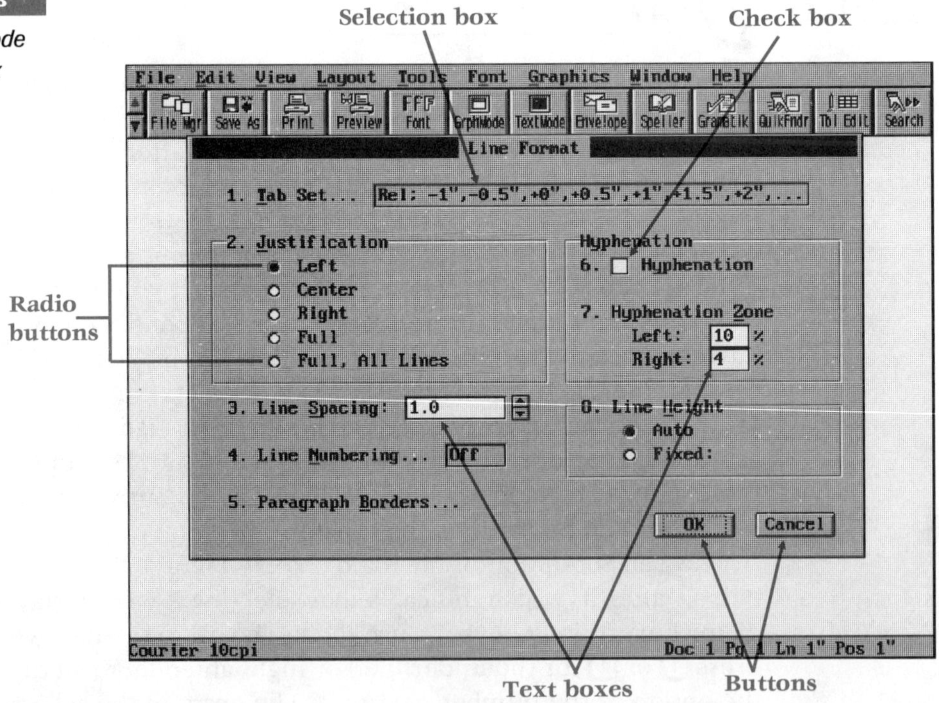

follows Tab Set changes when you finish making choices from a dialog box that is presented after selecting Tab Set. A *text box,* where you can type in entries, follows the Line Spacing option. Text boxes have an empty background color in graphics mode. In text mode, when you select an item with a text box, WordPerfect displays a box for you to fill with your entry.

The Hyphenation option is a *check box,* which toggles on and off as you select it. In text mode check boxes are represented with square brackets, and in graphics mode small boxes are used. Options with an *X* are selected; when the boxes are empty the options are not selected. You can choose as many of these boxes as appropriate.

The options below Justification are not selectable at the current time with the keyboard because they do not have numbers or letters next to each *radio button.* You press J to make these accessible. Only one radio button from the group can be chosen. In graphics mode radio buttons are small circles, and in text mode they are represented by an empty set of parentheses when not selected. Choosing one radio button removes the selection from the previously selected radio button in that group.

Buttons allow you to choose an action, such as canceling a request with Cancel or confirming selections with OK. You can click the button or press Tab until it is highlighted and press Enter. When a button has an outline around its text or is highlighted, pressing Enter selects the button.

Another type of selection is a pop-up list. When you select a pop-up list, you will see the possible choices listed. For example:

B.3 BUTTON BAR AND RIBBON

The Button Bar and Ribbon are optional elements that you can display at the top of your screen. You must have a mouse to use them. You can choose to display one or both elements with the View menu. Figure B-4 shows a screen with both elements visible. The Ribbon always appears directly beneath the menu bar when it is displayed, whether or not the Button Bar is displayed, and the Button Bar displays beneath the Ribbon.

FIGURE B-4

Button Bar and Ribbon

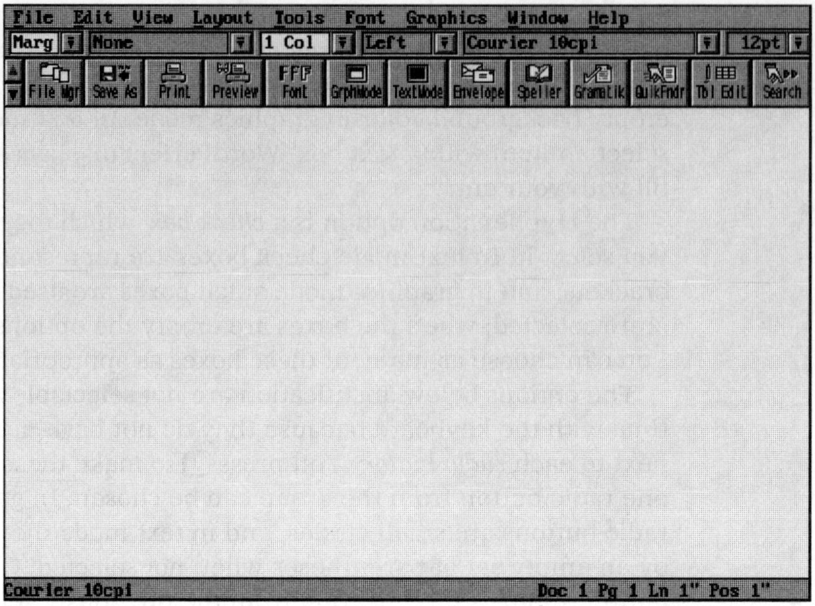

You can customize the Button Bar to create a bar that will be the most useful for your work. The options selected for the default Button Bar are as follows:

- Access the file manager
- Save the current document
- Print the current document
- Preview the current document
- Change the font
- Switch to graphics mode
- Switch to text mode
- Create an envelope
- Spell check the document
- Use the grammar checking features
- Search other documents
- Edit a table
- Search for text or codes

- Select a Button Bar
- Change Button Bar options

Not all of these appear immediately. You can select the up and down arrow buttons at the left of the Button Bar to scroll the Button Bar and display the missing buttons.

The Ribbon allows you to alter formatting. You can choose to create additional columns or alter the font style or size. The Ribbon does not allow customization. The features provided by the Ribbon are as follows:

- Setting the view magnification
- Adding character and paragraph styling
- Setting the number of columns
- Changing the text alignment
- Selecting a font
- Selecting a font size

Index

A

Abstract field. *See* Document Summaries
Adding rows and columns to a table, 475-479
Address labels, generating. *See* Merges
Alt key, use of, 6
Alt-F1 (Writing Tools) key, use of, 184, 188, 191
Alt-F2 (Replace) key, use of, 142
Alt-F3 (Reveal Codes) key, use of, 82
Alt-F4 (Block) key, use of, 87
Alt-F6 (Flush Right) key, use of, 106
Alt-F7 (Columns/Tables) key, use of, 231-232, 297, 301, 460, 471, 481, 483-484, 486-487
Alt-F8 (Style) key, use of, 404, 411, 415, 418, 421, 426, 428
Alt-F9 (Graphics) key, use of, 336, 342, 345, 351, 354
Alignment. *See* Justification
Appearance
  changing table cells, 483-487
  changing text, 74-78, 89-90, 251-255
  changing line, 80-81, 100-101, 102-105, 106-107
  changing page, 119-130, 199-201, 202-206
  changing paragraph, 97-99, 108-109, 110-111
Art. *See* Graphics
Arrow keys
  for moving the cursor, 11, 12-13
  with Ctrl key, 11, 13
  with Home key, 11, 13
  use of, 11, 12-13
Attributes. *See* Appearance
AUTOEXEC.BAT, and installation, 499, 501
Automatic timed backups, 40
  setting, 389-390

B

Back Tab feature
  use of, 100-101
  use of in outlines, 367
Backspace
  in Typeover mode, 35
  use of, 11, 12, 37-39
Backup copies, 215
  automatic timed, 389-390
  changing options for, 389-390
  creating, 215-217, 389-390
  deleting, 390
  renaming, 390
Backward search, 139-141
Beep sound, changing the occurrence of, 394-397
Blocked text
  applying special features to, 89-90
  copying, 157-159, 161-162
  copying from one document to another, 157-159, 161-162, 267-268
  deleting, 87-89
  moving, 157-159, 161-162, 267-268
Blocking text, 87-89
Boldfacing text, 77-78, 90
Bottom margin, changing. *See* Margins
Box types, WordPerfect, 335
Boxes. *See* Drawing lines and boxes; Graphics boxes
Bulleted lists, creating a style for, 408-409
Button Bar, 511-513
  default buttons, 512-513
  displaying, 22-23, 24
  using, 24
Buttons in dialog boxes, 511

C

Calculating
  multilevel totals, 301-306
  subtotals, 297-300
Cancel key. *See* Esc (Cancel) key
Caps Lock key, use of, 11, 19-21
Captions, 350
  adding to graphics boxes, 350-352
Case-sensitive search, 139-141
Cells (table), 458
  changing attributes of, 483-487
  changing justification of, 483-487
  joining, 481-482
Centering text
  on a single line, 80-81
  in paragraphs, 110-111
  on a page, 119-122
Changing file names, 225-226
Character styles
  creating, 403-410
  Enter in, 405
  modifying, 421-425
  using, 410-414
Check boxes, 511
Checking spelling
  of an entire document, 173-175
  and ignoring correct words, 179-180
  and replacing misused words, 169-172
  of a word, 169-172
Clearing the screen, 8-9
Clicking, 15
Closing a document, 8-9
Codes, hidden. *See* Hidden codes
Codes, merge. *See* Merges
Collapse an outline, 380-381
Colors, screen, 391-394
Column widths, changing, 471-474, 475-479
Columns
  adding to a table, 475-479
  calculating multi-level totals, 301-306
  creating newspaper or snaking, 435-442
  creating parallel, 444-449
  editing text in, 441-454
  modifying column settings, 452
  moving the cursor through, 452
  totaling numeric columns, 297-300, 488-491
  working with text columns, 433-454
  See also Newspaper columns; Parallel columns
Combining table cells, 481-482
Comments field. *See* Document Summaries
CONFIG.SYS, and installation, 499
Copies, printing multiple, 241-242
Copying
  a block of text, 157-159, 161-162
  documents, 41, 42-43, 215-217
  with drag and drop, 157-159
  text between two documents, 153-162, 267-268
Copies, printing multiple, 161-162
Ctrl key, use of, 11, 14
Ctrl-arrow keys
  to move cursor, 11, 13
  to change column widths, 471
Ctrl-Backspace key, use of, 38
Ctrl-End key, use of, 38-39
Ctrl-Enter key, use of, 13, 14
Ctrl-F2 (Speller) key, use of, 169, 173, 179
Ctrl-F3 (Screen) key, use of, 261, 263, 313, 316
Ctrl-F4 (Move) key, use of, 153, 157, 267
Ctrl-F5 (Outline) key, use of, 367, 374, 377, 380
Ctrl-F7 (Notes) keys, use of, 387
  Ctrl-F8 (Font) key, use of, 252
Ctrl-F9 (Merge/Sort) key, use of, 288
Ctrl-Home (Go To) key, 13
Ctrl-C (Copy) key, use of, 161
Ctrl-R (Repeat) key, use of, 11, 12
Ctrl-V (Paste) key, use of, 161
Ctrl-X (Cut) key, use of, 161
  for repeating characters, 11, 12
  using to control line length, 313, 316

Current document, printing, 57-59
Current time, inserting in a document, 396
Cursor, 5
  location displayed on status line, 10
  moving through a document, 11, 12-14
Customizing
  backup options, 389-390
  beep occurrences, 394-397
  date format, 395-397
  default codes for documents, 395-397
  display options, 391-394
  hard return characters, 392-394
  initial codes, 395-397
  screen colors, 391-394
  status line display, 392-394
  time format, 394-397
Cutting text. *See* Deleting; Moving

D

Data file. *See* Merges
Date display, changing, 394-397
Decimal tabs, setting. *See* Setting tabs
Default settings for documents, changing, 395-397
Del key, use of, 11, 12, 37-39
Deleting
  blocked text, 87-89
  a column in a table, 475-479
  files, 223-225
  a footnote, 207, 208-209
  graphics boxes, 345-350
  hidden codes, 84-86
  lines you have drawn, 319-320
  a row in a table, 475-479
  subdirectories, 223-225
  tab stops, 102-105
  a table structure, 38-469
  tables, 468-469
  text, 37-39
Descriptive Filename. *See* Document Summaries
Dialog boxes, 7, 509-511
Dictionaries, 179-180
Directories. *See* Subdirectories
Display options, changing, 391-394
Document, 5
Document Name. *See* Document Summaries
Document on disk, printing. *See* Printing
Document Summaries, 227
  creating, 227-230
  extracting entries from document, 227, 229-230
Document Type. *See* Document Summaries
Document windows, 46-52, 259-271
  changing the size of, 261-263
  moving, 263-266
  switching between, 48-52
  tiling, 50, 51-52
Documents
  changing default settings for, 391-394
  checking spelling in, 173-175
  copying, 41, 42-43, 215-217
  creating, 27-54
  looking at, 234-235
  new, 46, 47
  opening, 46-48
  previewing, 63-66
  printing, 27-42
  retrieving, 44-45
  saving, 40-43
  searching for text in multiple, 231-233
  switching between, 48-52
  viewing multiple documents at once, 50, 51-52
  working with multiple open, 48-52
  See also Merge documents; Multiple documents
Double-clicking, 346
Double spacing, setting, 108-109
Double words, checking for, 176-177
Down arrow key (↓). *See* Arrow keys

Draft-quality print output, 250
Drag and drop for copying or moving text, 157-159
Drag the mouse, 157
Drawing lines and boxes, 311-331
  adding text to boxes, 326-328
  automatic corners, 316
  boxes, 316-318
  erasing lines, 319-321
  inserting text in a box, 326-328
  lines, 313-315
  moving the cursor, 321-323
  using Ctrl-R, 313, 316
  using special characters, 324-325

E

Editing styles, 421-425
End key, use of, 11, 13
Ending a WordPerfect session, 5-6
Enter key, use of, 11, 12
  in character styles, 405
  in paragraph styles, 405
Entering text using defaults, 29-33
Envelopes, printing on, 128-130
Equations editor, 334
Errors
  correcting spelling, 167-172, 175
Esc (Cancel) key
  cancel commands, 11, 16-17, 17-18
  restoring text, 11, 17-18
Exiting
  a document, 8-9
  WordPerfect, 5-6, 7
Expand an outline, 380-381

F

F1 (Help) key, use of, 16
F2 (Search) key, use of, 135, 139
F3 (Switch To) key, use of, 49, 50
F4 (Left Indent) key, use of, 97
F5 (File Manager) key, use of, 215, 218, 221, 223, 225, 232, 234
F6 (Bold) key, use of, 77
F7 (Exit) key, use of, 8, 40
  to exit documents, 8-9
  to exit WordPerfect, 6
F8 (Underline) key, use of, 75, 90
F9 (End Field) key, use of, 278
F9 (End Field) key, use of, 278-281
F11 (Reveal Codes) key, use of, 82, 85
F12 (Block) key, use of, 87
Field, 278
Figures (graphics), placing in boxes, 335-340
File Manager, 215-226, 231-235
Filenames, rules for, 40
  changing display of on status line, 391-394
Files
  deleting, 223-225
  managing, 215-235
  printing from, 67-69
  renaming, 225-226
  See also Backup copies; Documents; Form file; Data file
Find text
  in the current document, 135-142
  in documents on disk, 231-233
  in documents on disk using logical operators, 233-234
Flush Right, setting text, 106-107
Fonts
  appearance, 252
  changing, 251-255
  monospaced, 312
  proportional, 312
  relative sizes, 252
  size, 254
  types, 251
Footers, 202-206

for even and odd pages, 202-203, 205-206
hidden codes for, 203-204
page numbers in, 204-205
using graphics in, 348-349
Footnotes, 206-209
Form file. *See* Merges
Form letters, 276
See also Merges
Format table column feature, 483-487
Formatting
changing default settings, 394-397
lines and paragraphs, 97-111
pages, 119-130
text appearance, 75-81, 89-90
See also Character styles; Paragraph styles; Open styles
Formulas, creating, 488-489, 490-491
Full justification, 111-112

G

Global replacement, 142-146
Go To command
selecting with menus, 13
selecting with keyboard, 11, 13
using, 13
Grammar-checking, 190-193
Grammatik, using, 190-193
Grand total, calculating, 301-306
Graphics
printing documents containing, 358-361
using in headers, 348-349
Graphics boxes
adding captions to, 350-352
changing the size of, 353-357
creating, 335-340
editing and deleting, 345-350
hidden codes for, 349
horizontal settings for, 353-357
moving, 345-350, 353-357
multiple boxes on one page, 338-339
numbering of, 335
placing figures in, 335-340
placing Lotus 1-2-3 graphs in, 339-340
placing text in, 341-344
positioning and sizing, 353-357
removing from a document, 346-350
removing filenames from, 348
types, 335
updating the contents of, 347-310
vertical settings for, 353-357
Graphics features, WordPerfect, 333-364
Graphics mode, 22-25
Grids. *See* Tables

H

Hanging indents. *See* Indentation, use of; Back Tab feature
Hard copy, creating. *See* Printing
Hard disk system
installing WordPerfect on, 498-501
starting WordPerfect on, 4-5
Hard page break
appearance on screen, 13
effect, 83
entering with keyboard, 13
entering with menus, 13
Hard return code, 83
Hard returns, 12, 38, 83
changing the character that displays, 391-394
Headers, 202-206
for even and odd pages, 202-203, 205-206
hidden codes for, 203-204
page numbers in, 204-205
using graphics in, 348-349
Headings
changing the style for, 411-412
creating a style for, 405-408

Help features
displaying with the keyboard, 16-17
displaying with the menus, 16-17
using, 17-18
Help key. *See* F1 (Help) key
Hidden codes
deleting, 85-86
for graphics boxes, 349
for headers and footers, 203-204
math, 298, 301
revealing, 82-84
searching, 137, 139-140
for tables, 462
High-quality print output, 250
Home key, use of, 11, 13, 14
with arrow keys, 11, 13
Homonyms, 181-183

I

IBM keyboard layout, 10
Indentation, use of, 97-99
Indents. *See* Indentation
Initial settings, changing, 394-397
Ins key, use of, 34-36
Insert mode, adding text in, 34-36
Installing WordPerfect, 498-505
in Windows, 504-505
on a hard disk system, 498-501
printer files, 501-503
documentation (Runtime program), 501
update files, 503-504

J

Justification
table, 483-487
text, 110-111

K

Keyboard layout, 10
Keys, special, 10-21
Keywords field. *See* Document Summaries

L

Labeling graphics boxes, 350-352
Left arrow key (←). *See* Arrow keys
Left margin, changing. *See* Margins
Letters, form. *See* Merges
Line spacing, changing, 108-109
Lines
changing the appearance of lines, 105-112
preventing widows and orphans, 199-201
Lists, creating a style for, 408-409
Ln (line) indicator, 10
Loading WordPerfect. *See* Starting a WordPerfect session
Locate text
in the current document, 135-142
in documents on disk, 231-233
in saved files using logical operators, 233-234
Logical operators, 233
Look feature, 234-235
Lowercase letters, entering, 19-21

M

Main dictionary, 179
Managing files, 215-235
Margins, 29
changing, 123-125
releasing, 100-101
Marking blocked text, 87-89
Math features, 295-310
using in tables, 487-491
Maximized document windows, 261
Medium-quality print output, 250

Menu bar, 5
Menus, 508
  activating, 6
  commands followed by arrows, 7
  commands followed by ellipses, 6-7
  displaying alternative key strokes, 7
  selecting from with keyboard, 6, 6-7
  selecting from with mouse, 15
Merge documents. *See* Merges
Merges, 273-293
  codes, 278-286
  data files for, 278-281
  doing, 287-289
  form files for, 282-286
  printing results of, 290-291
Monospaced font, 312
Mouse, using, 15, 508
  clicking, 15
  double-clicking, 346
  dragging, 157
Moving
  a block of text, 157-159, 161-162
  the cursor through the document, 11, 12-14
  the cursor through text columns, 452
  with drag and drop, 157-159
  graphics boxes, 345-349, 353-357
  a page, 153-156
  a paragraph, 153-156
  a sentence, 153-156
  text, 153-162
  text between two documents, 153-162, 267-268
Multiple copies, printing, 241-242
Multiple documents
  copying and moving text between, 153-162, 267-268
  opening a second document, 46-48
  switching between, 48-52
  working with, 48-52, 260-268

N

Names, adding to supplemental dictionary, 179-180
Newspaper columns, 434
  creating, 435-442
  entering text into, 435-442
  modifying, 451-454
Notes. *See* Footnotes
Num Lock key, use of, 14
Numbering
  pages in headers and footers, 204-205
  pages, 126-128
Numbering styles for outlines, 377-379
Numeric columns, totaling, 297-306, 487-481
Numeric keypad
  location, 10
  use of, 14

O

Open styles
  creating, 415-418
  modifying, 421-425
  using, 418-420
Opening documents, 46-48
  See also Retrieving documents
Option buttons. *See* Radio buttons
Orphan lines, preventing, 199-201
Outlines, 365-386
  adding items to, 374, 375
  changing, 373-376
  changing levels of entries, 376
  changing the numbering style, 377-379
  collapse levels, 380-381
  creating, 367-372
  default numbering for, 367
  deleting entries in, 374, 375
  expand levels, 380-381
  making changes to, 395-376

multiple levels in, 370-372, 376

P

Page numbers
adding, 126-128
in headers and footers, 204-205
Pages
centering text on, 119-122
changing size and type of, 128-130
copying, 153-156
moving, 153-156
numbering, 126-128
preventing widows and orphans, 199-201
printing single, 60-62
Paired styles. *See* Character styles; Paragraph styles
Paragraph styles
creating, 403-410
Enter in, 405
modifying, 421-425
using, 410-414
Paper, changing the size and type, 128-130
Paper-size options, 128-130
Paper-type options, 128-130
Paragraphs
changing the appearance of, 95-112
copying, 153-156
moving, 153-156
preventing widows and orphans, 199-201
Parallel columns, 434
creating, 444-255
entering text into, 444-255
Pasting text. *See* Copying; Moving
Pathname, 219
Pg (page) indicator, 10
Pg Dn and Pg Up keys, use of, 11, 13
Point sizes (fonts), 252-254
Pos (position) indicator, 10
Positioning graphics boxes, 355-357
Previewing before printing, 63-66
Primary file. *See* Merges
Print options, changing, 239-258
Print preview, 63-66
Print quality, setting, 250
Print queue, 240
canceling print jobs in, 246-247
changing order in, 246-247, 248-249
displaying, 243-245
rushing print jobs in, 248-249
Print request
canceling, 246-247
rushing, 248-249
Printers, installing, 501-503
Printing
the current document, 57-59
a document, 55-72
documents containing graphics, 358-361
from a file, 67-69
a merge document, 290-291
multiple copies, 241-242
and previewing, 63-66
a single page, 60-62
Proofing documents
alternate words, 183-187, 188-189
double or repeated words, 176-177
for mistakes WordPerfect can't recognize, 181-183
grammar, 190-191
spelling, 169-172, 173-175
Proportional spaced fonts, 251, 312
Pull-down menus. *See* Menus

R

Radio buttons, 61, 511
Records, 278
entering in data file, 278-281
Reference numbers for footnotes, 206
Releasing margins, 100-101

Removing rows and columns from a table, 475-479
Renaming
  backups, 390
  files, 225-226
Repeated words, checking for, 176-177
Repeating keystrokes, 12
Replacing text, 34-36, 142-146
Restoring deleted text. *See* Esc (Cancel) key
Retrieving a document, 44-45
  See also Opening a document
Returns. *See* Hard returns; Soft returns
Revealing hidden codes, 82-84
Ribbon, 511-513
Right arrow key (→). *See* Arrow keys
Right justification, 110-111
Right margin, changing. *See* Margins
Rows, adding to tables, 475-479
Runtime, installing, 501
Rush job (printing), 248-249

S

Save As command. *See* Saving a document
Saving a document, 40-43
  and clearing the screen, 40, 41-42
  and exiting WordPerfect, 40
  to multiple filenames, 42-43
  without clearing the screen, 40-41, 42
Screen, clearing, 8-9, 40
Screen colors, changing, 391-394
Screen display, 22-25, 391-394
  button bar, 22-25
  changing colors for, 391-394
  graphics mode, 22-25
  text mode, 22-25
Screen elements, 508-513
Search and replace options, 142-146
Searching
  backwards, 139-142
  from the beginning of a document, 134-138
  in blocked text, 146
  case-sensitive, 139-141
  and deleting, 142-143
  in documents on disk using logical operators, 233-234
  from the end of a document, 139-141
  for hidden codes, 137, 139-141, 144-145
  in multiple documents on disk, 231-233
  for part of a word, 138
  for a string, 135
  for whole words, 139-141
Secondary file. *See* Merges
Sentences
  copying, 153-156
  moving, 153-156
Session, 4-5
  ending, 4-7
  starting, 4-7
Setting margins, 123-125
Setting tabs, 102-105
Setup parameters, changing, 387-399
Shift key, use of, 11, 19-21
Shift-F1 (Setup) key, use of, 389, 391
Shift-F2 (Backwards Search) key, use of, 139
Shift-F3 (Switch) key, use of, 50
Shift-F4 (Left/Right Indent) key, use of, 97
Shift-F6 (Center) key, use of, 80
Shift-F7 (Print) key, use of, 57, 60, 67, 241, 243, 246, 248, 250, 290, 359
Shift-F8 (Format) key, use of, 108, 110, 119, 123, 126, 129, 199, 203
Shift-F9 (Merge Codes) key, use of, 278, 282
Shift-F10 (Open/Retrieve) key, use of, 46
Shift-Tab (Back Tab) key
  use of, 100
  use of in tables, 465
  use of in outlines, 367, 370-372
Short business letters, centering, 119-122
Single line at top or bottom, preventing, 199-201

Single page, printing, 60-62
Sizing graphics boxes, 355-357
Soft page break code, 83
Soft returns, 83
Sound. *See* Beep sound
Spacebar, use of, 11
Spacing, between lines, 108-109
Special characters, using to draw lines, 324-325
Special keys
  table of, 11
  use of, 10-21
Speller
  adding words to the supplemental dictionary, 179-180
  using, 169-181
Spreadsheet
  using a table as, 487-491
Starting a WordPerfect session, 4
Status line, 5
  displaying location of cursor, 10
String, to search for, 135
Styles, 401-432
  create a style library, 426-427
  create character and paragraph, 403-410
  create open, 415-417
  initial style, modifying, 394-397
  modifying, 421-425
  use character and paragraph, 410-414
  use from a style library, 427-429
  use open, 418-420
  See also Character styles; Paragraph styles; Open styles
Style libraries
  creating, 426-427
  using styles from, 427-429
  See also Styles; Character styles; Paragraph styles; Open styles
Subdirectories, 218
  changing, 221-223
  creating, 218-220
  deleting, 223-225
Subtotals, calculating, 297-306, 487-491
Supplemental dictionary
  adding words to, 179-180
Supplemental dictionary file, 179
Switching between documents
  with the keyboard, 49-50, 50-51
Synonyms, 184
System files, updating, 717-719
System styles, 426

T

Tab key
  use of, 14, 102
  use of in outlines, 367, 370-372
  use of in tables, 465
Tab stops
  changing, 102-105
  removing, 102-105
Table codes, 462
Table features, 458-494
Tables
  adding columns with Tab, 476
  adding rows and columns to, 475-479
  changing cell attributes, 483-487
  changing column widths, 471-474
  creating, 460-464
  deleting, 660-662
  deleting rows and columns in, 475-479
  entering data into, 465-469
  joining cells in, 481-482
  recalculating, 479
  use of Tab and Shift-Tab in, 465

using math features in, 487-491
Tabs, setting, 102-105
Technical terms, adding to supplemental dictionary, 179-180
Text
adding, 34-36
blocking, 87-89
boldfacing, 77-78, 90
boxes in dialog boxes, 511
centering, 80-81
centering on a page, 119-122
changing default settings for, 394-397
deleting, 37-39
editing column text, 451-454
entering using defaults, 29-33
formatting with styles, 410-414
in a graphics box, 341-344
inserting in a box, 326-328
justification of, 110-111
marking blocks of, 87-89
moving, 153-162
replacing, 34-36, 142-146
searching for, 135-141
string, 135
underlining, 74-76, 90
See also Blocked Text; Searching
Text boxes, 511
Text columns. *See* Columns; Newspaper columns; Parallel columns
Text mode, 22-25
Thesaurus, 183-189
looking up words, 183-187
replacing from, 188-189
Time, inserting current, 396
Timed backups, automatic, 389-390
Top margin, changing. *See* Margins
Totaling numeric columns, 297-306, 487-491
Totals, calculating multilevel, 301-306
Typeover mode
replacing text in, 34-36
using to insert text in a box, 326

U

Undelete, 18
Underlining text, 74-76, 90
Up arrow key (↑). *See* Arrow keys
Update installation, 503-504
Uppercase letters, entering, 19-21

V

Vertical center, pages, 119-122
Viewing documents
in graphics mode, 22-25
in text mode, 22-25
using the preview screen, 63-66

W

Widow lines, preventing, 199-201
Windows, 46-52, 259-271
changing the size of, 261-263
maximizing, 261
moving, 263-266
switching between, 48-52
tiling, 50, 51-52
Windows 3.0 or 3.1, installing WordPerfect in, 504-505
Word wrap, 29-30
WordPerfect
ending a session, 5-6
starting a session, 4-5
WordPerfect documents. *See* Documents

Words
  adding to supplemental dictionary, 179-180
  checking for double (repeated), 176-177
  checking spelling of, 169-172
  finding and replacing, 142-146
  looking for, 134-141
  looking up in thesaurus, 183-187
  replacing from thesaurus, 188-189
  replacing misused, 181-182
  searching for, 135-141
WPDOCS directory, setting up, 505
WYSIWYG display. *See* Graphics Mode